LATIN AMERICAN POLITICS

LATIN AMERICAN POLITICS

An Introduction

David Close

UTP

University of Toronto Press

LIBRARY AND ARCHIVES CANADA CATALOGUING IN PUBLICATION

Close, David, 1945–
  Latin American politics : an introduction / David Close.

Includes bibliographical references and index.
ISBN 978-1-4426-0137-6

  1. Latin America—Politics and government—Textbooks.
I. Title.

JL960.C56 2009   320.98   C2009-906227-5

We welcome comments and suggestions regarding any aspect of our publications—
please feel free to contact us at news@utphighereducation.com or visit our internet
site at www.utphighereducation.com.

North America
5201 Dufferin Street
Toronto, Ontario, Canada, M3H 5T8

2250 Military Road
Tonawanda, New York, USA, 14150

ORDERS PHONE: 1-800-565-9523
ORDERS FAX: 1-800-221-9985
ORDERS EMAIL: utpbooks@utpress.utoronto.ca

UK, Ireland, and continental Europe
NBN International
Estover Road, Plymouth, PL6 7PY, UK
TEL: 44 (0) 1752 202301
FAX ORDER LINE: 44 (0) 1752 202333
enquiries@nbninternational.com

This book is printed on paper containing 100% post-consumer fibre.

The University of Toronto Press acknowledges the financial support for its publishing
activities of the Government of Canada through the Book Publishing Industry
Development Program (BPIDP).

Designed by Zack Taylor.

Printed in Canada

Recycled
Supporting responsible use
of forest resources
www.fsc.org Cert no. SGS-COC-003153
© 1996 Forest Stewardship Council

Contents

Preface

Latin American politics changes, but it never gets any simpler. A course on Latin American politics in the late 1970s would probably have stressed the breakdown of democratic regimes and the rise of revolutionary movements. In the 1980s, the focus would have been the debt crisis, continuing guerrilla insurgencies, and the beginnings of transitions back to democracy. The 1990s marked a period of democratic consolidation and evaluation of the effects of structural adjustment policies. Now, a decade into the new millennium, the mix features the most severe economic crisis in three generations, a new crop of forceful leaders pursuing agendas of radical reforms, and more functioning electoral democracies than Latin America has ever known.

This continuous flux, brought by succeeding cycles of new problems and crises, makes it both easy and challenging to teach Latin American politics. What makes it easy is the array of issues and answers that emerges from the everyday business of governing Latin American nations. Students from Canada and the United States have little firsthand experience with revolutions, dictators, or coups; neither have they seen electoral democracies—the normal state of affairs for them—built from the bottom up. Such students naturally want to figure out what makes political systems try to resolve public problems in such dramatic ways, but they want even more to understand what kinds of problems have arisen that prompt those responses. The politics in most of Latin America's 20 countries, through most of their histories as independent states, present students here with a remarkable cluster of least-like cases to consider. And it is this novelty that engages many of them, just as it once engaged those who have become their teachers.

However, the distinctiveness of Latin American politics that attracts students also makes it a challenging subject to teach. When studying their own nation's politics and government, political science students throughout North America obviously learn about issues and leaders, but most of their time is dedicated to learning about how institutions work, processes operate, and policy is made. When encountering Latin America (or any other part of the developing world) in a class, students may see it as something exotic, not in any pejorative sense but simply as something too far outside of any existing framework to be more than an interesting datum. In short, it just does not fit that well with what they know about the political world and its workings. The challenge is to link Latin American politics to politics elsewhere.

Latin American Politics tries to make the challenging part a little easier by establishing the link between Latin American politics and politics in general more directly through the close examination of 11 different topics, allotting a chapter to each. Further, the text is self-consciously comparative, as each chapter uses cases from across Latin America and from other regions in order to explain and illustrate the concepts. Being organized around key themes has meant omitting the case-study chapters that are common in Latin American politics texts, thus making this book more like texts used in courses on Third World or African politics. I realize that this decision brings costs as well as benefits, but I believe that it is positive, on the whole, as I have organized my own course around these concepts for some time.[1]

Note

1. For those looking for a supplementary text that stresses country studies, there is Howard J. Wiarda and Howard F. Kline, eds., *Latin American Politics and Development*. 6th ed. (Boulder, CO: Westview Press, 2007).

Acknowledgments

You do not write a textbook without the assistance of a great many people, most of whom receive recognition only in the form of a bibliographic entry. However, there are still plenty who have had more active roles, but rather than attempt to list them all and omit someone by oversight, I shall select a few to represent everyone. First, I want to thank Greg Yantz, formerly of Broadview Press, for suggesting this project to me. As well, Anne Brackenbury of the University of Toronto Press has been very helpful and supportive throughout the entire process. And Heather Sangster wins my praise and thanks for her excellence as a copy editor. Among my colleagues, I especially want to thank Michael Wallack, who read the entire manuscript, and Osvaldo Croci and Steve Wolinetz, who each read sections. Further, the fine work of Heather Carton, an undergraduate student at Memorial, in preparing the bibliography and list of acronyms merits recognition. As well, a tip of the hat goes to my friend David Dye, who has observed and commented on Latin American affairs from his home in Managua, Nicaragua, since the 1980s. Above all, I want to thank my partner, Rosa Garcia-Orellan, who tolerated my too frequent grumpiness and self-absorption as I worked on this book.

Acronyms

AD: Democratic Action Party/Acción Democrática, Venezuela
AFP: Alliance for Progress
ALBA: Bolivarian Alliance for the People of Our America/Alianza
Bolivariana para los pueblos de neustra América
APRA: American Popular Revolutionary Alliance/Alianza Popular
Revolucionaria Americana, Peru
ARENA: Nationalist Republican Alliance Party/Alianza Republicana
Nacionalista, El Salvador
AUC: United Self-Defense Forces of Colombia/Autodefensas Unidas de
Colombia
BoP: balance of payments
BA: bureaucratic authoritarian regimes
CAFTA-DR: Dominican Republic–Central American Free Trade
Agreement
CI: counter-insurgency
CIA: Central Intelligence Agency
CIDA: Canadian International Development Agency
CMEA/COMECON: Council of Mutual Economic Assistance
COB: Bolivian Workers' Central/Central Obrera Boliviana
CONAIE: Confederation of Indigenous Nationalities of Ecuador/
Confederación de Nacionalidades Indígenas del Ecuador
COPEI: Political Electoral Independent Organization Committee/Comité
de Organización Politica Electoral Independiente, Venezuela
CTM: Confederation of Mexican Workers/Confederación de
Trabajadores Mexicana
ECLAC/CEPAL: United Nations Economic Commission for Latin
America and the Caribbean/Comisión Económica para América Latina
y el Caribe
ELN: National Liberation Army/Ejército de Liberación Nacional,
Colombia
EPL: Popular Liberation Army/Ejército Popular de Liberación
EU: European Union
EZLN: Zapatista National Liberation Army/Ejército Zapatista de
Liberación Nacional, Mexico
FA: Broad Front/Frente Amplio, Uruguay

FARC: Revolutionary Armed Forces of Colombia/Fuerzas Armadas Revolucionarias de Colombia
FHC : Fernando Henrique Cardoso, ex-president of Brazil
FMLN: Farabundo Marti National Liberation Front/Frente Farabundo Martí para la Liberación Nacional, El Salvador
FPTP: first past the post
FSLN: Sandinista National Liberation Front/Frente Sandinista de Liberación Nacional, Nicaragua
FTA: free trade agreement
FTAA: Free Trade Area of the Americas
GDP: gross domestic product
GNI: gross national income
GNP: gross national product
HDI: human development index
HIPC: Highly Indebted Poor Countries Initiative
IADB: Inter-American Development Bank
ICE: Costa Rican Electric and Phone Company/Instituto Costarricense de Electricidad
ICJ: International Court of Justice
IFE: Federal Electoral Institute/Instituto Federal Electoral, Mexico
IFI: international financial institutions
IGO: international governmental organizations
IIT: infant industry tariffs
IMF: International Monetary Fund
INGO: international non-governmental organizations
IPE: international political economy
IR: international relations
ISI: import substitution industrialization
M-19: 19th of April Movement/Movimiento 19 de Abril
MAS: Movement Toward Socialism/Movimiento al Socialismo, Bolivia
MDB: Brazilian Democratic Movement/Movimento Democrático Brasileiro
MNR: National Revolutionary Movement/Movimiento Revolucionario Nacional, Bolivia
MST: Landless Rural Workers Movement/Movimento dos Trabalhadores Rurais Sem Terra, Brazil
MVR: Movement for the Fifth Republic/Movimiento V (Quinta) República, Venezuela
NAFTA: North American Free Trade Agreement
NATO: North Atlantic Treaty Organization
NGO: non-governmental organization
OAS: Organization of American States
OECD: Organisation for Economic Co-operation and Development
PAN: National Action Party/ Partido Acción Nacional, Mexico

PDVSA: Petroleums of Venezuela (state oil company)/Petróleos de
 Venezuela, S.A.
PLC: Constitutionalist Liberal Party/Partido Liberal Constitucionalista,
 Nicaragua
PLN: National Liberation Party/Partido Liberación Nacional, Costa
 Rica
POS: political opportunity structures
PPP: purchasing power parity
PR: proportional representation
PRC: People's Republic of China
PRD: Dominican Revolutionary Party/Partido Revolucionario
 Dominicano, Dominican Republic
PRD: Party of the Democratic Revolution/Partido de la Revolución
 Democrática, Mexico
PRI: Institutional Revolutionary Party/Partido Revolucionario
 Institucional, Mexico
PRM: Party of the Mexican Revolution/Partido de la Revolución
 Mexicana, Mexico
PRN: National Revolutionary Party/Partido Revolucionario Nacional,
 Mexico
PRSP: Poverty Reduction Strategy Papers
PSUV: United Socialist Party of Venezuela/Partido Socialista Unido de
 Venezuela, Venezuela
PUSC: Social Christian Unity Party/Partido Unidad Social Cristiana,
 Costa Rica
SAP: Structural Adjustment Programs
SELA: Latin American Economic System/Sistema Económico
 Latinoamericano
SMC-P: single member constituency-plurality
UCR: Radical Civic Union/Unión Cívica Radical, Argentina
UNASUR: Union of South American Nations/Unión de Naciones
 Suramericanas
UNDP: United Nations Development Program
UNO: National Opposition Union/Unión Nacional Opositora,
 Nicaragua
UP: Popular Unity/Unidad Popular, Chile
USAID: United States Agency for International Development
WB: World Bank

1

Studying
Latin American Politics

For many North Americans, whether from Canada or the United States, the closest contact they will have with the Third World will be on a Latin American holiday. The resort they stay in will naturally be First World, indistinguishable from what exists in Florida. But on their way from the airport to the hotel, or on a shopping expedition to a local market, they will glimpse what life is like in a much poorer place than their own. Some may ask themselves how things got that way and why the people that live there have not made their government do something about it. However, few of us explore these issues much further. By reading this book and taking a course in Latin American politics, you are one of those few.

The reasons people become interested in Latin America obviously vary. For political science students, it could be as simple as migrating around the department, an interest in the politics of development, or from recent news stories coming out of Latin America. Students from other disciplines— anthropology, archeology, biology, comparative literature, economics, history, music, or sociology, for instance—will probably have conceived an interest in some aspect of the region and want to round out their knowledge by learning about its politics. Whatever your reason, you can be sure that somebody will ask you, "Why the heck are you taking that?" This chapter outlines some good reasons why you ought to study Latin American politics.

However, we will also go beyond *why* and address the question of *how* to study Latin American politics. At first blush, that might seem obvious: you study it in the same way you study anything else. But that intuitive answer is misleading. Political science regularly distinguishes between comparative politics, which deals with both individual foreign countries and comparisons between and among countries, and national or domestic politics. Making comparisons can be tricky, and it is easy both to miss and to misinterpret important features. This is especially true when examining cases drawn from political systems with different histories, structures, and dynamics from your own.

Why?

The election of George W. Bush as president of the United States in 2000 was supposed to raise Latin America's profile in that country, which would doubtlessly have put the region onto people's radar screens and would probably have made the world much more aware of Latin American affairs. Things did not work out quite that way. After the attacks on the United States in September 2001, North America's attention, and indeed the world's, became fixed on the War on Terror, especially as it has been waged in Iraq and Afghanistan. Occasionally, events in the rest of the world do catch our attention, but they have to be special to do so. Kim Jong Il's bringing North Korea into the nuclear club in 2006—then leading it back out two years later—and the cyclone that hit Burma in 2008 are just two examples, though all have been dwarfed by the global economic crisis that hit in autumn 2008. But among the events that did not often break through were political developments in Latin America.

Obviously, the 20 republics that constitute Latin America did not go into hibernation. Life went on, and political, social, and economic affairs continued evolving. Yet aside from rumblings about vexatious leaders (the most notable of whom in 2009 is Hugo Chávez, the president of Venezuela), the dangers of cocaine production in Colombia or Bolivia, or, in the United States, illegal immigration, Latin American affairs ceased to be newsworthy. This does not mean that nothing important has been happening there; only that, for people in Canada and the United States, Latin America has not been a significant source of concern over the past few years. Professor Claudio Lomnitz goes so far as to argue that since the end of the Cold War, Latin America "is as close to irrelevant for the United States, East Asia, and Europe as it had been since the First World War."[1] Under the circumstances, it is easy to fall into the trap of thinking that university students and their professors should apply their intellects to learning about places and issues that "matter": today's hot spots and hot topics.

This chapter begins by arguing that as attractive and persuasive as that argument might be, there are many valid and legitimate reasons for learning about Latin America and its politics. On the one hand, we will find pragmatic grounds for examining the western hemisphere specifically, and these grounds will encompass diplomatic, economic, and political concerns. On the other, we will encounter a host of conceptual or disciplinary reasons for being attentive to political questions in Latin America. These include problems of and prospects for further democratization, challenges that governments will be facing in the future, and the performance of alternative economic development policies.

What Makes Latin America Interesting and Important?

We can answer this question in two parts. The first part stresses basic data. Latin America's size—550 million inhabitants spread over 7.9 million square miles (20.5 million sq. km)—and the fact that it produced US$2.1 trillion in goods and services every year in the early twenty-first century make it significant—as does its proximity to North America. Latin America's historic political tendencies also make it a region of note: it has been seen by Washington, and other big powers, as both a source of problems and a region that an actual or aspiring great power needs to have on its side. Although these considerations are plainly significant, they are still not completely satisfying. Which brings us to the second part. Most of us need more than dry facts to convince us to invest the time and energy to learn about something. We want something that catches our eye, and when talking about a particular region of the world, that something is usually a headline or lead story on the evening news. In other words, what stories might make us pay attention to Latin America and its politics?

Let's consider three issues in the region that have been evolving since 2006: Cuba facing its post-Fidel future; the emergence of Venezuela's Hugo Chávez as a significant regional force; and the Pink Tide—the return of the left in Latin American politics. The first two stories, concerning Castro and Chávez, did receive pretty good coverage in the North American English-language press, certainly more than the growth of the Pink Tide did. Yet all three are significant developments in contemporary Latin American politics.

The significance of any change in Cuba's leadership hardly needs to be explained. On August 1, 2006, the Cuban government informed the world that Fidel Castro had undergone emergency surgery and handed over power temporarily to his brother Raúl. The Cuban exile community in Miami danced in the streets and speculated that Fidel had already died, meaning that their moment of triumph was at hand. Even where there was not such an immediate interest in the Cuban president's health, pundits began pontificating, and the Latin American desks in foreign ministries doubtless started examining their plans for dealing with Cuba's first new leader since New Year's Day 1959.

All this attention went to Cuba while a war between Israel and Hezbollah was raging in Lebanon. Cuba, small and poor, moved into the spotlight for a few days, reminding everyone that it remained a critical part of the broader international puzzle. It also reminded everyone that important things still happened in Latin America.

Of course, Fidel did not die; neither, however, did he return to office. Rather, a year and a half later, on February 24, 2008, Fidel passed the baton permanently to his younger brother. Raúl Castro was 76 when he took over as president; he aligned himself with economic modernizers and removed some of the onerous limitations on Cubans' personal freedom by allowing them to own cell phones and rent cars. What he did not do was threaten in any way the monopoly of the Communist Party. And although Fidel gave up his official positions, he began a column in *Granma*, the official daily paper of the Cuban Communist Party, and started developing a role as elder statesman.

This episode is important for several reasons. First, it signaled that the most stable government in the western hemisphere, with only one president in 49 years, was beginning to change. Second, since Fidel has stepped aside, it may become possible for Havana and Washington to take some very small and cautious steps toward normalizing relations. Finally, the ostensibly unproblematic passage of power from one Castro brother to the other may indicate that Cuba has avoided one of the greatest political problems a dictatorship can face: changing leadership without provoking instability. However, Raúl Castro's Cuba still must confront the delicate matter of generational change and find a way to transfer command over the state to men and women who did not make the Cuban Revolution but instead grew up with it.

Fidel Castro's departure from Latin America's political scene opened the way for Venezuela's president, Hugo Chávez, to step into the role of Washington's nemesis-in-chief and unofficial leader of the region's radical left. Chávez entered politics in 1992 as the leader of a failed left-wing coup attempt, something more common than many think, which was launched to put an end to the austerity politics being applied by the government. Jailed and later pardoned, Chávez returned to political life as a presidential candidate in 1998, taking 56 per cent of the vote and finishing 17 points ahead of the runner-up. He then held a referendum seeking public approval for a constitutional convention, won it overwhelmingly, gained a huge majority in the constituent assembly, and got a constitution tailored to his needs. The result was the Bolivarian Republic of Venezuela, whose name recalls Simón Bolívar, also known as the Liberator, whose goal had been to unite the newly independent Latin American republics into one state.

Chávez has been overwhelmingly re-elected twice already. He has followed a left-populist line domestically: greater focus on the needs of the poor, and hence more redistributive policies; a reassertion of the state's role in the economy, best seen in the renationalization of PDVSA, the national oil company; but his administration is also notable for its neglect of fiscal controls and, interestingly, of public security too. These are familiar trends in Latin America over the last 60 or so years, but the Venezuelan president's foreign policy has combined the familiar with some new touches. It blends anti-imperialism—focused on the United States—with a rejection of neoliberal free-market economics and an active attempt to build a "Bolivarian Alternative for the Americas." Chávez has found three solid allies in Latin America (Rafael Correa of Ecuador, Evo Morales of Bolivia, and Daniel Ortega of Nicaragua), and he has a good relationship with Iran's Mahmoud Ahmadinejad. Skyrocketing oil prices in recent years have provided Chávez with the resources needed to finance his plans. However, since the fall of 2008, the price of a barrel of oil declined by roughly two-thirds: from just over \$140 to around \$70.[2] This may hamper the Venezuelan president's ability to continue his policies.

In 2006, when Castro was taken ill, Chávez was pursuing his international goals, traveling the world and offering material support to Latin American politicians who shared his vision. Returned to office in 2006 with nearly 63 per cent of the vote, Chávez proposed another referendum for 2007, this time to amend the constitution to remove presidential term limits and generally strengthen the executive's already strong hand. In December 2007, Chávez suffered his first defeat in 15 years, as Venezuelans narrowly rejected his amendments by 51 to 49 per cent. Early in 2008, Chávez made the news again, this time after mobilizing his military forces against Colombia (see Chapter 10). A year later, in February 2009, he made headlines yet again by winning a rerun of the 2007 referendum on term limits (effectively winning the right to seek re-election as often as he wants)[3] and taking roughly 54 per cent of the vote.

The success of Hugo Chávez brought back to Latin American politics a style and substance not seen since the early 1990s, when neoliberal economics and electoral democracy gained the upper hand. Although the political left went into eclipse, it was not completely absent: the Chilean *Concertación*, an alliance of parties of the center and left, has governed continuously since defeating the chosen candidate of the Augusto Pinochet dictatorship in 1989, while Luiz Lula da Silva of the Workers' Party won in Brazil in 2002 and Nestor Kirchner carried Argentina in 2003. However, this was just the start of what has become known as the Pink Tide.

We can define the political left in very broad terms as favoring increased social spending, making greater efforts to redistribute wealth toward the poor, maintaining an independent foreign policy (in Latin America, this means not being in lockstep with Washington's wishes), and strengthening individual and collective rights. At any point during the 1990s, it would have been hard to find even five leftist governments in Latin America at any one time. By mid-2008, though, there were as many as 14, depending on how strictly the definition of *leftist* was applied (Table 1), and another two or three could arguably have been classed as centrist. The right's days of automatic victories may have ended.

Not all parties or governments of the left are the same. Cuba is resolutely Communist. Some—such as the Bolivarian Group of Venezuela, Bolivia, Ecuador, and Nicaragua—favor radical economic, social, and political changes but do so within the framework of electoral democracy. Most of the rest, notably Brazil, Chile, and Uruguay, are usually described

Table 1.1 Governments of the Left in Latin America, Early 2009

Country			
Argentina	Cuba	Guatemala	Paraguay
Bolivia	Dominican Republic*	Nicaragua	Uruguay
Brazil	Ecuador	Panama*	Venezuela
Chile			

* More centrist.
Source: Author's classification based on news reports.

as social democratic nations, and their policies can be compared to those of socialists in Spain, France, or Germany. Argentina, though best grouped with the social democrats, has had more conflictive relations with private enterprise than others in that class.

The one constant of politics is change; therefore, it is not surprising to see the left oust the right, just as one day the conservatives will replace the left again. This shift represents politics as usual in historically democratic countries. However, Costa Rica is Latin America's longest-lived democracy and it dates only from 1949. So the Pink Tide is not just about the left replacing the right as Latin America's leading political force, but it is also a story of democracy being allowed to work in ways that North Americans and Western Europeans think normal. If our media missed this, it is because other questions preoccupied us, and the merely interesting ceded to the pressingly important.

Why Would We Doubt That Latin America Is Important?

We need to put this question into historical perspective. In 1980, nobody would have asked, "Why Latin America?" because everybody knew why we had to understand what was going on in the southern two-thirds of our hemisphere. The 20 countries usually counted as forming Latin America—Argentina, Bolivia, Brazil, Chile, Colombia, Costa Rica, Cuba, the Dominican Republic, Ecuador, El Salvador, Guatemala, Haiti, Honduras, Mexico, Nicaragua, Panama, Paraguay, Peru, Uruguay, and Venezuela—were then either effectively one-party states, ruled by dictators, embroiled in guerrilla wars, in the midst of revolutions, or at least had next-door neighbors who were (see Text Box 1.1)

Countries of the Americas Not in Latin America

Latin America was a problem for the powerful of the world, so the world worried about Latin America, analyzed it, and sought to make it less troublesome. In short, Latin America was relevant.

By the 1990s, things had begun to change. Where a few years before authoritarian regimes had stood fast and guerrilla insurgencies had prospered, the last decade of the twentieth century saw experiments in conventional, constitutional, representative democracy. While this emerging new order attracted the attention of political scientists interested in studying regime transformation, it was less newsworthy. Further, whereas the 1980s had seen most of Latin America on the verge of economic collapse, the 1990s

---

Text Box 1.1 Countries of the Americas Not in Latin America

Besides Latin America, Canada, and the United States, there are another dozen independent countries in the western hemisphere:

Antigua and Barbuda	Guyana
Bahamas	Jamaica
Barbados	St. Kitts and Nevis
Belize	Saint Lucia
Dominica	Suriname
Grenada	Trinidad and Tobago

All but the formerly Dutch Suriname are former British colonies. Only two, Jamaica and Trinidad and Tobago, have populations of more than 1 million. One, Belize, is in Central America; two, Guyana and Suriname, are in South America; and the other nine are in the Caribbean. Strikingly, four of them—Bahamas, Barbados, St. Kitts and Nevis, and Trinidad and Tobago—rank among the 50 wealthiest countries in the world, according to the International Monetary Fund, and all are at least medium-income countries by World Bank standards. This is obviously an interesting array of countries, so why not group them with Latin America?

The reason is simply that that these nations are heirs to different political traditions and use different political institutions. Were this book about the countries of the Americas outside the United States and Canada, they would be there. However, these countries are worth studying in their own right, since examining them gives us more democratic countries to study, permits us to see how different governments resolve various challenges, makes us ask why those dozen states generally do better economically than the 20 Latin American republics, and allows us to study the effects of different colonial inheritances and different institutional structures.

---

witnessed signs of recovery, at times dramatically robust, throughout the region. And as if that were not enough, the Soviet Union passed from existence, ending the Cold War and the rivalry between East and West that made every spot on the globe of potentially critical strategic importance. From the perspective of the comfortable and powerful, especially in North America, Latin America ceased to be a problem. We could now relegate it to the category of "places we need not worry about." Of course, natural disasters would occasionally occur in the region to catch our eye and evoke our sympathy, and there was always the attraction of exotic new vacation spots for us to visit. Overall, however, Latin America slid quietly from the consciousness of North American policymakers and the general public alike.

Latin America disappeared almost completely from most of the world's radar after 9/11. The attacks made evident a new and serious problem facing the powerful, especially the United States, and that problem called forth a military solution. The fact that some Latin American states contributed to that military effort momentarily raised the profile of those specific countries, but on the whole, serious political and media attention was focused elsewhere. Benign neglect is not necessarily a bad thing; the region's economic, political, and social evolution continued nevertheless—but began turning for the worse. By 2006, the emergence of a new generation of left-wing populist[4] politicians, led by Hugo Chávez of Venezuela, put Washington, Ottawa, and other centers of power on alert: Latin America showed signs of again becoming a problem.

What you have just read is more than a description of how we in the global north—another name for the world's wealthy representative democracies, countries such as Canada, the United States, Australia, Japan, and France—have reacted to events in Latin America since 1980. It is also a sobering account of how strong countries have historically viewed weaker regions. When they cause us problems, we are desperately interested in learning everything about them that we can; otherwise, we will be unable to deal with them efficiently and effectively. But once the crisis is past, we can take things easy again, at least until the world's normally "unimportant" places start bothering us once more.

It is during those moments of crisis, when decision-makers in key capitals need to know about the until-then peripheral parts of the world, that people generally want to find out about these normally neglected regions. There are special reports on the evening news, feature articles in newspapers, long studies in magazines, and growing enrolments in university classes that deal with the problem area of the moment. Yet when those moments pass and our media shift to focus on new crises, it does not mean either that the places that have now dropped out of the headlines have solved all their problems or that they are not important. That is why we are now going to consider two distinct but related arguments to explain why we should study Latin America, even when the news tells us that it is someplace else that really matters. The rich tradition of political science is the source of both arguments, which we shall examine here before entering into them in detail.

Like many academic disciplines, political science has a two-sided personality. One side is concerned with matters of immediate practical importance. Political science is interested in finding solutions to concrete problems. For example, a political scientist could examine how a legislature's committees work in order to discover what changes might let them scrutinize the government's budget more effectively. One of her colleagues might try to figure out how more indigenous people might win elective office, while another would look for the most effective ways to resolve international trade disputes. These are all pragmatic concerns of the sort that governments and their citizens regularly have to confront. The study of Latin America both raises and helps answer myriad questions that arise in applied political science.

The other side of political science is its concern with more abstract conceptual issues. If one part of political science focuses on problem solving, the other concentrates on theory building. The political scientist who can suggest how to reform legislative committees is likely also concerned about broader questions of how legislatures function or of how they relate to the executive (that is, the concrete, practical questions often relate directly to more abstract, theoretical ones). Latin America's 20 nations, each with its singular history and path of development, offer extensive opportunities to analyze many of the discipline's conceptual issues.

The Pragmatic Argument

To decide what makes Latin America relevant to North Americans, especially Canadian and American university students, we need to discover what relevancy means. One common and widely accepted meaning of *relevant* is "topical." This is the "what do we need to know to understand today's news" perspective. Although I do not know this for sure, I would not be surprised to learn that a great many North Americans know a lot more about Islam than they did before 9/11; I certainly do. We need this information to make sense out of current events because there are Canadian and American soldiers in Afghanistan[5] and American and British troops in Iraq who regularly come under fire from Muslim guerrillas who want those forces out of their countries. Without entering into questions about the accuracy or extent of our understanding of the issues driving those who fight us, we, collectively, probably know more about this problem, than we do about Latin America, Africa, or any other place that does not pose an immediate threat to us.

So one way to think about relevance is in terms of its utility for "fire-fighting" (that is, what we need to cope with a crisis). In the early twenty-first century, there are no immediate crises in Latin America, but there are potentially several in the making. One of these is in Bolivia. President Evo Morales's efforts to give the country's indigenous people greater autonomy and a greater voice in Bolivia's politics has produced a strong reaction in the wealthier, resource-rich lowlands in the east of the country, which is seeking autonomy if not separation from the poorer Andean highlands in the west.[6] If a political settlement proves impossible, troops could be used to assert state control over the discontented region. A more widely recognized possible flashpoint is Venezuela, whose president, Hugo Chávez, has been at loggerheads with both the Venezuelan elite and the US government since he came to power in 1998. Since being re-elected in 2006, President Chávez has raised the stakes by finding allies in recently elected governments in Bolivia, Ecuador, and Nicaragua and ratcheting up his anti-elite and anti-American rhetoric.

Better than using knowledge to control crises is using that knowledge to think about avoiding crises. In the 1960s, the United States mounted the Alliance for Progress, with the aim of using aid and pressuring for progressive political reforms to reduce the appeal of revolutionary movements such as Castro's. Although that initiative failed, largely because too much emphasis went on military aid, the underlying idea was plausible. Although this sort of planning often produced direct interventions or gave the green light to coups in the past, more democratically persuasive incentives are available and we can hope that they will be used. In any case, knowledge of both past actions and present possibilities may help to moderate conflicts.

Latin America's economic power is another pragmatic reason for studying the region. A 2006 Goldman Sachs report predicted that Brazil and Mexico would be among the world's 10 largest economies in 2040,[7] and Britain's Institute of Petroleum lists Venezuela as having the sixth largest proven oil reserves in the world, with Mexico having the eighth largest.[8] There is obviously substantial potential for economic development here—but before you call your broker, you should also remember that the World Bank's *Global Economic Prospects 2007* listed Latin America as the slowest-growing region in the developing world, behind even sub-Saharan Africa.[9] Moreover, now that the global commodity boom, which lasted from 2004 to 2008, has ended, it is probable that growth will slow even further. In Chapter 8, we will investigate what lies behind this slow growth. For the moment, it is sufficient to note that slow economic growth can produce social unrest and political instability, and thus constitutes another potential hazard that can return Latin America to the lead story on the evening news.

Finally, although every region of the world has its own political dynamic, it is also true that there are interregional similarities. So, for example, the knowledge of how Latin American militaries have effectively lost their propensity to overthrow civilian governments since the 1980s should give us some hints about what might be needed to depoliticize militaries in sub-Saharan Africa. Similarly, an understanding of how winning open, honest elections became the only legitimate means to obtain the right to exercise state power in Latin America tells us something about the kind of process that would have to unfold to bring the Middle East to the same point.

Latin America and Political Science

With 20 countries, 18 of which have been independent for at least 180 years (the Dominican Republic became independent in 1844 and Cuba in 1898), Latin America is a treasure trove of data for political science. Every country, and really every polity—even a tiny municipality—has a unique history during which governmental machinery has been developed, political instruments have been invented and refined, and people have formed attitudes and beliefs about public affairs that are now part of a political tradition. Latin America's 20 republics obviously have 20 distinct political histories, processes, structures, and styles. However, there are a number of additional continuities that catch the political analyst's eye. As political science has several subfields, political scientists with different interests will be drawn to different phenomena.

One thing that some political scientists would see is that none of the 20 states is spectacularly rich, and that a few of them are pretty poor. That observation will lead analysts to ask why. They will think about resource endowments, social structure—including social class, of course, but also encompassing divisions based on ethnicity or legal status, domestic policies, and links to the international economy. Put differently, they will be examining Latin America's political economy.

Other colleagues in the same department might be more interested in institutions. The conventional definition of an institution says that it is a repeated pattern of interaction. Sometimes these patterns happen within formal organizations: administrative structures with legal bases, a roster of personnel, and a physical location. However, we find others in informal organizations that have none of those characteristics but that are just as effective in shaping people's behavior and attitudes. What these political scientists would find is that the formal institutions that have been crucial in North America—legislatures, parties, constitutions, elections, the rule of law—have had less influence in Latin America, while those that have little political weight here—the military, coups, dictatorships—have predominated historically there. Indeed, they will probably want to understand why constitutional democratic governments—the class to which the governments of Canada and the United States belong—have fared so badly in Latin America, at least until very recently.

Political scientists interested in political behavior—individual and collective—will also find plenty of questions to engage them. How do individuals express political views where democracy and the rule of law have not flourished? How has a history of *authoritarian government*—the term we currently apply to all forms of nondemocratic polities—affected political movements and civil society, when groups of individuals act together to pursue some public purpose independently of the state? And international relations specialists also have a range of issues to examine. These include US–Latin American relations; the position of relatively weak states in the international system; the reasonably low level of military conflict between and among Latin American states; and the various attempts at regional integration.

What the last two sections show is that there are lots of good reasons for studying Latin American politics that go beyond simple personal interest. We can now move to a question that is not asked very often: How should political scientists study Latin America? The answer is more complex that you might first imagine.

How Should We Study Latin America?

If your professor asked you this, you would probably think that it is some kind of trick question. We study Latin America the same way we study everything else. But the problem is that political scientists do not study everything the same way: they use different methods for different sub-fields. For example, you study the history of political thought by reading what influential political philosophers have written, but you employ statistical methods to study electoral behavior. The question is therefore a reasonable one, and it generates three distinct answers. One suggests that we should analyze Latin American politics through the lens of area studies, treating Latin America as a coherent whole and keeping our gaze firmly fixed on the 20 countries found there. Another comes at the issue from the opposite direction, saying that we need to be able to compare Latin American politics with politics everywhere and anywhere else. To do that, we need to look more at broad topics and less at the narrow particularities of individual countries. Obviously, the third response tries to find a way between the first two.

The Area Studies Approach

Area studies try to give an overall picture of a geographic (Latin America or Western Europe) or cultural (Muslim or Confucian) region of the world. Instead of talking just about politics or literature or the physical environment of a place, area studies seek to examine everything that makes that place work as it does. This is a tall order, for there is always a lot to learn. However, the simple understanding that we need a wide variety of information in order to comprehend a region fully can itself make the task less daunting.

For example, watching the news since the economic crisis of 2008 began, you might have noticed that the German chancellor (the equivalent of the prime minister), Angela Merkel, took stances very different from those of the US president or the British and Canadian prime ministers. To find out why, you would most likely intuitively follow an area studies approach. Your first step would probably be to pay more attention to the news. You would then look for books, magazines, and academic journals in the library. At some point you may realize that there is a lot of material in German that you would like to use but cannot because your German is a little shaky. So you would work on your German skills and eventually be able to read German-language newspapers, magazines, and books. After doing all this, you would have reached your original goal of learning more about why Chancellor Merkel has taken her particular stance. And you would have almost certainly learned things about Germany that go beyond the political and developed a broader vision of what makes that society work as it does.

Area Studies and Latin America

Though it sounds simplistic, in area studies, you would study Latin America in order to know about Latin America. At least part of any course on Latin American politics will take an area studies approach; some courses are based entirely on this method. However, if you were interested in knowing how political parties built around their leader's personality (personalistic parties) organize voters, run their campaigns, and raise money, you could certainly find this out in an area studies–oriented course, but you might not learn that those kinds of parties exist beyond Latin America. Later in this chapter we will see that a course with a stronger comparative politics orientation would be more likely to discuss personalistic parties from outside Latin America alongside Latin American examples to set you thinking about the conditions in which this kind of party prospers. Now, however, we will consider what you need to know specifically about Latin America in order to understand the region's politics.

History is the place to start. Think about the best domestic political commentators you see on television or read in the press and you quickly realize that they often situate their analyses in national or international history. Evoking the past to explain the present works because it lets us see how we handled some issue, confronted some challenge, or failed to manage some crisis in the past that resembles what we face now. Citizens have their version of history (for instance, that presidents have always betrayed our trust), which need not be true to be believed. Politicians also give their own readings to history (for example, that only strongman candidates win here), which shape their behavior and preferences. And history shows us how institutions and values have evolved.

In the case of Latin America, the course of history begins in fifteenth-century Spain and Portugal and then covers 300 years of colonial rule before developing into the national histories of the various republics. The objectives of the Iberian colonizers, the institutions of colonial rule, the class system that evolved, and the economy that grew up during those three centuries combined to form the birthright of the new nations. Wars for independence—some long and bloody, others less so—also contributed to building the foundation on which the Latin American republics would be built by making military forces key instruments of politics. In the aftermath of independence, all Latin American nations except Brazil suffered prolonged periods of political instability and autocratic rule, as the new governing classes could not agree on a formula by which to govern their states. The only thing the warring elites did agree on was that the masses and the fledgling middle sectors were not to be significant political actors, a condition that prevailed well into the twentieth century. The net effect of this experience was to delay the formation of lasting state structures and political processes, while reinforcing notions about the utility of violence as a political tool.

After considering these beginnings, a student taking an historical approach to Latin American politics would then pass to a more detailed examination of the past century. The objective would be to determine whether the paths laid down earlier continued influencing the shape and tenor of public affairs. The student would examine significant individuals, important movements and parties, dramatic events such as revolutions, the evolution of institutions, and key political issues, before moving into the analysis of individual countries and possibly of specific institutions and processes.

Underlying an area studies approach to politics is the belief that what needs to be taught and learned are the things that distinguish the area under examination—Latin America, Africa, Russia, or wherever—from the place the students live and know best. This approach requires emphasizing contrasts but also isolating those factors that do most to define how a given political system works. And Latin America produces a long list of themes.

Since these topics are treated in detail in other parts of this book, we will just identify a few of these themes briefly here. Most questions about Latin American politics are linked to the historic paucity of viable constitutional democracies in the region—states where the rule of law prevails, citizens' rights are protected and enforced, access to power is only through free and contested elections, and where oppositional activity and the media are free and unobstructed. More specifically, the list would also include the prevalence of military governments, the significance of violence as a political instrument, the difficulty new forces have in penetrating the political system and the concomitant longevity of traditional elites, the strength of personalistic leaders, and the related weakness of formal state institutions. In fact, these characteristics are found throughout the Third World, suggesting that poor countries find similar structures useful in governing themselves. However, it is important to note that this last point might not emerge in an area studies approach to the region's politics, since it is a comparative hypothesis.

Area studies teach facts about Latin America because they deal specifically with Latin America. The objective is to let you understand and appreciate the region and its politics, and to make you a more able interpreter of Latin American affairs. The skills this method emphasizes are highly valued, especially among journalists and government officials and business people who have to work in and with Latin American countries. They also apply very well to the study of history, literature, and culture. Although these skills are also important in political science, our discipline wants to go a little further in a somewhat different direction. Political science seeks to develop comparative frameworks that cross geographical and cultural regions and concepts that apply to politics as generally as possible. This is the approach of contemporary comparative politics.

Comparative Politics and Latin America

Comparative politics is one of the sub-fields of modern political science. Once, it was little more than descriptions of the formal machinery of foreign governments. Since the 1960s, however, comparative politics has also examined processes, institutions, historic development, and policies; it does not limit itself to countries but also looks at sub-national politics or at a single country at different times in its history. In doing so, the approach seeks to develop concepts that can become the building blocks of theory. For some, the objective is to develop a general theory that aspires to cover the entire political realm. Others set the more achievable objective of developing a mid-range theory that aims only to explain, for example, why personalist political parties are common in the Third World.

In practice, comparative politics often operates at a more concrete level. One reason for this is that we do not have enough empirical studies of existing political phenomena in enough places to make plausible generalizations that would lead to a general theory. Another explanation for comparative politics' more modest operational aims is that most of us who teach and study in this field do not feel comfortable going beyond mid-level generalizations. For example, someone who knows a lot about Canadian politics realizes how complex things are here and could sensibly decide that he is unlikely to have similar information about more than a few other places. Therefore he limits his comparisons and will not formulate concepts that apply to more than a carefully specified array of countries, institutions, processes, or problems. If such an approach is applied to Latin America, we are more likely to compare economic development policies in Chile, Argentina, and Brazil, or of political parties in Costa Rica, Nicaragua, and El Salvador than make efforts to construct even region-wide theories of economic policies or political parties.

In fact, comparative politics only discovered Latin America as a region of study when the field took its modern turn 50 years ago. Prior to that time, comparative politics studied Western Europe almost exclusively. It was only with the nearly simultaneous arrival of development studies, modernization theory, and the behavioral trend in political science that perspectives broadened and polities from outside Europe and North America became proper objects for study.

Behavioralism brought two changes. First, it aimed to make the study of politics more scientific. That meant thinking in terms of a general theory of politics, on the one hand, while proposing testable propositions about political action—instead of describing formal institutions—on the other. The other side of behavioral political science was its concentration on what individuals did politically. Although this led to a counterproductive disregard of state institutions, it provided increasingly sophisticated voting and public opinion studies that soon migrated to comparative politics.

Although all of Latin America was free of colonial rule by 1898,[10] it was the postwar wave of decolonization in Africa and Asia that excited political science and generated development studies.[11] Two questions drove development studies. One asked how the world's poor countries could become rich, while the other considered how they could govern themselves to become pluralist democracies. Modernization theory offered similar answers to both questions, namely, do what the most successful have done: in economics, follow a modified market model; and in politics, build representative, constitutional democracies. When this outlook proved unproductive, many researchers shifted to dependency theory, which argued that capitalist economics, and the politics it spawned, was the road to perpetual poverty and repressive government for many countries. Dependency theory counseled revolution and self-reliance as better options but found few takers.[12]

Another product of the 1960s thought was structural functionalism. This theory proposed linking state structures with functions governments had to perform. Unlike modernization and dependency theories, structural functionalism was not inherently prescriptive and could have contributed significantly to understanding how different governments did the things that all governments have to do. Unfortunately, both structures and functions were based overwhelmingly on the US model, so the approach disappointed in the end. From that point, in the mid-1970s, comparative work on Latin American politics has been more problem driven than theory driven. Perhaps the most significant exception to that rule has been the application of rational choice theory, which applies economics' rational actor model to political studies, to Latin American politics.[13]

Some of the problems in Latin America that political scientists have elected to study have been local instances of more general phenomena, among them economic policy issues. What began with the study of development by the modernization and dependency schools was picked up again in the 1980s by those analyzing Structural Adjustment Programs (SAPs). During the 1980s and 1990s, governments of countries with high foreign debts signed agreements with the International Monetary Fund (IMF) to enact SAPs in order to get low-interest loans. We examine SAPs in more detail in Chapter 9, so for now we need only note that they demanded dramatic cuts in government spending, privatization of state-owned enterprises, significant tariff cuts, and increased efforts to pay down foreign debts. An important adjunct of this policy emphasized state reform, how a government had to change to make the SAP work. This focused on sound administration, securing property rights, and basing economic policy on free-market principles. Although structural adjustment was applied globally, the majority of studies concentrated on a particular region, such as Latin America or Africa.[14]

The democratic transitions of the same period, which saw many countries around the world trade authoritarian rule for democracy, also received great attention. Although this process began in southern Europe in the 1970s,[15] democracy's Third Wave took root in Latin America after 1978. Since that time, 16 states[16] in Latin America have shifted to regimes where winning competitive elections is the only path to power. Most of the research on this wave of democratization has taken the form of specific country studies or comparative analyses of specific institutions (e.g., the military) within the region; however, some early studies of transitions from authoritarian to democratic politics were global in reach.[17] Nevertheless, comparative politics saw great debate in the late 1990s over "transitology," asking just how inclusive comparisons of democratic transitions could be.[18]

A question arises here: with whom or what should we compare Latin American political systems? Obviously, they can be compared with each other, and as with any comparison, one can focus on most-like or least-like cases. Similarly, comparisons between Latin America and other developing areas or regions experiencing democratic transitions should probably be more common than they are. And studies examining institutions, such as parties or executives, or policies, including foreign policy, in developed democracies and their Latin American counterparts would be fascinating and should be feasible, but few exist. In fact, most studies of Latin American politics are probably still single-country analyses built around a specific problem or issue.

Indeed, much of comparative politics retains a very strong area studies flavor. What that means is that a substantial part of what comparative politics does is based on what happens in particular countries or specific regions. This is hardly surprising, since the vast majority of political scientists who specialize in comparative politics tend to concentrate on a specific country or region, even when they also have a particular policy, issue, or institution that interests them. At a 1996 symposium that brought together some of the most innovative and productive scholars in comparative politics, it emerged that they placed themselves in "the methodologically messy middle," adopting methods, concepts, and theoretical frameworks to fit the study that engages them at the moment.[19]

Not everyone shares that approach. That same year, Robert Bates, an expert on Africa who works mainly within rational choice theory, suggested that area studies and social scientific inquiry were on divergent paths.[20] Text Box 1.2: Political Science and Area Studies sketches the debate that followed.

Where This Text Stands

The purpose of *Latin American Politics* is to introduce upper division, third- and fourth-year undergraduate students to Latin American politics. It has two related but distinct objectives: to cover material specific to the study of Latin America and to compare and contrast the political and economic situation of the region to others in the world.

Most texts introducing Latin American politics have either a series of case study chapters or refer to one or two cases throughout to illustrate their points. This one does neither. Rather, it picks out a few themes—nine of them, in fact—that will not just help you understand enough about Latin America to make you a far more able analyst of the region but will also allow you to build bridges to your other courses in political science. What you learn about Latin America will also sharpen your perception of domestic politics.

So this text offers a mix of area studies—the background you need to make sense of Latin America on its own terms—and conceptually oriented comparative politics. It gives you two different frameworks in which to organize the material you learn, but those frameworks share enough common ground to make it easy to bring together the knowledge you gain about Latin America into a coherent whole.

Text Box 1.2 Political Science and Area Studies

In 1996, Robert Bates, a political scientist from Harvard, wrote an article arguing that those who did area studies pursued goals that were not consonant with the enterprise of social science. His position rests on two related points: first, that area studies pursue a highly detailed view of particular political systems, and second, that as a result, they do little to search for the context-independent regularities that should be the concern of social science. Those from the opposing camp responded that without empirical evidence (from area studies, in this case) theory building would be an unrewardingly futile task—especially so if the data needed to come from places where English was not the mother tongue or where cultural practices would confound the uniformed. Both standpoints are logical and defensible, and neither side convinced the other.

But what difference do debates such as the one outlined above make to an undergraduate course on Latin American politics? Although these questions will affect how professors organize their courses, most students will find them peripheral to their immediate interests. The debates are about the current shape and future direction of political science as a professional, academic discipline, but even most majors will not become professional political scientists. There are more than 30 million people in Canada and only about 700 of them are political science professors; US numbers appear proportionally higher—there are just more than 10,000 nonstudent members of the American Political Science Association, but not all those are either professors or work in the United States—yet the point that most of you will not be professional political scientists is pretty clear.[21]

Nevertheless, students should know something about these disciplinary debates. The one we have been looking at asks how much detailed, Latin America–specific content we need to have to understand Latin American politics. Raising this question makes us, professors and students alike, reflect on how much of the political life of Latin America (or of Canada, the United States, or anywhere else) is unique and how much is part of a broader model of how human beings address the issue of governing their societies. As we want to know more about both Latin American politics and politics generally, the points raised by both Bates and his critics are ones we need to consider.

Conclusion

This chapter has presented two reasons why it is important for political science students to study Latin America. One of those is based on day-to-day utility—essentially the idea that studying Latin America will help you understand why the next international crisis has arisen and taken the form it has. The second reason for studying Latin American politics is that it is important for developing your knowledge of political science in general. In nearly two centuries of self-rule, these 20 countries have had many political successes and failures. They have experimented with an astonishing variety of laws, institutions, and ways of organizing power, all of which combine to offer much for political science to study.

The other task of this chapter has been to suggest that the framework you use to study the politics of a region or country makes a difference. An area studies approach directs your attention within Latin America, perhaps even to a particular country. Viewing Latin America and the politics of its 20 republics from the perspective of comparative politics, however, prompts you to cross national and regional boundaries. Putting the two together affords you the opportunity to develop an appreciation of this field that is both broad and deep.

Further Readings

Crow, John A. *The Epic of Latin America*. 4th ed. Berkley, CA: University of California Press, 1992.

Green, December, and Laura Luehrmann. *Comparative Politics of the Third World*. 2nd ed. Boulder, CO: Lynne Rienner Publishers, 2007.

Handelman, Howard. *The Challenge of Third World Development*. 5th ed. Upper Saddle River, NJ: Pearson Prentice Hall, 2008.

Munck, Ronaldo. *Contemporary Latin America*. New York: Palgrave, 2008.

Reid, Michael. *Forgotten Continent*. New Haven, CT: Yale, 2007.

Websites

Canadian Foundation for the Americas (FOCAL): www.focal.ca
Council on Hemispheric Affairs: www.coha.org
Inter-American Dialogue: www.thedialogue.org
Latin American Network Information Center: http://lanic.utexas.edu
Political Database of the Americas: http://pdba.georgetown.edu
Washington Office on Latin America: www.wola.org

Discussion Questions

① What sorts of information can you find in the specialized websites listed above that you cannot find in more general sources, such as newscasts, newspapers, or magazines? How is this specialized material useful?

② Why should combining an areas studies approach and facts about Latin America with a comparative politics approach, along with concepts and theories, help give you a better understanding of Latin American politics? Ask yourself this again when the term has ended.

Notes

1. Claudio Lomnitz, "Latin America's Rebellion: Will the New Left Set a New Agenda?" *Boston Review* 31:5 (September–October 2006): 7. http://bostonreview.net/BR31.5/lomnitz. html.

2. Unless otherwise noted, all financial figures are in US$.

3. Previously, the Venezuelan constitution, the one crafted by President Hugo Chávez, limited a president to two six-year terms.

4. Both the left- and right-wing variants of Latin American populism are discussed in Chapters 8 and 10.

5. In Afghanistan, they fight alongside troops from the UK and a number of other countries.

6. International Crisis Group, *Bolivia's New Constitution: Avoiding Violent Confrontation*. Latin American Report No. 23 (2007). www.crisisgroup.org/home/index.cfm? id=5044&l=1.

7. Cited in "The New Titans: A Survey of the World Economy," *The Economist*, 16 September 2006: 12.

8. Institute of Petroleum, "Where Is the Oil?" www.energyinst.org.uk/education/ natural/3.htm (accessed 7 January 2007). The institute's figures do not include the tar sands in the Orinoco oil belt, which are estimated to hold more than 200 billion barrels of oil. Since then, of course, Brazil and Cuba have reported important oil finds, which can only heighten Latin America's economic significance.

9. World Bank, *Global Economic Prospects 2007*. http://web.worldbank.org/WBSITE/ EXTERNAL/EXTDEC/EXTDECPROSPECTS/GEPEXT/0,,contentMDK:21021075~menu PK:51087945~pagePK:51087946~piPK:51087916~theSitePK:538110,00.html.

10. In 1960, there were still colonies in the western hemisphere: all of the British West Indian colonies, British Guyana (now Guyana) and British Honduras (now Belize), Dutch Guyana (now Suriname), and French Guyana (now La Guyane, as well as a Département d'outre-mer, an overseas department of France). There were also, and still are, Dutch and British colonies, the US Commonwealth of Puerto Rico, and the US Virgin Islands. Of all these, only Puerto Rico could conceivably be counted part of Latin America.

11. For a sense of what those early works were like, see Gabriel Almond and G. Bingham Powell, *Comparative Politics: A Development Approach* (Boston, MA: Little, Brown, 1966.)

12. A good introduction to dependency analysis is Ronald Chilcote and Joel Edelstein, eds. *Latin America: The Struggle with Dependency and Beyond* (Cambridge, MA: Schenkman Publishing, 1974).

13. At its simplest, rational choice argues that (1) individuals must be the center of social inquiry and (2) that the self-interested, utility-maximizing economic man is the best model

for understanding individual political behavior. This perspective is very strong in the United States but only one among a host of contending views on how to study politics in Canada and elsewhere in the world. As with any theoretical framework, there is a wide variety of interpretations within the rational choice school. Evelyne Huber and Michelle Dion, "Revolution or Contribution? Rational Choice Approaches in the Study of Latin American Politics," *Latin American Politics and Society* 44:3 (2002): 1–28, provides a valuable overview.

14. See, among others, Judith Teichman, *The Politics of Freeing Markets in Latin America: Chile, Argentina, and Mexico* (Chapel Hill, NC: University of North Carolina Press, 2001) and Kurt Weyland, *The Politics of Market Reform in Fragile Democracies: Argentina, Brazil, Peru, and Venezuela* (Princeton: Princeton University Press, 2002).

15. The first instances were Portugal and Greece (1974) and Spain (1976).

16. The following nations adopted competitive electoral democracy between 1978 and the present: Argentina, Bolivia, Brazil, Chile, Dominican Republic, Ecuador, El Salvador, Guatemala, Haiti, Honduras, Mexico, Nicaragua, Panama, Paraguay, Peru, and Uruguay. Costa Rica has had competitive elections since 1953, Venezuela since 1958, and Colombia since 1974. Cuba does not allow interparty competition for state power. Chapter 7 presents an analysis of democracy in Latin America that goes beyond holding elections.

17. Guillermo O'Donnell, Philippe Schmitter, and Laurence Whitehead, eds. *Transitions from Authoritarian Rule* (Baltimore: Johns Hopkins University Press, 1986).

18. Two articles by Valerie Bunce are particularly helpful. See "Comparative Democratization: Big and Bounded Generalizations," *Comparative Political Studies* 33: 6–7 (2000): 703–734 and "The Tasks of Democratic Transition and Transferability," *Orbis* 52:1 (2008): 25–40.

19. Atul Kholi, et al., "The Role of Theory in Comparative Politics: a Symposium," *World Politics* 48:1 (1995): 1–49, raises many useful points.

20. Robert Bates, "Letter from the President: Area Studies and the Discipline," *Newsletter of the APSA Organized Section on Comparative Politics* 7:1 (1996): 1–2. See also Robert Bates, "Area Studies and Political Science: Rupture and Possible Synthesis," *Africa Today* 44:2 (1997): 123–131 and the following interchange of ideas: Robert Bates, "Area Studies and the Discipline: A Useful Controversy," *Africa Today* 44:2 (1997): 166–169; Chalmers Johnson, "Preconception vs. Observation, or the Contributions of Rational Choice Theory and Area Studies to Contemporary Political Science," *PS: Political Science and Politics* 30:2 (1997): 170–174; and Ian Lustick, "The Disciplines of Political Science: Studying the Culture of Rational Choice as a Case in Point," *PS: Political Science and Politics* 30:2 (1997): 175–179.

21. The Canadian numbers come from Kim Nossal, "A Question of Balance: The Cult of Research Intensivity and the Professing of Political Science in Canada," *Canadian Journal of Political Science* 39:4 (2006): 735–754. The American data are from the American Political Science Association, *Membership Data: Current APSA Members, 2004.* http://apsanet.org/imgtest/APSAdata.pdf.

2

Why History Matters

This chapter considers how history affects politics and why it is necessary to know the rudiments of Latin American history to have a good grasp of Latin American politics.[1] This is not just names, places, and dates, although there is some of that. Rather, this is about broad themes and patterns that have emerged over time and influence the course of politics today. The tendency for those patterns to be reproduced and persist we call *path dependence*; and in most places, at most times, people do keep doing things generally as they have done in the past. These are paths that are well trodden and can be followed without much thought. In fact, what calls for serious thought is deviating from those established, institutionalized patterns of behavior or changing the structures of systems or organizations. Making these so-called off-path changes is hard work, and it happens no more frequently in Latin America than it does here.

To get a sense of what this means, think about how history has shaped politics in Canada and the United States. Although both are democracies, they use quite different formal state institutions. The operation of those institutions over time has affected how nonstate political institutions, such as parties, are organized and work. Moreover, the structures of the two societies have thrown up different problems for government to treat: the United States has no equivalent of Quebec and race politics are very different in Canada than south of the border. These are simple examples, but they indicate some of the ways that today's political structures, organizations, processes, and issues have historical roots. In a very elemental way, that is why political science, and above all comparative politics, is attentive to history.

Being attentive to history, however, does not mean that we should become historical determinists and hold that people and countries are slaves to their pasts. To say that change is hard is not the same as saying that it cannot happen. We study history to understand today's politics because we believe, based on good empirical evidence, that in most instances it is easier to follow established paths than it is to move off those paths. That is what most people do most of the time. So that is one reason why we need to know something about Latin America's history.

Another good reason for knowing some Latin American history is that there, like here or anywhere else, people allude to the past to explain the present. The past, in other words, is a source of symbols. For example,

Hugo Chávez, Venezuela's president since 1998, leads what he calls the "Bolivarian Revolution." He wants, first, to wrap his movement in the legitimacy that attaches to Simón Bolívar, the Venezuelan who is known as the Liberator for his role in the wars of independence waged by Spain's South American colonies. Equally important, however, is that President Chávez is signaling to everyone that he wants to take up the Liberator's dream of uniting all of South America under a single leader—himself in this case. Much the same thing happened in Nicaragua in the middle of the twentieth century, as a guerrilla organization fighting the dictatorship of the Somoza family took the name *Sandinista*. The guerrillas did so to indicate that they wanted to be linked to Augusto César Sandino, a guerrilla general who became famous in the 1920s for his struggle against the US Marines who then occupied Nicaragua. The guerrillas, thus, were representing themselves as the true nationalists, and the dictator was Washington's stooge.

The objective of this chapter is to present an overview of the historical factors that have contributed to forming the framework of Latin American politics. It begins by examining the Iberian background to give a sense of what the two colonizing powers, Spain and Portugal, were like and what their colonizing projects were. The chapter looks next at the two colonial regimes, giving greater emphasis to the Spanish case. Then it moves to the nineteenth century, which produced the independence movement, the age of *caudillos* (local politico-military leaders), and finally saw most Latin American countries develop political stability, though not democracy, and a degree of economic prosperity. The following section of the chapter reviews the developments of the twentieth century, which are still being worked through today. At that point we also take a more focused look at how the effects of history are clearly visible in the contrasting contemporary social and political realities of two neighboring countries, Nicaragua and Costa Rica. To conclude, the chapter raises a crucial question: do the countries of Latin America share enough of a common bond, a shared history, to make treating them as a cultural, political, social area feasible?

The Iberian Colonizers

If we take a romantic view, we can say that Latin America's history begins in 722, in the Asturian mountain range known as the Picos de Europa. There, in a cave located above the town of Covadonga, a Christian king, who was really little more than a local chieftain, planned a battle in which his men would defeat the Moors, the Muslims pushing up from what is now Andalusia. That victory set in train the longest civil war in Spain's history, if not the world's: la Reconquista, the Reconquest of Spain by the Christians, which was to last until 1492. What, though, does this have to do with Latin America?[2]

Text Box 2.1 Fragment Theory

Imperial states create one of two classes of colonies: colonies of settlement and colonies of occupation or exploitation. In settler colonies—all of the Americas, Ulster in Ireland, Australia, New Zealand, Manchuria and Korea under the Japanese, and Israel in the Middle East—the colonizer displaces, perhaps annihilates, the indigenous population and becomes the majority, or tries to. In colonies of occupation—India, for example, or most of Africa—the colonizer dominates the autochthonous population (which remains the majority), extracts valuable resources, and looks after the metropole's interests there.

In an attempt to understand the nature and direction of politics in settler colonies, especially when they diverge from the metropole's politics, political scientist Louis Hartz proposed the fragment theory.[3] This theory argues that immigrants bring a fragment of the political culture (that is, the ideas, beliefs, attitudes, and values people hold about who should rule and how they should do it) of the society that they have left to their new home. This fragment becomes the cornerstone of the political beliefs of the new society and shapes its future development. Applied to Latin America, particularly Spanish America, the fragment theory would suggest that the values and instruments of the Reconquest assume a critical importance. As the Spanish Conquest of America began the same year the Reconquest of Spain ended, it could hardly be otherwise.

It actually has less to do with Portuguese America (Brazil) than Spanish America (the rest). Although Portugal had its own reconquest, it ended earlier (1249) and involved the participation of many foreign crusaders, and thus was less of a proto-national project than Spain's. As a result, when the Portuguese made landfall in the western hemisphere in 1500, it had been two and a half centuries since the foreign occupiers had been expelled and Portugal began seeking new outlets for its energy, mostly in exploration and trade. In Spain, however, the completion of the work of reunification and its first contact with the New World occurred in the same year, just 10 months apart.[4] So the Spanish moved from Reconquest directly to Conquest (see Text Box 2.1) As one historian of the Reconquest puts it, "Spain was able to conquer, administer, Christianize, and Europeanize the populous areas of the New World precisely because during the previous seven centuries her society had been constructed for the purpose of conquering, administering, Christianizing, and Europeanizing the inhabitants of Al-Andalus (Muslim Spain)."[5]

What the Spanish brought with them was a combination of two factors. One factor was a mix of ideas, values, attitudes, and beliefs. Here we find a strong notion of religious purpose: they believed they were doing God's work. In behavioral terms, this translated into assuring the conversion of conquered peoples who were not Christians. In Spain, this meant Muslims and Jews—although the Jews were expelled from Spain in 1492, with the Muslims following a decade later. In the New World, it was the Native Americans who were brought to the Christian fold.

Besides this sense of religious mission, the Reconquest left a set of views on work and wealth that also crossed the Atlantic. Spain was emerging from eight centuries of warfare—thus the warrior, the specialist in organized violence, was highly esteemed. The military life was, indeed, the only suitable occupation for a gentleman. These gentlemen soldiers were in the main *hidalgos* (members of the nobility who were without lands and were thus like knights), who had to work at the only calling open to them: warfare. A successful commander could claim the lands and people he conquered, set the latter to work for him, and be assured of an income from his lands. Consequently, commerce and industry were disparaged, and actually working the land oneself was unimaginable. This outlook is essentially what would have been found among the landed classes of all Europe at the time.

The Reconquest also produced its own set of institutions. Some of these were formal and had a legal basis; others lacked legal sanction but were every bit as well established and hard to change. (We will discuss these in more detail in the next section.) One such institution was military organization, which counted on small units organized and led by *hidalgos*. As it was the *hidalgo* who recruited and equipped his force, hoping to recover his expenditures through conquest, the crown bore few costs. This model, the *adelantado*, successfully made the transition to the Americas, most famously in the conquests of Mexico and Peru. As conquered lands had to be worked, two more institutions emerged: the *encomienda* and the *repartimiento*, which governed the allocation and social organization of conquered people.

We have already noted that Portugal arrived in the Americas with its Reconquest far in the past. Fifteenth-century Portugal was a hotbed of exploration, creating commercial enterprises overseas from Africa to the Far East. Colonization was not part of Lisbon's repertoire entering the sixteenth century—it built trading posts instead—but historian E. Bradford Burns argues that the need to protect the brazilwood trade from the French convinced King João III to settle the long coast of Brazil.[6] Obviously, the Church also had a role in these explorations: Portuguese clerics made their way as far east as Japan but had their greatest success in Brazil. So even though the Portuguese did not bring with them ready-made templates for subjugating and ruling conquered peoples, the values of the metropole nevertheless made their way to the transatlantic possession.

To appreciate why the colonizers' domestic institutions and values were important, we need only think of the North American settler colonies, especially the English ones. Colonization began in the early seventeenth century, at a time when England was torn between two Protestant faiths, Puritanism and Anglicanism, as well as between two radically different political positions, royal absolutism and what soon became republicanism. Religious minorities—Puritans, Quakers, and Catholics—left their homeland to seek religious freedom in the New World. After the Glorious Revolution of 1689, political rights began entering the picture slowly, and within 100 years, the 13 southernmost of Britain's North American colonies had revolted and declared themselves a nation: the United States of America. Had England begun colonizing America when Spain and Portugal did, however, it too would have been under a powerful, centralized monarchy and a unified Catholic church. Its colonies would probably have followed a very different path.

The Colonial Background

Spain and Portugal kept their American colonies for more than 300 years—400 years in the case of Cuba. Even knowing nothing else, we would hypothesize that many patterns of social, economic, and political significance were established because three centuries is a long time. At a minimum, we would expect that colonial institutions, formal and informal, would influence the first years of independence. Three patterns matter most for the study of Latin American politics: economic, social, and governmental/political.

We usually explain the Iberian interest in the New World in terms of God, gold, and glory. God was represented by the friars, who accompanied explorer Christopher Columbus to the New World, the many priests, brothers, and nuns who followed them, and the strong Catholic faith that marked both Iberian societies at the turn of the sixteenth century. This was a militant faith, especially in Spain, where the fall of Granada brought not just the successful conclusion of the Reconquest but also the expulsion from the country of Muslims and Jews who did not become Christians. That the Church would be part of new endeavors was inevitable.

Still, although God came first, more worldly concerns were closer behind than the pious might have wanted to acknowledge. Remember that the Portuguese had spent most of the fifteenth century exploring and discovering new routes to support the spice trade. Along the way, they unfortunately also discovered that the trade in Africans as slaves was extremely profitable and well worth developing. The Spanish, with their project of national unification complete in 1492, sought their own way to those valuable resources as a logical next step. Besides this luxury trade, of course, both powers sought precious metals and soon found them in previously unimaginable abundance. There was wealth to be had, and with wealth came renown and power—hence glory. So the same motives that had been at work during the centuries of Reconquest found newly fertile ground in the Conquest of the Americas.

Neither Iberian power was looking for the western hemisphere. Everybody knows that Columbus was looking for China; it is less well known that the Portuguese got to Brazil in 1500 by having a ship blown off course on its way around Africa. Both sought the rich markets of Asia, and though the Spanish did find the enormously wealthy and highly sophisticated Aztec and Inca empires, everything else was a disappointment. Yet the Spanish soon found mineral deposits and set up huge agricultural estates where the native inhabitants of the conquered lands, the Indians, became miners and laborers. Although the Church forbade the enslavement of Indians (while approving it for black Africans), the indigenous population of Spain's colonies fell drastically during the colonial era. In the Antilles, the Indians were nearly exterminated. In Central Mexico, home of the Aztecs, it fell by at least 80 per cent and some estimates go as high as 95 per cent. The former Inca homeland of the central Andes saw the native population fall by about 80 per cent, while the overall rate most generally accepted points to a 60 per cent decline. Numbers for Brazil are similar, with most analysts settling on a two-thirds decline in the native population. While some of this carnage was caused by warfare, by far the greatest part came from overwork, disease, malnutrition, and the consequences of social and cultural dislocation.

The economy that overworked and ultimately killed so many displaced Indians had three important traits. First, it was based on the extensive exploitation of natural resources. With its huge landmass and equally huge reserves of precious metals, this was the most obvious economic base for America. Second, the economy was built around a repressive labor regime. Although wage labor existed, slaves and natives were obliged to work initially under the *encomienda* (Indians were granted by the crown to a Spaniard for whom they worked and by whom they were supposedly brought to Christianity) and *repartimiento* (the actual allocation of native forced labor), and later under forms of debt peonage; they formed the bulk of the workforce. Finally, the economies of the Ibero-American colonies developed within a mercantilist framework, in which the colonies existed to benefit the metropole or colonizer. Accordingly, in order to protect metropolitan interests, trade was strictly controlled until nearly the end of the colonial period and the colonies were prohibited from producing more than rudimentary manufactures.[7] These policies, common in imperial systems, not only stifled colonial economies but also delayed the emergence of new elites, thereby preserving colonial social hierarchies. All three characteristics—concentration on primary products, the use of a controlled labor force, and an externally oriented economy—are still found today in Latin America.

Colonial social structures paralleled those of their metropoles and were strongly hierarchical. The *conquistadores* (the conquerors) in Spanish America and the *donatarios* (those to whom land was given) in Brazil received huge grants of lands. Their *latifundia* (country-sized personal land-holdings) became the model for rural organization in Ibero-America, just as the family farm did in Canada and the United States. These *latifundios*[8] joined the higher clergy, top colonial officials, and the most important merchants to form a restricted elite that dominated the rest of society. This elite was white, either European-born or descended from Spanish or Portuguese families that had not intermarried with indigenous people. A "pigmentocracy" emerged that saw the European-born on top, followed by American-born whites, *mestizos* (of mixed native and European ancestry), *mulattos* (of mixed African and European descent), then natives, and finally blacks.

To govern the colonies, both empires deployed complex bureaucratic systems, the Spanish more so than the Portuguese. Given the distances involved and the slowness of transportation and communication during the colonial era, detailed orders from the center often bore little relation to conditions on the ground. From this arose the practice of *obedezco pero no cumplo* ("I obey my orders, but I don't carry them out.") More important for the future of Latin America, however, was the policy of both empires to restrict the top administrative posts to Iberians, leaving the American-born economic elites confined to municipal level politics. With representative politics existing only at the local level, the colonial elites of Latin America who would become national leaders after independence were unable to gain the experience in governing gained by their British North American peers, who had had active roles in the government of their colonies for many years before independence.

Independence

Although the Latin American colonial elites were constrained politically and economically by the imperial orders in which they operated, there was no continent-wide movement toward independence until Napoleon invaded Spain and set his brother on the throne in 1808. Perhaps this is not as unusual as it first seems, since even the more politically active colonists who made the American Revolution functioned under London's rule for well over a century before declaring their independence, while Canadians waited until 1982 to sunder their final constitutional ties with Britain. More interesting and important than the reasons for the delay in seeking independence, however, are the conditions in which the independence movements operated.

As in the 13 rebellious British American colonies that became the United States, both Spanish and Portuguese American colonies had a relatively large, native-born elite ready to take power. In all three areas, the bulk of the economy was run by Americans—those born in the Americas—although those Americans were notably wealthier than the vast majority of their compatriots and rather whiter than many of them, as well. Unlike the African and Asian colonies that became independent after World War II, the American colonies that revolted and gained their independence in the period between 1775 and 1825 had economies that were, in the main, the property of their own residents. As well, colonists throughout the Americas were tired of seeing their economies subordinated to the interests of colonizer and recognized that independence was the only answer. Finally, independence in the United States and most of Spanish America came after long military campaigns. Yet the two revolutionary contexts differed in important ways.

Perhaps the most obvious difference was the British Americans' greater experience with self-government. Even though in both cases colonials were excluded from the very top jobs, the British colonies had governed themselves substantially more fully and for longer than their counterparts in Ibero-America. Further, there were differences of social structure, with Latin America having a far smaller class of independent farmers, a notably less developed middle sector, and a larger proportion of very poor people.[9] Economic historians Stanley L. Engerman and Kenneth L. Solokoff argue that Latin America's factor endowment (climate, natural resources, and the availability of labor) favored the formation of large plantations and mines, both of which demanded large reserves of poorly paid workers. British American colonies, with the exception of what became the southern United States, however, possessed factor endowments that encouraged more egalitarian distributions of property and wealth. The latter was far better placed to permit democratic government than was the former.[10]

What sparked Latin America's independence movements was Napoleon's invasion of the Iberian peninsula. In Spain, the French leader removed the reigning king, Fernando VII, and set his brother Joseph on the throne in 1808. This gave the American colonists the chance to declare independence out of loyalty to the crown. As usual, things worked differently in Brazil. Under the protection of the British fleet, the Portuguese monarch, João VI, fled Lisbon in 1808 just ahead of Napoleon's troops and moved his family and the entire court to Rio de Janeiro. In 1820, João returned to Portugal, though his son Pedro stayed. Three years later, the Portuguese government of the day demanded that Pedro too return to Lisbon. He elected to remain, however, declaring Brazil independent and having himself crowned emperor in 1823.

Gaining independence was a longer and bloodier task in the Spanish colonies. Lasting from 1810 to 1825 (although they ended earlier in some places than others[11]), Spanish America's revolutionary wars of independence defined the political paths the new republics would follow for at

Text Box 2.2 Real and Typical Revolutions

As is true of so many concepts used in political science, there are several competing definitions of *revolution*. For some, it is any violent overthrow of a government. Others see it as any thoroughgoing political change, even if that change is not accomplished by violence, such as Quebec's Quiet Revolution of the 1960s. A third party reserves the label *revolution* for actions that not only topple governments but also significantly change the social and economic order. In this last class belong the French, Russian, Chinese, Cuban, and Iranian revolutions: what we normally call *social revolutions*.

Latin America has produced much political violence and many revolutions. Charles Anderson divided those revolutions into two classes: typical and real.[12] Into the former went the great majority of the region's revolutions. Anderson said that these did not produce fundamental changes to the class structure; at most they let new participants join the elites, often on the elites' terms. The latter class contains Latin America's social revolutions. This is a short list, one that took shape only in the twentieth century, and that features Mexico (1910), Cuba (1959), Nicaragua (1979), and possibly Guatemala (1944) and Bolivia (1952). However, if we are willing to be heretical, we can also add Chile (1973): General Pinochet's coup was violently anticommunist, which would lead some to declare it counterrevolutionary instead of revolutionary, but it certainly changed Chile radically.

least two generations. More so than in the United States, Latin America's wars broke down governing institutions and destroyed infrastructure—roads, schools, and the like. Moreover, and this paralleled the republic to the north, colonial militias were the starting point for the formation of the patriot armies; but in Latin America the commanders of those militias would emerge as *caudillos*: authoritarian, local politico-military bosses who would dominate public life for decades to come. So independence did not bring the bright future Spanish American revolutionaries desired.

We can even ask if it is correct to label these independence struggles *revolutions*. We have no trouble excluding Brazil from the class of revolutionaries: not only was the country still a monarchy, but it was also ruled by the same royal house. We might also want to leave Costa Rica out, since a courier from Guatemala brought word there that the country had become independent. But depending on how we define *revolution*, the rest could pose a problem. If a revolution must set in train far-reaching social and economic changes, Latin America's wars of independence were not revolutionary. Text Box 2.2: Real and Typical Revolutions discusses this question further.

The Era of Instability and the Rule of *Caudillos*

Much like what would happen in Africa over a century later, the newly independent countries of Latin America, with the notable exception of Brazil, fell quickly into either civil war and instability or authoritarian, one-man rule, if not both. For a minimum of 40 years, and in some places far longer, much of Latin America existed in a state of permanent political unrest. Elites agreed on neither governing philosophies nor models of governance and resorted to force to settle their disagreements. In fact, a few countries teetered on the edge of becoming what we now call failed states—those unable to perform the minimal functions of government— more than once. In the next chapter, we consider some explanations for why this happened. Here, though, our concern is with setting out some facts.

Once the wars ended, issues that had remained obscured during the conflict emerged. How would the now free countries be ruled? Who would rule them? Exactly what countries would there be? That last question is the most striking, so we shall start there. Movements in Mexico had visions of encompassing everything to the isthmus. Central Americans rejected this but then underwent 15 years of war to determine that they did not want to be joined together in a Central American federation either. Simón Bolívar, the Venezuelan known as the Liberator, dreamed of uniting all of Spain's former colonies under one flag, but this plan also failed. The political map that emerged closely followed the lines drawn by the colonial authorities, although these would change over time following wars, secessions, and other boundary adjustments.

Deciding who would rule and how they would rule occupied most of the new states for the better part of the next half-century. There were two basic contending views on these questions and they are associated with two broad ideological outlooks: liberal and conservative. Liberals, on the whole, were anticlerical, pro–free trade and free market, and in favor of constitutional government and dispersed authority. Put into practice, this meant taking away the Church's privileges, removing trade subsidies and putting communal lands on the market, and weakening the state. Conservatives wanted the opposite. They wished to let the Church keep its privileges, maintain existing subsidies to commerce, allow Indians to keep communal lands, and preserve a strong central government. When one side took power it would enact its agenda; when the other replaced it, the old rules were repealed and a new order erected. This sounds unexceptional; however, crucial issues of central importance were at stake and defeat was not accepted lightly. The result was frequent armed conflict.

Perhaps if the state had at its disposal a standing army the matter would have been settled decisively if not democratically. However, armed forces were usually little more than regional militias, loyal to their commanders.

And if the commanders were liberals they were loath to obey conservatives and vice versa. The outcome was *caudillo* rule.

Although the term is now conventionally applied to any political leader whose position derives from using personal appeal to attract followers and material resources to retain their loyalty, *caudillos* were originally regional chieftains who were able to become national leaders. These men—for a *caudillo* must be a man and a macho (stereotypically manly) one at that—thrived in conditions of disorder. Their principal political tools were violence (to gain resources) and patronage (distributing resources to keep his followers). The absence of a strong state meant that they would not meet overwhelming force, but it also meant that a *caudillo* who seized control of the central government could not expect to remain in power for long.

Caudillismo—more properly *caudillaje*—was then a political institution within a very particular political system. Divisions within the post-independence political elites in most of Latin America assured that control of the state would be violently contested. In turn, this guaranteed that a strong state would not be built, leaving substantial political space for entrepreneurs whose capital was based on leadership skills and the possession of military might. Until a potent central authority emerged the *caudillo* system would persist because it was so well adapted to its environment.

Not all of Latin America fell under *caudillo* rule. Brazil, with its monarchy, was the most obvious exception. From 1823 until 1889 that regime persisted. To be sure, there were strong regional elites in the person of the *coroneis* (colonels), dominant *fazendeiros* (owners of large estates) who commanded regional units of Brazil's National Guard, yet they did not challenge the emperor. Similar stability came to Chile by a different route, although it too was the product of a conservative regime. There, conservative politician Diego Portales played *éminence grise*, directing the political order from behind the scenes. This he did well, reducing the scope of a *caudillo*-led army and then replacing it with a more professional force. However, his most enduring legacy was the country's 1833 constitution, which lasted until 1925 and gave Chile a powerful central government, a trait that still characterizes its politics.

A third way to stability developed in Paraguay. From 1811 to 1840, the country was under the iron rule of Dr. José Gaspar Rodríguez de Francia.[13] Francia was a revolutionary. He attacked the Church, devastated the old colonial elite, built his system on the support of the peasantry, and effectively closed Paraguay off to the world. To replace commerce, the country developed a pre-Marxist socialism that served it well. After his death, the country experimented with other forms of government until investing Carlos Antonio López with dictatorial powers in 1844. When López died in 1862, his son Francisco Solano López assumed power and quickly led Paraguay into the disastrous War of the Triple Alliance, in which the tiny, landlocked country fought and was nearly destroyed by the armies of Argentina, Brazil, and Uruguay (see Chapter 10).

Order and Progress: From the End of the *Caudillo* Era to the Depression

A text on Latin American politics written 100 years ago would likely have lauded the region's economic and political progress. Development and the diversification of an economy into newer and more profitable areas were evident everywhere, and politics had in most places forsaken open warfare, left endemic instability behind, and moved toward constitutional government, if not yet democratic rule. The watchwords of this period were *order and progress*, the slogan found on Brazil's flag today. In the nineteenth century, they were linked to positivism, a philosophy-cum-ideology that proposed the scientific analysis of society. The outbreak of World War I in 1914 halted the international trade that had built prosperity and encouraged orderly government. Growth resumed in the 1920s, but another breakdown of trade in the 1930s led to the wholesale abandonment of the liberal experiment, which had emphasized free markets and stable political orders run by and for the beneficiaries of laissez-faire capitalism.

The elements that made this breakthrough possible were the end of *caudillo* dominance and the establishment of stronger central authorities. This did not imply the end of personal rule, however. Many of the new regimes were dominated by strongmen: Porfirio Díaz in Mexico, Justo Rufino Barrios in Guatemala, José Santos Zelaya in Nicaragua, and Antonio Guzmán Blanco in Venezuela are examples. The difference is that they not only controlled a stronger national government, but they also used government to build the country. But why did they do this and not keep on pillaging the national treasury as their forebearers had done?

Anthropologists Eric Wolf and Edward Hansen suggest that the arrival of significant foreign investment in the 1870s was the key factor.[14] Economic expansion in Europe and North America spurred demand for the cheap resources—in some cases minerals, in others foodstuffs—available in Latin America. However, before putting up the money needed to develop those resources, investors sought some guarantee of political stability. This, Wolf and Hansen argue, led to alliances between foreign and local interests in which the foreigners provided funds and the locals devised a policy that assured order.

Although the authors do not test their hypothesis, it is intuitively attractive. Capital would have been scarce after four or five decades of *caudillo*-induced stagnation, while Mexico, Chile, and Bolivia's mineral output, Brazilian coffee, and Argentine beef and wheat would have been attractive to industrial countries with capital to invest. This was particularly true of the United States in Mexico and Central America and Great Britain in

South America's Southern Cone. A few examples will show how this new system worked.

First, although governments became more stable, there was little that looked like what we could consider democracies, so we should follow political scientist Paul Lewis's lead and acknowledge that we are dealing with dictators and oligarchies.[15] Some of those dictators were military men, but unlike the *caudillos*, these generals led increasingly professional armies. Modeling Latin America's militaries on those of the most advanced European states—for example, Germany and France—was supposed to put an end to the use of armed might to win control of the state. Unfortunately, what it actually did was make the military more technically proficient, more aware of its distinction from the rest of society, and more impatient with what it deemed civilian misrule. Thus coups and military governments continued unabated.[16]

However, it was Porfirio Díaz, who controlled Mexican politics from 1876 to 1911, who was the apotheosis of the dictators of this era. His rule, nicknamed "Diazpotism," kept order through a judicious balance between the distribution of *pan* (bread) and the application of *palo* (the stick). Progress came through a foreign investment boom that built railways that carried increasing quantities of minerals (from gold to lead) and agricultural products to foreign markets. The political system was built around patronage, local bosses, and rigged elections. Yet this well-oiled machine somehow failed to notice a rapidly growing middle class that neither benefited from the concessions to foreign capital nor needed patronage handouts and that grew increasingly frustrated with the strongman's rule. When the 80-year-old Díaz won yet another fraudulent election in 1910, he loosed a storm of opposition that became the Mexican Revolution. In 1911, the dictator sailed into exile for the rest of his days.

An alternative model existed where parties engaged in limited competition for the votes of a restricted electorate. These were called "civic oligarchies," and they combined some aspects of constitutional rule with intra-elite competition. Though not democratic by contemporary standards, they did substitute minimally competitive elections for violence as the standard means of changing governments. The governments established within this framework understandably gave special attention to the concerns of the elite, national and foreign, but often also dedicated important sums to schools and infrastructure.

Perhaps the best model of a civic oligarchy was found in Chile. Built on the solid foundations left by Portales, it survived the shift in 1891 from an executive-centered system to a "Parliamentary Republic," which gave primacy to Congress. However, that change did not expand the political class but rather excluded the expanding middle and working classes. The parliamentary regime ended in 1920 with the election of Arturo Alessandri, and the last vestiges of the Portalian system were swept away by a coup in 1925.

A coup also revamped the Brazilian system. In 1889, the military revolted against the empire, mainly due to its failure to modernize the armed forces, and sought to break the power of the old elites and industrialize the South American giant. However, the 1891 constitution set in place a radically decentralized federalism that conferred far greater power on the states than on the national government. The resulting system lasted until 1930 and was dominated by the two most powerful states in the Brazilian union: São Paulo and Minas Gerais, both coffee states from the southeast.

What all Latin America shared was an export-oriented, staples-based economy. A staples-based economy is built on raw materials. Some of these are nonrenewable, such as minerals and petroleum, while others are renewable, such as coffee, sugar, and beef. Whatever the product, its market is foreign, leaving the producers dependent on the vagaries of the international economy, and shifting economic conditions and tastes far beyond their borders. During the last quarter of the nineteenth century, international communications became faster and more flexible as undersea cables were laid for telegraphic traffic. As well, steam navigation, which had existed since the start of that century, came to dominate world trade in that same period. Add to that growing international demand for cheap staples to feed industrial workers and fuel factories and you have the basis for rapid economic expansion in Latin America. However, World War I interrupted the trade circuits between Latin America and Western Europe. While these were restored during the 1920s, the Depression of the 1930s appeared to break them decisively.

The Great Depression to the Washington Consensus

Assigning a starting date to this period is reasonably easy. The obvious choice is Black Tuesday, October 29, 1929, the day the New York stock market crashed, but it is more prudent to select 1930, by which time the capitalist world was starting to reel from the effects of its latest crisis. Settling on a date to close this period is harder. Identifying it with the Washington Consensus is a natural choice, because the policies and practices gathered under that rubric—often labeled *neoliberal* for their embrace of free market orthodoxy—defined what was permissible in economic policy for Latin America and much of the rest of the world from the time the label emerged, in 1990, until perhaps the Pink Tide of elections that brought left-of-center governments to power in six Latin American countries in 2005 and 2006.[17] However, it appears wisest to close this era in 2001. That was when Argentina, the poster child of the Washington Consensus, saw its once-lauded economy crumble. Over these 71 years, Latin America would live through two significant economic experiments and see the dominant political model pass from limited constitutional democracy to authoritarianism to representative, electoral democracy. They are the foundation of modern Latin America.

Economics

Economically, these seven decades produced a rich array of experiments but still failed to secure North American levels of development for most of the population. From roughly 1870 to 1930, all Latin American nations passed through a process of liberalization. They embraced fully the principles of laissez-faire economics, including free trade (thus offering little or no tariff protection for local producers) and the universal use of individual titles to real property (thus initiating the abolition of communal lands). What made the model work was foreign demand for raw materials.

Latin America, like Canada and even the United States, was a staples-producing area. Places that have small populations, some access to capital, and a good supply of raw materials—fish, furs, timber, grains, ores, petroleum—are well placed to build their economies around staples. In Canada and the United States, as in Australia and New Zealand, the results have been excellent, as highly productive, thoroughly modern economies have resulted. Although Latin America has not made this qualitative leap, 100 years ago it certainly looked ready to do so. That it did not was due to factors that we consider more closely in Chapters 8 and 9, but here we can note that interruption of trade circuits during World War I and the Depression crushed the commerce that sustained the Latin American economies.

Like the rest of the world, Latin America responded to the collapse of the world economy with what Professor Jeffery Frieden calls "the turn to autarky."[18] What this translated to in practice was import substitution industrialization (ISI). The idea is simple and attractive. Take manufactured products that you import, have local firms start making those goods behind a tariff wall, and soon you have an industrial base. This model, too, proved successful in North America, where very high tariffs in the nineteenth century were key parts in the success of many industries. But the policy had other attractions for Latin American governments.

In its textbook format, ISI builds a class of industrialists who focus on the national market and are located in the cities. This class countervails the staples' exporters from the hinterlands. Moreover, ISI necessitates the growth of an industrial working class. The government that sustains ISI therefore finds itself with two useful allies, capitalists and industrial workers, strengthening its hand against factions tied to the old elite and preparing the country for a more prosperous future, less dependent on foreign markets. It looked like a winning proposition for government and business, and it produced good results for a time.

From its inception in the 1930s to the first oil shock of 1973 (if not somewhat earlier), the ISI model worked well in Latin America. This was particularly true in larger countries with big domestic markets, such as Argentina, Brazil, and Mexico. However, the system had built-in flaws, at least as it operated in Latin America.

Ideally, ISI is a short-term policy. After a few years, the protected industry should become efficient enough to withstand foreign competition and even to go in search of export markets itself. This did not happen, likely because the internal markets were too small and because domestic growth was too slow to add enough new clients to let the firms achieve economies of scale. Governments decided not to pressure the companies to become more competitive by withdrawing some tariff protection because the politicians feared the consequences of massive unemployment in the cities and the bankruptcy of the firms they had backed. The winning ticket of the 1930s became the no-win situation of the 1970s.

As if the exhaustion of the regional economic model were not enough, the 1970s also brought a foreign debt crisis. Latin America had known this problem before and many Latin American countries had defaulted on their debts in the past. This time, however, that option was ruled out, and Structural Adjustment Programs (SAP), a part of what would come to be called the Washington Consensus, were in. SAPs were run by the International Monetary Fund and offered debtor countries cheap loans in return for adopting a package of policies that would bring Latin America in the 1980s the unfettered free enterprise of the 1890s. Behind those policies were the objectives of avoiding default, assuring the participation of the debtor countries in the world economy, and seeing them implement policies that would avoid future debt crises and make the countries better off. The first three objectives were secured, at least in the short run, but the fourth was not. In the twenty-first century, most Latin American countries are still looking for ways to build a stable, productive economy.

Politics

The political side of the story has a more positive outcome, even though the road there was difficult and perilous. With the turn away from free trade in the 1930s came a similar shift away from political pluralism. Although politics during the 1920s remained elite-dominated, civic oligarchies did feature electoral competition within the elite. Democracy in North America and Western Europe had begun in similar conditions, so there was hope. The promise of evolution, however, was cut short in the 1930s: only three countries came out of the 1930s with same political system with which they entered the decade—Mexico, Costa Rica, and Colombia—and only the last two could be considered constitutional governments. In short, whatever progress had been made toward democratic government during the era of the civic oligarchies was rolled back in most of the region. Worse, in most places it would be a half a century before the democratic ball was picked up again.

Some of the cases of political breakdown were quite dramatic. In the 1920s, El Salvador was so well and moderately governed that it was looked upon as a model for all of Central America. In 1932, however, it produced *la Matanza*, the slaughter of at least 10,000 peasants who had resisted a military coup. The coup itself, led by General Maximiliano Hernández Martínez, was directed against newly elected President Arturo Araujo. Although Araujo came from an elite family (his father had been finance minister at the turn of the twentieth century), he had studied in England, where he was impressed by Labour Party doctrines, which worried the handful of coffee barons who dominated Salvadoran politics and society. Backed by the elite, Martínez[19] ousted the president in December 1931. However, in January 1932, a rebellion broke out under the leadership of the Communist Faribundo Martí. Although the rebels caused few deaths, the oligarchy destroyed them utterly.

Once El Salvador abandoned the limited pluralism (a situation marked by the existence of independent centers of influence beyond state control) that had characterized its politics in the 1920s, its elites apparently decided that even limited electoral competition among themselves was too much. Although Martínez was overthrown in 1944, the military and the elite were able to hold power until 1979. In that year, a reformist military coup ousted the sitting conservative military government before falling quickly to a countercoup. That brought a hardline military regime to power and marked the start of a dozen years of civil war involving the state, greatly aided by Washington, death squads linked to the state, and the Marxist guerrillas of the Frente Faribundo Martí de Liberación Nacional (FMLN, or Farabundo Marti National Liberation Front), named for the leader of the failed insurrection of 1932.[20]

The fighting produced a stalemate, leading to a negotiated settlement in 1992, which has left El Salvador with a two-party system built around the protagonists of the civil war. The Alianza Republicana Nacionalista (ARENA, or Nationalist Republican Alliance), the party of the right, dominant nationally through the 2009 congressional elections, has some of its roots in the death squads. The FMLN represents the left, and until winning El Salvador's presidential election in 2009 in a tight race (51.3 per cent of the vote to 48.7 per cent), it had done well in mayoral elections but had not won nationally.

Other countries experienced similarly significant changes. Argentina appeared to be leaving its era of limited pluralism behind in 1916 with the election of the Radicals (Unión Cívica Radical, or UCR) under Hipólito Yrigoyen. The Radicals were a middle-class party of social reformers and more in tune with an increasingly urbanized country with a large immigrant population. However, the UCR, like the political machines that developed in North America around the end of the nineteenth century, relied on patronage and a network of party bosses. As long as there was money in the treasury, the government was fine, but once the Depression hit, it had little to offer. This presented the old oligarchy the chance to turn to the military and return to power. Their stay, however, lasted only until 1943, when another coup brought them down. This second coup would become famous because it brought Juan Domingo Perón on to the Argentine political stage.

Although he was president of the republic for only 10 years (1946–55 and 1973–74), Perón dominated Argentina's political life in the second half of the last century. He not only mobilized labor and made it a political force but also gave the country's politics a strong nationalist and populist hue. Overthrown by conservative military officers in 1955, Perón remained in exile in Spain until 1973 when he was allowed back to confront a crisis of governability marked by high levels of violence; however, he died in 1974. Two years later, there was another coup, this one leading to the *Guerra Sucia*, the dirty war the military government waged against its enemies, a list including moderates and democratic conservatives. This regime, however, made the colossal blunder of attacking the Falkland Islands and allowing Prime Minister Margaret Thatcher to "put the Great" back in Great Britain by handing the Argentine generals a humiliating defeat in 1982. The next year, democracy returned to Argentina, and Raúl Alfonsín, a Radical like Yrigoyen, was elected president.

Democracy did not prove to be Argentina's promised land, though. Six years after beginning the country's transition, Alfonsín turned over the reins to his elected successor, Carlos Menem, six months ahead of schedule, with the nation facing a severe, inflation-fueled economic crisis. Menem dealt with inflation using the tools of structural adjustment, most notably pegging the peso to the US dollar, thus taking monetary policy effectively out of Argentine hands. This worked marvelously well to whip inflation and turn the country into the International Monetary Fund's star pupil, but it also destroyed Argentina's industrial base and spread poverty. The full consequences of this policy, or rather a mule-headed refusal to change it, became clear in December 2001 when the economy collapsed. That set off demonstrations, violence, and a remarkable record of five presidents in two weeks. What was more remarkable, however, was that no coup followed and democracy survived.

Brazil also saw its civic oligarchy fall to a coup in 1930. The proximate cause was the breakdown in the alternation of the presidency between candidates from the most important states, Minas Gerais and São Paulo, an informal institution that allowed the system to work. Specifically, the Paulistas refused to accept the candidate of Minas Gerais, Getulio Vargas, a nationalist with plans for industrialization. The military, though, liked Vargas's ideas and brought him to power through a coup.

Once in office, Vargas took two important steps. First, he established *O Estado Novo* (the New State), the same name used by Portuguese dictator António de Oliveira Salazar for his fascist regime. Like its Portuguese predecessor, Brazil's Estado Novo was corporatist. Thus, instead of letting a plurality of interests compete freely, the state organized them into hierarchies, sector by sector, all under state control. The most important of these sectors for Vargas was labor, which became his power base, as it would for Perón in Argentina. Although Vargas headed a political system with strong fascist traits, Brazil not only declared war on the Axis, something other states most often did to have the pretext for seizing property owned by Germans, but also sent troops to Europe to fight alongside the Allies. In 1945, Vargas's attempt to extend the New State and remain in office prompted the army to give him the choice of stepping down or being ousted. He left quietly and won election to Congress in the general elections of 1945.

From 1945 to 1964, Brazil maintained its Second Republic. During this period, a number of practices took root that still shape the country's politics (for example, the formation of parties with strong regional bases instead of national organizations). To knit these into a governing bloc, a president has to make regular trips to the pork barrel and broker the favor-swapping deals needed to keep the parties happy. However, it was not the corruption inherent in log-rolling politics that brought the Second Republic to its unscheduled appointment with a coup in 1964 but the decision of President João Goulart to press for land reform and the nationalization of oil. This time the military did not turn power over to civilians but rather stayed in power for 21 years, giving the world its first taste of bureaucratic-authoritarian rule.

Bureaucratic authoritarianism is the label applied to the four dictatorships that existed in South America's most developed states—Argentina, Brazil, Chile, and Uruguay—between 1964 and 1989. These were radically anticommunist military states, ruling through force and terror, and with a strong commitment to bring their countries into the ranks of developed nations. Brazil's generals and admirals stood out from their peers by being somewhat less repressive and by creating two official political parties to channel political activity, instead of banning political life altogether, as their colleagues did. The objective, of course, was to keep the military in power, but legitimated by elections. However, the attempt failed, and in 1985, a civilian president pledged to restore democracy, Tancredo Neves, was elected, albeit indirectly.

Brazil has not had an easy time under democracy since the withdrawal of the military, but it has remained democratic. The death of Neves before he took office was a bad omen, as was the impeachment, on corruption charges, of Fernando Collor de Mello, the first directly elected president under the new order. Worse, at first democracy seemed incapable of controlling inflation and sustaining the economy, but the naming of Fernando Henrique Cardoso, a former leftist sociology professor, as minister of finance led to economic stability. Cardoso then won two consecutive presidential elections. In 2002, he was succeeded by Luiz Inácio Lula da Silva. Lula, the one-time leader of Brazil's most militant union and head of the Partido dos Trabalhadores (Workers' Party), is the first self-identified leftist ever to lead Brazil. In the past, Lula's election might have sparked a coup, but not only did he take office, he also managed the economy carefully and well, withstood a corruption crisis in his party, and won re-election in 2006.

Even countries that preserved pluralism throughout the 1930s did not have a stable, democratic future guaranteed them. While Colombia has experienced just three military coups in its history (in 1830, 1854, and 1953), it has known the most political violence of any Latin American country, with six interparty civil wars in the nineteenth century and two in the twentieth. It is estimated that 100,000 people died in the War of a Thousand Days (1899–1902) and 200,000 lost their lives in *La Violencia* (1948–1958). Despite that background, Colombia not only maintained a constitutional government but also had a forcefully reformist administration under the Liberal Alfonso López Pumarejo (1934–1938). Within a decade of López Pumarejo's presidency, however, the country had again collapsed into chaotic warfare.

The spark that set off La Violencia was the assassination of the radical Liberal Jorge Eliécer Gaitán in 1948. The fighting that followed pitted Liberals against Conservatives, as it had since the earliest days of the republic. At stake were not abstract principles but the question of whether elites linked to the Conservative Party would win and govern or whether Liberal-aligned elites would prevail. A coup by General Gustavo Rojas Pinilla in 1953 ended the violence, but the military regime was ousted in 1957. At that point, Liberals and Conservatives combined to form the Frente Nacional (National Front). This was an ingenious bit of political engineering that let the Liberals and Conservatives alternate the presidency every 4 years for 16 years (the Front was extended for another 4-year period, thus ending in 1978), and share equally all other elected offices. This put an end to La Violencia but laid the foundation for the violence that afflicts Colombia today.

Although many reform projects began under the National Front, it did not address the concentration of political and economic power in the hands of the elites. Moreover, it led both parties to lose touch with the electorate, and the voters themselves to lose interest in politics. Worse, it was during the period of the National Front that guerrilla activity began in rural areas in defense of peasant demands for land.[21] Aggravating this long-running guerrilla conflict was the appearance in 1997 of well-organized paramilitaries, the Autodefensas Unidas de Colombia (United Self-Defense Forces of Colombia). Of course, the most important source of violence in recent Colombian history has been the rise since the 1980s of the cocaine trade and the drug lords it spawned. While the drug trade cannot be seen as a natural outgrowth of pre-existing tendencies, the more overtly political guerrilla violence does have its roots in social structures and the historic use of violence to settle political disputes.

Different Histories, Different Outcomes: Costa Rica and Nicaragua

Until now we have laid out broad themes that affected all or substantial parts of Latin America. To use these to argue that history matters for today's politics, we look at trends and tendencies that shaped and constrained choices made by contemporary citizens and the politicians they elect to office. As we observed at the start of the chapter, this is not historical determinism—the idea that history leaves you few, even no, choices about what kind of country you live in. Rather, the kind of viewpoint that has been developed here makes a more modest claim: things that happened long ago set in motion processes or gave power to classes or religious groups or races that still resound today. Power can be transferred to different groups and processes, and even lead to dead ends and expire, but at any given time the odds are that the way things are now will be how they are tomorrow. Looking at two Central American neighbors, Nicaragua and Costa Rica, provides some useful examples.

As a colony, Costa Rica held little attraction, as it had neither mineral wealth nor many natives to use as cheap labor. So instead of *latifundia*, Costa Rica saw the development of small, family farms. Nicaragua, however, was suitable for plantation agriculture. In fact, the native population was sufficiently great at the start of the colonial era to make Indians, shipped to the mines of Peru, Nicaragua's first big export item. One result of this difference was that Costa Rican society developed without racial differences that reinforced class divisions.

With independence, the differences grew. Nicaragua's two principal cities, León, a Liberal stronghold, and Granada, a Conservative bastion, were nearly constantly engaged in a civil war until 1856. In that year, William Walker, an American mercenary hired by the Liberals, turned against his employers, seized Nicaragua, and worked to have it admitted to the United States as a slave state. An alliance of the other four Central American states expelled Walker in 1858. Only then did the country settle in for three decades of stable, limited pluralism under the Conservatives. But in Costa Rica, the two old colonial centers, Cartago and Heredia, were vanquished by San José, producing a strongly centralized state that knew coups and insurrections but avoided civil war. In fact, it was stable enough that in 1824, the Nicaraguan province of Nicoya seceded and joined Costa Rica, where it remains.

Entering the twentieth century, Costa Rica had a stable civic oligarchy, dominated by big coffee producers, which would survive until 1948, interrupted only by a short-lived dictatorship (1917–1919). Nicaragua, however, again was convulsed by civil war. The Conservative republic, which earned Nicaragua the sobriquet "the Switzerland of Central America," fell in 1893 to a Liberal revolution, which was the only road to power open to a rising coffee elite. The leader of that revolt, José Santos Zelaya, harassed domestic opponents, meddled in the politics of neighboring states, and annoyed Washington grievously by trying to interest Germany and Japan in financing a Nicaraguan canal to rival Panama. In 1909, he fell to a United States–supported coup. That then produced the garrisoning of US Marines in Nicaragua for 23 years, an 18-year civil war, and another 6 years of guerrilla war against the Marines. The era ended with Anastasio Somoza muscling his wife's uncle out of the presidency in 1936 to begin 43 years of dictatorship by him and his sons.

It took a bloody revolution to rid Nicaragua of the Somozas and usher into power the Frente Sandinista de Liberación Nacional (FSLN, or Sandinista National Liberation Front) in 1979. Named for the guerrilla general who fought the Marines in the 1920s, Augusto César Sandino, the Sandinistas had no sooner begun their reforms to build socialism than they found themselves fighting an insurgency financed by Washington. Although the FSLN was not overthrown, a decade of hardship led Nicaraguans to vote them out of office in 1990 and make the Sandinistas the first revolutionary vanguard to leave office voluntarily. The Costa Ricans again fared better, because their revolution of 1948 both replaced the old elite of coffee barons and brought modern, democratic government. As a result, Costa Rica is Latin America's senior democracy, operating under the same constitution since 1949. Now *it* is the Switzerland of Central America.

Looking at these two countries side by side prompts a series of "what if" questions, which are more formally called counterfactuals. What if someone had imposed centralized rule over Nicaragua right after independence and forestalled 35 years of civil war? What if the 1917 coup in Costa Rica had ended up like the 1909 revolution in Nicaragua? How much of this was luck and unpredictable? How much is explained by path dependence (that is, structural elements that made what actually happened the most likely outcome)? How much could different leadership have changed the results?

Why Latin American History Matters

To see if there is enough shared history across the 20 republics that we call Latin America to let us treat them as a region in any sense beyond the geographic, we need to make a list of the things they have in common. First, there is the colonial heritage that, despite now being almost 200 years in the past, had economic, political, and social consequences, some of which are still felt today. Economically, we can point to the laying of the bases for a resource-exporting economy. Politically, the failure to develop participatory institutions for even the elites appears to have complicated the development of stable government after independence. Socially, a rather highly stratified class system emerged, which likely impeded later efforts to make political life more inclusive.

Applying the same criteria to the 120 years between independence and the Great Depression, Latin America's long nineteenth century, we could add to the list an economy still balanced precariously on international demand for staple products, but one that had grown and for a time prospered. Politically, the common ground was both more extensive and more pernicious. On the positive side of the equation, limited, quasi-democratic pluralism emerged toward the end of the nineteenth century, about the same time as in southern Europe. Yet this was outweighed by the rise of the *caudillo* and personalistic, authoritarian politics, the politicization of the military, and continuing utility and apparent legitimacy of violence as a regular governing instrument. These reached across the region and made constitutional rule and good governance rare commodities. Finally, society did begin to change, especially in countries that received substantial immigration, but it remained highly stratified and with fewer opportunities for mobility than in North America or northwestern Europe.

While the foregoing is not a seamless web, it still constitutes a substantial common heritage and one that should influence the shape and content of politics significantly. That being the case, we need a double focus. One part needs to ask why there are so many variations on these themes, while the other examines the cross-national continuities that we also find.

Further Readings

Bethell, Leslie (Ed.). *The Cambridge History of Latin America.* 10 v. New York: Cambridge University Press, 1984.

Journals

There are several academic journals that regularly carry articles about Latin American history and Latin American politics. You will probably find some of these, if not all of them, in your university's library.

Bulletin of Latin American Studies
Canadian Journal of Latin American and Caribbean Studies
Hispanic American Historical Review

Journal of Latin American Studies
Latin American Perspectives
Latin American Politics and Society
Latin American Research Review

Discussion Questions

① Here are two opposing views of the role of history in human affairs. The first is Henry Ford's, who said that history was bunk. The second is that of Mexican novelist Carlos Fuentes, who has argued that Latin America is at war with its past. What do you suspect each was getting at? How would each view affect how we perceive Latin American politics?

② To get a sense of how we use history in our daily understanding of how things work, take a fairly big public affairs story from the current news. This should be a local or national issue, not an international one. Analyze the central topic of the story in two ways: one without using historical referents, the other employing historical examples. Are there any differences?

Notes

1. Both Chapter 3, which looks at long-established political actors, and Chapter 4, which considers long-standing styles of governance and governing instruments, also have a significant historical element.

2. Harold B. Johnson, Jr., ed., *From Reconquest to Empire: The Iberian Background to Latin American History* (New York: Alfred A. Knopf, 1970).

3. Louis Hartz, *The Liberal Tradition in America* (New York: Harcourt, Brace & World, 1955) and Louis Hartz, ed., *The Founding of New Societies: Studies in the History of the United States, Latin America, South Africa, Canada, and Australia* (New York: Harcourt, Brace and World, 1964).

4. Granada fell on 2 January 1492, while Columbus arrived at what is now Watling Island, in the Bahamas, 12 October 1492.

5. Derek Lomax, *The Reconquest of Spain* (London: Longman, 1978) 178.

6. E. Bradford Burns, *A History of Brazil*. 2nd. ed. (New York: Columbia University Press, 1980) 29–31.

7. Although true of both colonial empires, Brazil had more room to maneuver than the Spanish colonies.

8. *Latifundista* is a generic term for someone holding vast tracts of agricultural land, a *latifundio*. More place specific terms include *fazendeiro* with a *fazenda* (Brazil), *hacendado* with a *hacienda* (Spanish America), and *estanciero* with an *estancia* (especially Argentina).

9. British American or British North American generally refers solely to Canada. However, it seems useful to include the United States under that rubric to emphasize how the levels of colonial self-rule they and, later, the Canadians enjoyed, contrasted with those extended to Portuguese and Spanish American colonies. The comparison could be taken further, for example, by noting the relative weight of independent small farmers versus plantation owners in the three systems or the relatively more open class structures of the British Americans, whether in the future Canada or in what became the United States.

10. Stanley Engerman and Kenneth Solokoff, "Factor Endowments, Institutions, and Differential Paths of Growth among New World Economics: A View from Economic Historians of the United States," *How Latin America Fell Behind: Essays on the Economic Histories of Brazil and Mexico*, ed. Stephen Haber (Stanford, CT: Stanford University Press, 1997) 260–304.

11. Cuba did not become independent until after the Spanish–American War 1898; Puerto Rico passed from being a Spanish colony to a US protectorate and now has the ambiguous status of a "commonwealth" within the American system. Panama is also an exception, as its independence came after secession from Colombia in 1903.

12. Charles W. Anderson, *Politics and Economic Change in Latin America: The Governing of Restless Nations* (New York: Van Nostrand Reinhold, 1967).

13. Francia's doctorate was in theology and came from the University of Cordoba, Argentina.

14. Eric Wolf and Edward Hansen, "Caudillo Politics; A Structural Analysis," *Comparative Studies in Society and History* 9:2 (1967): 168–179.

15. Paul H. Lewis, *Authoritarian Regimes in Latin America: Dictators, Despots, and Tyrants* (Lanham, MD: Rowman and Littlefield, 2006) Chapters 3–4.

16. The question of the political role of professional militaries in Latin America is discussed further in Chapter 3.

17. The Washington Consensus receives substantial attention in Chapters 8 and 9, while the Pink Tide is treated in Chapter 7.

18. Jeffry A. Frieden, *Global Capitalism: Its Fall and Rise in the Twentieth Century* (New York: W.W. Norton & Company, 2006).

19. Normally, Martínez would be known as Hernández in Spanish usage. The two last names commonly used in Spanish-speaking countries put the father's family name first and the mother's family name second, the children using the family name of the father. Occasionally, however, individuals prefer to use the family name of their mother. In Portuguese-speaking countries, though, the name of the mother's family comes before that of the father, so there it is the second of the last names that is generally adopted by the children.

20. Tommie Sue Montgomery, *Revolution in El Salvador: From Civil Strife to Civil Peace,* 2nd ed. (Boulder, CO: Westview, 1995).

21. At one time there were four guerrillas fronts in Colombia—Fuerzas Armadas Revolucionarias de Colombia (FARC, or Colombian Revolutionary Armed Forces of Colombia), Ejército de Liberación Nacional (ELN, or National Liberation Army), Ejército Popular da Liberación (EPL, or People's Liberation Army), and Movimiento 19 de Abril (M-19, or 19th of April Movement)—of which the first two still exist.

3

Latin America's Historic Power Elite: Stability and Change

For the first 150 to 175 years after independence, it was both common and fundamentally correct to describe Latin American politics as dominated by a power elite built around an iron triangle of economic interests: the landed classes (*latifundistas*, mine owners, and big commerce), the Roman Catholic Church, and the military. Together, they formed a formidable, generally coherent conservative bloc. One side of the triangle—the wealthy—affected a nation's material well-being; the second—the Church—addressed moral values and legitimated the existing social and political orders; the third—the military—kept unwanted change from occurring and served as the ultimate political arbiter. The specific roles these elites took differed over time and among countries. Economic interests sometimes squabbled among themselves, the Church might have been weakened by past anticlerical governments, and the military could be weak or even apolitical. However, every country in Latin America had its own version of this iron triangle.

Although we still speak of Latin America as a living political museum, by around 1975 this historic power elite begins losing its dominance. Landed classes had already begun turning to capitalist agriculture, changing their economic outlook and turning multitudes of peasants into rootless, rural proletarians. In addition, up to four decades of import substitution industrialization[1] had produced a substantial if somewhat artificial industrial sector to compete with the *latifundistas* in most countries. By the twenty-first century, the *latifundista* of old was no more, though large-scale agriculture was still very important; mining still dominated in some countries; and banking and commerce were swept up by the globalizing tide. The Church faced its own problems. First among them was liberation theology, a movement within the Catholic Church that preached a social gospel not far removed from Marxism. Then came the even greater challenge mounted by evangelical Protestantism, which has gained important numbers of converts throughout the region. Finally, even the military found its position challenged. Decades of economic mismanagement and exceptionally cruel human rights abuses, combined with a changing international order that no longer valued military governments, substantially reduced its clout. However, despite losing their predominance, all three forces remain significant political actors and are integral parts of the political power structure—the "who makes politics move and in what direction"—of most Latin American countries.[2]

This chapter examines the political evolution of these three forces from the earliest days of the independence movements to the present. It offers a regional perspective that covers all 20 republics and presents examples drawn from many of them. It then compares how these elites have functioned in Latin America with what has happened in other regions. By its conclusion, the chapter will have provided you with the material to answer four questions:

- · How can we best conceptualize this iron triangle?
- · How did these three groups become elites?
- · How did they manage to stay among the elite?
- · How and why did their power decline?

The first step is to select a conceptual framework, for that gives us a coherent way of examining the question and interpreting the answer. The chapter began by calling these three the *power elite* but rather than just define the term we will look at elite theory more generally to indicate why that label fits best.

Political Science and Political Elites

There has never been any doubt that individual political leaders and society's most politically influential groups are central to the study of politics. What has been less clear, even a source of conflict within political science, is just how they ought to be studied. We know that there *are* political elites: people, individuals and groups, who have more power, more ability to influence the course of public affairs than others in society. But are these elites best seen as a ruling class, a power elite, or just the people who happen to be running things at the moment?

How we answer the last question affects how we perceive politics. If we conclude that the political elite is the sum of those who occupy a country's top political posts, the ones who run things, we imply that these people can and will be replaced by others in the future. We do not always ask whether the replacements will have the same social characteristics because that is not our focus. Thus we will have a pluralist view of politics that emphasizes the existence of independent groups struggling for government power.

Alternatively, if we perceive the existence of a ruling class or a power elite, the implication is that even though the actual rulers will change, their successors will come from the same groups and reflect the same interests and values, obviously modified to suit changing conditions. We will view politics through the lens of elite theories and see the political arena as a sort of champions' league, where only the top teams compete. In fact, we may find that these elites compete less fiercely against each other than they do against those trying to enter this circle of the elect. Finally, if we discern a ruling class, we argue that a class, defined by its control over the means of production, dominates the state. In this Marxist subset of more general elite theories, the members of that class may govern directly or through proxies but always work to reproduce the social relations between and among classes that keep them on top. Our task is to examine these terms and explain why the power elite is the best concept for analyzing historic Latin American political elites.

Political science generally defines political elites as "persons who are able, by virtue of their strategic positions in powerful organizations, to affect national political outcomes regularly and substantially."[3] Political scientists Michael Burton, Richard Gunther, and John Higley estimate that large countries, such as the United States, might have 10,000 of these top decision-makers in government, political organizations, business, media, and professional organizations and movements, while a country the size of Chile, with about one-thirtieth the population of the United States, might have 1,000.[4] In either case, we are talking about no more than one-hundredth of 1 per cent of the population. Smaller countries, and presumably nondemocratic ones, which would not have extensive interest groups or an array of political parties, could even have proportionately smaller elites. None of this is surprising because the elites are those who hold a society's most prestigious positions.

It is important to note that political science usually identifies a pluralistic elite. Such an elite is drawn from various sectors and can include forces that are antagonistic toward one another and occasionally even toward the state itself. This is what we expect in consolidated democracies, which are permeable political systems[5] (that is, they allow forces to emerge and establish themselves relatively easily). However, all states necessarily have plural political elites in at least some sense.

First, there is the elite that runs the state, which itself has two parts: politicians and bureaucrats. Then there is the elite that influences but does not run the state. This, too, will have multiple parts, generally following functional lines but not always. Thus there will be at least economic, cultural, military, foreign policy, domestic policy and moral influentials. There will also be specific classes of individuals, founded on wealth, religions, ethnic and cultural groups, all of which stand at the apex of their particular hierarchies. Even in dictatorships, there are powerful social actors whose views need to be considered, even if they are not heeded. To complicate matters further, each of these categories of influentials is likely to have sub-elites who are at the top of a particular sector (for example, there are financial and industrial sub-elites within the economic elite).

Whether the political system is open and democratic or closed and authoritarian matters little; these groups and the individuals who compose them are political forces to contend with. They possess plentiful resources, both material and symbolic. Consequently, they can move the state to take action favoring them or hampering their opponents. Put these elements together and it is evident why political science has long given substantial attention to the study of elites. However, when looking at Latin America, this interest goes beyond knowing who these elites are and how they act to asking *how* and *why* the roster of elites changes or remains constant.

In the natural order of things, we expect to see elites rise and fall, reflecting broader social and political changes. Obviously, there will be some time lag before representatives of a rising group—which could be based on partisan affiliation, class, religion, ethnicity, or region—enter the upper ranks. Equally, an inertial lag should keep a group among the political elite even as its relative influence wanes. The latter observation is less apparent than the former but presumes that declining elites cede some space to newcomers rather than resisting until they are ousted. Although this is not always true, it is a reasonable rule of thumb.

Two questions arise from the foregoing. First, why might old elites not fall? For one thing, they still may hold key positions that control a lot of power: having been around for a long time lets them punch above their objective weight, because they know how to make the system work. Another possibility is that they draw support from other parts of the elite. This could be historically established actors banding together to resist newcomers or newcomers allying with the old guard to draw on its experience and legitimacy. The reasons in any real case will vary, but it is important to know that there are plausible reasons that account for the persistence of what look like superannuated political forces.

The second question is, What difference does this make? Why should the composition of a nation's political elite change? Many of the political instruments, actors, and institutions found in Latin America have their origins in the immediate post-independence era or even the colonial period. As every country in the region has been independent for at least a century and most are approaching 200 years of self-rule, clearly these are long-established, well-entrenched, solidly institutionalized patterns and practices (see Text Box 3.1). This suggests that we need to think in terms of power elites or ruling classes.

This is not to say that old is bad. Old can be both venerable and honorable. Parliaments and universities are both institutions formed in the medieval West, yet they have been adopted globally or nearly so and are usually held in high regard. What raises eyebrows about Latin America's array of long-lived political actors and institutions is their links to non-democratic politics. This has certainly been true in our three cases. But do these groups form either a ruling class or a power elite?

Text Box 3.1 The Really Permanent Elites

While individual members of an elite come and go, some groups seemingly have a permanent pass to the corridors of power. This chapter talks about three of those groups in detail: big landowners, the military, and the Catholic Church. However, there are two other sets of permanent participants whom we need to mention: men and nonindigenous people.

Although there have been a few women presidents in Latin American history (though none were elected before 1990), there have not been many: Violeta Chamorro of Nicaragua, who for a while also had a female vice-president, Julia Mena; Mirena Moscoso of Panama, Michelle Bachelet of Chile, and Cristina Fernández de Kirchner of Argentina. (North America itself has little to brag about, with only Kim Campbell's four months of service as Canada's prime minister in 1993 to offer.) Women thus are not a part of long-established power structures anywhere in the western hemisphere, nor have they really entered the ranks of the elites in substantial numbers even now. In fact, only in Scandinavia do women regularly hold even a third of legislative seats. Latin America is therefore hardly an exception.

Indigenous people are also beginning to make inroads into the ranks of the political elite. Although the first indigenous person to become president of a Latin American country was Mexico's Benito Juárez, who served five terms between 1858 and 1872, other countries with large indigenous populations waited until the twenty-first century to elect a person of indigenous descent to the presidency. Peru, whose indigenous population is just less than half the total, was the first, returning Alejandro Toledo in 2001, and Bolivia, which has an indigenous majority, followed with Evo Morales in 2005. Guatemala, which also has an indigenous majority, has yet to elect a native person to the country's highest office. Many other countries have relatively small indigenous populations today; however, that obviously was not always the case.

Ruling Classes and Power Elites

In discussing ruling classes and power elites, we presume that a country has stable, cohesive ruling groups, whose governance aims at preserving the structure of power and prestige that put them in command. The former argues that a dominant class, defined by its control of the means of production, is the preponderant force in a society's cultural, economic, political, and social realms. The latter holds that distinct groups can dominate these different social segments but that the apices of the relevant orders are closely interlinked and share common values. Though the practical consequence of being dominated by a ruling class instead of a power elite may be insignificant, analytically it points to divergent directions.

It is best to begin by examining the ruling class, because for most of human history, governing was the prerogative of a ruling class. Generally, this class also controlled the economy, and thus was a truly dominant force. For Marx and his followers, it is the capitalists, those who control the means of production and society's key economic decisions, who constitute the ruling class in contemporary society.[6] More significant politically is Marx's axiom that class conflict drives social change and is the sole route to real emancipation.[7] So accepting a ruling-class hypothesis means positing that there is a class, defined by economic characteristics, that is cohesive, conscious of its interests and power, and capable of acting across all sectors of society.[8] The advantage of conceiving the elite as a ruling class is that it makes us focus on how the interests of the various parts of this class, usually called fragments, converge. However, it also disposes us to see the ruling class as a monolith and thus ignore internal divisions.

Besides asserting that formally independent sectoral elites are interlocked, the power elite hypothesis[9] claims that these elites operate through established institutions. For example, religious elites work through churches, while economic elites work through business. This model offers a better way to examine Latin America's historic iron triangle and treat it as a long-lasting conservative bloc. Thinking of the elements of the triangle as a power elite lets us focus on shared interests and persistent dominance but not lose sight of their distinct institutional bases. Moreover, the term *power elite* itself suggests concentrated power exercised by some self-contained, self-interested faction.

The Economic Elites

Economic elites always count for a lot politically. They control investment, meaning they control jobs, and governments know that low unemployment rates make them look good. This relationship obviously applies in capitalist countries, where the economy is purposely left in private hands, but it also matters in Marxist regimes. Although governments in the latter category make society's investment decisions themselves and guarantee full employment, their citizens judge them by how well the economy works. Bad decisions by communist state planners over many years undermined popular support for Marxist rule in the old Soviet bloc and contributed to its downfall between 1989 and 1991.

Even though Latin America had one communist regime in 2008, Cuba, and a handful of radical, socialist-leaning governments—Venezuela, Bolivia, Ecuador, and Nicaragua—the region is essentially capitalist. Therefore, the economic elites we are examining control private wealth. One way to get a rough measure of the power of these elites is to look at income inequality. We can hypothesize (and eventually test our assumption against appropriate data) that economic elites are proportionally

Table 3.1 Comparative Inequality: Latin America and the World

Level of Income Inequality	Country	Gini*
High, World	Namibia	74.3
	Botswana	63.0
	Sierra Leone	62.9
High, Latin America	Bolivia	60.1
	Colombia	58.6
	Brazil	58.0
Low, Latin America*	Venezuela	44.1
	Ecuador	43.7
	Nicaragua	43.1
Medium, World	USA	40.8
	Spain	34.7
	Canada	32.6
Low, World	Sweden	25.0
	Japan	24.9
	Azerbaijan	19.0

* Gini data not available for Cuba.

Source: Adapted from United Nations Development Programme, *Human Development Report*, 2006, Table 15.

stronger where income inequality is greater, because they can apparently block redistribution of their wealth to the rest of society.

The usual measure of income inequality is the Gini index. A Gini score of zero would indicate perfect equality: everybody gets exactly the same income. At the other end of the scale, a score of 1 would mean that one person has everything and nobody else has any income. Using data from 2006, Table 3.1 shows the three highest (least equal distribution) and three lowest (most equal distribution) Gini index results from Latin America, the highest and lowest in the world, and the Ginis from Canada and the United States. These reveal that income distribution in Latin America is quite unequal, indicating that governments there have not had effective income redistribution policies, which, we can postulate, reflects the political influence of the economic elite.

No elite is homogeneous, least of all the economic elite. At minimum, it will include members from the primary (raw materials), secondary (manufacturing), and tertiary (service) sectors, and in practice there will be representatives from various subsectors. As Latin America's original economic elite was built around the *latifundistas*, we begin there.

Data from the *World Wealth Report* for 2008[10] indicate that these Gini figures are not becoming more equal. Between 2005 and 2007, those Latin

Americans with financial assets of at least $1 million saw their wealth grow by 20.4 per cent, the greatest percentage gain for any of the six regions the report tracks (Africa, Asia, the Middle East, Europe, North America, and Latin America). This gives the roughly 400,000 Latin Americans included in the report a total wealth of $6.2 trillion.[11] The fastest growth came in Brazil, Chile, and Venezuela—all three democratic and the last socialist! The main contributor to this explosion of wealth was high commodity prices, suggesting that landed elites and those who derive their wealth from minerals and petroleum still do very well economically in Latin America. Further, the Latin American middle class is smaller than the international average (accounting for 57 per cent of the region's total income, as opposed to 62 per cent worldwide), which is another indicator of the concentration of wealth.[12]

The Latifundistas

Latin America's landed classes have existed since the first days of the Spanish and Portuguese conquests. Throughout the colonial period, 1500 to 1800, the principal characteristics of this class and of its relations with the rest of society remained stable. Self-sufficient to a great extent and perhaps less important economically to Madrid and Lisbon than mine owners, though Brazil's sugar barons would have been an exception, *latifundistas* ran their holdings like feudal lords, dispensing justice and providing defense. The prevailing relationship on the *latifundia* was that of patron to client (see Text Box 3.2). Unlike feudal nobility, however, the *latifundista* did not owe fealty or service to an overlord, though he did eventually owe obedience to the crown. So when independence came, the landed classes had a centuries-long history of being both significant forces in society and autonomous powers in their regions. Two hundred years later, with agricultural products accounting for about one-sixth of Latin America's exports,[13] those who control vast expanses of land remain significant political figures.

Although "the great estates were the dominant economic institution in Latin America for nearly 300 years (and in some regions even longer),"[14] there were two other important players in the economies that developed in Ibero-America. One was obviously made up of groups such as mine owners, whose wealth rested directly on raw materials. However, commercial interests, such as banking and shipping, also played their part, because raw materials must get to markets to be transformed before anyone can make money.[15]

Staples exports formed a natural economic cornerstone for the newly independent Latin American states. Not only did they have favorable "man–land" ratios (that is, lots of land and low populations[16]), but their economic relations with Portugal and Spain also saw them specialize in

Text Box 3.2 Patron-Client Relations

In patron-client relationships there is a reciprocal exchange. The patron, the more powerful party, offers the weaker client a job, money, legal protection, or the like. In return, the client offers loyalty to the patron. This could mean simply working for him at low wages or it could mean being his political enforcer or even his soldier. A good example of how this worked is found in the works of Brazilian novelist Jorge Amado (1912–2001).

Amado's most famous political novel is *The Violent Land*[17] (*Terras do sem fim*, 1943). It tells the story of the early twentieth-century cacao barons of Bahia, in northeastern Brazil, especially the violent conflicts that marked their struggles for wealth and power. Particularly important to the barons were their *capangas*, their personal gunmen, thugs who were the foot soldiers in those wars for dominance. The *capangas* were the clients of the *barões*, who were of course the patrons of these "hard men."

Not all clients who do political service for their patrons become thugs. They could also be called on to stuff ballot boxes or just to vote for their protectors. At this level, the Latin American *patrón* looks a lot like an old-time North American city boss, who traded jobs and Christmas baskets for assured votes. However, the average rural *patrón* generally possessed a power more absolute than even the most powerful boss could wield, because the authority of the state often did not reach far into a country's rural areas. There it was the local big landholder who provided security for and meted out justice to his clients.

the production and export of raw materials. This meant that the newly independent countries entered the expanding world markets of the early 1800s with their economic vocation already mapped out. They would continue as staples producers both because it was what their economies were structured to do and because a combination of distance from markets and sparse and relatively unskilled populations left them few better options. Those who controlled the production of export staples became the economic backbone of the young states, and thus automatically members of their countries' emerging political elites.

Even in the twenty-first century, the role of staples exports remains significant in Latin America. Although the primary sector—agriculture, mining, fisheries, forestry, petroleum—only accounted for 11.64 per cent of regional gross domestic product (GDP) in 2004,[18] Figure 3.1 shows that the staples sector made up 50 per cent of Latin America's exports in 2005: 4.5 times greater than its share of GDP. More striking is the fact that the great estates still seem to be significant economic factors. Table 3.2 presents Gini coefficients assessing the concentration of agricultural landholding. Recalling that a higher score indicates more concentrated

Figure 3.1 Primary Products as a Percentage of Total Exports, Latin America, 1975-2005

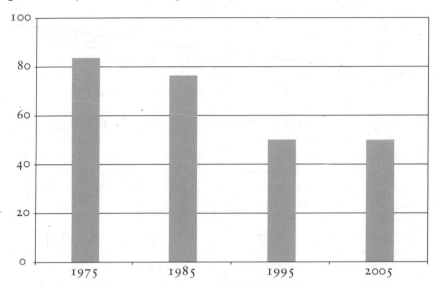

Source: Compiled by author from *ECLAC: Statistical Yearbook for Latin America and the Caribbean,* 2006, Table 2.2.2.1.

ownership, the numbers indicate that farmland is less equally distributed in parts of Latin America than in Canada and the United States, and is everywhere far less equitably divided than in Denmark and South Korea.

Political Consequences

The numbers by themselves do not tell us how *latifundistas* act politically. A few examples, both historical and contemporary, will do that.

The first case regards communal land. Indigenous Americans did not share the European view of private property and in many cases still do not. As a result, substantial swaths of land in Latin America were not under individual title. However, the liberal reforms of the nineteenth and twentieth centuries removed legal protection from communal land, throwing it open to purchase by white landholders. And unlike in North America, where once communal lands went first to family farmers, in most of Latin America, it was the landed classes who profited.[19] The most recent step in this process of privatizing land occurred in 1992 in Mexico with the amendment of article 27 of the constitution, which effectively put *ejidal* (communal) lands on the market.

Just as elites try to get laws passed that reflect their interests, they also work to keep newcomers off their turf. This is politics as usual, but it has occasionally had extremely serious consequences in some countries. From

Table 3.2 Concentration of Land Distribution

Country	Gini coefficient of concentration
Latin America	
Argentina	.83
Bolivia	.56
Brazil	.85
Chile	.64
Colombia	.79
Costa Rica	.66
Dominican Republic	.70
Ecuador	.69
El Salvador	.58
Guatemala	.72
Honduras	.66
Panama	.87
Paraguay	.93
Peru	.86
Mean	.74
North America	
Canada	.64
USA	.74
The Most Equitable	
Denmark	.24
South Korea	.34

Sources: Compiled from Food and Agriculture Organization, *Census of Agriculture, 1990 Round.* Table 1, www.fao.org/ES/ess/census/gini/table1.asp; and Mariana Herrera, *Land Tenure Data and Policy Making in Latin America.* Paper presented at the Conclusive Expert Meeting on FAO Normative Work on Land Tenure Data, September 2005, Rome, Italy, 2; www.oas.org/dsd/Documents/LTDpolicysummary_LATIN%20AMERICA.pdf.

1858 to 1893, Nicaragua enjoyed a rare period of peace and prosperity: the *trentenio,* or 30 years of Conservative Party rule.[20] The Conservatives were successful because they managed to balance the claims of regional elites from León and Granada, whose conflicts had embroiled the country in nearly constant civil war from independence (1821) until 1858. However, the finely struck balance did not allow new elites to enter the political game as full partners. Consequently, the rising class of coffee growers from outside the two established areas had to fight their way to power in the Liberal revolution of 1893. Although the revolution did bring the new elite into national politics, it also brought a dictator, José Santos Zelaya, and set Nicaragua en route for nearly a century of instability, civil war, and dictatorship.

Finally, there is the matter of land reform. Land reform can have two meanings. One, perhaps better called agrarian reform, centers on technical questions—for example, mechanization, seeds (hybrids, genetically modified, natural); irrigation, fertilizer use (organic, mineral, chemical), crop rotation or new crops, and land use. This is the sort of thing that agricultural extension services concern themselves with, as do official development agencies such as Canada's Canadian International Development Agency (CIDA) or America's United States Agency for International Development (USAID). The vocation of these types of organization is to make existing farms work better by producing more. This kind of reform, though, can produce social consequences that have democratic effects, by making small farmers better off and more independent, or antidemocratic ones, by promoting capital intensive agriculture that drives smallholders from the land or introducing crops and techniques that make rural laborers expendable.

More interesting to us is land reform that changes the social relations of rural areas by redistributing land from those with a lot to those with little or none. This is self-consciously democratic in three ways. One, it advances economic and social equality by giving the poor more material resources. Two, redistributive land reform empowers the rural poor by giving them more independence: they no longer rely exclusively on the great estates for sustenance. Three, and a corollary of the last, the very fact that a government would strengthen the hand of the peasantry and weaken the position of powerful rural interests connotes a realignment of forces by putting the state on the side of the poor. For these reasons, land reform has been a central tenet of revolutionary movements in Latin America and the rest of the Third World since the dawn of the twentieth century.

Evidently, land redistribution was necessarily a foundation stone of Latin America's great twentieth-century reform movements: the social revolutions in Mexico, Bolivia, Cuba, and Nicaragua and the democratic revolutions of Guatemala (1944–1954) and Chile (1970–1973). Peru also undertook a significant land reform under a reformist military government (1968–1975). In fact, most countries have an agrarian reform institute or agency that continues to redistribute land, usually on a modest scale. Nevertheless, early in the twenty-first century only Cuba's land reform program remains intact and even it has essentially substituted state ownership for that of private landholders.

Two pessimistic conclusions emerge from the foregoing. One is that land reform only persists under governments strongly committed to egalitarian principles. And it may even be that making land redistribution stick demands a regime change: altering the bases of a political system's legitimacy, how and to whom government is accountable, who influences governments and has privileged access to them, and how the state relates to civil society and private citizens. Yet even where that has happened, namely in Cuba, the second troubling conclusion remains: the individual peasant farmer still does not have land. Substituting state-owned agricultural for privately run *latifundia* changes the elite and how the products of the land are distributed but leaves the ownership and control of land even more concentrated.

Latin America's landholding elite seems to be surviving well, but what of the rest of the economic elite? We consider the questions of neoliberal economic policy, its origins, and its consequences in Chapter 8, but we can make the following observations now. From the origins of the debt crisis in Latin America in 1982 until the Pink Tide elections of 2005 and 2006 that saw the left make a political comeback,[21] economic policy and the general drift of politics favored the right. Labor and peasant unions, and popular organizations generally, lost whatever foothold they had and again became political outsiders. The winners in this realigning of political power were those with the money to take advantage of the global free market. Many of these were multinational firms, but domestic capitalists big enough to play globally profited as well. The fruit of their labor is a political agenda that firmly entrenched their economic model and its social correlates. However, the election of Hugo Chávez as president of Venezuela in 1998, Argentina's economic meltdown at the end of 2001, and the failure of the robustly pro-capitalists to produce results dramatically better than anyone else has opened the door to other options.[22] Big business remains the central economic elite everywhere but Cuba, but its dominance is now more disputed.

A Comparative View

Economic elites matter politically everywhere. They generate much of the income that produces the taxes that lets government run. Some of this they do directly through the products and services they sell. Another part of this income takes the form of wages paid to employees. Their investment decisions shape the prospects of countries and the communities within them.

Governments are attentive to the demands of economic elites for reasons that go beyond the resources those elites control. Where elections determine who governs, a significant part of the electorate's evaluation of an incumbent is based on the general state of the economy. If there are lots of jobs and plenty of money around, voters are likely to give a sitting government another term. Citizens believe, rightly or wrongly, that their economic well-being reflects a government's skill in managing the economy. If heeding the advice of economic elites keeps an economy humming, which is only sometimes true, a government would be foolish to ignore or annoy them. For when economic elites are discontented, they do not invest, or perhaps even move to other jurisdictions, and are not shy about identifying the government and its policies as the cause of their malaise.

What applies in democracies also exists in dictatorships, if in a different form. Unless the economy is state owned, private investors can leave a dictatorship with bad economic policies as quickly as a democracy. So even in authoritarian systems, economic elites are generally influential.

If Latin America is not exceptional in counting the economically powerful among the political elite, we still want to know if the persistence of the landed elite among the dominant is unusual. There are two points to bear in mind. First, a sector of the economy with diminished weight nationally can still be preponderant regionally and locally. Thus a landed elite could retain its place at the national table due to its significance in specific regions. Second, landed elites are linked to other elites with whom they deal (for example, banking and transportation). They are part of interlocking elites, so their persistent presence among Latin America's politically powerful is not surprising.

The Roman Catholic Church

Until the 1970s, political science generally treated the role of religion in politics as being of declining importance. The Iranian Revolution of 1979 changed all that, and the rise of religiously based political movements in the Muslim world and a powerful Hindu, religious nationalist party in India have also assured that we remain attentive to how religion affects politics. However, students of Latin American politics never lost sight of the religion-politics link. The continued political power of the Roman Catholic Church, from the Conquest to the late twentieth century and beyond, has intrigued analysts over the years.[23]

The Church's centrality in the region's political life can be traced to the medieval doctrine of the Two Swords. The doctrine, which dates from the fifth century, held that there are two swords, spiritual and temporal, that rule the world. In its more moderate form, the doctrine recognized Church and state as equal. A stronger version had the Church wielding both swords. The priest holds the first, while the second is in the king's hands, but is only to be used with the permission of the priests. Perhaps still self-evident in fifteenth-century Christendom, the doctrine had a strong operational presence in both the Reconquest of Spain and Portugal, and the Conquest of America. Although both were military campaigns, each had the triumph of the Christian faith as a central objective.

From this follows the prominent role assumed by the Catholic Church in Latin America's colonization. There were, in the view of the Church, countless souls to be brought to Christianity and saved. For this the Church needed, at least occasionally, the persuasive arm of the state. Thus, much as during the Reconquest in Spain, the Catholic Church and the Spanish state, as well as its Portuguese counterpart, continued working in tandem, at least usually. This last qualification is necessary because at times the Church asserted its moral primacy by protecting the natives it was converting. Perhaps the best known defender of indigenous Americans among the churchmen was Fray Bartolmé de las Casas (1484–1566). This brought him and the Church into conflict with the *encomenderos,* who benefited from having natives assigned to them to work their properties in return for assuring the Indians' conversion to Christianity. Similarly, the Jesuits who built communities, called *reductions,* for the indigenous people in parts of Argentina, Brazil, and Paraguay were also vigorously opposed by colonists who wanted cheap, servile workers.

Generally, however, the Catholic Church got on well with the colonial elites. It provided moral legitimation for the regimes constructed in Ibero-America and brought almost all of the population under the same religious roof. Perhaps because of its close ties to the old regime, the Church became a controversial institution after independence throughout Latin America. Liberals, influenced by the Enlightenment, wished to curb its powers and create a secular society guided by the dictates of reason. Somewhat less noble were the views of economic liberals, partisans of the free market. Over the years, the Church had become a great landowner, as many of the wealthy faithful would endow the church with land and money. Although the liberals doubtless believed that privately-held land was more productive than that held by a pre-capitalist, charitable institution, the desire to possess the Church's lands, along with communal lands held by Native Americans, also played a role. Thus for a variety of reasons the Roman Catholic Church in Latin America has been ceaselessly involved in political conflicts since independence.

Religion and Politics

Given the Church's integration with the colonial regime, people commonly believed that it has never played a significant role in promoting democratic, egalitarian politics. This is inaccurate, as the following cases illustrate.

The first dates from 1810 and concerns two priests who were the founding fathers of Mexican independence, Miguel Hidalgo and José María Morales. It was Hidalgo who set the independence movement in motion with the *Grito de Dolores* (Cry of Dolores) that he issued in his heavily

Indian parish of Dolores. Hidalgo was a social revolutionary who wanted to change not only the government but also the entire structure of society. His program included confiscating land held by Europeans, the abolition of slavery, and ending taxes that applied only to Indians. Although Hidalgo had many armed followers, they were quickly subdued; and he was captured and executed in 1811. Father Morales, however, quickly seized the banner of revolution and led a four-year military campaign for Mexico's independence, proclaiming his country's first constitution along the way in 1814. He was then captured and executed in 1815.

Our second case marks the latest instance of a rapprochement between religion and revolution. Liberation theology combined Christian social thought, emphasizing social justice, with Marxist analysis and methodology (that is, it spoke of classes and class struggle). Its greatest prominence came from the middle 1960s though the 1980s. As a social-religious movement, liberation theology was very strong in Brazil and played a prominent role in the Nicaraguan revolution and the insurgency in El Salvador.

Theologically, this movement viewed God, the Christian faith, and society through the eyes of the poor and downtrodden. The formation of Christian Base Communities offered the poor opportunities for self-realization, which liberation theology saw as part of the divine purpose for humans. Further, it maintained that Christian teachings as found in the Gospels demand a "preferential option for the poor" and the involvement of the Church in struggles for social justice. Throughout Latin America priests and nuns began living in poor neighborhoods both to share more fully the lives of their flocks and to do hands-on work for social justice (see Text Box 3.3).

This made liberation theology extremely controversial and far from universally accepted. Political conservatives believed the movement was little more than communism, while theological conservatives within the Catholic Church viewed it as a dangerous challenge to the Church's historic rights to teach and lead the faithful in moral matters. Although neither liberation theology nor liberation theologians met the fates of Fathers Hidalgo and Morales—though some priests were stripped of their religious functions—the established elite won out in the end. Pressures from the Vatican reduced the freedom of liberation theologians to preach, teach, and practice their views, which eventually took the priests and nuns away from the poor with whom they worked, vitiating the social side of liberation theology.

There are obviously other instances where the Latin American Catholic Church took the part of the weak against the powerful, but the overall picture of its political role since independence sees it aligned with other conservative elites. That is not surprising. Organized religion is usually one of the pillars of society, a stabilizing force that lends legitimacy to a social order by bestowing some form of divine approval on it. In Christian

Text Box 3.3 Two Practitioners of Liberation Theology

Dom Hélder Câmara (1909–1999) was for many years archbishop of the poverty-stricken Brazilian city of Recife. Though a man of the Church, he was not really a theologian. Rather, he put theology's abstract principles into practice. He was known for his commitment to the poor, a commitment that politicized him and saw him branded a radical. One of his most famous works, *Spiral of Violence*,[24] argued that the structural violence of everyday life pushed the oppressed to revolt, and the elite to repress the revolt, thus sharpening the structural violence of daily existence. He is remembered for saying, "When I give food to the poor, they call me a saint. When I ask why the poor have no food, they call me a communist."

Gustavo Gutierrez (1928–) is a Peruvian priest who is generally considered the founder of liberation theology. His book *A Theology of Liberation: History, Politics, Salvation*[25] gave spiritual liberation a political and social content that demanded the emancipation of the poor. This emphasis on the poor and its implications for justifying an energetic participation in leftist politics by the Church would earn the rebuke of the Vatican. Although Gutierrez himself was never sanctioned, Cardinal Joseph Ratzinger, before he was elected Pope Benedict XVI, did order some liberation theologians to cease expounding their doctrine. As a result, by the end of the 1980s, liberation theology had lost its practical force.

societies, like those found throughout the Americas, this has historically taken the form of assuring the marginalized that their rulers enjoy God's favor, or at least that those rulers are legitimate and that everyone should obey them, and that the poor and excluded will eventually reap eternal rewards that immeasurably outweigh their temporal suffering. However, in Latin America, the Catholic Church did more than that. It ran schools, hospitals, and other charities; it was society's social service sector long before the welfare state's creation. Further, as already noted, at the time of independence, it was rich.

Conservatives were pro-clerical and wanted to keep the Church strong. That meant, first, making it an established church or state religion, thus giving it the state's official support. Through much of the period, this implied restricting the freedom of other religions, or at least their ability to proselytize. Moreover, a conservative regime would sign or renew a concordat—a sort of treaty between the Vatican and a government that grants the Church certain rights, for example, regarding education. They would also invite certain orders of priests (often the Jesuits) to come and run schools or other social service institutions. Finally, general legislation would be shaped to the Church's interests (for example, laws governing marriage and divorce).

Text Box 3.4 Church and State in Contemporary Chile and Nicaragua

Nowhere in the world are religion and politics separated. Same-sex marriage causes Church and state to clash in the United States and Canada, and the governments of Muslim countries regularly deal with the various currents of politicized Islam. Therefore, it is no surprise to find that the Catholic Church and state still cross swords occasionally in Latin America. Two recent examples can be found in Chile, where the Church was on the losing side, and Nicaragua, where it won.

In 2004, Chile left the declining ranks of states prohibiting divorce—only Malta and the Philippines remain. Previously, a legal end to marriage came only via annulment, a civil process in Chile but a complicated and expensive one. Twelve previous attempts to reform the civil marriage act had failed. It was the socialist administration of Ricardo Lagos that pushed for the change, and the Catholic Church resisted with all its might. In the end, the government carried the day and simpler means to end a marriage are now available to Chileans.

In Nicaragua, however, in 2006 the Catholic Church won its battle to criminalize therapeutic abortion (that is, abortion to save the mother's life). What made this instance of church-state politics notable, aside from the change itself, was the fact that it was supported by not just the conservative parties but also by the Frente Sandinista de Liberación Nacional (FSLN, or Sandinista National Liberation Front). This is the same FSLN that made the Sandinista Revolution in 1979 and found in the Catholic Church an implacable foe during its first period in power, 1979 to 1990. Observers saw political opportunism underlying the Sandinistas' support of the Church's project, a view reinforced when Sandinista presidential candidate Daniel Ortega received no opposition from the Catholic Church on his way to electoral victory in 2006.

Liberal governments tended to be anticlerical and did just the opposite. They would declare freedom of religion; abrogate the concordat signed by their conservative predecessors; expel the Jesuits; strip the Catholic Church of its powers over education and the administration of social services; secularize laws governing marriage, divorce, the registry of births and deaths; and establish nondenominational, public cemeteries. In this, Latin American anticlericals were very much like their counterparts in nineteenth-century Europe, above all in France. Yet sometimes they went further, for both Guatemala and Mexico banned clerics from wearing religious habits in public. And where in Europe the clerical versus anticlerical political fault line largely disappeared after World War II, in Latin America it is still present (see Text Box 3.4).

Obviously the Roman Catholic Church has been near the center of politics in Latin America for a long time. Nevertheless, with the exception of Chile, Christian Democratic parties have not been strong in the region. Two factors explain this. One, the Church in Latin America has generally been able to count on other political organizations to defend its interests and represent its values, and thus it did not need Christian Democratic parties. Two, there is the fact that for a very long time electoral politics were not the key to power in many countries, again obviating the need for a modern political party founded on Catholic social principles.

Protestant Churches in Latin America

If the 1970s and 1980s were the era of liberation theology, the religious story of the 1980s and 1990s in Latin America was Protestantism. Although not new to the region, prior to the last decades of the twentieth century, Protestantism was not only a minority faith but also often an almost invisible one. It was only when Pentecostal churches became active in the 1960s that Protestant congregations began to expand and become the faith of a significant minority of the population in several countries. In fact, estimates suggest that the number of Protestants in Latin America grew from about 50,000 to at least 40 million, more than one-tenth of the total population, during the twentieth century.[26]

As it is the Pentecostal churches that have accounted for most of this growth, we need to know what they stand for. Many supporters of liberation theology view the rise of the Pentecostals with suspicion. They believe that this branch of Protestantism favors conservative politics because it discourages political engagement. A strong emphasis on personal salvation and an associated stress on self-improvement turn people's energies away from political activities. And as the Pentecostal churches are particularly successful in obtaining converts among the very poor, this would appear to take potential adherents away from leftist political parties.

Although it is true that the Pentecostals and other evangelical, fundamentalist Protestant denominations have generally been inactive politically, this does not mean that they are without political effect. For example, by placing personal reading of the Bible at the center their faith, Pentecostals may develop greater self-reliance and eventually be less likely to follow authoritarian political leaders. Similarly, by identifying moral uprightness with abstinence from tobacco, liquor, and gambling, male Pentecostals could leave their families more material resources, leading to future generations that are healthier and better educated.[27] Further, the individualism, self-reliance, and self-determination often seen as attributes of the Pentecostal faithful might be part of a recipe for economic success.[28]

Despite accounting for a substantial part of the population (at least 30 per cent in Guatemala, the country with the highest proportion of

Protestants, and somewhat more than 10 per cent in the region), there is still no distinct Protestant politics. Nevertheless, Guatemala has elected two Protestant presidents, Efrían Ríos Montt and Alfonso Portillo, and Alberto Fujimori won Peru's presidency with the support of Protestant votes, just as Brazilian Protestants backed Fernando Collor de Mello and later Luiz Lula da Silva.[29] There have also been several other high-profile Protestant politicians in Brazil. However, this has not translated into a Protestant vote; neither has the presence of a Protestant party, like the Nicaraguan Christian Way, produced a clear Protestant political agenda. Further, the Catholic Church has not lost its place among the political elite. What we are likely seeing is a pluralization of Latin American religious life that may in the midterm, 10 to 20 years, have more tangible political effects.

A Comparative View

In much of the world, religion drives politics. The United States has a constitutional bar separating Church and state, but since 1970, the political potential of organized and mobilized born-again Christians has been amply demonstrated. Thus candidates seeking the 2008 presidential nomination in both the Democratic and Republican parties made their personal religious convictions as clear as their stands on foreign policy. We could include numerous other global examples involving Islam, Hinduism, Judaism, and Buddhism, but the point is the same: religion matters politically. Because of this, we should be neither shocked nor surprised to find religious leaders among a state's political elite.

What likely strikes North Americans is the religious monism or uniformity that characterized Latin American society for nearly five centuries. We are used to very high levels of religious pluralism. We live among multiple Protestant denominations, Roman Catholics, Orthodox Christians, Jews, Muslims, Hindus, Buddhists, and those who adhere to spiritualist religions. Each of these occasionally makes its claims on the state, and though government need not respond favorably, there is little question that a religious group has the right to petition government. But historically, we in North America have been an exception. Looked at from a perspective that accepts that one faith should dominate society, it is Latin America's increasingly pluralistic present and not its monistic past that appears odd.

The Military

"The question of questions about the Latin American military establishments concerns not their combative but their political capacity and role. These capacities are large. ..."[30] Ever since independence, some would say ever since the Conquest, soldiers have been enormously influential political actors in Latin America. There is not one country that has not experienced a coup or a military dictatorship, although some have distinctly more experience with this than do others. Yet now, at the start of the twenty-first century, the military's political role is substantially reduced throughout the region. Some military establishments still possess a political veto of sorts, but even those exercise their influence from the barracks and do not seize the presidential residence. To discover how this has happened, we need to review the history of Latin American military politics, suggest what has prompted their withdrawal from the political arena, and finally survey current trends.

Before beginning, though, there is one thing to bear in mind throughout this section. Although Latin America has a longer history of military rule than any other part of the world, other regions also have politically active militaries. Most modern African states became independent in the 1950s and 1960s, and since then very few have escaped military rule. Similarly, in South Asia, Pakistan and Bangladesh have experienced numerous military governments, while Myanmar (Burma) has scarcely known any other form of rule since gaining independence in 1947. Farther east, Thailand has had many coups and military juntas over the years, Indonesia lived for 31 years under General Suharto's military government, and South Korea had episodes of military rule from the 1960s to the 1980s.

Military rule is not rare. Thus what we want to understand about politically active Latin American militaries is not why they emerge there but rather what sort of conditions permit their existence. Above all, we need to know why they stopped around 1990 and how confident we can be that military rule in Latin America is now consigned to the museum of archaic political practices.

A Brief History of Military Rule in Latin America[31]

We could start this history with the role of armed force in the Conquest or with the fact that colonial creole elites were able to take military commissions before they could enter colonial politics or with the knowledge that independence came to most places only after prolonged military struggle. Each of these probably played a part in giving the military a prominent social role. However, to find the roots of its political ascendency, we must consider the post-independence political disorder that reigned for decades in practically all of Latin America. Lawlessness sparks a tendency to seek the reimposition of order, and that search ends up pointing to someone who controls a substantial armed force. Here we need to add one final note: not all armed forces are what we would call a military today. In nineteenth-century Latin America it was often a semi-organized armed band.

Thus the story of the origins of military force as a political instrument in Latin America resides in the failure of political elites to channel conflict through state institutions. Had they done so, more disputes would have been settled without resort to arms. There are several plausible explanations for why this proved impossible. One is the lack of experience with self-government under colonial rule. Another is the ideological chasm separating the main political camps, be they Liberals or Conservatives, centralists and federalists, or urban and rural dwellers. Some point to a political culture that devalued compromise, sometimes expressed as "*somos todos toderos*" ("we all want it all").[32] Finally, the presence of armed troops, not all controlled by the state, made armed might handily available. For whatever mix of reasons, in all of Spanish America except Paraguay, Costa Rica, and Chile, where strongmen centralized power rapidly, the half-century after independence was marked by chronic political instability and frequent resort to force.[33] Brazil avoided military rule until 1889.

Military activity in those early years was not solely internal and aimed at grasping political power. International wars were waged to settle boundaries (Rio de la Plata, 1817–1860; Gran Colombia, 1821–1830; Central America, 1824–1838; Colombia–Peru, 1828–1830) and confront imperial encroachment (Mexico, unsuccessfully against both the United States, in 1846–1848, and France, from 1862–1867). Yet these were not armies like those found in Europe or even the United States at the same time. They were far less professional, and less well trained and equipped. It was only in the last third of the nineteenth century that military professionalism, with its specialized training and attendant corporate identity began to take root; and then only in the larger, more economically developed nations. In the industrialized world, professional militaries were important politically as interest groups, not as governors. However, becoming professional did not diminish military intervention in Latin American politics, but only changed its rationale.

Whereas earlier armed interventions in politics were to put a new *caudillo* in power, once a country developed a professional military, different objectives—all linked to its institutional interests—predominated. Among these was the belief that civilian politicians were incapable of developing the nation. Professional soldiers, here meaning officers, had received the latest technical training from foreign experts and many had been abroad to Germany or France. Thus they knew what modernity looked like and how it worked. Most politicians, many of them backcountry *caciques* (local bosses), did not. Even worse from the soldier's perspective, those few politicians who did understand what had to be done were insufficiently patriotic to take the necessary steps. Thus it became the military's responsibility to oust the miscreants and assume the reins of government until suitable civilians could be found (see Text Box 3.5).

Text Box 3.5 The Military Ends the Brazilian Empire

Brazil was unique among the Ibero-American colonies in that its break with the metropole, Portugal, was peaceful. Indeed, although it split from the Portuguese crown, Brazil constituted itself an empire and named the crown prince its first emperor. Thus where Hispanic American states knew highly conflictive transitions to independence that were followed by decades of strife and instability, Brazil sailed smoothly on through most of the nineteenth century. Nevertheless, Brazil's military was far from inactive, fighting Argentina in the 1820s over control of what is now Uruguay, repressing a republican rebellion in Brazil's south in the 1830s, and then joining with Argentina and Uruguay in the Triple Alliance that devastated Paraguay in the 1860s.

Yet Brazil's military only became active politically after that last war, when it felt that the country's rulers, the imperial nobility and its allies, failed to give the armed forces due respect. There ensued a series of minor disputes that became affairs of honor and the military became staunchly republican. In 1889, convinced that the imperial state could not be reformed, the military moved—and the emperor abdicated and went into exile. This was not the last time Brazil's military would act against the state. In 1930, it toppled the increasingly decrepit republic that succeeded the empire. Then in 1964 it moved again to put an end to what it deemed civilian incompetence, remaining in power for 21 years.

If there is anything positive to be said about the military's frequent seizures of control of the state, it is that they did not last long and were generally accomplished with minimal violence. A modal military takeover would last for a year or two, occasion few casualties, although a number of those tied to the old regime would go into exile, and end with the military convening elections engineered to assure the success of its favorites. Occasionally, and especially in the smaller, less-developed countries, a coup would launch a new dictator. Yet until the 1960s the institutionalized pattern of military intervention was almost "gentlemanly." And though military rulers often sided with the established elites, there were exceptions. For example, the Peruvian military junta that governed from 1968 to 1980 undertook a substantial redistribution of land, nationalized the petroleum industry, and promoted the use of indigenous languages, although it censored the media.

The military regimes that arose in the Southern Cone nations of Argentina (1976–83), Brazil (1964–85), Chile (1973–89), and Uruguay (1973–84) were of an entirely different sort. They deviated from the historic model of Latin American military governments in three ways:

- They all planned to retain power indefinitely.
- All undertook radical political, economic, and social reforms to remake their countries.
- Each was uncommonly brutal.

Part of the cause of this phenomenon, labeled *bureaucratic authoritarianism*, rests in the national security doctrine. The doctrine was of US origin and consisted of "an interrelated set of concepts about the state, development, counterinsurgency warfare, and, above all, security."[34] It focused on the enemy within, normally called "Communist subversives," and permitted the state to use exceptional powers to destroy that enemy, regardless of the cost to human rights and the price in human lives. To officers in countries experiencing internal insurrection and urban guerrilla warfare (Argentina and Uruguay), or with an ineffective civilian president who was encouraging enlisted soldiers to form unions (Brazil), or an increasingly radical, Marxist-oriented government increasing its electoral support in mid-term elections (Chile), the doctrine made a lot of sense.

In the end, though, the bureaucratic authoritarian regimes yielded to democratic governments, though essentially under conditions of their own choosing. Since 1990, the nature of military politics has changed dramatically in the region, so much so that civilian defense ministers are now the rule rather than the exception. None of this means that the military is without political influence or even that there will never be another military coup in Latin America—the 2002 coup attempt against Venezuelan president Hugo Chávez, which divided the military, is proof of that.[35] Nevertheless, whereas in the mid-1970s, military governments or authoritarian governments headed by military men ruled in 13 states, in 2009, there are none.[36]

Why Has the Military Withdrawn from Politics Since the 1990s?

The 1980s were Latin America's Lost Decade economically. Every country but Colombia saw its economy shrink. Even the much-touted minimally regulated market of General Augusto Pinochet's Chicago Boys[37] in Chile had a bad decade. Thus, part of the explanation for the military's region-wide exit from active governing is that it failed the test of economic management. In fact, military governments have historically done a poor job managing economies. However, there are other factors in play.

One of those factors is neoliberal economic policy. This comes under a variety of names, such as structural adjustment or the Washington Consensus, which we examine later, but at the policy's core was a double-barreled prescription: cut spending and balance the budget. Technocrats from the International Monetary Fund saw only budget allocations and the bottom line, and only those sectors that promised high-export earnings could expect the slightest mercy. As the military had contributed mightily to the economic problem with weak management, it had to contribute to the solution by accepting shrunken budgets.

In the four nations of the Southern Cone—Argentina, Brazil, Chile, and Uruguay—which suffered particularly cruel military regimes in the 1970s and 1980s, military rule lost its legitimacy. Unable to govern either humanely or even particularly competently, the military establishment now finds far fewer civilians calling for the armed forces to seize control of the state. In addition, the end of the Cold War in the late 1980s reduced the value of military governments to the world's great powers. In the Latin American case, the United States, which had long accepted military dictatorships as guarantors of stability and repressors of revolution, abandoned its former paladins.

A Last Comparative Look

Military leaders are part of the political elite in most countries, including highly developed, consolidated democracies.[38] Defense is a key part of the state's responsibilities everywhere, so military figures—more broadly, the national security services—will be important figures in their special realm of the policy process. What distinguishes Latin America, along with Africa and parts of Asia, is military government as a common form of rule. Why?

A definitive answer is probably impossible. However, there are two plausible hypotheses with which we can start. The first is that civilian politicians in many countries have been unable to agree on how their states should be structured, what the state should do, and who should have the right to govern. In short, there is no consensus on basic rules, probably because there is not enough trust among the various subdivisions of the political elite. This creates conflicts and instability that the military feels it has to sort out. From this there arises a second likely factor: military rule becomes an institution in and of itself. It may have come to be seen as part of the normal course of politics and a suitable way to resolve certain recurring problems. The move away from direct military intervention since 1990 may, though, indicate that a corner is in sight, although it may yet to be too soon to say that it has been turned.

Conclusion

Like everywhere else, Latin American politics features certain elites. This chapter has looked at three of them that have proven particularly persistent. In itself, persistence is neither newsworthy nor particularly interesting. It is only the relation of the elites—*latifundistas* among the economic elites, the Catholic Church, and the military as governor—to long periods of nondemocratic, even antidemocratic, rule that draws attention. Early in the twenty-first century, Latin America is experiencing its most promising democratic opening ever. These elites will either learn democratic ways, fall by the wayside, or once again undermine democracy.

Further Readings

Camp, Roderic. *Mexico's Mandarins: Crafting a Power Elite for the Twenty-First Century*. Berkeley, CA: University of California Press, 2002.
Higley, John, and Michael Burton. *Elite Foundations of Liberal Democracy*. Lanham, MD: Rowman and Littlefield, 2006.
Freston, Paul. *Evangelical Christianity and Democracy in Latin America*. New York: Oxford University Press, 2008.
Bowman, Kirk. *Militarization, Democracy, and Development: the Perils of Praetorianism in Latin America*. University Park, PA: Pennsylvania State University Press, 2002.

Discussion Questions

① Can there be a public-spirited democratic elite? What characteristics would it have? Can there be a democracy without a democratic elite?

② What would a democratically inclined elite have to do to turn a nondemocratic political system into a democratic one?

Notes

1. See Chapter 8.
2. It is most countries instead of all of them because two, Costa Rica and Panama, do not have militaries. However, both had their quota of military governments in the past.
3. Michael Burton, Richard Gunther, and John Higley, "Introduction: Elite Transformations and Democratic Regimes," *Elites and Democratic Consolidation in Latin America and Southern Europe*, ed. John Higley and Richard Gunther (Cambridge: Cambridge University Press, 1992) 1–37.
4. Burton, Gunther, and Higley, "Introduction," 8–9.
5. The term is William Gamson's; see William Gamson, *Power and Discontent* (Homewood, IL: Dorsey Press, 1968).
6. Obviously, in pre-capitalist or simply noncapitalist states, there has to be a different class that rules; but in Marxist thought, it will still be the class that controls the means of production.
7. This reflects the belief that a society divided into classes can never permit all individuals real freedom. The political corollary of this position is that political democracy in a class-divided social order—including one directed by a communist party after a socialist revolution—is at best incomplete and at worst a sham. It should be noted, though, that one can use class conflict as an analytical theme without being a Marxist.
8. Contemporary statements of this position can be found in the work of American Paul Sweezy, especially the magazine *Monthly Review*, which he founded; and Briton Ralph Miliband, *The State in Capitalist Society* (London: Quartet Books, 1973). It is also useful

to consult Leo Panitch and Colin Leys, eds., *The Socialist Register* (Halifax, NS: Fernwood Publishers), which is published yearly.

9. This is most clearly identified with C. Wright Mills, *The Power Elite* (New York: Oxford University Press, 1956), but also with G. William Domhoff, *The Power Elite and the State: How Policy Is Made in America* (New York: A. de Gruter, 1990) and Thomas R. Dye, *Top-Down Policymaking* (New York: Chatham House, 2001).

10. Andres Oppenheimer, "Report on Wealthy Latins Is a Bit Troubling," *Miami Herald* 17 August 2008. www.miamiherald.com/news/columnists/andres-oppenheimer/story/645347.html; Capgemini and Merrill Lynch, *World Wealth Report, 2008*. www.ml.com/media/100472.pdf.

11. *World Wealth Report*, 3.

12. Oppenheimer.

13. Patrice Franko, *The Puzzle of Latin American Economic Development* (Lanham, MD: Rowman and Littlefield Publishers, 2003) 234.

14. Marshall Eakins, *The History of Latin America: Collision of Cultures* (New York: Palgrave Macmillan, 2007) 96.

15. The nature of staples-centered economies is considered in Chapter 7.

16. Discussions of staples-led growth are found in Melville Watkins, "A Staple Theory of Economic Growth," *Canadian Journal of Economics and Political Science* 29 (1963): 141–158 and Albert O. Hirschman, *The Strategy of Economic Development* (New Haven, CT: Yale University Press, 1958).

17. Jorge Amado, *The Violent Land* (New York: Knopf, 1965).

18. ECLAC, "Table 2.1.1.23," *Statistical Yearbook for Latin America and the Caribbean.* www.eclac.org/cgi-bin/getProd.asp?xml=/publicaciones/xml/4/28074/P28074.xml&xsl=/deype/tpl-i/p9f.xsl&base=/tpl/top-bottom.xslt.

19. The important exceptions to the rule of the dominance of estates in Latin America are the central plateau (*meseta central*) of Costa Rica and Antioquia, the region of Colombia around Medellin. Both were coffee zones with rough terrain.

20. Arturo J. Cruz, *Nicaragua's Conservative Republic, 1858–93* (Houndmills, UK: Palgrave, 2002) cf. Andres Perez, *Entre el estado conquistador y el estado nación: providencialismo, pensamiento político y estructuras de poder en el desarrollo histórico de Nicaragua* (Managua: Fundacion Frederich Ebert, 2003).

21. The Pink Tide is the name given to the round of 12 presidential elections from late 2005 through to the end of 2006, 7 of which went clearly to the left—joining 2 previously elected and Cuba, 3 to the centrists, and only 2 to the Conservatives. We return to this matter in Chapter 7.

22. Chile is something of an exception here, as the center-left governments of the Concertación have managed the country's economy so that it has grown strongly while at the same time instituting social programs to reduce poverty.

23. Rather than try to catalog the vast literature on church-state issues in Latin America, I shall note here a few useful starting points for further reading: Lloyd Mecham, *Church and State in Latin America: A History of Politico-ecclesiatical Relations* (Chapel Hill, NC: University of North Carolina Press, 1966); Phillip Berryman, *Liberation Theology: Essential Facts about the Revolutionary Religious Movements in Latin America* (New York: Pantheon, 1987); David Martin, *Tongues of Fire: The Explosion of Protestantism in Latin America* (Oxford: Basil Blackwell, 1990); Jeffery Klaiber, *The Church, Dictatorships, and Democracy in Latin America* (Maryknoll, NY: Orbis Books, 1998).

24. London: Sheed and Ward, 1971.

25. Maryknoll, NY: Orbis Books, 1973.

26. The numbers given for the Protestant population of Latin America vary wildly according to the sources, ranging from 40 million to 75 million. I use the most conservative numbers available.

27. David Martin, *Pentecostalism: The World Their Parish* (Oxford: Blackwell, 2002).

28. Bernard Martin, "From Pre- to Postmodernity on Latin America: The Case of Pentecostalism," *Religion, Modernity and Postmodernity,* eds. Paul Heelas, David Martin, and Paul Morris (Oxford: Blackwell Publishers, 2004 102–145).

29. Newton Gaskill, "Rethinking Protestantism and Democratic Consolidation in Latin America," *Sociology of Religion* 58:1 (Spring 1997): 69–91, examines the cases of Fujimori and Collor de Mello; for Lula, see "Historical Overview of Pentecostalism in Brazil," *Pew Forum on Religion and Public Life.* http://pewforum.org/surveys/pentecostal/countries/?CountryID=29 (accessed 21 September 2007).

30. Robert Wesson, et al., *The Latin American Military Institution* (New York: Praeger Publisher, 1986) 157.

31. Among the many sources one can consult on the Latin American military, the following will provide a foundation: Alain Roquie, *The Military and the State in Latin America* (Berkeley, CA: University of California Press, 1987); Karen Remmer, *Military Rule in Latin America* (Boston, MA: Unwin Hyman, 1989); Bruce Farcau, *The Coup: Tactics in the Seizure of Power* (New York: Praeger Publishers, 1994); Brian Loveman and Thomas Davies, eds., *Apolitical Politics,* 3rd ed. (Wilmington, DE: Scholarly Resources, 1997); J. Samuel Fitch, *The Armed Forces and Democracy in Latin America* (Baltimore: Johns Hopkins University Press, 1998); Brian Loveman, *For La Patria: Politics and the Armed Forces in Latin America* (Wilmington, DE: Scholarly Resources, 1999); David Pion-Berlin, ed., *Civil–Military Relations in Latin America: New Analytical Perspectives* (Chapel Hill: University of North Carolina Press, 2001); Thomas C. Bruneau and Scott D. Tollefson, eds., *Who Guards the Guardians and How: Democratic Civil–Military Relations* (Austin: University of Texas Press, 2006).

32. See Howard Wiarda, ed., *Authoritarianism and Corporatism in Latin America* (Gainesville, FL: University Press of Florida, 2004); and Glen Caudill Dealy, *The Public Man: An Interpretation of Latin American and Other Catholic Countries* (Amherst, MA: University of Massachusetts Press, 1977).

33. Paraguay and Costa Rica both had periods of instability with military rule later in the nineteenth century, while Chile had brief episodes of military political activity in the 1920s, 1930s, and an extended spell under General Augusto Pinochet from 1973 to 1989.

34. David Pion-Berlin, "The National Security Doctrine, Military Threat Perception and the 'Dirty War' in Argentina," *Comparative Political Studies* 21:3 (1988): 385.

35. The failed 2002 coup attempt in Venezuela is discussed in more detail in the next chapter.

36. The calculation for the mid-1970s excludes Cuba's Fidel Castro and Nicaragua's Anastasio Somoza from the roster of military leaders of authoritarian governments, just as the 2009 list classes Raúl Castro as a civilian. Of course both of these decisions are disputable and reasonable arguments could be made for treating all three as military figures.

37. The Chilean economists who advised the Pinochet dictatorship on economic policy are called the Chicago Boys because so many of them did graduate degrees at the University of Chicago, a bastion of free-market economic thinking. We return to this question in Chapter 9.

38. The exceptions are countries where there is no military force, as in Costa Rica and Panama. Even there, however, security forces—such as the police, border guards, or the coast guard—are likely to have prominent political roles. This is especially true in the post-9/11 world where terrorism has joined drug smuggling as a great international security concern.

4

Historic Modes of Governing: The Politics of Patrimonialism, Violence, and Instability

Latin American politics has long been noted for its high levels of political violence. Whether it is a *caudillo*—a charismatic boss, usually with an armed following—or a general leading a *golpe de estado* (a military seizure of state power), or an authoritarian government using force to repress its opponents, we conceive of Latin America as a region ruled by force. Along with violence, we have also focused on the region's reputation for political instability (actually a consequence of it)—its endless rounds of musical governments as coup followed coup and general followed general to become supreme leader for an undetermined but not infrequently short length of time. Governments were more often changed by force than electoral results.

Although the description presented above is now showing signs of passing into history, and perhaps has even already made the journey in a few countries, we should neither ignore these long-standing habits of rule nor assume that they are gone forever. Take, for example, patrimonial or personalist politics, which are leader-centered, often to the extent of placing the leader above the law. This characterized *caudillo* politics. Contemporary Latin America still has a number of high-profile, personalist presidents, such as Venezuela's Hugo Chávez, who embody much of the *caudillo* tradition. And although political violence has played a diminishing role in Latin America since 1990, it has not vanished. Because of this, we need to see how *caudillo* rule and political violence came to be policy instruments and what let them keep their usefulness for so long. How, that is, did they become political institutions? This is a way to try to understand why political actors, institutions, and instruments have such long lives in Latin America.

In this chapter, we treat the politics of *caudillos*, coups, and revolutions as parts of a model of rule, a political tradition. Doing this means placing these phenomena in a broader theoretical framework. Two perspectives offer the best possibilities. One treats personal rule and high levels of political violence, as well as the political instability that often accompanies them, as political institutions: well-established, rule-bound structures and processes of governing. The other sees them as manifestations of political culture: the values and attitudes people hold about politics. Using these tools will enable you to understand how these instruments of rule developed, how they have persisted, and how they are changing.

Introduction: Modes and Models of Governing

In 1952, political scientist William Stokes published an article titled "Violence as a Power Factor in Latin American Politics," in which he wrote that

> [v]iolence seems to be institutionalized in the organization, maintenance, and changing of government in Latin America. The methodology of force is found in advanced and in backward countries, in Indian, *mestizo*, and white republics, in large states and in small ones, in urban and in rural areas, in agricultural and in industrial organization, in the beginning of the twentieth century, in the present period, and in the early, middle, and late nineteenth century—in a word, wherever and whenever Hispanic culture is to be found in the Western Hemisphere.[1]

A half-century later, historian Robert H. Holden published *Armies without Nations: Public Violence and State Formation in Central America*, in which he speaks of "public violence":[2]

> The boundaries of ... state power, constituted not so much by structural boundaries but by fluid social relationships, vary over time and space. The killing, maiming, and destruction that take place in this field is "public violence," owing to this compatibility with all the conventional senses of the word "public" ... its wide visibility, potential to affect great numbers of people, and connections with government.

Plainly, violence has been an important political commodity in Latin America. Therefore, those who are skilled in the use of violence—sometimes called "specialists in violence"[3]—have been well placed to gain the power to rule. It also means that other political instruments, such as building electoral political parties to mobilize voters, were long underdeveloped. One can also ask whether the conditions noted by Stokes and Holden also point toward a particular mode of organizing government, namely personal rule. This question arises partly because personal, one-man rule has long been common in Latin America and partly because specialists in violence come mostly from extremely hierarchical institutions, where leadership is called command. In short, one has to consider whether the

relationship one man ruler
violence

FOUR Historic Modes of Governing: The Politics of Patrimonialism

correlation of these factors points to them reinforcing each other, giving both rule by violence and one-person rule special institutional viability.

Political Institutions and Their Relation to Modes of Governing

Politics works in and through political institutions. On hearing "political institutions" what generally comes to mind is the formal machinery of government: executives (presidents or prime ministers and their cabinets), legislatures, courts, and bureaucracies. These are clearly political institutions, but they are not the only ones. We also include parties, groups and movements, the media—especially when they treat political affairs—and even well-established practices that may not have any legal status (for example, how patronage is used). To understand political institutions we need more than a list. We need to know what characteristics define them. Although there is no universally accepted definition, there are components that appear repeatedly.

A common way to identify institutions is by searching for repeated patterns of interaction among people. "Repeated" implies both that the interactions happen over a period of time (hence that an institution is long-lived), and that they are not random but rather intentional or systematic, implying that they reflect rules. Indeed, some argue that institutions are rules,[4] but it is more prudent to say that they lay down rules that shape the behavior of individuals who work with them. This makes institutions "deliberate attempts to channel and constrain human behavior."[5] In the case of political institutions, the rules will establish who gets to make decisions, about which issues, limited by what restraints, and with what penalties for breaking the rules. Seen in this light, the link between political institutions and modes of governing becomes clear. How rulers govern will shape political institutions, even start them, but the institutions will also affect how rulers rule. Institutions offer a selection of mechanisms with which to govern, but also set some limits on their use.

But how are these institutions formed? One view suggests that they began as instruments that people devised to achieve some objective.[6] Over time, an instrument—a combination of rules and processes—can metamorphose into an institution by becoming more autonomous, setting more rules to govern people associated with it, and being valued in its own right instead of simply as a tool to do a job. Alternatively, people can set out to establish organizations that will direct human activity in given directions.[7] In either case, institutions begin with a conscious decision by someone to find a way to do something.

Historical Institutionalism and Informal Institutions

There are other questions that arise in connection with political institutions. How do they change? Is formal, legal recognition necessary for a political institution to exist? How should we study them? To examine the question of institutional stability and change, many political scientists, along with sociologists and historians, use the theory of historical institutionalism.[8] Central to this theory is the concept of path dependence.[9] Path dependence refers to why institutions tend to adhere to established ways of doing things, or paths.[10] How an institution works often reflects previous outcomes rather than current conditions, unless a significant off-path change has shifted the direction of an institution's evolution.

Applied to the central question of this chapter—how *caudillo* rule, violence, and military insurrection remained instruments of rule in Latin America for so long—path dependence suggests two answers. One is that an outcome at a "critical juncture" can significantly shape the future evolution of an institution. For example, Robert Holden argues in another context that "[t]he core event in the Central American state formation process was the gradual knitting together of dispersed power centers into coherent organs of coercion."[11] Thus, some action produces results that literally change the course of history. So if using violence as a method of rule works by bringing some desired end when first employed, this raises the chances that violence will become a normal, institutionalized instrument in a ruler's toolbox.

The other point is that once a path is embarked upon, it becomes progressively harder to shift direction, as a form of institutional inertia comes into play.[12] In terms of violent politics in Latin America, path dependence would suggest that rulers would see that their predecessors used violence to take and keep power, note that violence worked, and continue with this successful strategy.

But does any form of institutional analysis really apply to *caudillos*, military rule, and political violence? If being an institution demanded having formal rules and publicly known structures, the answer is no. However, historical institutionalists argue that formal, legally defined organizations are not the only institutions. There are informal institutions (see Text Box 4.1) that cover phenomena ranging from legislative folkways to how bureaucratic corruption operates. They, too, have rules than can be enforced (think of any mob movie), persist over time, and shape the behavior of people associated with them. What informal institutions do not have is published rules that are legally enforceable, official tables of organization, or the ability to trace their origins to legislation. Political science has always known that informal institutions exist and affect how politics works, and has studied them over the years.[13]

Text Box 4.1 Formal and Informal Political Institutions

Formal political institutions are easy to define. They are official state organizations, with publicly known rules and regulations, and a legally, sometimes constitutionally, specified place in the political process. Examples include constitutions, bureaucracies, legislatures, electoral systems, and security agencies, but also political parties and interest groups, as these also have formal legal structures. Since the advent of the New Institutionalism in the 1980s,[14] political science has emphasized how institutions, and their design and operation, affect political actors and outcomes.

Informal institutions are harder to pin down. Helmke and Levitsky define them as "socially shared rules, usually unwritten, that are created, communicated, and enforced outside of officially sanctioned channels."[15] Yet like their formal counterparts, informal institutions are durable and influence official political actors and the actions of government. An example of an informal institution that is often given is the *dedazo*, literally "pointing a finger," which is how Mexican presidents were chosen from the 1930s to the 1990s. The incumbent president, always a member of the Partido Revolucionario Institucional (PRI, or Institutional Revolutionary Party) or its lineal predecessors from 1929 to 2000, selected his successor from the party's ranks. As the PRI, the official party of the Mexican Revolution, controlled the electoral apparatus, the designated heir always won. Never enshrined in law, the *dedazo* was nevertheless very real and unchallengeable in practice. It was dropped in the late 1990s as the PRI moved to more open and conventional methods of candidate selection to adjust to the increasingly open and honest Mexican electoral system.

Political Culture

If we treat *caudillos*, coups, and violence as institutions, it means that we see them as well-established, widely accepted instruments of government whose use is governed by informal but enforceable rules. This reminds us that the three mechanisms became standard ways to take and hold power. As a result, those who became governors accepted these institutions as normal parts of the political process. There is, however, another way to account for the same phenomena: political culture.

Political culture is conventionally defined as a people's political values, attitudes, and beliefs. It is thus more about preferences than rules, although in many cases the line dividing preferences from informal rules is faint and shifting. The concept of political culture has been part of political science for some 50 years; but it has come to be seen as having limited explanatory power. Nevertheless, there is a significant school of Latin Americanists who use political culture as their central analytical variable. Their argument is that Latin America possesses a distinct political tradition that is best understood through the prism of political culture.

One of the central figures of this school is Howard Wiarda. He argues that understanding why Latin American politics does not work like those of the historic democracies requires understanding the region's political culture. This culture is organic, corporatist, Catholic, and authoritarian. Thus it is dramatically different than the political culture of the United States and Canada.[16] The work of Glen Caudil Dealy, another forceful advocate of the centrality of political culture, puts the matter more starkly. Whereas North America and northwestern Europe share a tradition of pluralist politics, a tradition encouraging the existence of centers of power independent of the state, Latin America's tradition is monist, thus favoring the concentration of power in the state.[17] Certainly, Dealy's view helps explain the longevity of highly centralized, presidentialist political systems in Latin America.

Looking at the institutional and political culture schools of interpreting Latin American politics lets us see their complementarity. There can be no political tradition without both institutions—long-lived sets of rules, processes, and organizations—and a political culture whose values and preferences are congruent with those institutions. To grasp the lasting power of personal rule and the pervasiveness of violence as an implement for governing we need to take both institutions and culture into account.

Personal Rule or Patrimonialism

Personal rule is most easily defined as a government of men, not of laws. It is a political system in which the will of the ruler—whether a monarch, dictator, or president—counts for more than do laws and institutions. In fact, personal rule is almost anti-institutional, because there is no way to turn an individual's preferences into long-standing processes and organizations. However, personal rule as a political system can become institutionalized if it comes to be seen as the natural way to govern.

Although personal rule demands executive-centered government, not all executive-centered government is the product of personal rule. As long as there are institutions that countervail an executive's power and enforce accountability on a nation's chief political executive, constitutional government prevails. So if an exceptionally strong president or prime minister still has to struggle with the legislature, obey the courts, tolerate the critical media, and, if in a federation, deal with the provinces or states, he or she will remain under the ultimate control of the rule of law. Under these conditions, the next leader may not be able or willing to push the limits of executive rule so far, and the interinstitutional balance of government will re-equilibrate itself.

> **Text Box 4.2** Patrimonial and Neopatrimonial Politics
>
> *Patrimonial* refers to an inheritance. The early twentieth-century German sociologist Max Weber adopted that term to indicate that the state apparatus is the personal property of the ruler—thus the whole machinery of government is the ruler's to use as he or she sees fit. This is personal rule in the strictest sense, for the levers of state power are solely in the ruler's hands.
>
> Neopatrimonial politics entered the political science vocabulary in the 1960s to describe political systems evolving in newly independent African states. It refers to the ruler using public resources to win or hold the loyalty of citizens. It is a large-scale edition of the patron–client relationship examined in Chapter 3. As with patrimonialism, the ruler uses the state for personal ends; it differs in its focus on patron–client ties. Both, however, are forms of personal rule, because an individual is able to use public resources and state power to secure personal objectives, untouched by institutional or constitutional restraints.

To distinguish cases like the above, which are what we have always found in Canada and the United States, from instances where the individual ruler really does escape the control of both state institutions and the law itself, we need another term. The obvious candidate is *patrimonialism* (see Text Box 4.2). It and its near relation, neopatrimonialism, are used in formal social-science discourse as synonyms for personal rule.

Personal and Patrimonial Rule in Latin America: *Caudillos* and *Caudillismo*

Rule by one person who controls the state and uses it as a private resource is not unique to Latin America. Absolute monarchies epitomize personal rule and they have existed for thousands of years. Personal dictatorships are equally ancient—one of the six forms of rule identified by Aristotle was tyranny: a state in which a single ruler governs in his or her own interest. Both forms of government still exist. Saudi Arabia and the Gulf States are absolute monarchies; and although one-person dictatorships are far rarer than before 1990, they are found in some post-Soviet states (for example, Belarus).

How does personal rule become institutionalized? Obviously an absolute monarchy will invest its ruler with a legal mandate, and thus personal rule will be a formal institution. Personal dictatorships may also have formal institutions recognizing the leader's rights and privileges. For example, it is common to declare a dictator president for life. Prior to the 1990s, it would have been normal to find at least one or two personal dictatorships in Latin America, and up to the 1970s they were rather common. However, when Fidel Castro passed control to his brother in 2008, the last

Text Box 4.3 *Caudillos, Coroneis,* and Big Men

Our focus is the *caudillo,* but there are other strongmen who have governed with little regard to law. Brazil contributed the *coronel* (pl. *coroneis*) and *coronelismo.* The *coroneis* were *fazendeiros* (*latifundistas*) with huge expanses of land who, after independence, held commissions in the National Guard. They combined the social prestige and wealth of landowners with the right to command military forces. They controlled Brazil's vast rural areas and were a potent force in national politics until the 1930s. Unlike their Spanish American counterparts, the *coroneis* did not emerge from political chaos but from the empire's inability or unwillingness to extend its rule to the country's remotest corners.

Much closer to the *caudillo* in terms of his origin is the African Big Man. These figures emerged as leaders in post-independence Africa, because they, too, filled power vacuums left when other elites could not agree how best to govern their countries. Practically every country in sub-Saharan Africa has had at least one Big Man as its ruler, with South Africa, Botswana, and for some years the Gambia as the only exceptions. Like the early *caudillos,* Big Men are tyrants, ruling by force and fraud, and who often saw their political careers end by the same violence that first brought them power. Among the more recognizable of these rulers are Idi Amin (Uganda), Jean Bedel Bokassa (Central African Republic), Omar Bongo (Gabon), and Robert Mugabe (Zimbabwe).

personal dictatorship in Latin American may have ended. Nevertheless, there is no doubt that constitutions in Latin America give great power to the executive. So the question becomes whether an informal institution—or tradition or cultural predisposition—favoring the politics of strong leaders exists in Latin America. Whatever we decide, we have to begin our analysis with the figure of the *caudillo.*[18]

Independence brought personal rule and the *caudillo* to all Latin America except monarchical Brazil. Interestingly, independence also brought personal rule to almost all of sub-Saharan Africa and to a number of Asian states. We have alluded to this in Chapter 3 but need a closer look.

Generally speaking, when a colony becomes independent it experiences a form of revolution. Even if many of the former governing structures are held over, they will be run by different people with different agendas. The nature of the state itself changes. It no longer seeks to control the population for the benefit of foreigners; at best it will seek the welfare of its citizens; at worst the population will be controlled by and for a domestic ruler.

What is most closely related to the emergence of personalist, *caudillo,* rule is the breakdown of consensus among domestic political elites that

---

Text Box 4.4 Famous *Caudillos*

The best-known Latin American *caudillo* is Juan Facundo Quiroga (1788–1835), who ruled northwestern Argentina from 1825 to his death in 1835. His fame comes mainly from being the central figure in Domingo Sarmiento's *Life in the Argentine Republic in the Days of the Tyrants, or Civilization and Barbarism*.[19] For Sarmiento, a teacher who was president of Argentina from 1868 to 1874, Facundo was the barbaric tyrant who, along with others of his sort, kept Argentina poor and backward.

But if Facundo Quiroga has literary cachet, it was Juan Manuel de Rosas (1793–1877) who was the most significant Argentine *caudillo*.[20] Governor of the province of Buenos Aires from 1835 to 1852, Rosas led the *Federales*, who favored decentralized government, and opposed the *Unitarios*, who, as the name implies, wanted a strong central administration. A ruthless dictator with an efficient secret police force, the *Mazorca* ("ear of corn" because its members were as united as kernels on an ear of corn), Rosas brought law and order through force and coercion. Overthrown in 1852, Rosas spent the rest of his life in exile in England.

There are many others who merit mention. Antonio Páez of Venezuela (1790–1873) was a leader in Venezuela's struggle for independence, first from Spain and then from Gran Colombia—Simón Bolívar's ill-fated attempt to sustain the Viceroyalty of New Granada (now Colombia), Venezuela, Panama, and Ecuador. Like Rosas, Páez died in exile. Equally interesting was Mexican José Antonio López de Santa Ana (1794–1876), known as Santa Ana. He was president of Mexico on 11 different occasions, retaining office for 22 years.

---

existed when everyone worked to oust the colonizers. With no foreigners to fight, the elites turn on each other. The newly independent state is often weak, and thus not able to apply the law effectively, and frequently deemed illegitimate, as it is seen by some significant part of society as not deserving to govern. Law and order break down, the economy falters, and society seems on the brink of disintegrating. It is at this juncture that personalist, patrimonial, strongman leaders enter the picture.

After a period of turmoil, people want stability. They want to see order imposed to make them more secure physically and psychologically. This is what Hobbes said in *Leviathan*. To leave behind the state of nature, where life was "solitary, poor, brutish, nasty, and short," people cede even their right to defend themselves to Leviathan, an omnipotent ruler. They quite reasonably trade liberty for security. And this applied in early nineteenth-century Latin America or mid-twentieth-century Africa, just as Hobbes thought it would in seventeenth-century England (see Text Box 4.3).

The original *caudillo* was a military figure who gained prominence in the wars for independence. Military skill would remain essential to a *caudillo*'s success for many years. The state was weak and could not enforce the law in large parts of even small countries. A *caudillo* would have a regional base where he would build his initial support. He would also be a charismatic leader who exuded personal magnetism. Further, the *caudillo* looked after the material needs of his followers and their families, acting as a patron to his clients (see Text Box 4.4).

Having seized power, the *caudillo* staffed the state with his loyalists and used government to preserve his power. However, the same weaknesses at the center that let one *caudillo* take power would let others rebel and eventually depose him. Thus government did not settle into established routines or develop structures that could function independently of the desires of the ruler. *Caudillo* rule prevented the building of stable government institutions. This is why, as time passed, opposition to *caudillo* government arose and support for stronger, centralized authority grew. Nevertheless, traditional *caudillos* could still be found in Latin America's smaller, poorer countries, such as Nicaragua or the Dominican Republic, until the second half of the twentieth century.

Although *caudillos* and *caudillo* rule began disappearing from Latin America's political scene in the 1850s, the label *caudillo* still is widely applied to charismatic, patrimonial political leaders, even elected ones. In part, this just pins a well-established name on what political science calls a patrimonial, personalistic ruler. But it also draws our attention to what has changed since the 1820s in how *caudillos* rule. Contemporary *caudillos* do not employ force to gain power and use violence sparingly to keep power. The coercive mechanisms of choice are now bureaucratic and legal measures (inspections, licensing, or court cases) when governing and strikes and demonstrations if in opposition. Nicaragua offers an example.

Nicaragua's 1996 elections pitted Arnoldo Alemán of the Partido Liberal Constitucionalista (PLC, or Constitutionalist Liberal Party) against Daniel Ortega of the Frente Sandinista de Liberación Nacional (FSLN, or Sandinista National Liberation Front), with the Liberal winning. Both dominated their parties, raised money, distributed their resources to gain support, and knew how to pressure and manipulate to maximize their power.[21] Ortega used his party's presence in university politics to direct protests against the government's funding of postsecondary education and influenced Sandinista-aligned judges to render decisions unfavorable to the government.[22] For his part, Alemán used tax inspectors to harass nongovernmental organizations (NGOs) he felt were aligned with his opponents. The main difference between them and old-time *caudillos*, however, is that these two leaders recognized that power could be taken legitimately only through elections. Therefore, they can be called electoral *caudillos*, the modern Latin American version of the US city bosses of 100 years ago.

Caudillo-style personal rule is thus still possible in Latin America, albeit in a renewed form. There are several plausible reasons to explain its persistence. First, most countries in the region still have many people who count on government-controlled handouts; thus patronage politics, or clientelism, dominates. Although patronage can be handled by an impersonal party apparatus, it is traditionally the leader who decides who gets what. Second, political culture plays a role to the extent that people expect to need a leader's personal good will to get benefits. Many political scientists and journalists who work in Latin America have seen poor people in party offices waving party membership cards at officials as they sought jobs, pensions, or help with some other problem. Third, political professionals may believe that only a *caudillo*-like figure can win elections and manage government. Their national histories will have provided many examples of successful strongmen but relatively few cases of low-profile institution builders who rank among the nation's greats.

Personal and Patrimonial Rule in Latin America: Dictators and Dictatorship

Dictators are individual rulers who are not constrained by law. They differ from absolute monarchs in that the latter are legitimated by descent from a ruling family whereas dictators base their legitimacy on a revolution, winning a civil war, or providing stability. Like any unaccountable ruler, dictators generally rely more on force and coercion than do democratic governments. Thirty years ago, there would have been dozens of examples from around the globe. In 2009, we have a far shorter list: Raúl Castro of Cuba, Muammar Gadaffi of Libya, Bashar al-Assad of Syria, Kim Jong Il of North Korea, and a few others.

Caudillos and dictators are not identical. John Lynch, a historian who has written extensively about *caudillos*, said this about Simón Bolívar, the Liberator of South America: "Bolívar was a dictator (but) ... Bolivarian dictatorship was not *caudillismo*. It was less personal and more institutional; it dealt in policies as well as patronage ... and restored law as well as order."[23] Obviously, some dictators were *caudillos* and many *caudillos* were dictators. What matters is that dictators have also been extremely common throughout Latin American history.

The best way to understand what dictators and their governments do is to examine several cases. There are three types of dictatorships: personal, institutional, and a mix of the two that sees a powerful individual dominate an institutional dictatorship. A personal dictatorship is a one-man government, and it is usually a man who runs it. This does not mean that there is not a bureaucracy, political party, and security apparatus but rather that these and all other parts of government respond in the final analysis to the leader's will. It is a patrimonial regime.

An institutional dictatorship is different. It is usually run by the military or a ruling party, although one can imagine a religion or an ideologically driven group at the helm. The institution could be represented by a committee (the familiar military *junta*—the Spanish word for board or committee—is the easiest example), or it could have an individual as presiding officer. Institutional dictatorships differ from personal ones in that the institution that set up the dictatorship normally makes the government accountable to it. Should an especially strong figure emerge to control the government and escape to some degree institutional control, the third or hybrid form of dictatorship emerges.

All dictatorships are unaccountable to the general public. They place themselves above the law. Dictatorships use coercion freely. Individual rights and liberties are defined by government and enforced or ignored as it sees fit. Such regimes may enrich themselves at the people's expense or they may provide citizens reasonable public services and fairly efficient government. Finally, dictatorships commonly end in collapse, although there are cases where a dictatorship scripted its departure with some success.

Personal Dictatorships

Latin American history offers many examples of personal dictators, three of whom we will examine closely: Francia of Paraguay, the Somozas of Nicaragua, and Cuba's Fidel Castro. Francia is a classical personal dictator, but the Somozas managed to sustain a personal dictatorship for two generations. In addition, Francia represents the first generation of dictators, coming to power with his country's independence. The Somozas, whose rule ended only in 1979, are one of the most recent personal dictatorships to fall. Castro could also be placed with either institutional or hybrid systems, for although he took power as a charismatic individual leading a guerrilla movement, he soon added the Communist Party to the framework of his regime.[24]

José Gaspar Rodriguez de Francia (1766–1840) ruled Paraguay from 1814 to 1840 with as tight a hand as any imaginable. The man who styled himself "El Supremo" came from a comfortable background and was extremely well educated. Yet he was to persecute the old colonial elites and cut his country off from the rest of world. In fact, Francia was one of the harshest dictators in Latin American history. Despite his cruelty and isolationism, Francia made Paraguay self-sufficient and took radical steps to overcome the country's grave inequality (for example, through a miscegenation law that demanded that whites marry nonwhites and vice versa).[25]

The Somozas, Anastasio (Tacho) and his sons Luis and Anastasio, Jr. (Tachito), ruled Nicaragua from 1936 to 1979. They, along with Carlos Antonio and Francisco Solano López of Paraguay (1844–1870) and François and Jean-Claude Duvalier of Haiti (1957–1986), are Latin American examples of the rare phenomenon of intergenerational dictatorships. The Somozas got started when Tacho overthrew the sitting president, who happened to be his wife's uncle. Then, through a combination of force, fraud, co-optation, and absolute control of the National Guard (Nicaragua's military), he ruled his country and built the family's fortunes. Tacho also cultivated a relationship with the United States, and Franklin Roosevelt supposedly said of the first Somoza that "he's a son of a bitch, but he's our son of a bitch!" An assassin's bullet ended Tacho's rule in 1956, but the dynasty continued for another 23 years.

Luis, the elder son, was as ruthless as his father and as shrewd a politician. He hoped to take the family out of the spotlight by retiring from active politics and retaining indirect command through the family's party, the Nationalist Liberals. However, Luis died of a heart attack and his younger brother Tachito assumed control. More vicious and less politically adept than either his father or brother, the last Somoza alienated even Nicaragua's upper class and was overthrown by the FSLN in 1979. He died in exile in Paraguay at the hands of a team of assassins in 1980.[26]

Before handing control to his brother in 2006, Fidel Castro was the last classical dictator in Latin America. He took power in Cuba in 1959, ousting another dictator, Fulgencio Batista, after a three-year guerrilla insurgency. Proclaiming his nationalist and anti-imperialist credentials, Fidel moved quickly to expropriate American property, thereby earning the enmity of the US government, which imposed an economic embargo on the island nation in 1961. In that same year, Cuban exiles living in the United States and supported by Washington mounted an unsuccessful invasion of the Bay of Pigs. By then, Castro had declared himself a Communist and established a one-party state.

In his 47 years in power, Castro built a reputation as an extremely able international politician. He has survived some 600 attempts by the CIA to assassinate him, and also (more figuratively) the collapse of the Soviet Union, which heavily subsidized his rule. Cuba has only one party and many political prisoners, but although Castro is seen by his enemies as a bloodthirsty tyrant, he is seen by his supporters as the first Cuban ruler to look out for the nation's poor and marginalized. He is also an icon among the Latin American and international left, due to his defiance of Washington and his long-standing assistance to revolutionary movements.[27]

Although Castro was the last personal dictator in Latin America, it would be premature to think that there will never be others. One-man rule emerges in times of conflict, especially in countries with weak political institutions. And we have the example of Hitler to remind ourselves that dictators can arise even in developed countries. Although Latin American politics is now reasonably stable, a serious economic recession, such as that which began in 2008, or even just a very powerful ruler who declines to leave office could bump a country back into the ranks of dictatorial rule.

Institutional Dictatorships

Institutional dictatorships are built around a well-established organization, such as the military or a political party. Whereas individual dictatorships die with the dictator, or with his son in rare cases such as the Somozas, an institutional dictatorship can theoretically last forever. It can certainly outlive the individuals who founded it. And that is often the objective.

Why would an institution, military or party, want to govern? There are two usual reasons. One is to get rid of a bad government, where bad can mean corrupt, feckless, or prejudiced against the institution in question. This is what underlays most institutional military governments in Latin America.

The other is to seize and hold power for a long time in order to change society. Communist parties are the best-known practitioners of institutional dictatorships. Militaries, however, can also act this way, and from 1964 to 1989 there were four such regimes in Latin America: Argentina, Brazil, Chile, and Uruguay. We consider Brazil here and then all of them together below in the section on coups.

Brazil was the first of these institutional dictatorships.[28] When military rule began in 1964, after the overthrow of João Goulart, it was not a long-term project—it was originally to last for just the term of the president who was ousted—but hardliners in the military demanded more and settled in until 1985. Two things about this dictatorship catch the eye. First, leadership circulated among various general and admirals; it really was the _military institution_ that ruled. Second, the regime created two political parties to channel political activity.

There was a government party, Alianza Renevadora Nacional (ARENA, or Alliance for National Renewal), and an opposition party, Movimento Democrático Brasileiro (MDB, or Brazilian Democratic Movement). These two organizations ran in elections (at first with predetermined results) and existed until 1979. At that time, they were abolished, in line with a policy of gradual liberalization (_distenção_) and political opening (_abertura_) implemented by the military government of the day. The military regime, that is, sought to create conditions that would let it leave power with the state and leave society relatively stable. It did so in 1985, after indirect but freely competitive presidential elections.

Hybrids

Some dictatorships that begin as institutional regimes change into personalistic ones as a dominant figure emerges and monopolizes power. Soviet dictator Joseph Stalin (who ruled 1927–1953) may be the best example produced in the twentieth century. Latin America's best-known recent contribution to this sub-class of dictators is Augusto Pinochet, who ruled Chile from 1973 to 1989.[29]

When Chile's military toppled the government of Salvador Allende, a Marxist whose Popular Unity Alliance won a narrow victory three years earlier (see Chapters 5 and 7), it was evident that the military would be in power for some time. As in Brazil, the governing junta that ruled the country after the coup contained representatives from the three military services, as well as the national police. However, one figure soon emerged on top: General Augusto Pinochet.

In his 16 years governing Chile, Pinochet was involved in multiple human rights abuses. He expected never to have to face charges, however. First, the 1980 constitution, drafted by and for the dictatorship, appeared to offer the general the chance to govern until 1996. However, a referendum in 1988 rejected the dictator's bid for another eight years in power. Then competitive elections in 1989 were won by Pinochet's opponents. Yet things still looked good for the general, since the 1980 constitution made him a lifetime senator with parliamentary immunity from prosecution.

Obviously, Pinochet did not foresee being arrested in 1998 while in England for medical treatment and charged with torture, murder, forced disappearances, and illegal detention. Although he did not stand trial in England, the House of Lords found that an ex-head of state was not immune to arrest and extradition for acts committed while a head of state.[30] He returned to Chile, where in 2000 the courts stripped the ex-dictator of his immunity from prosecution. Pinochet never stood trial, though, because the Chilean Supreme Court dismissed the indictments on the grounds that he was mentally unfit to stand trial.

The court battles continued until the dictator's death in 2006. One of the proceedings saw him charged with tax evasion after a US Senate investigation of money laundering found that Pinochet had $11 million secreted in foreign bank accounts, some under assumed names. The retired general's reputation for probity was in tatters. Then in 2006, shortly before his death, most of the 1980 constitution was amended, leaving another part of Pinochet's legacy in ruins. Although Augusto Pinochet died in 2006 never having been convicted of any of the crimes with which he was charged, he had lived to see much of his life's work undone.

Personal Rule: An Overview

We shall never see an end to personal rule. Neither should we expect to see an end to presidents and prime ministers, even in democracies, doing all they can to avoid the limits the law places on them. Nevertheless, the world's historic democracies have an advantage because there are both well-designed legal limitations on the executive and a substantial array of individuals and institutions ready to assert their rights to constrain the activities of the nation's top political leader. In other nations, including most of Latin America, the restraints are weaker and the predisposition to accept an untrammeled executive as natural is stronger.

Many of those democracies, though, were governed by absolute monarchs in the not-too-distant past. Over time, newly powerful actors and interests emerged to curb executive power while carving a niche for themselves in the political system. We have suggested that the extremely powerful executive has achieved institutional status in Latin America. Both constitutions and citizens' expectations reinforce the president's hand. Yet as we discuss in Chapter 6, other institutions and actors—legislatures, civil society, media, courts—are growing in power, which should make personal, patrimonial rule increasingly harder to implement.

Violence and Politics in Latin America

English political scientist Bernard Crick speaks of the "political method of rule."[31] Politics is built around negotiations and the reconciliation of differences. It is about conflict resolution. Violence has no place as an instrument of governing in the political method of rule.

People who live in one of the world's historic democracies would accept Crick's observation as self-evidently true. When political violence occurs in democracies, we think it aberrant. Yet our concurrence with Crick's dictum does not alter the fact that violence is commonly used for political ends. Governments use it, and so do those who challenge government.

One characteristic of a state is that it possesses a monopoly on legitimate violence. That is, states should be the only organization in society that is permitted to use violence when necessary, and then only in prescribed and well-known ways. National defense and policing are the obvious examples. Yet states regularly use violence to suppress dissent and opposition, and some states do this far more than others. Further, it is not only states that use violence and claim to do so legitimately. Citizens may argue that they need to resort to force to protect themselves from an abusive state or to remove a tyrannical regime.

Violence has long been and will long be a useful political tool. It can defend, influence, or overthrow governments. Governments use violence to establish and maintain order, at home and abroad. The question is not whether violence has a place in politics but rather what that place actually is in particular cases.

But why use political violence? Why does the political method of rule sometimes not work? Perhaps a minority feels threatened and uses violence to repress a majority. Or state violence is the only way to restore order that has broken down. And there are the obvious cases of forceful overthrows of government, from coups to popular insurrections. Each of those instances will spin off numerous variations, and thus there are plenty of plausible reasons for using political violence.

This variety of reasons becomes evident when looking at Latin America, which has long had an unenviable reputation for violent politics. Dictatorial governments have employed violence to keep themselves in power. Revolutionaries and insurrectionists have used violence to get themselves into power. Militaries stage coups for the same reason. There is not one country in the region without a significant degree of violent politics in its history.

One part of this section describes the part violence has played in Latin America's politics. Another suggests why it has had a larger role there than in the United States and Canada. Finally, it asks about the consequences of relatively high levels of violence, from instability to the institutionalization of violence as a political instrument.

Political Violence at Work

Countries can go through long periods of turmoil when violence reigns and the ordinary institutions of government function badly, if at all. England was like that from the fifteenth through to the seventeenth centuries, somewhat more time than Latin America has been independent. Between 1455 and 1689, the country knew two lengthy and bloody civil wars; saw two monarchs executed and a third exiled; lived through at least four far-reaching constitutional transformations; and experienced religious changes that sundered the country for 150 years. Now that is a record of instability and violence! England—more accurately the United Kingdom—has known violent politics since then, too, most recently in the form of terrorism. But now it has a governing formula acceptable to the vast majority of its population and has developed institutions that channel most of society's conflicts into paths leading to peaceful resolution. History is not fate and institutions do change and develop along new paths.

What brought the English two and a half centuries of instability, conflict, and violence was a simple but deadly combination of questions: Who should rule? How should the ruler govern? And in whose interests should the ruler govern? Being unable to answer those questions to the satisfaction of a significant proportion of a country's political elite (and their followers) means that there is no generally accepted governing formula, hence no political method of rule. That makes violence an attractive option. A look at Nicaraguan and Colombian political history shows how this has worked in two especially difficult Latin American cases.

Nicaragua

Although all of Central America has known turmoil and violence since independence in 1821 (1903 for Panama), Nicaragua seems especially cursed. From independence until 1855, the country knew near-continuous civil war, waged not by professional armies but by peasants following their landlords into battle. Liberals from León and Conservatives from Granada fought to control the state and impose their vision of the politically good. There were ideological divisions in play, but there were also personal rivalries and ambitions.

This tumultuous period ended not because the warring factions struck a peace, but because William Walker,[32] a mercenary from New Orleans who was hired by the Liberals, captured the country. He wanted to introduce slavery and have Nicaragua become a slave state. The combined armies of Central America defeated Walker in 1857, and Nicaragua entered what remains its longest period of peaceful, constitutional rule: 1858 to 1893.

That period of Conservative dominance was based on interregional elite pacts. Things were fine until a new region emerged as an economic power and wanted commensurate political force. When that was not forthcoming, a Liberal *caudillo*, José Santos Zelaya, led a successful revolution and built a dictatorship that would last until 1909. Although Zelaya introduced many much-needed modernizing reforms and brought Nicaragua's Atlantic Coast (until then a British protectorate) under Managua's rule, he was not a democrat. Finally, in 1909 a US-backed Conservative revolution sent Zelaya into exile and Nicaragua hurtling toward 18 years of civil war.

Conservatives and Liberals confronted each other once again from 1909 to 1927. However, unlike a century earlier, this time Washington sent the US Marines to be peacekeepers, to "protect American lives and property," and to train a nonpartisan Nicaraguan army, the National Guard. Although the United States brokered a peace in 1927, one that led to Nicaragua's first honest elections in 1928 and another free vote in 1932, one combatant did not recognize the deal. Augusto César Sandino, a Liberal general during the wars with Conservatives, began a seven-year guerrilla struggle against the Marines and the National Guard. The Marines withdrew in 1934, but Sandino was dead within two months, assassinated by order of the Guard's commander, Anastasio Somoza García.

By 1936, Tacho Somoza had set up his own dictatorship. His would endure until 1979, passed down to his two sons, Luis and Tacho, Jr. Although the Somozas gave Nicaragua political stability, they also restricted freedom and repressed opponents. There were several attempts to overthrow the dictators. Tacho was assassinated in 1956, but it was a revolutionary movement that took Sandino's name that finally toppled the dynasty: the FSLN.

Founded in 1961, the Marxist-oriented but later surprisingly pluralistic FSLN gained power in 1979. The new regime, and basically all Nicaraguans who had not been directly linked to the Somozas, were looking forward to peace, recovery, and putting the country on a new road. That did not happen. In 1981, the US government began waging what it called "low-intensity conflict"[33] against the Sandinista government. This *Contra* (for "counterrevolutionary") war ended only after the FSLN lost the 1990 elections and became a democratic opposition. By then, however, some 31,000 Nicaraguans on both sides of the conflict had lost their lives.

Since 1990, Nicaragua has been spared large-scale violence. Indeed, it has even had a measure of political stability, as there have been five straight open and free elections to determine who governs until the next vote. In 2006, the FSLN itself won, coming back after 16 years out of power. There is still considerable disagreement among Nicaraguans about how those three perniciously dangerous questions—who governs, how, and for whom—should be answered but for now electoral results provide satisfactory responses.

Colombia

Colombia's past has been even more tragically violent than Nicaragua's. Though it has had fewer dictatorships than the Central American country and likely the fewest military coups of any country in the region, Colombia has known great and bloody civil wars, eight of them in the nineteenth century alone. Worse, the country is still gripped by violence today.[34]

The origins of political violence in Colombia lie in political ideas and the organizations founded to mobilize those ideas and turn them into policies: political parties. As in Nicaragua, ideological differences were compounded by personal ambitions and animus. But in Colombia, both the Liberals and the Conservatives were able to capture the state and dominate it for long periods, leading the other party to rebel and plunge the country in civil wars. First was the War of the Supremes, from 1839 to 1842, so called because the local *caudillos* who led the revolt always referred to themselves as the supreme leaders of their respective localities. They rebelled against the central government's increasing concentration of power. The Supremes foreshadowed the Liberals, and the central government the Conservatives.

Civil wars were fought from 1859 to 1862, in 1876, and again in 1885, all with the aim of one party, whether Liberal or Conservative, excluding the other from having a real chance of taking power by elections. But the most serious nineteenth-century civil war in Colombia was the Thousand Day War, from 1899 to 1902, which took some 100,000 lives—about 2.5 per cent of the population. After that war, the Liberals and Conservatives sought to reduce friction between them. And they succeeded until 1948 when the last of Colombia's partisan wars erupted.

La Violencia (The Violence), from 1948 to 1953, began after the assassination of Liberal leader Jorge Eliécer Gaitán. A riot broke out in Bogotá and quickly spread to the rural areas. There, the fighting took place, as it always had, between peasants who followed their landlords. Before Colombia's only military coup of the twentieth century brought the bloodshed under control, an estimated 200,000 people had died.

As in 1902, Colombia's political elites sought to put a permanent end to civil wars. This time they devised the National Front, from 1958 to 1974, an ingenious plan which saw Liberals and Conservatives alternate the presidency every four years and share equally between them all elected offices. Although this did end Liberal-Conservative violence, the failure of the National Front to solve the problems of the rural poor saw the emergence of the guerrilla groups that still operate in the country.

Since 1974, the nature of political violence in Colombia has changed. First, there are the guerrilla groups. Once, there were four but now only two remain: the Fuerzas Armadas Revolucionarias de Colombia (FARC, or Revolutionary Armed Forces of Colombia) and the Ejército de Liberación Nacional (ELN, or National Liberation Army). Emerging to fight the guerrillas are paramilitaries, the Autodefensas Unidas de Colombia (AUC, or United Self-Defense Forces of Colombia). And then there are the drug lords, the *cocaleros*.

Colombian governments have tried various approaches to deal with those forces, insurgents, counterinsurgents, and plain criminals. They have tried repression, they have set up demilitarized zones, and they have even placed co-optation on the table. Further, there was an attempt to bring the leftist guerrillas into the political process, beginning in 1985, but it failed as the right assassinated more than 3,000 candidates and elected officials from the radical parties.[35] Despite continuing high levels of violence, Colombia nonetheless maintains a functioning electoral democracy.

The Instruments of Political Violence

Political violence takes many forms. These range from breaking windows to assassination, insurgency, terrorism, coups, armed overthrow, and social revolution. There is enough material here for several books, so we will only consider two that have been prominent in Latin America's history: military coups and social revolutions.

Coups

In military coups, the military, acting as an institution, overthrows a government. This distinguishes the coup, *golpe de estado*, from a *caudillo*-led armed revolt. The distinction is important, because Latin American political elites believed that establishing a professional military, one that saw itself as an independent state institution, would end political violence and instability.

Starting about 1870, as *caudillo* politics waned in the larger and more developed countries, professional militaries began to appear. Their models were the most sophisticated armies of Europe, namely those of Prussia and France. Not only were those forces well trained and armed, but they also stayed clear of overt politics. Yet what worked in Europe did not work in Latin America. Why?

In developed European countries professional, well-equipped militaries were part of a generalized modernity. In Latin America, even in relatively wealthy nations such as Brazil or Argentina, they were the country's most advanced institution. Officers commanded sophisticated machinery and had the most up-to-date technical training, often at European military academies. They were the technological elite of their countries.

Faced with low levels of economic and social development, not to mention politics built on patronage, spoils, and corruption, the military professionals were repelled. They could not see why bumblers who were so unpatriotic as to tolerate their nation's underdevelopment should remain in office. All that was needed was a spark—prolonged disorder, a fraudulent election, or some real or imagined insult to the military itself—and a coup would ensue.

Most *golpes de estado* were carried off with relatively little violence. There would be a *pronunciamento* (a declaration of the military's intention to act), followed by the mobilization of troops. Then the presidential palace or the congress would be surrounded and left incommunicado. Next, the president and whatever other officials the military found culpable would be offered the chance to go into exile. With luck, they accepted this offer and the coup would be bloodless. A military government would then be formed, govern for two or three years, and then, convinced that the original problem had been solved, hand power back to a different set of civilians.

Although events did not always follow the above script, it was the general model for Latin American *golpes de estado* until the mid-twentieth century. Things changed with the Brazilian coup of 1964, which set the pattern for similar takeovers in Uruguay (1973), Chile (1973), and Argentina (1976). The militaries of these four countries felt compelled to act to save their countries from the threat of communist takeover. They set up what were called bureaucratic authoritarian (BA) regimes and committed themselves to retaining power until the danger they perceived had been extirpated.[36] Unlike earlier military governments, these governed with exceptional brutality.[37]

During the 1970s, when those military dictatorships were strongest, it was feared that they were the wave of the future. However, not only had all four passed from the scene by 1989, but their disappearance also coincided with at least the temporary end of military rule in Latin America. Since 1976, there have been only three *golpes* in Latin America: in Ecuador (2000), which did not result in a military government; in Venezuela (2002), which failed; and in Haiti (2004), where the coup did oust the elected president Jean-Bertrand Aristide.[38] Although that is a good sign, it is too soon to declare Latin America freed from the threat of coups.

Revolutions

Students of revolutions distinguish between social and political revolutions. That is, beyond defining a revolution as violence used to bring down a ruling elite, they ask whether the result was to expel just the governors—a political revolution—or whether it changed social and economic relations and structures as well. To consider political revolutions in Latin America would be a daunting task. However, there have been only three social revolutions in Latin America, all in the twentieth century: Mexico, Cuba, and Nicaragua.[39] In all three cases, there were high levels of violence and, after the revolutionary seizure of power, a total overhaul of the political system and serious attempts to restructure economic and social hierarchies.

The Mexican Revolution is the most complex of the three. It began in 1910 as a consequence of the last of many rigged elections by Porfirio Díaz, the country's dictator since 1876. Soon, agrarian reform was added to the agenda, which would eventually embrace the wide range of socialist and liberal reforms found in the 1917 Constitution. Though the worst of the fighting ended by 1920, sporadic violence continued until 1929.

Often called the last bourgeois revolution because it attacked absolutist rule and inherited privilege, the Mexican Revolution entered a new phase in 1929 with the founding of the Partido Revolucionario Nacional (PRN, or National Revolutionary Party) as the official party of the Revolution. The party was renamed the Partido de la Revolución Mexicana (PRM, or Party of the Mexican Revolution) in 1938 and became the Partido Revolucionario Institucional (PRI, or Institutional Revolutionary Party) in 1946. It governed Mexico from 1929 until 2000. Over time, the official party became corrupt, bureaucratic, and coercive. Nevertheless, the Mexican revolution set Mexico on a new path that saw the country assert its independence.

Nicaragua's Sandinista Revolution (1979) was the only *fidelista* (inspired by Fidel Castro) revolution to take power outside of Cuba. The revolutionary movement, the FSLN, was founded in 1961, split into three factions or tendencies in 1975 and reunited, thanks to Castro's mediation, only five months before taking power on July 19, 1979. Although the FSLN tried rural guerrilla warfare and organizing a proletarian rising to overthrow the Somoza dictatorship, it was a strategy built around a multiclass alliance of the dictatorship's opponents that carried the Sandinistas to power. As a result, the Sandinista Revolution was more pluralistic, politically and economically, than Castro's, even though the FSLN was a self-declared, revolutionary vanguard party with distinct Marxist leanings.

Nicaragua's pluralism, however, did not keep Washington from trying to overthrow the revolutionary government. Although the United States did not invade Nicaragua as it had Mexico in 1914 and 1916, Washington did raise and arm a proxy insurgent force, the *Contras* or counterrevolutionaries, to do the same work. The insurgents could not topple the Sandinista government, however. That was achieved by the Unión Nacional Opositora (UNO, or National Oppositional Union), a broad electoral alliance of anti-FSLN parties (including some to the revolutionaries' left) in 1990, in the second national elections held under the revolutionary government.

Even though the FSLN regained Nicaragua's presidency in 2006, it is tempting to class Nicaragua among the world's failed revolutions. Its social, economic, and political reforms did not long survive the defeat of the revolutionary government. Though the Sandinistas attempted a social revolution, they were able to take only a few steps in that direction. Fidel Castro's Cuban Revolution, though, is a different story. Its longevity, its transformation of Cuban society, and Castro's own unswerving dedication to his revolution's goals clearly mark it as a social revolution.

After only three years of guerrilla operations, Castro's Movimiento 26 de Julio (July 26 Movement)[40] became Cuba's government on New Year's Day 1959. Whether the revolutionaries were committed Marxists or just radically democratic Cuban nationalists, the *fidelistas'* systematic nationalization without compensation of US-owned properties in Cuba—everything from sugar plantations to mob-run casinos—earned Washington's wrath. An economic embargo that still exists, an attempted invasion of the island by Cuban exiles in 1961, and numerous attempts by the United States to assassinate Castro are the fruits of that displeasure.

For nearly half a century, Castro kept power in his hands and those of the Communist Party. While Castro occasionally permitted some limited market reforms in Cuba, he steadfastly refused to let them take root or to compromise his monopoly on power. However, in 2006, Castro fell seriously ill and handed power to his brother Raúl, making the transfer official in 2008. In the long run, after Fidel Castro's death, there may be political openings and further economic experiments. One thing is certain, though, and that is that Latin America still lives in a revolutionary age.

In the first decade of the twenty-first century there are nonviolent revolutions underway in Venezuela, Bolivia, and Ecuador. Because they are nonviolent, they are not treated here but rather in Chapters 5 and 7. If Latin Americans are able to discover how to produce profound and lasting

> **Text Box 4.5** Cops and Drug Traffickers in Rio: The Movie[41]
>
> *Elite Squad* is a Brazilian cop movie that is a little edgier than what we usually see in North America. Premiered at the 2007 Rio de Janeiro International Film Festival, the film focuses on the operations of a special unit of the Rio police that deals mainly with drug trafficking. The drug dealers are bad guys, killing people with impunity. But the police are not much better, since they regularly use torture to get information from prisoners.
>
> Rio's poor neighborhoods, the *favelas*, are awash in crime and drug-related violence. Shoot-outs between gangs and between criminals and the police take many innocent victims who are literally caught in the crossfire. The drug traffickers terrorize the people to keep them under control and have to be stopped. But a shooting war between the traffickers and the cops is a bloody, costly process. Worse, when the police act with impunity—the belief that they can get away with whatever they do—the line between good guys and bad guys is hard to find.

social, economic, and political change without violence, they will truly make history.

Other Forms of Violence

Governments are not only permitted to use violence, but they are also expected to employ violence to maintain order and protect citizens from threats external and domestic. Yet governments can rely too much on violence, and those who challenge government can turn too easily to violence. People living where Crick's political method of rule is the only legitimate way to govern are intolerant of political violence and unlikely to condone its use. Looking beyond our borders and outside our own times, however, we see that others have a different perspective.

This different viewpoint may come from having to confront more violence. Why there *is* more violence is the question to address first. If the cause is crime (see Text Box 4.5), what are authorities using besides violence to lower crime rates? If a government uses violence to repress an insurgency, we need to ask why an insurgency exists. An insurgency that grows from misgovernment, which includes too much reliance on violence, is different from one sponsored by another state to get its favorite into power.

Regarding state violence, the 1980s saw a profusion of death squads in Latin America. These are unofficial hit squads, usually with links to government that are sufficiently vague to be deniable, who assassinate those assumed to be enemies of the state. In general, the enemies came from the political left, those who propose diluting the power of current elites.[42] More recently, the phenomenon of extra-judicial killings has become prominent. In these cases, teams not unlike death squads, often formed by off-duty police or soldiers, go around eliminating "undesirables": street kids, drug addicts, or petty crooks.[43]

At a more obviously political level, the three questions that bedeviled the English for two and a half centuries remain key:

- Who gets to rule? Who is seen as a legitimate, rightful governor? What makes a governor legitimate? What does he or she have to do to be legitimate?
- How does the ruler rule? Violence? Rule of law? Does he or she rule effectively and maintain order? Or ineffectively, with chaos reigning?
- On whose behalf is the country ruled? An elite? A religious group? A class or social sector? A party? The ruler's family and cronies? The community as a whole, in as far as possible?

Where there is no consensus on these points, at least among those who count—people who control lots of resources—conflict ensues. Where whatever political institutions exist to channel conflict toward peaceful resolutions are weak, corrupt, biased, or nonexistent, violence can erupt. Throughout much of Latin America's history, there has been neither consensus on the basic question of rule nor state institutions capable of keeping conflict in bounds.

Conclusion: Personalism, Violence, and Democracy

Personalisitic politics and historically high levels of political violence are important, because in Latin America's past they have impeded democracy and favored authoritarian rule. Personalized rule produces strong executives and weak legislatures and courts. In turn, this encourages a politics that discounts popular opinion and opposition, while turning law into a simple instrument of rule and politicizing justice. A history of personal rule can also lead a country's people to look for strongman saviors instead of forming lasting political organizations, and to view concentrating power in one person's unaccountable hands as normal. Finally, as the executive controls the forces of order, the military and police, personalistic rule privileges recourse to violence to take and keep power. And this of course stifles the development of other methods of conflict resolution and discourages seeking bargained, negotiated settlements to disputes.

To the extent that these practices are institutionalized, formally through constitutions that vest enormous powers in a president or informally through a predisposition to think first of coercion as the way to solve political disputes, they condition contemporary politics. These patterns can and do change but generally do so slowly and unpredictably.

Further Readings

Honderich, Ted. *Three Essays on Political Violence*. Oxford: Basil Blackwell, 1976.

Lewis, Paul. *Guerrillas and Generals: The Dirty War in Argentina*. Westport, CT: Praeger Press, 2002.

Linz, Juan, and H.E. Chelabi, eds. *Sultanistic Regimes*. Baltimore, MD: Johns Hopkins University Press, 1998.

White, Richard. *Paraguay's Autonomous Revolution: 1810-1840*. Albuquerque, NM: University of New Mexico Press, 1978.

Discussion Questions

① On the one hand, most citizens in most countries, regardless of how democratic those nations are, want strong leadership, which means strong leaders. On the other, especially in historic democracies such as Canada and the United States, those same citizens fear the excessive concentration of power in a leader's hands. Is it possible to resolve this contradiction?

② This text hypothesizes that violence is likely to become a viable governing instrument when political elites disagree about basic questions of governing. What could cause such profound splits? Is there any means to resolve such profound differences short of violence?

Notes

1. *Western Political Quarterly* 5: 3 (September 1952): 445.

2. (New York: Oxford University Press, 2005) 11.

3. Harold Lasswell, "The Garrison State," *American Journal of Sociology* 46 (1941): 455–468.

4. For instance, Douglass North, *Institutions, Institutional Change and Economic Performance* (Cambridge: Cambridge University Press, 1990).

5. Michael Atkinson, "Governing Canada," *Governing Canada: Institutions and Public Policy*, ed. M. Atkinson (Toronto, ON: Harcourt, Brace, Jovanovich Canada, 1993) 6.

6. Carroll Quigley, *The Evolution of Civilizations: An Introduction to Historical Analysis* (New York: Macmillan, 1961).

7. This is called "rational choice institutionalism." We discuss it in greater length in Chapter 7.

8. There are two good introductions to historical institutionalism: Sven Steinmo, Kathleen Thelen, and Frank Longstreth, eds., *Structuring Politics: Historical Institutionalism in Comparative Analysis* (New York: Cambridge University Press, 1992) and Kathleen Thelen, "Historical Institutionalism and Comparative Politics," *Annual Review of Political Science* 2 (1999): 369–404.

9. See Paul Pierson, "Increasing Returns, Path Dependence, and the Study of Politics," *American Political Science Review* 92:4 (2000): 251–267.

10. In Chapter 3 we encountered this problem in a different guise when examining the relative continuity of actors constituting Latin America's political elites.

11. Holden, 47.

FOUR Historic Modes of Governing: The Politics of Patrimonialism

12. There is a danger that historical institutionalism can become historical determinism. Current debates among historical institutionalists increasingly focus on how much political processes and structures change, thus de-emphasizing institutional stability.

13. Gretchen Helmke and Steven Levitsky, "Informal Institutions and Comparative Politics: A Research Agenda," *Perspectives on Politics* 2:4 (2004): 725–740.

14. James G. March and Johan P. Olsen, "The New Institutionalism: Organizational Factors in Political Life," *American Political Science Review* 78:3 (1984): 734–749.

15. Helmke and Levitsky, 727.

16. Howard Wiarda and M. MacLeish Mott, "Introduction: Interpreting Latin America's Politics on Its Own Terms," *Politics and Social Change in Latin America: Still a Distinct Tradition?* 4th ed. eds. Howard Wiarda and Margaret MacLeish Mott (Westport, CT: Praeger Publishers, 2003) 1–2.

17. Glen Dealy, "The Tradition of Monistic Democracy in Latin America," *Journal of the History of Ideas* 35 (1974): 616–630.

18. On *caudillos*, see John Lynch, *Caudillos in Spanish America, 1800–1850* (Oxford: Clarendon Press, 1992); Hugh M. Hamill, ed., *Dictatorship in Spanish America* (New York: Knopf, 1966); Hugh M. Hamill ed., *Caudillos: Dictators in Spanish America* (Norman, OK: University of Oklahoma Press, 1992).

19. Domingo F. Sarmiento, *Life in the Argentine Republic in the Days of the Tyrants, or, Civilization and Barbarism*, tr. Mary Mann, 1868 (New York: Haffner Publishing, 1960).

20. A splendid biography of Rosas is John Lynch's *Argentine Dictator: Juan Manuel de Rosas, 1829–1852* (Oxford: Clarendon Press, 1981).

21. David Close, "Undoing Democracy," *Undoing Democracy: The Politics of Electoral Caudillismo*, eds. David Close and Kalowatie Deonandan (Lanham, MD: Lexington Books, 2004) 1–16, cf. Kalowatie Deonandan, "The *Caudillo* Is Dead: Long Live the *Caudillo*," eds. Close and Deonandan, 183–198.

22. We return to Sandinista control of the Nicaraguan judiciary in Chapter 6.

23. Lynch, *Caudillos*, 60.

24. Some will object to labeling Castro a dictator. However, Cuba does not permit competition for power and any Marxist knows that all states are dictatorships.

25. On Francia, see Paul H. Lewis, *Authoritarian Regimes in Latin America: Dictators, Despots, and Tyrants* (Lanham, MD: Rowman and Littlefield, 2006) 31–39 and Richard Alan White, *Paraguay's Autonomous Revolution: 1810–1840* (Albuquerque, NM: University of New Mexico Press, 1978). For a fictional account of the dictator, see Augusto Roa Bastos, *I, the Supreme*, tr. Helen Lane (New York: Vintage Books, 1987).

26. On the Somozas, see Bernard Diederich, *Somoza* (New York: New York Press, 1981).

27. There is a huge body of literature on Castro and Cuba. Some useful sources are Hugh S. Thomas, *The Cuban Revolution* (New York: Harper Torchbooks, 1977); Sheldon B. Liss, *Fidel: Castro's Social and Political Thought* (Boulder, CO: Westview Press, 1994); and Isaac Saney, *Cuba: A Revolution in Motion* (Black Point, NS: Fernwood Publishing, 2004).

28. See Thomas E. Skidmore, *The Politics of Military Rule in Brazil, 1964–85* (New York: Oxford University Press, 1988).

29. The best work on Pinochet is Carlos Huneeus, *The Pinochet Regime* (Boulder, CO: Lynne Rienner Publishers, 2007).

30. *Regina v. Bartle and the Commissioner of Police for the Metropolis and others EX Parte Pinochet* (on appeal from a Divisional Court of the Queen's Bench Division). *Regina v. Evans and another and the Commissioner of Police for the Metropolis and others EX Parte Pinochet* (on appeal from a Divisional Court of the Queen's Bench Division), 1998. www.publications.parliament.uk/pa/ld199899/ldjudgmt/jd981125/pino01.htm (accessed 29 January 2008).

31. Bernard R. Crick, *In Defence of Politics* (London: Weidenfield and Nicholson, 1962).

32. Walker receives further treatment in Chapter 10.

33. A good place to start is Michael T. Klare and Peter Kornbuth, eds., *Low Intensity Warfare: Counterinsurgency, Proinsurgency, and Antiterrorism in the Eighties* (New York: Pantheon, 1988) cf. Ivan Molloy, *Rolling Back Revolution: The Emergence of Low-Intensity Conflict* (Sterling, VA: Pluto Press, 2001).

34. The section on Colombia is based on David Bushnell, *The Making of Modern Colombia: A Nation in Spite of Itself* (Berkeley, CA: University of California Press, 1993).

35. Suzanne Wilson and Leah A. Carroll, "The Colombian Contradiction: Lessons Drawn from Guerrilla Experiments in Demobilization and Electoralism," *From Revolutionary Movements to Political Parties: Cases from Latin America and Africa,* eds. Kalowatie Deonandan, David Close, and Gary Prevost (New York: Palgrave Macmillan, 2007) 81–106.

36. See Guillermo O'Donnell, *Modernization and Bureaucratic-Authoritarianism: Studies in South American Politics* (Berkeley: University of California Press, 1972); David Collier, ed., *The New Authoritarianism in Latin America* (Princeton, NJ: Princeton University Press, 1979).

37. The four South American military dictatorships are described more fully in Chapter 3.

38. In 2009 the Honduran army ousted President Manuel Zelaya but did not assume power. Four months later a deal was reached to restore Zelaya to power but the details of his return were not completed in time to be included here.

39. Some argue for adding the Bolivian Revolution of 1952 and the independence struggle in Haiti. Experts on revolution who do not study Latin America can exclude Mexico and Nicaragua, leaving only Cuba as a social revolution; see Stephen K. Sanderson, *Revolutions: A Worldwide Introduction to Political and Social Change* (Boulder, CO: Paradigm Publishers, 2005). In fact, beyond the French (1789), Russian (1917), Chinese (1949), and Cuban (1959) revolutions, there is no consensus about who belongs in this category.

40. The name comes from the date in 1953 of Castro's failed attack on the Moncada Barracks in Santiago de Cuba.

41. Isabel Vincent, "Where Even the Good Are Bad," *Maclean's* 121:4–5 (February 4–18, 2008) 33–35.

42. Jeffrey A. Sluka, ed., *Death Squad: The Anthropology of State Terror* (Philadelphia: University of Pennsylvania Press, 2000) cf. Bruce B. Campbell and Arthur D. Bremmer, eds., *Death Squads in Global Perspective: Murder with Deniability* (New York: St. Martin's Press, 2000).

43. Michael Taussig, *Law in a Lawless Land: Diary of a "Limpieza" in Colombia* (New York: New Press, 2003); see also the Project on Extrajudicial Executions webpage at www.extrajudicialexecutions.org and the reports of the Special Rapporteur on extrajudicial, summary, or arbitrary executions of the United Nations High Commissioner for Human Rights at www2.ochr.org.

5

Political Change, Political Contention, and New Political Contenders

Chapter 3 discussed how key Latin American elites, namely the *latifundistas*, the military, and the Church, maintained their political predominance over time. This chapter looks at how new interests enter Latin American political systems and who today's newcomers are. Chapter 3 was about political stability. Chapter 5 is about political change.

When political science first began systematically studying Latin America about 50 years ago, one of the central concepts was political change. Like so many social-science concepts, political change was never precisely defined, no doubt because political change can take so many forms. Going back and examining the works political scientists were publishing in the 1950s and 1960s, however, shows that they were particularly interested in what appeared to be a promising trend of democratization in much of Latin America. They shared this focus with colleagues who were examining the newly independent states in Africa and Asia. The times were hopeful, and political science, above all in the United States, wanted to analyze how countries built political systems, in Africa and Asia, and how they restructured existing systems, in the case of Latin America.

What all of these researchers shared was the conviction that political change, big or small and wherever it occurred, meant more democracy. There were plausible reasons for this belief. First, as Chapter 7 shows in more detail, there was movement toward democracy in Latin America. Peter Smith, a political scientist whose speciality is Latin America, notes that from the 1930s through the 1950s, mass politics—the meaningful involvement of ordinary citizens—arrived in the region, and nearly half of Latin America's countries elected their leaders democratically.[1] And the new states of Africa and Asia all began their existences with both a strong dedication to self-determination and political machinery that had built and sustained robust democracies in Western Europe. But what really caught the attention of political science was social mobilization, which was another, broader form of political participation.

That concept refers to "... an overall process of change, which happens to substantial parts of the population in countries which are moving from a traditional to a modern way of life ... [and that] tend[s] to influence and sometimes to transform political behaviour."[2] It directs our attention to how social changes bring new actors with new claims face to face with government. By expanding the population of political actors to include newly emerging and newly empowered groups, the cause of democracy was served. Yet for social mobilization to produce democratic effects, there had to be an already-functioning democracy that could convert numbers into a political asset. If votes did not actually bring power, mobilized citizens would only be frustrated by their largely futile efforts to influence government.

Failing that, the new arrivals would have to fight their way into the system. Sometimes they did so with violence, using revolutions and guerrilla insurgencies as their instruments. Other times they could use the contentious but fundamentally nonviolent mechanism of movement politics. Most important political change has demanded high levels of conflict.

The above, of course, are different answers to the question facing us of how new forces enter the political system, make themselves heard, and possibly enter the ranks of the politically powerful—the elite. One useful way to think about this is by using the concept of political opportunity structures (POS). The concept is not new, having been introduced by political scientist Peter Eisinger in 1973.[3] It refers to the possibilities a political system offers an outsider group to get power and manipulate the system to its benefit. As originally conceived and as it is still most frequently used, the POS describes openings available to those who use political protest. Although we apply the concept to other forms of political action later, the reference to protest is very useful, for it is by using contentious, confrontational, disruptive tactics and strategies that most newcomers get their first whiff of political power. There are good reasons for this.

No political elite, anywhere, has ever gladly welcomed new members. At a minimum, those in the elite do not want to see their power diluted by sharing it. However, elites can also see outsiders who seek entry as illegitimate. Those outsiders could be considered incapable of governing, because they are from the wrong class, ethnic group, religion, gender, or whatever. Alternatively, they could want free elections, decided by universal suffrage, to be the only way to earn the right to govern. Or they could demand that government no longer be the private reserve of existing power holders. They could even want to destroy the current political order entirely.

Yet sometimes those outsiders get in. Writing in the 1960s, political scientist Charles W. Anderson[4] spoke of power capabilities—political resources that give their holders influence—and these capabilities have to be put to use and shown to be effective before whoever is using them enters the ranks of those who count. In fact, Anderson argues that an outsider "must demonstrate possession of a power capability sufficient to pose a threat to existing [elites]."[5] Once they have done that, they become what he calls "power contenders": individuals and groups recognized as having the resources to influence political outcomes. And if the newcomer agrees to let existing elites preserve some share of the power they already have, admission to this power contenders' club is then secured.

Anderson notes two things that are unexceptional and should form part of everyone's political common sense: outsiders have to show they belong and insiders are more disposed to admit outsiders who accept much of the status quo. The bigger the changes sought, the greater the resistance. That is the difference between reform and revolution. Both still have their place in Latin American politics.

This chapter examines how new political actors have emerged in Latin American politics. A few have been co-opted (that is, given a quota of power to bribe them into good behavior). Most have had to fight for their place in the system. Historically, most of those have involved violence or at least highly confrontational protest. However, as there are now more democracies, it is increasingly possible to struggle for political change within the system.

Analysis begins with the most violent and contentious, revolutions and insurgencies, and moves to movement politics and political protest, before ending with instances of co-optation. In addition to describing how different sectors came to claim a share of political power, the chapter also looks at the political changes that resulted from the admission of new actors.

Contentious Politics and Political Change

Contentious politics involve advancing claims on the state or some non-state actor to recognize rights, cede privileges, or remove some disability or burden, or some combination of the foregoing.[6] Although contentious politics can take place in and through established state institutions, they are more commonly associated with disruptive, confrontational, conflictive actions, usually involving direct contact between whoever makes the claim and the state or, less frequently, the third or nonstate party referred to above. Further, contentious politics are often linked to political protest and movement politics. Contentious politics thus are identified with politics carried on outside normal channels by political actors who are not part of the established power structure, using unconventional methods, and with objectives that elites may deem illegitimate. Those who use contentious political action to advance their claims may break the law in doing so but they can also carry on their work within legal bounds. Indeed, they can combine legal and illegal action.

Using contentious politics usually implies attempting to offset official or entrenched power. This further implies that entrenched power is used to the detriment of those advancing their claims contentiously. It also suggests that those using these methods insist on making their claims themselves.

They may do so because they do not trust others to represent them or because they think it imperative to speak for themselves.

In general, it is reasonable to begin an examination of contentious politics hypothesizing that those making the claim have found the political system impermeable. Permeability refers to the ease with which someone wishing to make a claim on government can get a hearing, build a coalition, and secure the reforms thought necessary.[7] Where a political system is not very permeable, those making claims often have to use forceful, even violent means to get action. All Latin American countries have had quite impermeable politics through much of their histories, and it is only within the last 25 years that many of them have begun to open the channels leading to power.

Violent and Lethal Contention

Chapter 4 introduced the theme of political violence and its place in Latin American history. Although violence in international relations is seen as unexceptional—think of nineteenth-century Prussian soldier and military theorist Karl von Clausewitz's observation that war is the continuation of politics by other means—in domestic politics, violence seems nearly deviant. A standard introductory political science text will explain that politics is about both conflict and conflict resolution,[8] meaning that people compete for power and dispute how power should be used, but that government offers mechanisms for settling those disputes. These means can be courts, legislative debates, negotiations, or elections, and all are designed to keep competition for power within commonly agreed-upon rules. Violence should be unnecessary in a democracy's internal politics. And you will recall that Bernard Crick's "political method of rule" excluded violence.[9]

Yet even in democracies there can be political violence. Conflict resolution mechanisms do not always work. It may be because they are too weak, people do not trust the government to act impartially, or the government just decides that it will get more of what it wants through conflict. If political violence can occur in democracies, authoritarian political systems that are unaccountable to their citizens and are generally readier to use force to settle disputes are particularly liable to see violent politics. And where there is a long history of using violence to seek political ends, violence itself can be seen as a normal way to win and wield power.

In such cases, which would include most countries of Latin America through long stretches of their histories, being a political outsider can seem like a life sentence. Since being an outsider can mean having no rights other than those the government decides to give you, and which the government can take away immediately, it is easy to imagine how drastic action looks like the only way out. The most visible response is revolt, a decision that leads to lethal contention.[10]

Revolutionary Political Change

Revolutions bring new actors and new issues into political life. Sometimes they displace most of the old system and its personnel, other times not. That is, revolutions do not always move a country's political trajectory far off its previous path. Revolutions can be the work of massive insurrections, guerrilla insurgencies, and even nonviolent, electoral politics.

Revolutionary Insurrections, Guerrilla Insurgencies, and Peaceful Revolutions

Revolution now has two meanings. One is older: the forceful overthrow of a government. The other is newer: any thorough, radical change, especially if quickly accomplished. The former has to involve violence; the latter does not.

Violent revolutions in Latin America have taken two forms. The first and more established is by insurrection. A newer model, from the twentieth century, is built around a guerrilla insurgency. Latin America has also seen several attempts at peaceful revolutions. In fact, in 2009, there are at least three ongoing: in Venezuela, Ecuador, and Bolivia. All follow the Bolivarian Model that was developed by Hugo Chávez, the president of Venezuela. This examination begins with the instances of violent political change first and then turns to the nonviolent ones. In each case, the objective is to determine what new actors entered the political system and how effective they proved to be.

Most revolutions can be classed as insurrections. An insurrection does not have to be a spontaneous, popular uprising. Indeed, if it is, it will likely fail. It is, after all, a revolt against established authority and if it is to succeed, it must be well planned and well coordinated. Many if not most instances of revolutionary insurrections turn into protracted conflicts. This was certainly the case of the Mexican Revolution and the revolts that led to the wars of independence.

Some would argue that Latin America's wars for independence do not merit the name *revolution*, as the social and economic structures of the new countries differed little from the colonial structures they replaced. However, the simple act of expelling the Spanish colonial rulers meant that the native-born would now exercise power. It may be true that most of the first generation of new rulers was drawn from among the wealthy, but some later *caudillo* leaders did come from the popular classes. What is important here is that, without the revolt against Spain, the *criollo* elites had no immediate prospect of governing. Thus violent insurrection brought new actors into a changed political system.

The Mexican Revolution (1910–1920) offers a clearer example. As with the wars of independence, the roots of this revolt were political, centering on the last fraudulent election of a long-time dictator, Porfirio Díaz. However, there was more at stake. Díaz's regime, the Porfiriato, had brought Mexico stability and prosperity, but it also ceded much of the country to foreign interests, notably those from the United States. Therefore, the Mexican Revolution had a strong nationalist component and brought nationalist politics back to the country's political agenda. And if the foreigners could be displaced and the dictatorship brought down, there would then be new political and economic opportunities for an increasingly frustrated Mexican middle class.

But it was not only the Mexican middle class that would use the revolution to enter the political system. As the old regime broke down and order gave way to chaos, Mexico's peasants pushed their claims for land while the working class looked for better wages and the right to organize. Both groups, as well as Mexico's indigenous people, would receive some political recognition as a result of the revolution. However, they would not emerge as independent actors but rather as sectors of the official party of the revolution, which eventually became the Partido Revolucionario Institucional (PRI).

Other insurrectional revolutions (see Text Box 5.1) produced similar results; that is, they did create new power contenders by allowing some new actors into the system. As well, they restructured the state and redefined its role to better suit the interests of the new arrivals. This is what revolutions do in practice, even when they propose to completely restructure economy, society, and state because there is little else they can do in the short run.

After 1959, a new medium of revolutionary insurrection arose in Latin America: the guerrilla insurgency.[11] Guerrilla war was already well established as a mechanism for a revolutionary movement to seize power, having been used by Mao Zedong in China between 1927 and 1949. As those dates suggest, guerrilla warfare requires patience, although the first Latin American guerrillas to overthrow a government, Fidel Castro's Movimiento 26 de Julio (July 26 Movement) in Cuba, were only in the field for three years. Perhaps it was this relatively quick return on investment that led a generation of Latin American revolutionaries to embrace not just guerrilla strategies but also the specific Fidelista model. Nevertheless, although many embarked on this path, only one of those who followed Castro's lead succeeded: the Sandinistas of Nicaragua.

Guerrilla warfare is a complicated undertaking. For an insurgent, it demands blending military and political strategies. Militarily, it involves small units, light arms, and hit-and-run engagements with the enemy. Politically, the task is to work with local populations to gain their support or at least their neutrality. This presumes minimizing the violence used against local populations, even if they are unfriendly to the guerrilla.

Guerrillas thus seek their supporters among those the government ignores or suppresses. Taking the case of the Sandinistas as an example, this

Text Box 5.1 Two Cases of Political Change by Insurrection in Central America

Two Central American cases, one from nineteenth-century Nicaragua and the other from twentieth-century Costa Rica, help exemplify how new actors use violence to enter the political system.

In Nicaragua, the 1893 revolution came after an unprecedented 35 years of stability. However, that stability was based on a careful balancing of the regional interests that had kept the country convulsed in civil war for the first three-plus decades after independence in 1821. Though the resulting political system, called the *trentenio* because it lasted about 30 years, brought the country peace, prosperity, and the label "la Suiza centroamericana" ("the Switzerland of Central America"), its operation demanded that no new forces become political contenders. As a result, an emerging *cafetelero* (coffee-growing) elite, concentrated in a part of Nicaragua with little presence in government, became restless. And as the Liberal Party was also marginalized under the *trentenio*, the *cafeteleros* had a political vehicle.

To start that vehicle, though, there needed to be the first signs of breakdown in the existing system and then a rising led by Liberal general José Santos Zelaya in 1893. Zelaya won and brought the new elite a government more attuned to their needs. However, it also brought them a dictatorship that endured until 1909.

Costa Rica's experience started from a similar base but had a very different outcome. From 1906 to 1948, the country was governed by an elite, the Olympians, who maintained a limited democracy that relied heavily on electoral fraud. When the last Olympian, the maverick Rafael Ángel Calderón Guardia, became president in 1940, he instituted a welfare state that had the support of both the Catholic Church and Costa Rica's Communists (the Partido Vanguardia Popular, or Popular Vanguard Party). Yet Calderón kept manipulating elections and added harassment of the opposition to his political arsenal.

This led a group of reformers, organized as the Center for the Study of National Problems, to push for clean elections, but they also turned to violence. The 1948 election was particularly fraudulent and when Calderón was returned to power, the reformers rebelled. There followed a short (six-week) but bitter civil war, which the reformers won. The victors, under José Figueres, set up a junta that ruled for 18 months, crafted a constitution that has sustained electoral democracy since 1949, and then handed power over to the ultraconservative who was the legitimate winner of the 1948 contest. The reformers won the presidency in 1953 and then lost it in 1958, proving their respect for clean elections.

As in Nicaragua 55 years earlier, Costa Rican political outsiders resorted to violence to change a political system that excluded them from power. In both countries, the winners put in place political systems that responded to their needs. Costa Ricans, however, had the good luck to have the victors of their country's revolution install an electoral democracy.

meant peasants, the rural proletariat, the urban working class, women, students, and even businesses whose owners opposed the dictatorship of the Somoza family (see Chapter 4). Most of these groups had to be mobilized, some even had to be politicized (made aware of political issues and of their inherent rights). Many individuals from these sectors served with the Sandinistas as either combatants or underground workers.

When the dictatorship fell in 1979, these marginalized sectors finally had a government that was responsive to their wants and needs. However, they had to work through the party, the Frente Sandinista de Liberación Nacional (FSLN, or Sandinista National Liberation Front), and not as independent pressure groups. Thus when the FSLN lost elections in 1990, the weakest of these groups—the rural and urban poor—lost access to government and suffered greatly during years of economic austerity. With the FSLN's return to the presidency in 2006, the poorest Nicaraguans could again hope that their political prospects would improve, although they would still be dependent on the party and not have their own resources with which to pressure government.

Unlike revolutionary uprisings, guerrillas do not have to overthrow the state to achieve at least some of their political aims. First, sound counterinsurgent strategy has two parts: repression, the military side, and reform, the political element. To undermine a guerrilla insurgency, governments often address the political problems that gave the movement its start. Obviously, this does not always happen: it did not in Nicaragua. However, since the late 1980s there has been increasing activity by the United Nations and other interested outsiders to bring protracted guerrilla-government conflicts to a negotiated end.

Twelve years of civil war between the Frente Farabundo Martí de Liberación Nacional (FMLN, or Marti National Liberation Front) and the government of El Salvador ended with the signing of peace accords in January 1993. These called for restructuring the state's security forces and strengthening democratic institutions. This created an opening for the FMLN to become a political organization that would seek power only through elections. In was 2009 before the FMLN won the presidency under Maricio Funes with 51.3 per cent of the vote. They also outpolled their main conservative rivals, ARENA (Alianza Republicana Nacionalista, or Nationalist Republican Alliance), in the 2009 legislative elections by 42.6 per cent to 38.6 per cent, although ARENA and its allies took more seats and retained control of El Salvador's Congress.[12] As a result, those who support the FMLN, especially the rural and urban poor, have representation at the center of Salvadoran politics.

Of course not all guerrilla movements have the success of the FSLN and FMLN. When Colombian guerrillas tried to make the transition to electoral politics in 1985, with the formation of the Unión Patriótica (Patriotic Union), the party became the target of right-wing paramilitaries, and more than 2,000 of its members were killed in its 10 years of existence.[13] Since then, the main guerrilla forces, the Fuerzas Armadas Revolucionarias de Colombia (FARC, or Revolutionary Armed Forces of Colombia) and the Ejército de Liberación Nacional (ELN, or National Liberation Army), have supplemented their political activities with kidnapping and also have a hand in the drug trade. Although they obviously affect Colombian politics, the guerrillas are still outside the state.[14]

Peaceful Revolutions?

Finally, there are peaceful revolutions. This sounds odd because revolutions are supposed to smash the old regime. If the old regime remains, how can it be stopped from undermining attempts to make radical changes? This is precisely the problem that felled the first attempt at a peaceful but profound revolution in Latin America: President Salvador Allende's experiment in Chile from 1970 to 1973.

Although Chilean politics has long been noted for respecting the constitution and avoiding violent conflict, until the 1960s the country's political system remained dominated by the elite. This was a benign, responsible, and relatively responsive elite, but the poor and working classes had little influence over it. Things began changing when the Christian Democrats, a new party founded in the 1950s, took power in 1964. Its program, the Revolution in Liberty, included a significant agrarian reform initiative, which was an important step toward empowering the country's poor. But it was the next step that pushed the possibilities for peaceful revolution to the limits.

Despite winning the presidency with only 36.2 per cent of the vote in the 1970 presidential election, Salvador Allende, a socialist with Marxist convictions who led the Unidad Popular (UP) coalition, decided to treat his party's minority victory as a mandate for revolutionary change. Seeing a Marxist president at the head of a radical alliance that was set on bringing Chile a peaceful socialist revolution was too much for the United States. President Richard Nixon committed his government to overthrowing Allende. At first, Washington and its allies tried using political pressure, but when the UP won 43 per cent of the vote in the 1973 legislative elections it was evident that Allende remained popular. In the end, Chile's military acted, striking on September 11, 1973, killing the president[15] and setting the country on the path to a harsh 16-year dictatorship under General Augusto Pinochet.

Besides incurring Washington's wrath, which took the practical form of suspending all but military aid and giving material support to Allende's opponents, this attempt at peaceful revolution also encountered other problems. One that proved very serious was not of the government's making: the price of copper, Chile's main export, fell 27 per cent between 1970 and 1973. However, the government's economic policies, which sought a rapid redistribution of income toward the working classes by raising wages and freezing prices, produced runaway inflation. These policies also led to food shortages, as many producers stopped producing for the market, which further heightened tensions. The Chilean Path to Socialism was heroic but ill conceived and faced too many enemies, foreign and domestic.

It would be another 25 years before Latin America witnessed another attempt at peaceful revolution. This one came from Venezuela, was led by Hugo Chávez, and is still operating in 2009. His Bolivarian Revolution, which gets more extensive treatment in Chapter 7, differed from Allende's revolution in several ways. First, Chávez, an ex-lieutenant-colonel who led a failed coup attempt in 1992, maintained good relations with the military. Second, although the government has serious redistributive policies and is frankly socialist, it was at first generally respectful of property rights, although this has changed with time and there have been conflicts. Third, Chávez has had the good fortune to see the price of his country's major export, petroleum, rise ninefold between 1998 and 2008, which assured the government a reliable source of export earnings. However, with the economic crisis that began in the fall of 2008, the price of oil began falling, going from just over $140 a barrel to around $40 six months later. As long as the slump continues, the price of oil is likely to stay low, thus hampering Chávez's reform plans. Finally, the president has also benefited from Washington's preoccupation with its military engagements in Iraq and Afghanistan: although the US government spoke approvingly of, and almost certainly backed, if very unofficially, a coup attempt against Chávez in 2002, it has contented itself with using political pressure to oppose the Venezuelan leader. In this, the US government has had little short-term success, as elections in 2005 and 2006 saw allies of Chávez take power in Bolivia, Ecuador, and Nicaragua.

Latin America now has several governments pursuing peaceful paths to significant social, economic, and political restructuring—in a word, revolutions. It is too early to know how they will fare or how long they will last. However, the fact that experiments in radical political change can begin with elections and proceed through peaceful political processes—as will be seen in Chapter 7—bodes well for democracy.

Beyond Violent and Lethal Contention: Social Movements and Political Protest

This review of the role of violent contention as a means of political change points to three conclusions. One is that political change is often accompanied by violence, even lethal violence. Another is that violent politics can assume various forms. Finally, violence is used to get the ability to restructure the state so that it better suits the needs of the outsiders who brought the challenge.

Obviously, there are other ways to challenge authority and change how a political system works; in relatively democratic systems with permeable institutions, nonviolent means are both more legitimate and work better. The structure of political opportunities found in democracies offers especially attractive incentives for peaceful methods of political change. Demands for inclusion and change are still made contentiously and often with disruptions and confrontations, but government resistance is not so unwavering as to be overcome only by violence. A number of familiar organizations and methods figure in nonviolent contentious politics—for example, social movements, ad hoc coalitions of groups, protest politics (demonstrations, sit-ins, or petitions), lobbying, and electoral politics. These, however, have occasionally been joined to violent contention.

Principally we are referring to social movements—also called protest movements or mass movements—and political protest. We have already noted that social movements mobilize people for sustained campaigns that make claims on government. The claims can be sweeping, such as demanding votes for women, or narrow, such as agitating to preserve a particular wetland. They can be advanced through conventional means (such as peaceful mass marches) or can be more openly conflictive modes of protest (building occupations or physical clashes with authorities). What distinguishes movements is that they work outside established government channels, although they may also work within them simultaneously.

Social movements date from eighteenth-century Western Europe. They are products of the early age of industrialization and of the first serious stirrings against absolutist and aristocratic rule. One of the earliest movements was the English antislavery movement. In the nineteenth century, there came movements for workers' rights, the expansion of the franchise, and the independence of peoples subjected to the yoke of imperialism. Movements thus have established themselves as prominent and effective political actors. Part of their effectiveness comes from operating outside the usual channels.[16] They develop *performances*, which are standardized ways of making claims on political actors (for example, demonstrations or petitions). Sometimes an array of performances emerges as a *repertoire of contention*. In Latin America, the *cacerolazo* (people banging on pots to protest something) is often bundled with strikes and demonstrations, as in Argentina in 2001. Over time these performances and repertoires change as new ideas emerge to help movements make their claims more effectively. These "outside strategies" can also be combined with conventional lobbying and electoral work, or "inside strategies," when that is what is required.

Movement politics are plainly about political change and equally plainly about getting power to those who do not have it. Movements begin from

Text Box 5.2 Movements and Parties

Both movements and parties want to influence policy, and some movements even want to take and exercise power. But there are more points of
divergence than of convergence. First, movements are less disciplined than
parties and usually have weaker formal structures. Second, they encourage
greater participation by their members. Third, movements do not contest
elections unless they have become political parties. They usually focus on a
more specific policy change, perhaps land rights for indigenous people, and
do not have a broad-spectrum agenda. Political parties, for example both
the Sandinistas and the Liberals of Nicaragua, sometimes argue that movements should not promote policies or criticize government if they do not
want to run for office, but that argument is transparently self-serving.

Sometimes, however, movements do become parties. In 2008, the governing parties of Venezuela, Bolivia, Ecuador, and Argentina all had movement
roots. Even armed movements, such as El Salvador's FMLN and Nicaragua's
FSLN, have transformed themselves into political parties in order to run for
office and administer the state should they win. Green parties also do this.
A movement that becomes a party generally displays characteristics of both
forms: it will usually provide more opportunities for its members to have a
hand in running the organization than is true of most parties, but it will also
have a stronger central structure than is usually found in movements.

what is conventionally called civil society: people outside government organizing themselves to take action on a matter of public concern.[17] Although
governments can and do organize their own movements, especially in
dictatorships, movements for change come from outside government. And
although there are parties that have grown from movements, movements
and parties are distinct phenomena (see Text Box 5.2).

Saying that movements spring from citizens' concerns does not mean
that they must be organizations run by amateurs. A serious movement has
to be as professional as the government (or sometimes the industry) that
it opposes. Movements want to see important aspects of a political system
changed and cannot, therefore, afford a cavalier approach. The opponents
of movements often argue that this professionalism makes movements
somehow illegitimate when what it really does is level the playing field.

Finally, it is wrong to assume that all movement politics are left wing.
A movement can seek more equality and liberty for more people, the hall-
mark of the political left, but it can as easily pursue the right-wing goal of
greater social inequality. What matters is that it mobilizes people to take
collective action, using contentious forms, to change something government does or even to change the government itself. If there are more social
movements from the left, it is because the left is more often politically

marginalized than the right, thus more likely to need conflictive outside strategies.

Knowing how these methods have worked, and where and when they have succeeded or failed, demands examining cases. The clearest way to present cases is to select broad classes of outsiders who seek to become political contenders and see what each has done to press its case and how far it has succeeded in making itself an important political force. Women, native people, and the economically marginalized are the three groups that historically have been denied access to the seats of political power—thus, they will be the focus of our attention.

Saying that women, indigenous people, and the poor in the past have not been important political actors in any Latin American country simply puts all of Latin America on an equal footing with the rest of the world. The point, therefore, is not to examine the overall record of Latin American countries in terms of when these marginalized sectors began to achieve some quotas of power. Those are interesting data that we will note, but they are less important than how this happened and what results have been recorded.

Women

Women everywhere have confronted legal and cultural barriers to equality, and like working-class men and indigenous people, women have had to fight their way into the political system.[18] Like their companions in marginalization, women have had to mobilize themselves into movements to demonstrate their potential as political contenders; that is, their capacity to make it harder to exclude them from the political process than to let them enter as full players in their own right. Where the women's movement has differed is that it has used violent contention less frequently than some other excluded sectors. Why that might be so is a matter meriting more analysis that it can receive here, as our objective is to survey women as actors in Latin American politics. We begin with the suffrage.[19]

In 1929, Ecuador became the first Latin American country to enfranchise women. This came eleven years after Canada, nine years after the United States, but only one year after Britain. Paraguay waited until 1961 to give women the vote, beating Switzerland by ten years. Table 5.1 gives the dates when women got the vote in each country. There are some interesting patterns.

For instance, it was Ecuador, not revolutionary Mexico or the more developed Argentina, that was the first to grant women the right to vote. This happened because a constituent assembly, convened after a coup in 1925, gave the country a constitution that guaranteed extensive individual rights. In several other countries—for example, Guatemala, Argentina, Venezuela, Costa Rica, and Bolivia—women won the vote after a reformist

Table 5.1 Voting Rights for Women in the Americas: National Elections

Country*	Year†	Country*	Year†
Canada	1918	Venezuela	1947
United States	1920	Chile	1949
Ecuador	1929	Costa Rica	1949
Brazil	1932	Haiti	1950
Uruguay	1932	Bolivia	1952
Cuba	1934	Mexico	1953
El Salvador	1939	Honduras	1955
Dominican Republic	1942	Nicaragua	1955
Guatemala	1945	Peru	1955
Panama	1945	Colombia	1957
Argentina	1947	Paraguay	1961

* National elections only. Women received the vote earlier in US states and Canadian provinces than they did at the national level.

† Date at which women received the vote on the same basis as men.

Source: Compiled from June Hannam, Mitzi Auchterlonie, and Katherine Holden, *International Encyclopedia of Women's Suffrage.* Santa Barbara, CA: ABC-CLIO, 2000. 339–340.

or revolutionary government took power. In other cases, such as Brazil, it was a conservative government that expanded the suffrage to women because women were thought more likely to support conservative parties.

Despite starting later, Latin American nations have recently made progress in two areas: the number of female chief executives and quotas for women's representation in the legislature. Regarding chief executives, there have been four women elected as president of their respective countries, all since 1990 (Table 5.2). However, it should be noted that one (Kirchner) succeeded her husband; another (Moscoso) was the widow of a former president; and a third (Chamorro) was the widow of an assassinated newspaper editor, although she had her own personal political profile. Only Michelle Bachelet of Chile was elected without having immediate kinship to a famous male political figure. Further, neither Chamorro nor Moscoso was especially concerned with promoting gender equality. Nevertheless, Chamorro is the only woman president in Latin America to have ever served with a female vice-president (see Text Box 5.3).

Turning to the question of quotas, political scientists Maria Escobar-Lemmon and Michelle Taylor-Robinson find that having a quota law is the best predictor of the number of women in a Latin American legislature.[20] At present, some kind of quota for women candidates (a law or an internal party rule) exists in 17 Latin American countries.[21] Another political scientist, Mala Htun, presents an analysis of 11 countries with laws establishing quotas for women legislative candidates which reveals that

Table 5.2 Women Elected President of Latin American Countries

Name	Country	Date Elected
Violeta Chamorro	Nicaragua	1990
Mireya Moscoso	Panama	1999
Michelle Bachelet	Chile	2006
Cristina Kirchner	Argentina	2007

Source: author

"[f]rom an average of 9 percent in 1990, by 2005 women's representation in the lower houses of national parliaments had increased to 17 percent. Women's share of [senate] seats ... grew from an average of 5 percent in 1990 to 13 percent in 2005."[22] The two North American countries do somewhat better. In the US Congress in 2006, 16.8 per cent of the members of the House of Representatives were women, as were 16 per cent of the Senate. In Canada, 21.3 per cent of the House of Commons seats were held by women in 2006 and women occupied 34.4 per cent of the seats in the appointed Senate.[23]

Besides gaining the vote and serving as elected officials, women have also used contentious forms of participation to influence their nations' politics. One of the best-known examples of women engaged in political

---

Text Box 5.3 Choosing a Female Vice-President in Nicaragua[24]

Nicaragua's constitution demands that a sitting vice-president who wants to run for president must resign a year before the next presidential election—thus, Vice-President Virgilio Godoy stepped down in October 1995. It fell to the National Assembly to pick his successor. The media in the capital, Managua, bruited the names of four men as possible replacements. One of them, Fernando Zelaya, was President Violeta Chamorro's first choice.

Yet neither Zelaya nor any of the other three men won. The new vice-president was Julia Mena. This came about because Dora María Téllez, house leader of a small opposition party, had developed allies, especially among the other women in the assembly. While the four men were lobbying, so was Téllez. She built a majority of deputies, men and women, who would support Mena over any of her opponents. Sensing this, the supporters of Zelaya tried to get their colleagues to leave the floor and have the house counted out for want of a quorum so they could reorganize. They failed: Julia Mena became Nicaragua's first female vice-president and Nicaragua became the first country in the western hemisphere to have two women as its top executive officers.

protest comes from Argentina: the Madres de la Plaza de Mayo. These were women whose children, husbands, or other relatives had been "disappeared" in the "dirty war" the military junta waged against its citizens. The military denied any knowledge of the disappeared's whereabouts, leaving the women not knowing whether their loved ones were dead or alive. On Thursday afternoon, April 30, 1977, 14 women began a silent march around the Plaza de Mayo, in the heart of downtown Buenos Aires, in front of the Casa Rosada, the presidential residence. Eventually, 3 of the original 14 were also disappeared, and it was only after the fall of the military regime in 1983 that answers to what happened to some of the more than 10,000 Argentines who were kidnapped by agents of the state were provided.[25]

The Madres formed one of a number of movements led by women, or at least involving the participation of many women, that arose in the 1970s and 1980s in the military dictatorships of South America and that played significant roles in the transition to democracy. These can be divided into human rights groups, such as the Madres, and consumer organizations, such as the communal kitchens that developed during the economic crisis of the 1980s and 1990s.[26] Organizations of both types were often run exclusively by women, giving the participants the opportunity to develop a wide range of skills and substantial experience in dealing with government officials. With the coming of democracy in the 1990s, many of the groups involved in the struggle for democracy demobilized, in great part because political parties assumed many of the functions the movements had previously performed. However, the movements left a base on which other civil society organizations have been able to build.

Experience of a different kind was gained by women who participated in guerrilla movements. Although there are only a handful of examples (the Fidelistas in Cuba, Guatemala's Unidad Revolucionaria Nacional Guatemalteca [UNRG], the FMLN in El Salvador, Nicaragua's FSLN, the Zapatistas in Mexico, Sendero Luminoso in Peru, and Colombia), they are extremely important because they show women stepping far outside of traditionally "feminine" roles and acting as warriors. Although estimates of the number of women combatants for all groups are not easily available, for the Sandinistas of Nicaragua, the FMLN of El Salvador, and the Zapatistas experts suggest that women accounted for about a third of each force. There is also a consensus that Cuba's *Fidelistas* had very few women fighters. What happened after 1959?

Karen Kampwirth, a political scientist who has examined the role of women combatants in revolutionary struggles, suggests that a combination of four factors account for the change.[27] Like all theorists of revolution, Kampwirth starts with structural factors, such as men leaving their homes to look for work, leaving more women heading households, as well as changes in political opportunity structures. She then looks at ideological changes (for example, the rise of liberation theology) and changes in the structure and tactics of guerrilla movements, with the Cuban emphasis on rural focus giving way to more emphasis on mass mobilization. Finally, there is a consideration of personal factors, including a family history of political resistance, youth, and membership in groups likely to mobilize for guerrilla warfare, perhaps a church group attuned to liberation theology. Yet even though many women participated in these movements, the upper ranks remained preponderantly male, and in Nicaragua at least, the revolutionary regime frequently pushed women's concerns to the back of the line.

The evidence suggests that women have made a breakthrough in Latin American politics. Women are contenders, recognized actors, but they still have not really got a sure place at the policy-making table. It is still too soon to tell whether this is a case of newcomers having to serve an apprenticeship or male politicians consciously limiting women's political role.

Indigenous People

Our conclusion about the political status of women unfortunately applies as well to indigenous people.[28] Latin America's indigenous populations began mobilizing for political action in the 1970s, about the same time that aboriginal political movements began in Canada and the United States. Obviously, there have been risings and revolts by natives and minorities throughout the region's history: the movement led by Túpac Amaru II against the Spanish in Peru in 1780 stands out, though there were similar risings against national governments in the 1800s. It is only now, however, at the start of the twenty-first century, that these long-marginalized groups are emerging as regular political actors, part of the normal political process. Why now? What has changed? What resources give at least some indigenous groups the capacity to become serious political contenders?

Historically, Latin America's indigenous peoples (First Nations)[29] have been second-class citizens. At times, they have had defenders among the elite—for example the Church in colonial times and during the nineteenth century—but often the best First Nations could hope for was to be ignored and left to live as they wished. Starting in the 1970s, however, indigenous people in Latin America became more assertive in demanding and defending their rights. They may seek land rights, individual and collective rights (civil, cultural, economic, and social), or a measure of political autonomy (see Text Box 5.4).

It is best to start with a famous case: the Zapatistas.[30] The Ejército Zapatista de Liberación Nacional (EZLN, or Zapatista National Liberation Army) first made headlines on New Year's Day 1994 by declaring war on the Mexican state. The group, from the southern Mexican state of Chiapas, was composed of both Mayan Indians and other poor peasants not of

---

Text Box 5.4 The Unfulfilled Promise of Autonomy on Nicaragua's Atlantic Coast

Until 1893, what is now the Atlantic Coast of Nicaragua was a British protectorate known as the Miskito Kingdom. However, even once it officially became part of Nicaragua, most Nicaraguans ignored the easternmost part of their country. It was principally English-speaking, inhabited overwhelmingly by indigenous people and Afro-Caribbeans, who had come from the West Indies to work on banana plantations. Until the 1980s, the Pacific and Atlantic parts of the country lived as two solitudes.

The 1979 Sandinista Revolution promised greater freedom and equality for Nicaragua's poor majority. Unfortunately, the Sandinistas could not imagine that cultural minorities in that great majority might have different views about what freedom and equality looked like in practice. Thus when the counterrevolution began in earnest in 1981, this eastern region was one of its main theaters and the Miskito people one of the main protagonists.

The Sandinistas were able to recognize their error and rectify it by granting the Atlantic Coast region, which occupies half of Nicargua's territory but has only 11 per cent of its population, a significant measure of self-government with an Autonomy Statute in 1987. This document established the two regional governments and gave them administrative responsibilities in health, education, culture, transport, and natural resources, which they shared with the central government. Further, the 1987 constitution guaranteed the right of the Coast's indigenous peoples to preserve and develop their identities and cultures. Finally, there was the 2003 Communal Property Act, which addressed the matter of communal titles and control over natural resources.

These should have given the people of the Coast the guarantees they needed to flourish but they did not. When the Sandinistas lost power in 1990, for 16 years their successors essentially abandoned the region. As well, land hunger has forced *mestizos* (people of mixed European and indigenous descent) from Nicaragua's west into the eastern zones, where they pushed the indigenous peoples and Afro-Carribeans from their lands. The *meztizos* now constitute a majority of the population of the Atlantic Coast region, which may mean that even the return of the Sandinistas to office in 2006 could be insufficient to see the Autonomy Statute fulfill its intended purpose.

---

indigenous origin and was dedicated to resisting the encroachment of modern, globalized capitalism. Its particular target was the North American Free Trade Agreement (NAFTA) that linked Mexico to the United States and Canada. But even more so its enemy was the government of Mexico, which had brought the country into NAFTA as part of a broader strategy of aligning Mexico more fully with the rest of the capitalist world.

There are three traits of the EZLN that merit special mention. First, although the Maya of Chiapas are its main constituents, it is not a purely ethnic movement. Rather, the Zapatistas incorporate the support of women's issues, peasant and other class-based issues, human rights questions, land tenure problems, liberation theology, social justice, autonomy, and resistance to neoliberalism—the package of economic policies comprising free trade, reduced social programs, and fiscal austerity. Because of this, some have called the EZLN the world's first postmodern guerrilla movement. Second, the Zapatistas were pathbreakers in their use of the Internet and in their ability to mobilize support transnationally. Third, they produced an iconic representative in Subcomandante Marcos, their pipe-smoking, ski mask–wearing spokesman.

Yet 14 years after the EZLN introduced itself to the world, its success is still far from assured. This is hardly unique among guerrillas: the Sandinistas fought for 18 years and Mao Zedong for 22 years. Nevertheless, it is useful to ask why the Zapatistas have not made greater headway. Is it because they are identified as an indigenous movement or have such a strong regional identity that it is difficult for them to expand? Or could it be due to the intransigence of the Mexican government and the elites of Chiapas? Whatever the case, the EZLN showed enough political capacity to become a reasonably regular actor in Mexican politics, but it has still not been able secure key policy goals, notably autonomy, or force its way into the councils of the nation on a regular basis.

It is the problem of converting political capacity into political presence that the peaceful revolutions of Bolivia and Ecuador are attempting to address. There are three points to consider in examining these cases:

· Two-thirds of Bolivians and 43 per cent of Ecuadoreans are counted as belonging to First Nations (see Table 5.3).
· The projects underway in both countries involve drafting new constitutions—documents defining the countries' basic laws which apply to all.
· Each peaceful revolution grew from a contentious protest movement.

In Ecuador, the movement dates from 1990, when a massive protest led by the Confederación de Nacionalidades Indígenas del Ecuador (CONAIE) against a structural adjustment program (see Chapter 8) sought recognition of indigenous land claims. Further protests led to the formation of an indigenous political party, Pachakutik, which was instrumental in securing the adoption of a new constitution in 1998 that recognized the country's multicultural character and which played a central part in pushing two presidents from office (in 1997 and 2000). In 2006, a new electoral alliance, Alianza País, 2007–2011, led by Rafael Correa, who holds a PhD in economics from the University of Illinois, swept to power. Although Correa is not a member of an Ecuadoran First Nation, his government

Table 5.3 Latin American Countries with Indigenous Populations More Than 5% of Total

Category	Country	% Indigenous
>40 %	Bolivia	71
	Guatemala	66*
	Peru	47*
	Ecuador	43*
10–20%	Honduras	15
	Mexico	14
5–9%	Chile	8
	El Salvador	7
	Panama	6
	Nicaragua	5

Data from the United Nations Economic Commission for Latin America (ECLA) give radically different numbers based on censuses conducted between 2000 and 2002: Guatemala, 39.5%, Peru, 15.3%, and Ecuador 6.8%. See the Political Database of the Americas, http://pdba.georgetown.edu/InddigenousPeoples/demographics.html. As it was not possible to determine how the category of indigenous peoples was defined in each case, the disparities could not be explained.

Source: Adopted from International Labour Organization, Indigenous Peoples, 1999. www.ilo.org/public/english/region/ampro/mdtsanjose/indigenous/cuadro.htm.

is closely aligned with the indigenous movement and the draft of a new constitution reflecting the values of his alliance was adopted in 2008.

Bolivia's situation is somewhat different. In 2006, Bolivians elected their first indigenous president, Evo Morales. Morales entered public life in the 1980s as the head of Bolivia's *cocoleros*, farmers who legally grow coca, whose leaves have always been consumed by Andean natives but are also the basic ingredient of cocaine. Coca eradication campaigns, promoted by Washington, threatened the producers' livelihood and thrust Morales into national prominence. In 1997, Morales was elected to Congress but was expelled by the majority. In 1999, he returned as the head of the Movimiento al Socialismo (MAS, or Movement Toward Socialism), which had become the country's second-largest party under his direction. Using continuous parliamentary and extra-parliamentary pressure, the MAS forced the sitting president from office and in 2005 rolled to a convincing majority victory.

Part of Morales's platform promised a constitutional convention. This began in August 2006, and the draft was completed in December 2007 and ratified via referendum in January 2009. The document itself acknowledges the right of First Nations to self-determination within the framework of the state (Art. 2), grants official status to all indigenous languages (Art. 5.1), recognizes the collective rights of First Nations (Arts. 30,

31), as well as authorizing the operation of indigenous systems of justice (Arts. 191–193). If implemented fully, this would mark an unprecedented devolution of power from the state to its citizens.

The three movements presented here show Latin American indigenous people pursuing their goals at least to some extent with allies who face common economic challenges. Thus these movements have an anti-neoliberal element, as policies rooted in that perspective have proved particularly costly to the poor. Obviously not all goals are shared, as questions of communal land titles, indigenous justice systems, and language rights interest solely the First Nations. However, winning power nationally has meant forming alliances, even in Bolivia, where the country's various First Nations account for between two-thirds and seven-tenths of the population. Whether the indigenous groups will be able to advance their agendas in the arena of coalition politics remains an open question.

As in the case of women, it looks as though indigenous people in at least some Latin American countries have emerged as significant political actors. However, the inability of the Zapatistas to consolidate their position is troubling. It suggests that established, entrenched elites may resist the emergence of First Nations as serious political contenders.

The Poor: Workers and Peasants

Women are marginalized by gender, the First Nations by ethnicity, and the lower classes by poverty. Although it may be true that the poor will always be with us, it is also true that the poor will always struggle to be less poor and to be treated with more respect. The poor all have numbers on their side: in most of the world, they are the majority. But sheer numbers are never enough. Over the years, sectors of the poor have organized themselves in movements, unions, and parties to press the state for the rights their wealthier peers enjoyed. Numbers, plus organization, plus contentious political action give the poor a chance to advance.

Historically, the largest sector of the poor in Latin America has been the peasantry. As the term is used in the region, the peasantry includes wage laborers, sharecroppers, tenants, and families who own a small plot of land that barely meets their needs, if that. Until large-scale agriculture became more fully capitalist and began modernizing around the middle of the last century, *latifundistas* depended on cheap labor. And as those with massive landholdings formed a central part of the governing elite, peasants were kept from organizing. Yet there was an insatiable land hunger among the peasantry, and land for the landless became a rallying cry of the great Latin American revolutions of the twentieth century.

This drive for land still continues. It is at its strongest in Brazil, home of the Movimento dos Trabalhadores Rurais Sem Terra (MST, or Landless Rural Workers Movement).[31] It is considered the largest social movement in Latin America, reportedly having 200,000 to 400,000 members,[32] and has been active since the late 1970s, although it emerged as a formal organization only in 1984. It is important to observe that the MST has been an effective political instrument for a quarter-century, making it an institutionalized part of Brazilian politics. In that time, it has had to adapt to changing circumstances and changing demands from its members.

Behind the formation and continued operation of the MST is the concentration of land ownership in Brazil. Chapter 3 reported data showing a very unequal distribution of land in the country. In concrete terms, the MST reports that two-thirds of Brazil's arable land is held by 3 per cent of the landholders.[33] To change this situation, the MST developed a specific strategy: massive land occupations.

Organizers search out a large property, which can be public, with a substantial segment of uncultivated land, a condition that makes it eligible for land reform. The MST then spends months carefully recruiting families who will participate in the occupation. These are mainly smallholders, sharecroppers, and rural wage workers. Anywhere from 50 to several thousand families arrive at the property late at night, set up makeshift shelters, and hope to settle in while the MST tries to get titles for the occupiers through the Brazilian federal government's land reform institute. Sometimes the occupiers meet with violence from the landowners or the police and have to abandon their occupation.

Finding this kind of highly contentious form of political participation during conservative administrations is not surprising. Seeing it continue under centrist and leftist governments, however, is. Since 1995, Brazil has had federal governments from the center, Fernando Henrique Cardos (1995–2003), and the left, Luis Inácio Lula da Silva (2003–), yet the MST has continued its land occupations. They have done so partly because both presidents have pursued relatively conservative economic policies and partly due to the realities of Brazilian politics, which combine the intricacies of federalism with a complex and fractionalized multiparty system to render policy-making slow and uncertain. Were the MST not well established, it would be unable to work effectively.

Just being organized does not guarantee success, however. Organized labor in Latin America has often fallen under the control of government. The clearest examples are Argentina during the Perón administration (1947–1955), Brazil under the Estado Novo of Getulio Vargas (1930–1945), and Mexico's Confederación de Trabajadores Mexicana (CTM, or Federation of Mexican Workers) from 1941 until today. In all cases, a supposedly union-friendly administration placed the union movement under tight state control, manipulating organized labor for political ends. An exception to this is Bolivia, where the Central Obrera Boliviana (COB, or Bolivian Workers' Central), one of whose founders was the legendary

Juan Lechín, was active in the revolution of 1952 and has continued its militancy to this day.

It is important to remember that among what are usually classed as the major Latin American revolutions of the last century—Mexico, Bolivia, Cuba, and Nicaragua—only in Bolivia did organized workers, from the miners' union, play a decisive role. The other three are generally considered peasant revolutions because so much of the fighting occurred in rural areas and was carried out by rural people.[34] Yet the relative marginality of organized workers as a political force did not stop death squads in El Salvador and Guatemala, paramilitaries in Colombia, or the brutal, bureaucratic-authoritarian, military dictatorships of the 1970s in South America from killing and disappearing hundreds if not thousands of labor activists. Further, high levels of political contention by unions against the bureaucratic authoritarian state in Argentina, Brazil, and Chile contributed to the fall of the dictatorships and the return of democracy.

Up to now contentious politics have been presented in their planned, organized, almost formal version. However, political protest can start spontaneously from the grassroots. In 2001, the Argentinean economy collapsed, provoking massive protests that saw five presidents governing in two weeks. A massive debt default produced a run on the banks, which in turn brought restrictions on currency withdrawals. From that came weeks of protest, looting, and even deaths. Two distinct groups took high-profile roles in the conflict.

One of these came mainly from the middle classes who lost much of their savings as the Argentine peso, maintained at par with the US dollar for a decade, lost two-thirds of its value in massive devaluations and as the banks restricted the withdrawal of US currency. The favorite instrument here was the *cacerolazo* (a mass demonstration accompanied by loud banging on pots and pans). Other groups came from the working classes, especially those left unemployed by a recession that had been gathering strength for several years. These were the *piqueteros,* who blocked roads asking for work or food. In the short run, neither class of protesters got what they wanted. It was only after the election of Nestor Kirchner in 2003 that things began to improve.[35]

Another important case of spontaneous protest took place in Costa Rica in 2000. Latin America's senior democracy (dating from 1949), Costa Rica built an impressive welfare state with a wide range of public services during the 1950s and 1960s. However, as in most of the rest of the region, the 1970s brought an end to growth and the 1980s brought an austerity program—structural adjustment—from the International Monetary Fund. A central component of this program was privatization: selling state-owned enterprises to the private sector.

Costa Rica had many of these, including a cigarette factory and liquor bottler. But it also had the Instituto Costarricense de Electricidad (ICE, or

Costa Rican Electrical Institute), which supplied not just electricity but telephone services too. Unlike public utilities in the rest of Latin America, the ICE worked and even the poor in Costa Rica had lights and phones; and the service was reliable. Thus when in 2000, President Miguel Ángel Rodríguez of the center-right Partido Unidad Social Cristiana (PUSC, or Social Christian Unity Party), backed by the center-left Partido Liberación Nacional (PLN, or National Liberation Party) proposed a package of bills to privatize the ICE, the Combo ICE, he set off a wave of protest.

There was a march of 100,000 people in the capital, San José; protests in smaller towns and in the countryside saw roads blocked with barricades, a common feature of Costa Rican protests. Within a short time, the government convened meetings with the main groups involved in the protest—unions, the universities and university students, women's groups, and small, leftist political parties. The result was a new bill that apparently guaranteed the ICE's future as a power company, at least.

Conclusion: How Much Is Latin American Politics Changing?

There are new political forces contending for power throughout Latin America. However, they have arrived on the scene as effective, independent political actors only in the recent past, with most having less than 40 years on the scene. Thus they are still establishing themselves.

One factor that has favored the arrival of women, indigenous people, the economically disadvantaged—indeed, of citizen politics in a broad sense—has been the return of democratic government to Latin America. Since 1982, open electoral politics and the citizens' rights that such a system presupposes have become more common than ever before. This has changed the structure of political opportunities outsiders face in their attempts to become contenders for influence. Yet there has been another element to consider.

Since the 1980s, economic policy in Latin America, as everywhere else, has been decidedly antistatist as the neoliberal model rose to dominance. There are now challengers in Venezuela, Bolivia, Ecuador, Nicaragua, and to a degree Argentina, but the prevailing orthodoxy has been a noninterventionist state maintaining an open economy. It is the marginalized who suffered most from these policies, yet in the cases presented above they were able to find openings through which to make their claims. Where those claims involved material benefits, the results have been disappointing. With the coming of a grave economic crisis in 2008, neoliberalism had lost its allure, but the severity of the downturn meant that there was still little money available for redistributive policies. In terms of getting a seat at the policy-making table, however, women did not fare badly, thanks to winning electoral quotas in several countries, and First Nations in Ecuador and Bolivia were instrumental in ousting conservative governments and seeing them replaced by reformers sympathetic to indigenous demands.

Overall, though, it has been difficult for the new entrants to translate political openings into economic and social gains. The question now has to be whether women, indigenous people, the economically marginalized, and ordinary citizens regardless of gender, ethnicity, or class will be favorably positioned to take advantage of better times, whenever they arrive.

Further Readings

Balive, Teo, and Vijay Prashad (Eds.). *Dispatches from Latin America: On the Frontlines against Neoliberalism.* Boston, MA: South End Press, 2006.
Johnston, Hank, and Paul Almeida (Eds.). *Latin American Social Movements: Globalization, Democratization, and Transnational Networks.* Lanham, MD: Rowman and Littlefield, 2006.
Veltmeyer, Henry, and James Petras. *The Dynamics of Social Change in Latin America.* Houndsmill, UK: Macmillan, 2008.

Periodicals

Mobilization: The International Quarterly Review of Social Movement Research
NACLA Report on the Americas: http://nacla.org; probably also available in your university's library

Websites

Latin American Working Group (LAWG): www.lawg.org

Discussion Questions

① Now that elections are the main instrument for political participation in Latin America, can we justify a significant role for movement politics? Thinking about what political movements do in the two North American democracies or in the states of Western Europe will help focus your thinking.

② How do political movements affect what political parties do? What impact do they have on the executive part of government? To what extent does the North American and Western European experience provide a guide?

Notes

1. Peter H. Smith, *Democracy in Latin America: Political Change in Comparative Perspective* (New York: Oxford University Press, 2005) 32–33.
2. Karl Deutsch, "Social Mobilization and Political Development," *American Political Science Review* 15:3 (1961): 493.
3. Peter Eisinger, "The Conditions of Poorest Behavior in American Cities," *American Political Science Review* 67 (1973): 11–28. For the term's contemporary usage, see Charles Tilly and Sidney Tarrow, *Contentious Politics* (Boulder, CO: Paradigm Publishers, 2007).
4. Charles W. Anderson, *Politics, and Economic Change in Latin America: The Governing of Restless Nations* (New York: Van Nostrand Reinhold Company, 1967).
5. Anderson, 105.
6. Tilly and Tarrow, Chapter 1.
7. William Gamson, *The Strategy of Social Protest* (Homewook, IL: Dorsey Press, 1975). ·
8. For example, Eric Mintz, David Close, and Osvaldo Croci, *Politics, Power, and the Common Good* (Toronto: Pearson, 2005) 4–7.
9. Bernard Crick, *In Defence of Politics* (London: Wiedenfield and Nicholson, 1962).
10. Tilly and Tarrow, Chapter 7.
11. See Timothy P. Wickham-Crowley, *Guerrillas and Revolution in Latin America* (Princeton, NJ: Princeton University Press, 1992); Ian Beckett, *Modern Insurgencies and Counter-insurgencies* (London: Routledge, 2001); William R. Polk, *Violent Politics: A History of Insurgency, Terrorism, and Guerrilla War, from the American Revolution to Iraq* (New York: Harper, 2007; and United States Army, *Counterinsurgency* FM3-24 (Washington, DC: Department of the Army, 2006).
12. Electoral data from El Salvador, Tribuna Suprema Electoral, "Elecciones 2009, Resultados Electorales: Diputados." http://elecciones2009.tse.gob.sv/page.php?51 (accessed 12 March 2009).
13. Suzanne Wilson and Leah A. Carroll, "The Colombian Contradiction: Lessons Drawn from Guerrilla Experiments in Demobilization and Electoralism," *From Revolutionary Movements to Political Parties: Cases from Latin America and Africa*, eds. Kalowatie Deonandan, David Close, and Gary Prevos. (New York: Palgrave Macmillan, 2007) 81–106.
14. There are other guerrillas that have failed. The most famous and probably the most deserving of failure was Peru's Sendero Luminoso, the Shining Path. This group was uncommonly violent and employed terror at levels that were not seen in other guerrilla movements. Cynthia McClintock compares Sendero Luminoso and the FMLN in *Revolutionary Movements in Latin America: El Salvador's FMLN and Peru's Shining Path* (Washington, DC: United States Institute of Peace Press, 1998).
15. There is some dispute over whether Allende was killed resisting the coup or whether he committed suicide rather than be captured.
16. For more details, see Tilly and Tarrow, Chapter 1.
17. This is not the only definition of civil society. The question will be discussed later.
18. In general see, among many others, Lynn Stephen, *Women and Social Movements in Latin America: Power from Below* (Austin, TX: University of Texas Press, 1997); Karen Kampwirth, *Feminism and the Legacy of Revolution: Nicaragua, El Salvador, Chiapas, Cuba* (Athens, OH: Ohio University Press, 2004); Dana Frank, *Bananeras: Women Transforming the Banana Unions of Latin America* (Boston: South End Press, 2005); Nelly P. Stromquist, *Feminist Organizations and Social Transformation in Latin America* (Boulder, CO: Paradigm Publishers, 2007).
19. There is no general study that examines how women got the vote in all Latin American countries. However, Asuncion Lavarin, "Suffrage in South America: Arguing a Difficult Case," *Suffrage and Beyond: International Feminist Perspectives*, eds. Caroline

Daley and Melanie Nolan (New York: New York University Press, 1994) 184–209, gives an account of how the suffrage was won in Uruguay, Chile, Argentina, and Colombia.

20. Maria Escobar-Lemmon and Michelle Taylor-Robinson, "How Electoral Laws and Development Affect the Election of Women in Latin American Legislatures: A Test 20 Years into the Third Wave of Democracy," Paper presented to the 2006 Annual Meeting of the American Political Science Association, Philadelphia, PA.

21. Calculated from International Idea, Global Database of Quotas for Women. www. quotaproject.org (accessed 22 February 2008).

22. Mala Htun, "Women, Political Parties and Electoral Systems in Latin America," *Women in Parliament: Beyond Numbers, A Revised Edition*, eds. Julie Ballington and Azza Karam (Stockholm, SE: International IDEA, 2006) 112–121.

23. International Parliamentary Union, *Women in Parliaments: World Classification*. www.ipu.org/wmn-e/classif.htm (accessed 22 February 2008).

24. For more details, see David Close, *Nicaragua: The Chamorro Years* (Boulder, CO: Lynne Rienner Publishers, 1999) 105–107.

25. In 1986, the Madres split into two factions. One, the Founding Line, worked to bring to justice those responsible for the kidnappings but also accepted compensation from the government. The other, the Association, has taken a more radical political line. A third associated group, the Abuelas (grandmothers), not only lost their children but also had their grandchildren stolen and given to members of the military regime to adopt.

26. See Nikki Craske, *Women and Politics in Latin America* (New Brunswick, NJ: Rutgers University Press, 1999) 114–118.

27. Karen Kampwirth, *Women and Guerrilla Movements: Nicaragua, El Salvador, Chiapas, Cuba* (University Park, PA; Pennsylvania State University Press, 2002).

28. To begin further research on indigenous people and politics in Latin America, see two works by Donna Lee Van Cott, *The Friendly Liquidation of the Past: The Politics of Diversity in Latin America* (Pittsburgh, PA: University of Pittsburgh Press, 2000) and *From Movements to Parties in Latin America: The Evolution of Ethnic Politics* (New York: Cambridge University Press, 2005); as well, consult David Maybury-Lewis, ed., *The Politics of Ethnicity: Indigenous People in Latin American States* (Cambridge, MA: Harvard University David Rockefeller Center for Latin American Studies, 2002) and Erick D. Langer and Elena Muñoz, *Contemporary Indigenous Movements in Latin America* (Wilmington, DE: SR Books, 2003). For those interested in the politics of black Latin Americans, the starting point is George Reid Andrews, *Afro-Latin America, 1800–2000* (New York: Oxford University Press, 2004).

29. "First Nations" is used in Canada to refer to indigenous peoples, especially those who signed treaties with the state. Here I use the term interchangeably with indigenous peoples.

30. There is a lot written on the Zapatistas. Among the places to start looking are: Harry M. Cleaver, Jr., "The Zapatista Effect: The Internet and the Rise of an Alternative Political Fabric," *Journal of International Affairs* 51:2 (1998): 621–40; Tom Hayden, *The Zapatista Reader* (New York: Nation Books, 2002); Karen Kampwirth, *Feminism and the Legacy of Revolution: Nicaragua, El Salvador, Chiapas* (Athens, OH: Ohio University Press, 2004); special issues of the *Journal of Peasant Studies* 32:3–4(July/October 2005) and of *Latin American Perspectives* 33:2 (March 2006); and John Ross, *¡Zapatista! Making Another World Possible: Chronicles of Resistance 2000–2006* (New York: Nation Books, 2006).

31. For more on the MST, see Angus Lindsay Wright and Wendy Wolford, *To Inherit the Earth: The Landless Movement and the Struggle for a New Brazil* (Oakland, CA: Food First Books, 2003) and Sue Branford and Jan Rocha, *Cutting the Wire: The Story of the Landless Movement in Brazil* (London: Latin American Bureau, 2002).

32. Harry Vanden, "Brazil's Landless Hold Their Ground," *NACLA: Report on the Americas*. 38:5 (2005), 21–27.

33. "About the MST," *MST*. www.mstbrazil.org (accessed 5 March 2008).

34. Nicaragua was the least rural of the three, as a great deal of combat in the revolution's final years (1978–1979) of fighting took place in urban zones. All the same, prior to that point the struggle had a strongly rural character.

35. On the Argentine crisis, see Edward Epstein and David Pion-Berlin, eds., *Broken Promises? The Argentine Crisis and Argentine Democracy* (Lanham, MD: Lexington Books, 2006) and Paul Blustein, *And the Money Kept Rolling In (and Out): Wall Street, the IMF, and the Bankrupting of Argentina* (New York: Public Affairs, 2005).

6

Political Institutions and the Machinery of Government

We can think of political institutions and the machinery of government as the framework for a country's politics. They define how laws are made and applied. They prescribe what rights citizens and governors possess and how each may use those rights. They provide the pathways for much of everyday politics.

Institutions are important, but they sometimes have been overlooked or given short shrift in the study of Latin American politics. For many years, that was because formal political institutions (courts, executives, legislatures, electoral authorities) either did not work in long-established democracies or simply did not exist. And since the study of informal political institutions (see Chapter 4) has only emerged recently, not a great deal of energy went into studying how military juntas or personal dictatorships actually worked—though, to tell the truth, those kinds of governments are not known for cooperating with researchers. However, since the 1980s, there has been increasing interest in political institutions everywhere, and analysts now produce useful studies of Latin American governmental machinery.

Chapter 4 set out some of the questions involved in examining political institutions, but these need another look and some expansion because the focus there was on informal institutions. From the perspective of theory, and thus of understanding principles and basic relationships, political institutions are defined very abstractly. Political science sees them as repeated patterns of interactions designed to influence people's behavior. That gives us a general idea of what institutions do but tells us almost nothing about how they do it.

A better strategy for analyzing political institutions is to bear the abstract definition in mind but actually work with concrete examples. For instance, all governments have some identifiable organization that most observers would say is an executive. That organization would, at least, attend to the implementation of laws and regulations, collect revenues, spend money and account for money spent, conduct foreign relations, and wage war. This is managing government operations. How the executive would be structured, what internal rules it would follow, and how it would be staffed could vary radically from case to case; still, we have a little better idea of what the executive part of government is actually about.

Executives are one of several formal political institutions. Unfortunately, there is no standard, universally accepted definition of a formal political institution. However, a composite view would yield something like the following: it is an organization with some kind of legal status that is a recognized, official part of the state. This produces a list that includes constitutions, executives (which comprise presidents and/or prime ministers, cabinets, and bureaucracies), legislatures, electoral systems and elections themselves, judiciaries, local and regional governments, federalism—where it exists, and the relations between and among the above.

However, it is possible to extend the roster of formal political institutions by removing the requirement that they be an official part of the state. It is impossible to imagine politics anywhere today working without political parties, and parties are generally recognized in law and subject to regulations dealing with financing, how they receive official recognition, and so on. But they are unlikely to be formal parts of the state, outside of dictatorships that designate a single party as official. Parties thus belong on the list of formal institutions, even though they are not part of the formal machinery of government. In fact, democratic theory asserts that they should not be because in democratic countries they are private organizations not under the control of government, and as such must be conceptually and legally separate from the governments they run.[1] This principle also extends to interest groups.

Rather than add further entries to this inventory, it is better to amend slightly our initial definition of a formal political institution. It should now read: a formal political institution is an organization with some kind of legal status that is either an official part of the state or is widely recognized as integral to the functioning of the state. Those organizations, rules, and processes that fall under the first heading—official parts of the state—are better called the machinery of government. They should receive separate treatment.

In the present chapter, this definition is applied conservatively to limit the array of institutions treated to those mentioned above. Further, the chapter looks mostly at contemporary institutions, although it places them in their historical settings where necessary. And it does not attempt comprehensive coverage of all countries but rather examines only selected cases. Finally, recalling points raised in Chapter 1, this analysis of Latin American state machinery and political institutions features a comparative element. The machinery of government is treated first and then political parties are considered.

Machinery of Government

Governments are very complex organizations. They are often the largest organization in a country in terms of people employed and money controlled. Because government, as a concept, is central to political science, the discipline uses the word carefully. In particular, it takes pains to distinguish government from the state, even though everyday usage treats the terms as interchangeable.

The state is the broader of the two concepts. It is "an independent, self-governing political community whose governing institutions have the capability to make rules that are binding on the population residing within a particular territory."[2] Another definition, that of early twentieth-century German sociologist Max Weber, describes the state as having the monopoly over the legitimate use of physical force. The state, however, is also an abstraction. It is the government of a state that actually deals with people and issues; and when speaking of interstate conflict, which we do in Chapter 10, it is really governments that carry on the dispute.

Government is therefore far more concrete. It can be defined as "the set of institutions that makes decisions and oversees their implementation ... on behalf of the state for a particular period of time."[3] It is what most people think of when they hear the word *politics*. How government is structured and how well it works has a lot to do with how free and secure people actually are.

One hundred years ago, political science was mostly about studying the formal rules and regulations within which governments operated. Today, its focus has broadened. Yet even if institutions are now only a part of the political mosaic, their importance is recognized because they are seen as influencing the behavior of those who work in them, which in turn affects how the institutions work. Politicians have long realized that revising how people in different parts of government do their jobs can be critical to securing their goals. As a result, much effort goes into deciding how to tailor institutions to maximize the probability of achieving that desired end. In short, everybody agrees that institutions matter.

This section of the chapter examines the governmental machinery Latin American political systems have configured and used. It concentrates on the machinery currently in use in different countries but also provides the background needed to understand how institutions have changed. The machinery treated here falls into five categories: constitutions, executives, legislatures, judiciaries, and elections.

Constitutions

Constitutions set forth the basic rules and principles of government. They are complicated legal instruments and, as such, are normally constructed by the political elites who will work within them. This does not preclude broad consultation or even directly involving ordinary citizens, often called non-elites, in the process of constitutional construction. It is nevertheless true that most people find much of what their national constitution says to be opaque, due to its legal language, and generally of little practical concern to them. In fact, in the world's poorer countries ordinary citizens may scarcely be aware that their country has a constitution; much less that it grants them rights that they can use to better their lives.

Any constitution has to do four things. First, it provides a statement of the principles on which a state is founded or that it wants to secure. Second, constitutions establish a basic legal framework for the state. This includes the specifying the rights and duties of governors and citizens, indicating those areas where the government may act and defining the state's territorial structure—federal or unitary, centralized or decentralized. Third, constitutions map political power by describing both what offices and organizations may do but also what steps they must follow in doing them. Finally, constitutions set out how they may be changed: the requirements for adopting constitutional amendments are almost always more rigorous than the rules that apply to ordinary legislation. In doing these four things, constitutions define a regime.

Although *regime* is another concept that is used interchangeably with *state* and *government*, careful usage limits it to covering only the fundamental aspects of how political authority is composed and operates. What, for example, are the bases of a state's legitimacy: Divine right? Popular sovereignty expressed through elections? Revolution? How and to whom governors are held accountable is another aspect of a regime. Do the rulers answer to God or history; to a particular race, class, or religion; to the military; or to the electorate? Another factor is the question of who has influence over and access to the governors and is similar to the issue of accountability. The last element to mention is the relationship between state and civil society, on the one hand, and the individual, on the other. How do the rulers treat private citizens? How do they respond to citizens organizing themselves to petition government or protest its behavior?

These are questions that constitutional drafters everywhere address. Taken together, they define a political system. In Latin America, it seems that national elites or some part of them are compelled to define their political system far more frequently than in the world's historic democracies. Table 6.1 presents the number of constitutions each nation has had.

Given that the United States has had one constitution since 1789 (with 27 amendments) and Canada has had one since 1867 (with multiple amendments, a major one in 1982), readers from those two countries will find Latin America's record inexplicable. Nevertheless, there are explanations, and they begin with political instability and personalized politics.

Recall that for the first 40 to 50 years of their existence, most Latin American countries suffered *caudillo* rule. New rulers brought new constitutions to legitimate their rule. This was especially the case where Conservatives replaced Liberals, or vice versa, as the new ruler would have to undo the legal framework of the old regime to let him change the legal status of the Catholic Church. In other cases, the number of constitutions is related to the structure of the nation's constitutional law: Venezuela's having had 25 constitutions is attributable in part to the absence for many years of a formula permitting the partial amendment of its constitution. All this would be of historical interest only, useful for charting the development of political institutions and reflecting upon political cultures, if the practice of regular constitutional revision were not still widespread.

| The fall of authoritarian regimes in the 1980s is part of the story of Latin America's continuing constitutional revisions. This would apply in at least Brazil, El Salvador, Guatemala, and Paraguay. Other new constitutions or significant amendments arrived with neoliberal politics that required revising the economic role of the state. Nicaragua's 1995 constitution belongs in this category as does Ecuador's revision of 1998. Simply put, significant political changes demanded new constitutions to let the state and its government do their new jobs. Looking at three cases—Nicaragua, Venezuela, and Bolivia—will provide a more detailed view of how constitutional politics works in Latin America.

Table 6.1 Number of Constitutions for Each Latin American Country

Country	Number of Constitutions
Argentina	5
Bolivia	17
Brazil	7
Chile	8
Colombia	13
Costa Rica	13
Cuba	8
Dominican Republic	6
Ecuador	24
El Salvador	15
Guatemala	10
Haiti	23
Honduras	19
Mexico	6
Nicaragua	14
Panama	4
Paraguay	5
Peru	14
Uruguay	7
Venezuela	25

Sources: Author's compilation from *Constituciones hispanoamericanas,* www.cervantesvirtual.com/portal/constituciones/constituciones.shtml, and *Bob Corbett's Haiti Page,* http://www.webster.edu/~corbetre/haiti/haiti.html.

Nicaragua's recent constitutional history begins in 1987, when the governing Sandinistas (Frente Sandinista de Liberación Nacional, or FSLN) sought to institutionalize the revolution they had been building since overthrowing the Somoza family's dictatorship in 1979. That document blended liberal democratic and radical democratic elements, reflecting the nature of the regime. The former consisted of descriptions of ordinary government machinery and elaborating citizens' rights. The latter assigned a very substantial economic role to the state, spoke of preserving the conquests of the revolution, recognized the existence of a Sandinista army and a Sandinista police, and gave the president enormous decree powers.

With the electoral defeat of the FSLN by the conservative Unión Nacional Opositora (UNO, or National Oppositional Union), a constitutional change was expected. It only came in 1995, however, and was not backed by either the president, Violeta Chamorro, the bulk of the UNO, or the FSLN leadership. This substantial reworking of the 1987 constitution stripped the text of its revolutionary language and brought it into line with the capitalist-centered economic policy backed by the new government. The amendments also took away much of the president's decree power and strengthened the legislature, courts, and independent agencies that oversee and control the executive, such as the comptroller and the electoral authority, which explains why the president did not support the changes.

The 1995 version of Nicaragua's constitution lasted until 2000, when the FSLN combined with the far more conservative governing Partido Liberal Constitucionalista (PLC, or Constitutionalist Liberal Party) for another overhaul. These amendments strengthened the executive, weakened the independence of the courts, comptroller, and electoral authority, and tried to lay the foundations for a permanent FSLN-PLC duopoly over Nicaraguan politics. Though still in opposition, the Sandinistas pushed through another set of amendments in 2005, this time weakening the president again, and strengthening the National Assembly, where the FSLN was the best-organized party. Regaining the presidency in 2006, the FSLN is again proposing reforms, this time to allow the immediate re-election of the president, something it refused to back in 2000 when another party held the presidency. In Nicaragua, the constitution became a political instrument like any other.

Venezuela offers another example of constitutional engineering to let a governing party build the regime it envisions. In 1998, Hugo Chávez became president of a country whose political system was in an advanced state of decay. An outsider who had led a failed coup in 1992, Chávez promised that he would call a referendum on constitutional congress if elected. He was elected and did hold a referendum in which the voters approved the constituent assembly. In the subsequent election of representatives to that assembly, Chavez's party won 121 of 131 the seats. At the end of the constituent assembly, the president emerged with the 1999 Constitution of the Bolivarian Republic of Venezuela, the framework for his new regime.

The assembly itself was important because it became a model for later full-scale reforms in Bolivia and Ecuador. Its work was done quickly, taking only six months, which indicates that it was well organized and that the president's followers were well disciplined. Having no real opposition probably expedited matters too. The assembly used 22 committees to do its work, a common practice in any deliberative body.

Equally important is the constitution proper. It marked the first break with the then-prevailing neoliberal orthodoxy. "Title VI: The

Socioeconomic System" returns an expanded role to the state, charging it with promoting "... the solid, dynamic, sustainable, continuing and equitable growth of the economy to ensure a just distribution of wealth through participatory democratic strategic planning with open consultation" (Art. 299). And "Title III: Human Rights, Citizens' Duties, and Constitutional Guarantees," places great emphasis on direct citizen participation. This is using the constitution both to establish the legal framework that will let a government build and maintain the political system it wants and to send citizens a message about the government's aspirations.

Conditions in Bolivia, which completed its latest constitutional process in 2009, were similar to those in Venezuela. The earlier model, in place since the 1980s, was a mix of liberal democracy and radical free-market economics. In the first years of this century, there were fierce confrontations over the privatization of water and the nationalization of gas in Bolivia. The government also generated conflict by pursuing a program of coca eradication—coca is the raw material for cocaine—that focused on legal growers.[4] This brought Evo Morales, the leader of the coca growers, into national politics.

Like Chávez, Morales campaigned on a platform of radical change, promising a constituent assembly if elected. He won the presidency and took a majority of seats (135/255) in the constitutional convention. However, constituent assemblies normally require a qualified majority of three-fifths to two-thirds to approve the resulting constitution, and Morales fell 35 seats short. This opened the way for a much more contested and contentious assembly and a constitution that was approved by the Bolivian Congress while the opposition was kept from entering the chamber by the president's supporters.

This is another constitution that is the foundation for a radically new regime. Chapter 5 noted some of the articles of the draft constitution that addressed the rights of Bolivia's First Nations. The draft also specifies a much more active economic role for the state, including the promotion of economic democracy and self-sufficiency in food (Art. 310.4). Although policies pursuing those ends might well have been achievable under the old 1995 constitution, entrenching them in the 2009 version signals their centrality in the new order.

Of course, any Bolivian government could simply ignore the constitution and do as it wished. In the past, many independent states proclaimed their devotion to the highest principles of freedom and justice, and then went along their old elitist ways. However, the twenty-first century is a more democratic era and its constitutions often give more opportunities for citizens to act for themselves and to control their governors. This shows in the Venezuelan and Bolivian constitutions.

Federalism

In the early post-independence period, the federal question occupied the minds of political thinkers and activists (often the same people) throughout all Latin America, except Brazil. Conservatives were generally centralists who wanted a unitary state, with all governing authority concentrated at the center. Liberals were usually federalists, because they wanted to decentralize authority and diffuse power. However, the new nations of Latin America were not in the same situation as the United States in 1789, which had to knit together a number of colonies that had formerly enjoyed a substantial level of domestic self-government. Nor did they face the predicament of incorporating an ethnoterritory, such as French-speaking Quebec, an issue that would confront Canada in 1867. Both North American nations had pragmatic and philosophical reasons for entering the complex world of federalism. Their Latin American counterparts had fewer practical arguments to adduce, and where they did, as with the often-attempted Central American federation, they met with failure.[5]

Nonetheless, federalism did eventually come to a number of Latin American countries. Argentina, after decades of conflict and bloodshed between the Buenos Aires–based proponents of a unitary state and the supporters of decentralized federal rule who came from the peripheral provinces, settled on a "centralized plural" system, a center-dominant federal system. Brazil, which even under the empire gave substantial de facto responsibility to the provinces, in 1889 instituted a very decentralized federal state, the Velha Republic, which endured until 1930. Although the authoritarian governments of Getúlio Vargas (1930–45) and then the bureaucratic authoritarian dictatorship (1964–1985) radically centralized power, the democratic constitution of 1988 restored more power to the states. In Venezuela, federalism existed in name only until 1989, when state governors came to be directly elected instead of appointed by the president. Finally, Mexico, another federation in name only for many years, also entered the ranks of functional federations following electoral reforms.

Executives

Latin American governments have always been strongly executive-centered. In fact, they have often been called hyper-presidential. There have been some exceptions, which receive treatment in the next section on legislatures, but what is more interesting is that among governments in other countries of the Third World there is a similar preponderance of executive–dominated administrations. In fact, most governments in the history of the world have been dominated by the executive, in addition to being authoritarian.

It helps to know that contemporary Latin America is not alone in having very powerful political executives, if only because it eliminates political culture or some quirk of history as the cause. It does not, however, give any hint about how to address this problem or even why it is a problem. Surprisingly, the latter question is easier to deal with.

It was in the seventeenth century that European political thinkers became concerned about concentrated political power. In their day, the problem was the absolute monarch—the king or queen who ruled unconstrained by parliaments or courts—and this problem had both abstract and concrete expressions. The practical side of the problem was that an absolute monarch could repress religious dissidents, stifle economic endeavors, and march the country off to war without having to convince anyone else that it was a good idea. The philosophical side, of course, grew from notions of natural law and natural rights. Solving the problem took revolutions, civil wars, risings, and wrenching socioeconomic change; and the solution was over two centuries coming.

Today's executive-centric regimes pose a similar challenge: unaccountable leaders can distort, even destroy, democracy and get their countries and people into trouble. That is why political science gives so much attention to the concept of accountability[7] as an integral element of democracy. It also is one of the reasons why Latin American political activists and analysts have long been preoccupied with keeping presidents under control. The most obvious means they have is legally limiting how long a president can serve. *term years*

The practice of presidents amending the constitution to give themselves another term is so common in Latin America that it has a special name: *continuismo,* continuance in office. It is usually accomplished by simply changing the rules to let a president have another term in office. Where these changes have to go before the public in a free referendum, the results are not assured (see Text Box 6.1). When they go through a legislature controlled by the president's party, however, success is more likely.

To deal with the problem of concentrated presidential power and its arrogation by one person, Latin American states have imposed a number of legal restrictions. The most common is some kind of term limit. Guatemala, Honduras, Mexico, and Paraguay have absolute prohibitions on presidential re-election. In Paraguay, even a vice-president must sit out one term before running for president. There can be costs associated with such a policy. Costa Rica recently amended its constitution to allow re-election of a president after a two-term, eight-year lapse, thus permitting successful chief executives the opportunity to serve a second term. In both Brazil and Colombia, the constitution's no–re-election provision was amended to permit a president's immediate re-election for a second term and so let a popular and effective president continue in office.

Text Box 6.1 Presidents Chávez and Menem Fail to Get Third Terms

Continuismo, the endless extension of a president's term, is something Latin American democrats want to avoid. That is why most of the region's constitutions have some manner of term limit. Increasingly, re-election in some form is allowed, but usually there must either be a term out of office or there is a strict two-term limit in place. However, some presidents want more. The two most recent cases are Argentina's Carlos Menem and Venezuela's Hugo Chávez. Both failed in their quest—at least initially, in Chávez's case.

Menem, whose presidency saw Argentina master its longstanding problems with inflation, was able to get the constitution amended in 1994 to permit him a second consecutive term. Ten years was not enough, though, and Menem wanted to run again in 1999, in what Argentines called his "re-re," or re-re-election. His dream ended when the courts found his proposed candidacy unconstitutional. He did run again in 2003 but mustered only 20 per cent of the vote and declined to participate in a run-off against frontrunner Nestor Kirchner.

Chávez has had a greater impact on Venezuela than Carlos Menem had on Argentina. The leader of a failed coup staged in 1992, Chávez returned six years later to win the presidency. After also winning a referendum on holding a constituent assembly and then seeing that body draft Venezuela's Bolivarian constitution, Chávez was re-elected under the new charter in 2000, withstood a coup attempt in 2002, and survived a recall vote in 2004. In 2006, he won his second term—his final, according to the Bolivarian constitution. Like Menem, though, Hugo Chávez wanted more and proposed a package of constitutional amendments, one of which removed all term limits on the president. The vote held on December 2, 2007, saw the president's amendments defeated. However, Chávez did not abandon his quest and in February 2009, the president won the referendum on his second try.

Another device used to limit presidential power is a consanguinity prohibition. This means that a close relative, by blood or marriage, cannot succeed the current president. The logic behind such a law is that the brother, wife, or first cousin of an ex-president is likely to be little more than a placeholder, leaving the past president the power behind the throne. Not all countries have this constitutional provision. Argentina, where Cristina Fernandez de Kirchner succeeded her husband, Nestor Kirchner, as president of the republic in 2007, is obviously one that does not.

Despite the problems overly powerful chief executives have brought Latin American countries in the past, all 20 republics have presidential systems. There are no parliamentary systems similar to Canada, Spain, or India in Latin America. Brazil did give serious thought to adopting a parliamentary system, however—even holding a plebiscite on the question in 1993, in which those in favor of presidential government carried 59 per cent of the vote.[8]

Although presidents are the most important and most visible parts of the executive, they are not the entire executive. There are also cabinet ministers, the men and women who are the political heads of the various departments of government. And there is also the bureaucracy, the appointed staff that manages and operates government departments. Governments are large organizations charged with important tasks: educating people, looking after at least the rudiments of public health, maintaining highways and other transportation links, protecting citizens from their less law-abiding neighbors (foreign and domestic), and defending the country's interests abroad. This is obviously not a one-person job.

As a rule of thumb, ministers in presidential governments have a lower profile than their counterparts in parliamentary regimes. The latter are almost always elected politicians with substantial personal followings, whereas the former not only may come from outside government but, except in some US states, are also not elected to office. Nevertheless, it is usually just as hard to name the minister of municipal affairs or public works in a parliamentary system as a presidential one. And where political chief executives are exceptionally strong, often the case in Latin America, ministers are correspondingly weak.

Despite such obstacles, there are some cabinet ministers worthy of note. In the 1980s and 1990s, finance ministers achieved very high profiles. In Argentina, for example, there was Domingo Cavallo, who was the architect of the 1990s austerity program there. In a very different way, Ricardo Lopez Murphy, finance minister in 2001, became famous for presenting a belt-tightening plan in the midst of Argentina's worst-ever economic crisis. In Brazil, Fernando Henrique Cardoso became finance minister in 1993, making a name for himself that led him to the presidency in 1994. Similarly, Michelle Bachelet, elected president of Chile in 2005, also began her climb to her country's top job by holding the health and defense portfolios in her predecessor's administration.

The final part of the executive is the civil service or bureaucracy. In most Third World countries, the civil service is ill paid and understaffed: in 1999, in the developed countries of the Organisation for Economic Co-operation and Development (OECD), 15.6 per cent of the economically active population worked for government; in Latin America that figure was only 7.3 per cent.[9] This leads to three unfortunate outcomes: 1) public services are not delivered effectively; 2) corruption is not uncommon; 3) the bureaucracy has little policy capacity, which translates into incompletely thought-through programs. In general, poorer, smaller countries (Nicaragua, Haiti, or Ecuador) are more affected than larger, wealthier ones (Chile, Argentina, or Mexico), but all Latin America knows how hard it is to have good government with a weak public service.

In the 1990s, during the period of structural adjustment and under the austerity programs prescribed by international financial institutions such as the International Monetary Fund (IMF), some energy was directed toward strengthening the bureaucracy. However, the focus was on reducing the size of the state, so most departments lost personnel and funding. In 2003, however, countries from throughout the region adopted the Ibero-American Charter on the Civil Service, which committed the signatories to supporting the establishment of a more professional civil service and so increase the state's managerial capacity.[10]

Legislatures

Latin American legislatures are usually styled "reactive," which means that historically, with the exception of Chile (1891–1925), the legislative branches of Latin American governments have not assumed the law-making powers found in the US Congress. In this respect, the Latin Americans are like the rest of the world, as the powers of the US Congress constitute a clear case of American exceptionalism. More important than not initiating much legislation is the lack of independence shown by Latin American representative assemblies.

A legislature has other functions besides law-making. It can and should oversee and control the executive, making the president and cabinet accountable for their actions. This can be done not just through formal mechanisms but also by the legislature's daily work, which should shine a light on all parts of government. And the legislature is also one of the sites where a democracy's continuing election campaign is carried out, as parties parry among themselves, seeking the edge that will bring them to power when citizens next vote.[11]

There is also the question of whether legislators in all Latin American countries actually act as representatives of their districts. Large districts with multiple representatives elected by a party-list proportional representation system seem to produce a disconnect between the deputies and those who should be their constituents. For this reason, in 1994, Bolivia changed how its citizens elected their legislators with a new law assuring that 68 of 130 congressional deputies would be selected by the single-member constituency-plurality system that is used in Canada and the United States. This experiment was just one of many attempts to strengthen Latin American legislatures in the 1980s and 1990s.

Those two decades were the era of democracy promotion. Also called *democratic strengthening*, the concept refers to a form of foreign aid, principally from Washington, directed toward building stronger democratic institutions in countries that had recently abandoned authoritarian rule. Elections, parties, courts, civil society, and legislatures were among the political forces targeted for assistance. In the case of legislatures, the objective

---

Text Box 6.2 Contentious Legislative Politics in Nicaragua

During the 11 years of the revolutionary Sandinista government, a great deal of property was expropriated and redistributed to some 170,000 families. With its defeat, the FSLN passed three bills to regularize the titles to those redistributed properties. One of the biggest problems facing Violeta Chamorro when she became Nicaragua's president in 1990 was the property question. Chamorro took a go-slow approach to try to sort out the thorny issue, but some legislative members of the alliance she led to power wanted faster action and moved to repeal the Sandinistas' laws in 1991. The ensuing conflict was defused but worse was to come.

In September 1992, National Assembly president (speaker) Alfredo César reintroduced the bill to repeal the Sandinista titling laws. To show their displeasure, the FSLN and some allies from a centrist party walked out of the Assembly, leaving the legislature without a quorum. César responded by summoning substitutes for the centrists who were boycotting (every Nicaraguan deputy is elected with an alternate who can assume the seat if it is vacated) to get a quorum. He then passed the repeal act. The president declared she would not recognize any actions taken by the National Assembly since the majority of deputies had walked out, and the question was settled when the courts held that the Assembly could not act because it did not have a legal quorum. This ended Nicaragua's first legislative insurgency.

Its second began late in 2004. This time the initiative came from the Sandinistas, the second-largest party in the house. It took the form of a constitutional amendment reducing the president's power of appointment by requiring that all cabinet ministers and heads of autonomous state agencies (for example, the public utilities board) be approved by 60 per cent of the National Assembly. The objectives of the amendment were (1) to give the legislature a veto over top level presidential appointments and (2) to guarantee that the support of at least two parties would be required to approve a candidate. This amendment was adopted, but the FSLN then succeeded in having a bill adopted delaying the amendment's enactment for two years, to avoid further conflicts with the sitting president, Enrique Bolaños.

In both cases, political interests that were strong in the legislature used the National Assembly to achieve results that might have been impossible otherwise.[12]

---

was to build their capacity by giving deputies greater technical skills and a better understanding of their roles and responsibilities. Concretely, these projects were concerned with stressing bill-drafting skills, assisting in the design of oversight mechanisms, conducting media relations programs, and contributing to upgrading the physical space where legislators work.[13]

Obviously, legislative-strengthening projects can give a legislature better tools to work with and suggest new ways for legislators to conceive of their roles. Such projects cannot, however, make them either use those tools as the donor wishes or change their behavior in any way. For the latter to occur, there must be an incentive. That often happens when a group that has little access to the executive has a power base in the legislature. It has been going on since the 1300s in England, and the process has been playing itself out again in Nicaragua (see Text Box 6.2).

As Text Box 6.2 shows, empowering a legislature need not strengthen constitutional government or advance democracy. Yet even in such instances, if there were some assurance that the nondemocratic effects of usurping power would be temporary and that the reformed institutions would be adaptable to democratic and constitutional ends, the risk might be justified. Most observers, however, would prefer smaller, slower changes that were entirely within democratic bounds.

Judiciaries

If you live in Canada or the United States, you are used to having a judiciary that is a central part of the political system. In both countries, the Supreme Court makes decisions that determine what the state can do. Most countries, however, do not have such politically powerful courts. This does not mean that their courts never make politically significant decisions, but rather that it would be a mistake to assess them by standards developed in Washington or Ottawa.

Similarly, although issues of judicial independence, impartiality, and competence—all of which produce public confidence in the court system—as well as administrative questions, such as overloaded dockets, figure prominently in any context, many Latin American judiciaries have been dominated by the executive. Historically, there existed the supposition that judges, especially superior court judges, followed the wishes of the chief executive. As constitutional government expanded, this trait became less evident. However, there are countries where a politically sensitive judiciary is still the rule.

The best contemporary example of a politicized judiciary in contemporary Latin America may be Nicaragua. As a result of a political deal (the Pact) struck in 2000 between the then-ruling Partido Liberal Constitucionalista (PLC, or Constitutionalist Liberal Party) and the Sandinistas, Supreme Court appointments are divided between those two parties in proportion to their relative electoral strengths. In Nicaragua, Supreme Court justices are elected by the National Assembly to serve five-year terms and, since the Pact, the National Assembly approves a slate that has already allotted the available positions to the proper number of Liberals and Sandinistas.

The partisanship of the judiciary was seen most clearly in the corruption charges brought against former president Arnoldo Alemán of the PLC.

Since Nicaragua's constitution forbids consecutive presidential terms, Alemán arranged for his seemingly compliant vice-president, Enrique Bolaños, to head the PLC's ticket in 2001. Bolaños won easily, beating the Sandinistas' Daniel Ortega by 10 points—and then set about charging his old boss with various counts of fraud and corruption. Ortega, who had a legislative seat thanks to a constitutional provision granting one to the runner-up in the presidential election (the past president has one too, so Alemán himself was in the Assembly, acting, in fact, as its speaker), decided to back Bolaños and weaken the man with whom he had negotiated the Pact. The Sandinista did this by having the Sandinista Supreme Court justice who assigned judges to hear cases name a strong Sandinista partisan to try Alemán, and the former president was convicted and sentenced to 20 years imprisonment. Alemán would likely have been convicted in a fair trial, but if a Liberal judge had heard the case, the ex-president could well have gone free.[14]

But the story had not ended. When, two years later, President Bolaños became an obstacle to the FSLN leader's objectives, the same judge who had tried Alemán opened an investigation into charges that Bolaños had violated the campaign finance law.[15]

Justice for top politicians in other countries, however, is less political. Chile, Argentina, and Costa Rica provide examples.

The Chilean case revolves around Augusto Pinochet. The dictator was detained in Britain and judged by British courts in 1999. Spain sought his extradition for trial on charges of murdering Spanish citizens, but London allowed him to return to Chile due to his age and ill health. Once home, however, the Chilean courts removed his parliamentary immunity—ex-presidents became lifetime senators, thus enjoyed immunity from prosecution—and the general spent the rest of his life trying to avoid trial, doing so by being declared incompetent.[16]

Argentina's courts acted similarly to bring to justice the men who waged the Dirty War against their countrymen. From 1987 to 2001, many military officers were protected by the Law of Due Obedience—"I was following orders so I am not guilty": the so-called Eichmann defense. However, a judge struck down that and another immunity law in 2001 and the country's Supreme Court upheld his decision in 2005. In 2007, the life sentences of one-time head of the Argentine junta, retired General Jorge Videla, and former naval chief of staff Eduardo Massera were confirmed.

Finally, in Costa Rica, three former presidents have been charged with graft. In 2004, the three presidents who had served between 1990 and 2002—Rafael Ángel Calderón, José María Figueres, and Miguel Ángel Rodríguez—were implicated in taking money to influence government decisions, or influence-peddling. Figueres, who was out of the country, never returned to face charges, but Calderón and Rodríguez did. Both were convicted and each served nearly a year in prison before being released.

There are, then, cases where courts acted independently in high-profile cases, as well as instances where they were used as political instruments. Obviously, cases involving ex-presidents do not make up much of any judiciary's workload and what matters most to ordinary citizens is the treatment they can expect at the hands of their country's courts. All the same, it is a positive sign if high-profile defendants neither get preferential treatment nor are subjected to political justice.

Elections and Electoral Systems

There was a time when papers in some Latin American countries could publish headlines reading, "Here are the winners of tomorrow's elections" and get every last one right. That was because many countries ran elections according to the principle of "the one who counts wins." Elections were not left to chance, so fraud, dirty tricks, and coercion were normal parts of the electoral process. Now, however, all Latin America, except Cuba, uses open, competitive, and acceptably clean elections to choose those who will govern.

With the spread of electoral democracy in the 1980s, a great deal of attention went to electoral systems, the institutions that turn votes into results. An electoral system can be seen as having two parts. One is the machinery established to run elections. It is the norm in Latin America for this machinery to be run by organizations with constitutional status that are labeled "the fourth branch of government." These bodies, often called electoral tribunals or councils, also generally administer the law governing the recognition of political parties, a status that lets parties run for office and receive some campaign funds from the government; sometimes the electoral tribunals also handle voter registration.

The other part of an electoral system is the method for determining who won. As noted above, Canada and the United States use the single member constituency-plurality (SMC-P) system. Also called *first-past-the-post* (FPTP) or just *plurality*, this system returns one representative per district, and the candidate with the most votes, not always a majority, wins. The system is simple to use, easy to understand, and works well in a two-party system such as the one that exists in the United States. No Latin American country uses this system exclusively, although Honduras, Mexico, Panama, Uruguay, and Venezuela use it for presidential elections. Most presidential contests, however, provide for a second round if the first-round leader does not reach a stipulated minimum percentage of the vote. This is normally a majority but can be as low as 35 per cent, with a 5-point edge on the runner-up, the model Nicaragua uses.

Most legislative elections use some form of proportional representation (PR), which assigns a number of legislative seats that corresponds to the percentage of the vote a party receives. The most common form of PR in Latin America is a party-list system. Mexico and Bolivia use a mixed-member system, which has a proportion of seats elected by SMC-P and the rest by PR. As noted above, the objective is to combine the presumed personal responsiveness of representatives from single-member districts with the party-strengthening traits associated with PR. Special notice must be taken of the Chilean electoral system, binomialism, for it is both unique to that country and a fine example of electoral engineering: adjusting the electoral system to secure partisan ends.

Under the binomial system, members of both Chile's Chamber of Deputies and Senate are returned from two-member districts. Parties or electoral alliances present lists with two names. If the list carries two-thirds of the vote in its district, both candidates are elected. However, if the leading list falls below the two-thirds threshold, it gets only one, while the second-place list gets the second seat, no matter how many votes it wins. This system was set up in 1988 by the outgoing Pinochet regime intentionally to benefit the largest minority and not the majority. The military foresaw that the right would not be a majority force, and thus they tailored the electoral system to overstate its strength.

Other governments have also used electoral engineering successfully. For example, the revolutionary Sandinista government in Nicaragua designed an electoral system for its first vote in 1984 that made it relatively easy for small parties to win seats in the National Assembly. Bringing more parties into the legislature enhanced the Sandinistas' democratic credentials while fractionalizing the opposition.

The final aspect of electoral politics in contemporary Latin America that we note here is the emergence of domestic election observer groups.[17] When authoritarian governments yield to democratic ones, the first (transition) elections are almost uniformly observed by outsiders whose job is to determine whether the election meets democratic standards. In Latin America since the 1990s, the work of ensuring electoral probity has been increasingly assumed by domestic groups. These nonpartisan organizations not only report on the conduct of elections but also give many citizens a solid grounding in the mechanics of elections. Further, they are becoming institutionalized: in Mexico, the Alianza Cívica (Civic Alliance) has monitored the last three presidential elections as has its Nicaraguan counterpart, Ética y Transparencia (Ethics and Transparency).

Political Parties

Political parties are not only essential parts of democracy: in their guise as organizational weapons, they are critical elements of any political system.

Table 6.3. Electorally Significant Political Parties Formed Pre-1970

Country	Party
Argentina	Radicals and Peronistas
Bolivia	MNR (Movimiento Revolucionario Nacional/National Revolutionary Movement)
Chile	Socialists and Christian Democrats
Colombia	Conservatives and Liberals
Costa Rica	PLN (Partido Liberación Nacional/National Liberation Party)
Dominican Republic	PRD (Partido Revolucionario Dominicano/Dominican Revolutionary Party)
Honduras	Conservatives and Liberals
Mexico	PRI (Partido Revolucionario Institucional/Institutional Revolutionary Party) and PAN (Partido Acción Nacional/National Action Party)
Paraguay	Colorados and Liberals
Peru	APRA (Alianza Popular Revolucionaria Americana/American Patriotic Revolutionary Alliance)
Uruguay	Blancos and Colorados

There are very few polities without parties. Military dictatorships often suspend them; traditional and absolute monarchies, such as Saudi Arabia or Qatar, ban them;[18] but otherwise, parties are part of politics everywhere. They have been part of the political scene in all Latin American countries since independence, giving them a pedigree as long as can be found anywhere in the world. Yet studies comparing Latin American parties to those in Europe, North America, or even other developing countries are scarce.

A partial explanation exists in the tendency of political science to concentrate the comparative study of political parties on Europe, leaving Latin America as a residual category of interest principally to Latin Americanists.[19] Perhaps more important is the fact that, even for Latin Americanists, parties in the region did not seem to do what parties in democracies were expected to do. Looking back to 1977, the apex of authoritarianism in recent Latin American history, finds only three countries where open elections decided who governed: Colombia, Costa Rica, and Venezuela. Whatever parties did then, most of them did not run in elections.

With the arrival in Latin America of the Third Wave of democracy in the 1980s, that changed. Parties had to develop electoral skills, as well as learn how to forge coalitions, produce coherent policies to meet public demands, and either manage the governing of a country or oppose a government in innovative ways that did not include violence. Some already had these skills, whereas others had to pick them up. Unsurprisingly, some parties have made the adjustment better than others. And some of the longer-established parties are in the ranks of those which have encountered problems.

The Current State of Parties

There are a good number of long-lived Latin American parties that continue to do well in the twenty-first century. Some of these, among them Costa Rica's Partido Liberación Nacional (PLN, or National Liberation Party), the Chilean Socialists and Christian Democrats, Liberals and Conservatives in Colombia, Peru's Alianza Popular Revolucionaria Americana (APRA, or American Popular Revolutionary Alliance), and Uruguay's Blancos and Colorados have long histories of democratic electoral activity. Others, such as Mexico's Partido Revolucionario Institucional (PRI, or Institutional Revolutionary Party), Paraguay's Colorados, and the Liberals and Conservatives of Honduras have been around a long time but are either recent converts to electoral democracy or never had much chance to develop democratic skills due to frequent military coups. A few, like the two sets of Liberals and Conservatives, and the Blancos and Colorados, reach back to the nineteenth century. All the same, a list of the parties formed before 1970 that are still among the two or three most important in their countries produces a somewhat disappointing inventory, because nearly half Latin America's nations are not on it (Table 6.3).

Some of the parties in Table 6.3 have always been electoral parties: the Argentines, the Chileans, the Costa Ricans, the Dominicans, the Peruvians, and the Uruguayans. Others, like the Colombians, have been mainly electoral organizations but fought bloody civil wars against each other from shortly after independence until the 1950s. The Hondurans are somewhat similar because those two parties were often vehicles for *caudillos* until the 1980s. Paraguay's Colorados were the party of General Stroessner, the country's dictator for 35 years. Bolivia's MNR, however, arose as a revolutionary party, and the PRI was Mexico's official governing party for seven decades. Yet all now contest free elections, winning some and losing others. In a number of cases, the party has changed its function.

Just as a number of parties have survived, some have failed. The most notable casualties are Venezuela's Acción Democrática (AD, or Democratic Action) and Comité para Electores Independientes (COPEI, or Committee of Independent Electors). They were the lynchpins of what most commentators saw as a robust democracy that was launched in 1958. However, by the 1990s both were living on borrowed time and after the landslide victory of outsider Hugo Chávez in 1998, neither was more than a shadow of its former self. The fate of the Partido Unidad Social Cristiana (PUSC, or Social Christian Unity Party) in Costa Rica was equally dramatic. Three of the four presidents of Costa Rica between 1990 and 2006 carried the PUSC's colors, but in 2006 the party garnered but 3.55 per cent, of the presidential vote and 7.8 per cent of the legislative. In this case, the cause of the party's slide may be found partly in the fact that two of three former chief executives from the PUSC have served prison terms for corruption and that the third, himself under investigation for allegedly violating election spending rules, was widely adjudged Costa Rica's least effective president in 30 years. Individual parties can thus deinstitutionalize and decompose.

What the two sets of cases just presented suggest is that while political parties are well-established political actors, neither individual parties nor any particular role for parties (electoral, revolutionary, dictatorial) is a permanent, institutionalized feature of a given system. As was noted in Chapter 4, institutions start out as instruments, tools to do a job. The fundamental job of a party is to win, organize, and exercise power, and it is a job that can be done in myriad ways. Three new parties, all parts of peaceful revolutions, demonstrate one alternative.

Hugo Chávez of Venezuela, Evo Morales of Bolivia, and Rafael Correa of Ecuador represent a trend in Latin American political parties (and political leadership) that is both new and old. The old part is that all three are personalistic leaders with parties that are their personal political vehicles, advancing a populist agenda that puts them on the side of the people against the interests—the powerful, sometimes referred to in North American populism as "the aristocrats, the plutocrats, and all the other rats!"—and who turn elections into plebiscites on themselves. What is new is more significant, because these three presidents who claim to be leading peaceful revolutions are using parties as mechanisms to win legitimate power through elections. Even if their parties did nothing but mobilize each president's supporters to campaign and vote for him, it would be a task familiar to other parties throughout the democratic world. In fact, it would not be greatly different from the role assumed by parties in Canada and the United States. However, in the past, strong leaders—for example, Argentina's Juan Domingo Perón—have used parties to secure their personal dominance.

As parties rise, fall, or simply reshape themselves to meet new challenges, party systems change too. Party systems are defined by the number of parties with real influence, patterns of party support, the presence or absence of antisystem parties that oppose the regime, and how stable those elements are. However, they also change as the general framework for a country's politics is altered. In the 1980s, for example, Venezuelan politics was defined by vigorous competition between AD and COPEI, whereas in the first decade of the twenty-first century, Chávez's Movimiento V (Quinta) República (MVR, or Movement for the Fifth Republic) is the dominant force in national politics. The change came about due to the weakening of the two formerly dominant parties and the rise of the charismatic and energetic President Chávez, who has rebuilt the country's political system to promote his values and secure ends he believes vital. So of course the party system changed.

This sounds like common sense, but political science has at times become infatuated with stability and seen party system realignment and restructuring as symptoms of terminal illness. Though they can be, it is more probable that what we are seeing in the early 2000s does not presage disaster. Rather, changes in parties and party systems, like the ongoing reconfiguration of the machinery of government occurring in many countries, might better be conceived of as sequels to the political and economic changes of the final 20 years of the last century, which are treated in Chapters 7 and 8.

Conclusion

Although the machinery of government and other formal political institutions tend toward stability and do not change much or do so quickly under normal circumstances, they are not static. If they did not evolve or sometimes undergo a complete overhaul, they would eventually stop working. Over the last three decades, however, all the nations of Latin America, even Cuba, though to a lesser degree, have been particularly active in re-engineering their governmental organizations and structures. At the same time, most of the 20 have also seen substantial reconfigurations of their political parties, as old parties decline, new ones emerge, and the balance of power among parties shifts.

On balance, the changes are positive. One of the great tragedies of Latin American history is that the strongest political institutions in most of the region's nations have done less to diffuse authority and empower citizens than to concentrate authority and marginalize citizens politically. However, the trend toward accepting that elections decide who governs may be a sign of a new order. The central characteristic of this new regime is emerging as the deinstitutionalization of violence as a legitimate political instrument. This is not yet democracy, but it is a necessary first step.

Formal political institutions have contributed to this transformation and will be critical to what happens next. If the machinery of government is designed and run to accommodate more interests, and if parties do not seek only short-term gains, it should be possible to build on the foundation that has been laid. Badly designed structures and processes, and parties pursuing nothing but their own self-interest, though, could slow, stop, or reverse existing trends.

Further Readings

Gandhi, Jennifer. *Political Institutions under Dictatorship*. New York: Cambridge, 2008.

Lora, Eduardo (Ed.). *The State of State Reform in Latin America*. Stanford, CT: Stanford University Press, 2007.

Rhodes, R.A.W., Sarah A. Binder, and Bert A. Rockman (Eds.). *The Oxford Handbook of Political Institutions*. Oxford: Oxford University Press, 2006.

Discussion Questions

①   Governments are forever reconfiguring the official structures within which they work. Why would this task interest politicians? How much of their motivation comes from partisan ends? How much derives from wanting to make it easier to achieve some desired policy goal—for instance, addressing climate change? How much is the product of the search for general organizational efficiency? Might one of these elements count for more in the hypothetical average Latin American country than in Canada or the United States? How could we find out?

②   It is often said that Latin American governments are cursed by weak institutions. How would we find out whether the governmental institutions of a particular country are strong or weak? How would you define the terms? How would you measure strength and weakness?

Notes

1. That, at least, is the ideal. Sometimes, however, there has arisen "party-state" confusion. This can be as familiar as governing parties scheduling public works projects just before elections, which is probably unfair but not a threat to democracy, but it can also include legislating specifically to harm opponents or using the courts to harass them.

2. Eric Mintz, David Close, and Osvaldo Croci, *Politics, Power and the Common Good: An Introduction to Politics*, 2nd ed. (Toronto: Pearson Education Canada, 2008) 29.

3. Mintz, Close, Croci, *Politics*. 29.

4. Until coming under pressure from the US Drug Enforcement Agency toward the end of the last century, Bolivia had always allowed the cultivation of coca for local use. Native Bolivians have always chewed coca leaves to relieve hunger, and a tea made from the leaves is used as an antidote for altitude sickness.

5. This was also true of the Federation of the West Indies, which lasted from 1958 to 1962.

6. Edward L. Gibson and Tulia Falletti, "Unity by the Stick: Regional Conflict and the Origins of Argentine Federalism," *Federalism and Democracy in Latin America*, ed. Edward Gibson (Baltimore, MD: Johns Hopkins University Press, 2004) 226–254. Military governments, however, were highly centralized.

7. On accountability, see Andreas Schedler, Larry Diamond, and Marc F. Plattner, eds., *The Self-Restraining State: Power and Accountability in New Democracies* (Boulder, CO: Lynne Rienner Publishers, 1999).

8. For an introduction to the debate over the virtues of presidential versus parliamentary government, see Juan Linz and Arturo Valenzuela, eds., *The Failure of Presidential Democracy: The Case of Latin America* (Baltimore: Johns Hopkins University Press, 1994) and José Antonio Cheibub, *Presidentialism, Parliamentarism, and Democracy* (New York: Cambridge University Press, 2007).

9. Bernardo Kliksberg, "Public Administration in Latin America: Promises, Frustrations and New Examinations," *International Review of Administrative Sciences* 71:2 (2005): 312.

10. Kilksberg, 324.

11. The list obviously is taken, with some modifications, from John Stuart Mill, *Considerations on Representative Government*, 1861 (Whitefish, MT: Kessinger Publishing, 2004).

12. The material is drawn from David Close, *Nicaragua: The Chamorro Years* (Boulder, CO: Lynne Rienner Publishers, 1999), 164–66 and Gabriel Alvarez Arguello and Joan Vintró Castells, "Constitutional Evolution and Institutional Change in Nicaragua," *The Sandinistas and Nicaraguan Politics Since 1979*, eds. David Close and Salvador Mati i Puig (University Park, PA: Penn State University Press, forthcoming).

13. On legislative strengthening in particular, see USAID Center for Democracy and Governance, *USAID Handbook on Legislative Strengthening* (Washington, DC: United States Agency for International Development, 2000). For an introduction to democratic strengthening more generally, see the following works by Thomas Carothers, *Aiding Democracy Abroad: The Learning Curve* (Washington, DC: Carnegie Endowment for International Peace, 1999) and *Critical Missions: Essays on Democracy Promotion* (Washington, DC: Carnegie Endowment for International Peace, 2004).

14. David R. Dye, *Democracy Adrift: Caudillo Politics in Nicaragua* (Managua, NI: Prodeni, 2004); see also Elena Martinez Baharona, "Nicaragua's Politicized Judiciary." *The Sandinistas and Nicaraguan Politics Since 1979*, eds. David Close and Salvador Mati i Puig (University Park, PA: Penn State University Press, forthcoming).

15. For details, see David Dye and David Close, "Patrimonialism and Economic Policy in the Alemán Administration," *Undoing Democracy: The Politics of Electoral Caudillismo*, eds. David Close and Kalowatie Deonandan (Lanham, MD: Lexington Books, 2004) 119–141 and David Close, "President Bolaños Runs a Reverse, or How Arnoldo Alemán Wound Up in Prison," *Undoing Democracy*, 167–181.

16. For background material on Pinochet, see Roger Burbach, *The Pinochet Affair: State Terrorism and Global Justice* (London: Zed Books, 2003); Madeleine Davis, ed., *The Pinochet Case: Origins, Progress, and Implications* (London: Institute of Latin American Studies, 2003); and Naomi Roht-Arriaza, *The Pinochet Effect: Transnational Justice in the Age of Human Rights* (Philadelphia: University of Pennsylvania Press, 2005).

17. Eric Bjornlund, *Beyond Free and Fair: Monitoring Elections and Building Democracy* (Washington, DC: Woodrow Wilson Center Press; Baltimore: Johns Hopkins University Press, 2004); also Neil Nevitte and Santiago Canton, "The Role of Domestic Observers," *Journal of Democracy* 8:3 (July 1997): 47–61.

18. For completeness, it should be noted that the Vatican City also is governed without political parties.

19. Richard Gunther, José R. Montero, and Juan José Linz, eds., *Political Parties: Old Concepts and New Challenges* (Oxford: Oxford University Press, 2002) is a good summary of current thinking and research on political parties.

7

Democracy and Democratization

For most of recorded history, people have been ruled. They have not governed themselves. Thus democracy is not the historic default option for a political regime. People living in long-established democracies, such as Canada or the United States, may find this counterintuitive, but it is the historical record. To use the language of historical institutionalism, democracy is an off-path change and a big one.

Not only have most people not governed themselves through the ages, but history also suggests that authoritarian governments have been the norm. Authoritarian government is the label under which political science currently groups all governments that rely on arbitrary rule not constrained by the law. Thus, the category includes bloodthirsty dictatorships as well as polities that treat their citizens benignly but engage in electoral fraud and administrative malversation more generally. Giving everyone equal rights, treating all with equal respect, and limiting the use of coercion to enforce the government's will are fairly new ideas.

To complicate matters further, what counts as a democracy is constantly changing and, more importantly, is dramatically different from what it was a century ago. Take the simple doctrine of one person, one vote. Not only was it one *man*, one vote until the arrival of women's suffrage, but the slogan was not applied across the board. The United States granted full and unrestricted suffrage to all its citizens, other than certain classes of prisoners, in 1965, when the Voting Rights Act became law. Canadians will be pleased to know that they achieved universal suffrage a full five years before the Americans, when, in 1960, Indians living on government reserves got the vote. Yet nobody thought Canada or the United States to be anything but democracies in the 1950s.

Obviously, democracy is a complex affair in both theory and practice. Accepting this, however, does not change the fact that Latin America has not done well in creating and sustaining democratic governments. Even if we exclude from consideration the first 50 years of independence, to 1875, to account for the age of *caudillos* (Chapter 4) and allow some time for the nations to get democratic government right, the region's record is hardly inspiring. Political scientist Peter H. Smith presents data indicating that of the 1919 country-years from 1900 to 2000, 47 per cent were accounted for by autocratic governments, 18 per cent by constitutional oligarchies, 10 per cent by semidemocracies, and 26 per cent by electoral democracies.[1] Yet we could apply the same calculus to Spain and Portugal and find something not too different, as electoral democracy only became established there in the last quarter of the twentieth century. Once again, it is the handful of historic democracies,[2] those with electoral democratic rule throughout the twentieth century—except when under military occupation during war—that are the outliers.

Putting Latin America into global context shows that the region does not suffer from some antidemocratic pathology. The 20 republics are not alone in the world as relatively recently arrived democracies. What does set them apart from all but a few others is their lack of a recent colonial history. By 1825, 17 of these 20 countries were independent; the 18th, the Dominican Republic, in 1844; the 19th, Cuba, gained formal independence in 1898; and the 20th, Panama, in 1903. The question this chapter asks has two parts: why did democracy come late to Latin America and will it be sustained?

Before addressing those questions, though, there is another, more central one: why should it matter whether a country has a democratic form of government? Everyone knows Sir Winston Churchill's quip about democracy being the worst form of government, except for all the others. But what makes the alternatives less desirable?

Democracy, by allowing all adults who meet certain requirements (such as citizenship and age) to choose their country's rulers, allows for governments to succeed one another peacefully. In lands with long histories of revolutions, coups, and the use of violence as a political instrument, this is a signal advantage. But a well-functioning democracy goes further, for if it is to work as it should, people have to enjoy a wide array of political and legal rights, the media must be free, and political organizations need to be free to form and operate. Obviously, none of these rights and freedoms is absolute, but democracy requires that more be permitted than excluded. Put differently, democracy gives ordinary citizens tools they can use to claim and secure greater liberty and equality. So if democracy is a "hurrah word," there is good reason for it.

However, a working democracy needs more than just citizens: the state has to accept the same terms. It does so by agreeing to follow the directives of the electorate and to be bound more generally by the law. The state, which monopolizes the legitimate use of force and which directs the legally constituted instruments of coercion (police, military, intelligence services), cannot be compelled by force so to act, except in the rare cases of successful revolution. Rather, it has to accept the authority of *concepts*—nothing but ideas and words that convey control of the state to the mass of the people.

Further, the state needs a government structured to facilitate democracy. In practice, that means that there are ways for people to participate in government directly, mainly through elections and various forms of citizen action, and indirectly, via representative institutions. Setting up representative institutions means that other parts of government—especially the executive but also the courts—listen to them and agree to be overseen by them, just as representative bodies are counterbalanced by the other branches. This is hard to achieve. In fact, throughout history very few governments have greeted the prospect of democracy with hurrahs.

How Many Kinds of Democracy?

For much of its existence as a political concept, democracy was linked with class politics. Aristotle listed democracy as a corrupt form of rule because it was rule by the many in their self-interest. Elites subscribed to this view for centuries; however, contemporary views of democracy are more diverse and have a much broader empirical base.

Political science has accepted a procedural definition, also called a minimal definition, of democracy. In this view, democracy is first and foremost a way to select leaders. It was the economist Joseph Schumpeter[3] who first made a strong, sophisticated argument for a purely political definition. In operational terms, emphasizing the procedures used to make democracy work directs attention to the machinery used to organize and hold elections, assure citizens have access to enough information to let them make informed choices, count and report the results accurately, and see that the winner actually takes office.

This is a substantial task because the electoral process is complex. Voters have to register. Parties have to organize and get on the ballot. Poll workers have to be trained. Voting procedures—the form of the ballot and polling hours are two of many—have to be chosen. The electoral system—proportional representation, plurality, or a mix—must be selected. All this has to happen before the vote is held, counted, and reported. Further, holding free, meaningful elections requires that guarantees of free speech and assembly are applied, and that voters exercise their franchise in a secure environment free from intimidation or threats of reprisals. And they must be decisive: the winner takes office and governs for his or her constitutionally stipulated term.[4] Those are significant prerequisites.

Nevertheless, emphasizing elections has advantages. It focuses attention on what is arguably the central feature of democratic politics, namely being able to vote someone out of or into office. As voting is the peak of most individuals' political involvement, an electoral focus also reflects the reality of citizen participation. And as elections put parties, platforms, and campaigns into the spotlight, they necessarily bring in policy issues and make us think about the media's political role.

Electoral-centered definitions of democracy derive from the theory of liberal democracy. This is the democratic tradition of Canada and the United States, whose origins are in seventeenth- and eighteenth-century

Western Europe. At the core of this philosophy is the idea of individual equality that gets practical recognition in what would become legal and political rights applied to all men and women. Although liberal democracy per se does not address questions of social and economic equality, its advocates assume that people will use the legal and political right to press for economic and social rights.[5]

However, there are other democratic traditions with different conceptions of democracy. These alternatives all point in one way or another to viewing democracy as more than a means of selecting leaders, even as more than a political theory. These stress economic and social democracy and judge the quality of a democracy by the socioeconomic outcomes it achieves rather than its procedures for processing inputs. Often, political systems that seek democratic outcomes are called *real democracies*, while those that focus on procedures are labeled *formal democracies*. Formal democracy is what is found on the books and only on the books. This was the case in much of Latin America for many years: constitutions replete with grand-sounding guarantees of rights and liberties, and manifold opportunities for citizen participation that were never applied. In this, they were like the Soviet constitution of 1936, which guaranteed every political right imaginable at the height of Stalin's terror.

A democracy that is only formal scarcely qualifies as a democracy. However, disregarding processes is dangerous. Although democratic outcomes, in the form of greater economic and social equality among people, are clearly desirable and something any democracy worthy of the name should work toward, too many regimes that boast of their democratic results—such as health care, education, an egalitarian distribution of income, and real opportunities for women and minorities—have one-party states that make it impossible for their highly equal citizens to expel them from office.

Recently, the United Nations Development Program (UNDP) published *Democracy in Latin America*,[6] which develops the concept of a citizens' democracy. The document speaks of Latin America moving from a voters' democracy, built on what it terms "political citizenship," to a broader citizens' democracy. The starting point is politics, and within the political sphere the foundation of such a democracy is built on free and fair elections, with universal suffrage, and elected public officials able to take office and serve a full term. Here, the 18 countries surveyed (all but Cuba and Haiti) do well. That said, there are some problems with weak judicial independence, oversight agencies (comptrollers or auditors) that are not as strong as might be desired, and the mechanisms of direct democracy that are still not widely employed.[7]

The UNDP finds what it styles "civil citizenship"—the rule of law (which demands that government be as fully subject to the law as any citizen), functioning and enforceable guarantees of personal freedoms, personal security, and freedom of information—to be more problematic. This is not for want of a legal framework but rather because there are areas in which progress toward real equality before the law has been slow. There are similar problems in the sphere of social citizenship—the system of social services and supports for citizens. This area is proving problematic in no small part because the dominant economic policy since the 1980s has stressed a smaller state sector and balanced budgets.[8] As result, those who need social supports to be active citizens are at a disadvantage.

What the UNDP proposes is a view of democracy that goes beyond elections and that sees democracy's political component as only one part of the concept. The citizens' democracy it envisions conceives of democracy as a way to organize and manage a society to make it easier to extend and safeguard individuals' rights and freedoms. As this necessarily involves a substantial role for government, it stresses democracy's political content more than some other views. And while the UN agency's notion of citizens' democracy is far from being a reality in Latin America, there is movement toward that end.

Having at least two notions of democracy present in discussions of Latin American politics raises serious questions for political science and for anyone interested in how governments work. From one angle, the debate is positive, because it reminds us that democracy has many components. However, it also complicates attempts to analyze trends in countries throughout the region, as changing the definition of democracy can alter a study's conclusions. It would be tempting to consign this issue to the realm of scholarly disputes, but doing so would affect our understanding of both how governments work in Latin America and what democracy can be expected to do anywhere.[9]

Latin America's Experience with Democracy

In looking at Latin America's experience with democracy, we should recall that it is really only since 1945 that the majority of the world's states and political leaders have embraced even the notion of democracy. Latin America was actually ahead of the curve, because, since independence, its principal models were the French and American revolutions. Thus the principles of democracy and liberty have always been part of the region's political discourse, even if not always of its practice. Once past the era of *caudillo* rule, though, the road away from authoritarianism opened, and tentative steps were taken toward full enfranchisement, broad participation, increasing equality, and extending the reach of the rule of law.

This first step has many names but *civic oligarchy* and *oligarchic democracy* are the best known and the most descriptive. The system's oligarchic label came from its domination by elites and its maintenance of a restrictive franchise, often based on literacy. Its civic side refers to the elite's acceptance of electoral outcomes, although this meant acknowledging that some degree of manipulation, such as vote-buying, was normal practice. Of course, it was the acceptance of electoral outcomes that earned it the adjective *democratic*. An example will show how this system worked.

From 1858 to 1893, Nicaragua was known as "the Switzerland of Central America," because of its stable, effective government. This system emerged after 37 years of nearly constant warfare, the last two of which saw the country occupied by US mercenaries who had come to Nicaragua to assist one side in one of the civil wars. Much of the underlying conflict grew from regional differences that were magnified through the lenses of ideology and personal animus. The failure of the Nicaraguan state, which is today's term for what happened, prompted the feuding regional elites to find a way to manage their differences without violence.

The regime that managed this had a government dominated by Conservatives (the Liberals had invited the mercenaries) and addressed through its constitution the two gravest problems of the era of instability.[10] First, it addressed the question of presidential succession by having the Senate propose the names of five of its members to be presidential designates. Each of these went into an envelope and the five envelopes went into an urn. A child picked two names, which were discarded, and then the remaining three envelopes were numbered 1, 2, and 3 at random, giving the country three successors, should the president resign or die in office. It then dealt with the problem of regionalism by demanding that each of the nation's 570 electors (out of a population of some 200,000) vote for two presidential candidates, one of whom could not be from the elector's district.

Scarcely democratic, the system ran by interelite accommodation, restricting popular participation, and balancing the interests of Nicaragua's two most important cities, León and Granada. It endured until 1893 and only fell when a president sought and won re-election. This produced a revolution, emerging from a region of the country not included in the 1858 system.

Political arrangements similar to the above were as close as Latin Americans got to democracy in the nineteenth century. Smith,[11] who traces the growth of electoral democracy in twentieth-century Latin America through three cycles (1900–1939, 1940–1977, and 1978–present), found no democracies—either electoral, featuring free and fair elections, or liberal, stressing individual rights—in the region until 1916. The dominant regime type was oligarchic, and even semidemocracies—systems that have either rigged elections or elections that do not actually decide who governs—did not appear until after 1910. It is only toward the end of World War II that the number of democratic states starts to rise. With the exception of a series of coups in the early 1950s, it continues this trajectory until 1960. At that point, the second cycle moves away from democracy and by its end there are just three electoral democracies: Colombia, Costa, Rica, and Venezuela. By the start of the twenty-first century, however, the picture had changed dramatically (see Table 7.1), yet the newness of the electoral democratic systems is striking.

Smith's third cycle corresponds to the arrival of Samuel Huntington's "third wave of democracy" in Latin America. Huntington argued that democracy did not expand at a steady pace across the world but rather grew in three large long-lasting waves, two of which ended in similarly large reverse waves.[12] The third wave began with the fall of dictatorships in Portugal and Greece in 1974, continued as Spanish fascism died with the dictator Francisco Franco in 1975, and by 1982 had landed in the western hemisphere. Today, only Cuba has withstood the push to adopt free, fully competitive elections.

Choosing a country's leaders by election and then actually letting those leaders govern does not make a country a democracy, however. There are

Table 7.1 Twenty-First-Century Electoral Democracies in Latin America

Country	Current democratic regime installed
Argentina	1983
Bolivia	1983
Brazil	1990
Chile	1989
Colombia	1990
Costa Rica	1953
Cuba	n/a
Dominican Republic	1978
Ecuador	2000
El Salvador	1994
Guatemala	1996
Haiti	1990
Honduras	1982
Mexico	2000
Nicaragua	1984
Panama	1994
Paraguay	1993
Peru	2001
Uruguay	1985
Venezuela	1958

Source: Author

questions of individual rights and freedom to consider, along with questions regarding the rule of law, controlling government officials, and the ability of citizens to use democracy to secure greater social and economic equality that must be considered. Nevertheless, seeing electoral democracy nearly universal in Latin America would have seemed impossible at the end of the 1970s. Before we all cheer, though, we should ask what a minimum of 20 years of democracy has brought to the countries of Latin America. Democracy has had the misfortune to arrive in three-quarters of the electoral democratic states of Latin America at the same moment as the austerity policies of structural adjustment. Structural adjustment receives fuller treatment in Chapter 8, so it is enough for now to observe that the policy radically reduced the state's economic and social presence. The areas the state vacated were colonized by the market. One result has been a generalized political weakening of the lower classes, who counted on their numbers to win redistributive policies from government. For many Latin Americans, democracy came to be associated with hard times.

This revised role for government, in many ways a throwback to the night-watchman state of the 1890s, carried a special label: *governance*. Governance has two meanings. One is more common in the developed world, where the term refers to how government coordinates its activities with those of non-governmental actors, from businesses to voluntary organizations. Because this version of the concept deals with government interacting with its non-governmental partners, its democratic character is unquestioned.

However, as the concept evolved in Latin America and other parts of the developing world, its impact on democracy was less clear. Governance there was not internally generated but externally imposed as part of struc-tural adjustment programs. Its content focused mainly on building stron-ger, more independent administrative institutions that are transparent and accountable. This is a more limited, even nonpolitical view of governance. And since what came to be called "good governance" came paired with deep cuts to government spending that shredded social programs and imposed disproportionate costs on the poor, it is easy to understand why Latin Americans might think differently about governance than North Americans do.[13]

In summary, the austerity programs, necessary to confront high infla-tion, led to a generalized reduction of the size and scope of government as the state gave back to the market (that is, private enterprise) many func-tions related to social and economic regulation. This has made the state less useful to those who lose more under the market than they do dealing with government. The overall result is the social deficit seen plainly in poverty figures, which showed 36.5 per cent of Latin Americans classed as poor by the United Nations and 13.4 per cent as indigent.[14] Translated into numbers, that means 195 million poor and 71 million indigent.[15] Those figures help explain why Latin Americans have a less sanguine view of democracy than we might expect.

Every year the polling firm Latin Barometer (Latinbarómetro) publishes a report that gives important information about the state of democracy in Latin America. Table 7.2 reports the levels of support for and satisfac-tion with democracy recorded in 18 countries (Cuba and Haiti are not included). The results, with an overall level of support for democracy of 55 per cent and satisfaction with democracy of 36 per cent, are lower than the values in the high 70 per cent range usually reported in the United States and Canada.

It is, of course, impossible to posit a causal relation between structural adjustment and its form of governance, on the one hand, and low levels

Table 7.2 Levels of Support for and Satisfaction with Democracy in Latin America, 2007

Country	Support (%)	Satisfaction (%)
Argentina	63	33
Bolivia	67	41
Brazil	43	30
Chile	46	36
Colombia	47	32
Costa Rica	83	47
Dominican Republic	64	49
Ecuador	65	35
El Salvador	38	33
Guatemala	32	30
Honduras	38	31
Mexico	48	31
Nicaragua	61	43
Panama	62	38
Paraguay	33	09
Peru	47	17
Uruguay	75	66
Venezuela	67	59
All Latin America	55	36

Source: Adapted from Corporación Latinobarómetro, Informe Latinobarómetro, 2007: Banco de datos en linea. Santigaro, Chile: Lationbarómetro, 2007, 80.

of satisfaction with democracy in Latin America, on the other. Yet it is equally impossible not to wonder if the economically straitened conditions in which free elections and improved legal and political rights came to much of the region will not affect citizens' opinions about democratic government for at least a generation. Democracy, like any other political system, has to prove itself.

From Authoritarian to Democratic Government: Democratic Transition

In 1978, *The Breakdown of Democratic Regimes* appeared,[16] examining how democratic political systems failed. Just eight years later, *Transitions from Authoritarian Rule* came out.[17] A great deal had obviously changed. The changes continued through the 1980s, Latin America's decade of democratic transition.

Political science developed a subspecialty in transitions during the 1980s and 1990s. Of special interest were democratic pacts and the resulting pacted democracies. In these cases, which were the dominant form in Latin America, democracy came not after a revolution or a mass popular movement, as was true in most of the ex-Soviet bloc, but after negotiations among a country's established elites—linked to an authoritarian system— and challengers who wanted democracy.[18] The essence of these deals was to protect the interests of the elites to a degree that convinced them to accept free competition for political power. Although pacts allow countries to establish democratic constitutions, they are not without their weakness. More than 20 years ago, political scientist Terry Karl[19] observed that pacts are made to fit the immediate needs of those who negotiated them. As time passes, not only do the needs of the original parties to the contract change, but new forces also emerge who are not easily accommodated in the pacted system. With a modicum of luck, the political system will have gained sufficient strength and flexibility to deal with new demands, but the case of Venezuela, whose pact Karl analyzed in the 1980s and which is discussed below, shows that this outcome is not inevitable.

One of the most striking facets of Latin America's democratic transitions was the success that the bureaucratic authoritarian military regimes of the Southern Cone (Argentina, Brazil, Chile, and Uruguay) had in arranging their exits. Even in Argentina, where the ruling junta provoked a costly war with Great Britain that ended in an ignominious defeat for the South Americans, the military wrote its own ticket to a substantial extent. When the military lost power in Argentina, Uruguay's dictators agreed to elections, but only after disqualifying perhaps the most popular and powerful contestant. The Brazilians, who had a carefully planned program of liberalization (*distenção*) and political opening (*abertura*) that was supposed to institutionalize the achievements of the military regime, did not secure their objective but the military did not leave in disgrace. And in Chile, where General Augusto Pinochet saw his 1980 constitution become the basis of a democratic regime, it seemed for a decade that the military would suffer no consequences for their years of iron rule. However, as already described in Chapter 6, in Argentina and Chile, at least, members of the bureaucratic authoritarian military governments are being brought to justice. The pacts the authoritarians struck in the 1980s have come undone.

Toward Consolidation?

The theory of democratic transitions developed in the 1980s and 1990s held that a transition ended with a transition election that returned a democratic government. After that, a country entered a phase of democratic consolidation. This concept refers to the process of strengthening the machinery of democratic government and the non-governmental institutions of democracy to the point where no important political actors espouse authoritarian alternatives. Democracy becomes the only game in town. In the past, Latin Americans had seen plenty of democratic governments rise on the ashes of authoritarian regimes and then fall soon afterward to a fresh dictatorship. Consolidating democracy would require stopping the pendulum that swung between authoritarianism and democracy.

At present, in 2009, the swings have stopped and electoral democratic regimes have remained even in the face of substantial governmental instability.[20] There is a further question, however, whose answer is only now taking shape: what does a consolidated democracy look like? It obviously has to focus on elections as the only way power can be gained and lost. Yet to work well, democracy needs the rule of law, accountable government and transparent administration, active protection of human rights, and the ability to assure that citizens' demands are fairly represented and responded to without discrimination.

Electoral democracy is the first step, and there is no guarantee that a given political system will go much beyond what is necessary to make an electoral democracy work. Nevertheless, this should not be disparaged. Elections give citizens the opportunity to participate in the most basic decision about government—who will run it. That people's choices may be more limited than they ought to be is a problem that all democracies have faced. Yet elections both contribute to making governors accountable to the governed and solve the problem of succession of rulers in a way that minimizes disruption and maximizes a ruler's legitimacy, assuming the vote is honestly run. Given Latin America's historic use of violence as a political instrument, the institutionalization of electoral democracy is very welcome.

Recently another issue has arisen in the context of consolidation, namely populism. At its simplest, populism is a political movement of "the people versus the interests," where "the interests" are "the aristocrats, the plutocrats, and all the other rats." This at least was its essence in North America, from its origins in the United States in the 1870s to the peak of its power in Canada in the 1920s and 1930s. Although North American populism had its antidemocratic facets, notably in the United States where it eventually became a vehicle for the politics of racism, it has a strong democratic character, seen in its promotion of policies to benefit farmers, who then formed the largest subordinate class in the two countries.[21]

However, populism has another connotation: that of a leader mobilizing a mass of people to take political power. There are certainly numerous examples of this kind of populism in Canadian and US history, but leader-based, top-down populism is more often associated with Latin America.[22] Juan Domingo Perón, twice Argentina's president (1946–1955 and 1973–1974), is generally thought of as the prototypical Latin American populist because he mobilized the Argentine working class against the country's establishment of landholders, financial interests, and the Church. Yet his character as a personalist leader who arrogated power to himself has over-shadowed his redistributive policies.

More importantly, it is this marriage of *caudillismo* and a mass fol-lowing that is the default definition of Latin American populism for most North Americans. And today it is regularly applied to Venezuela's Hugo Chávez and the rest of the Bolivarian Group: Evo Morales of Bolivia, Rafael Correa of Ecuador, and Daniel Ortega of Nicaragua (see Text Box 7.1). Although each of these leaders identifies himself as either a socialist or at least a radical opponent of neoliberal capitalism, the four are often presented as populists, and thus as strongman, *caudillo*-style leaders.

Each of the four leaders in the Bolivarian Group is a personalist leader, like old-time *caudillos*. However, the fact that all work within an elec-toral framework and that two of them, Ortega and Chávez, have accepted electoral defeat (the former in three presidential elections and the latter in a critical referendum), is more significant than their leadership styles. Instead of looking at these four leaders as throwbacks to an authoritarian age, we should ask if they could represent the democratization of a politi-cal style long institutionalized in Latin America.

Cases

The best way to get a sense of the state of democracy in contemporary Latin America is to survey a selection of cases. Ten countries are included in this survey, representing five distinct categories.

Pacted Democracy: Colombia, Venezuela, and Nicaragua

As political scientist Valerie Bunce has noted, all of Latin America's tran-sitions to democracy since 1978 grew from pacts.[23] Pacts, however, are not new to Latin America but have also figured in authoritarian and pre-democratic systems, and can still be used for ends potentially subversive of democracy. Two examples of transitional, even transformational pacts were struck in 1958: the Liberal-Conservative accord establishing the National Front in Colombia and the Pact of Punto Fijo that gave Venezuela more than three decades of stable electoral democracy. The most recent Latin American pact was concluded in Nicaragua in 2000 between the Liberals and Sandinistas, with the objective of reducing the accountability of government and cementing the duopoly over power enjoyed by those two parties. Although all have been alluded to previously, each merits a brief examination.

The Colombian case stands out, because the National Front put an end not to just the decade-long *Violencia*, a civil war that killed 200,000 people (1.5 per cent of the population), but also to the violent struggles

Text Box 7.1 The Bolivarian Model

When Hugo Chávez was elected president of Venezuela in 1998, he initiated the Bolivarian Model, named after Símon Bolívar. Chávez, whose only earlier try for power was a failed coup in 1992, built a political movement (Movimiento V [Quinta] República/Fifth Republic Movement) around himself, campaigned on a platform of completely changing the existing and desperately enfeebled political order, and promised to hold a referendum on whether the country should have a constituent assembly to write a new constitution. Chávez won the election, held a referendum in which Venezuelans voted overwhelmingly in favor of a constitutional convention, saw his party elect a large majority of the representatives to that convention, and emerged with a new constitution designed to let him build a Venezuelan state that would let him develop both his Bolivarian Revolution and twenty-first-century socialism.

In 2005, Evo Morales followed a similar electoral path to power in Bolivia and saw a new constitution drafted. A year later, Rafael Correa began the same process in Ecuador. The fourth member of the Bolivarian Group, Nicaragua's Daniel Ortega, won re-election in 2006 after three straight losses; although he began concentrating power in the presidency, by 2009 the former guerrilla commander had not changed Nicaragua's constitution. All four members of the Bolivarian Group appear to believe that political change beneficial to society's poor and marginalized can be achieved by taking power at the polls, and thus they have maintained a commitment to respect electoral results.[24]

It is still too early to make definitive judgments about the long-term evolution of this new model Latin American left. However, the fact that radical reformers now find it plausible to use elections to gain and shape power constitutes an important break with the past.

between Liberals and Conservatives that had brought so much death and destruction to Colombia since its independence. To keep the two parties from again resorting to violence to settle which of them would exercise power, the Liberal-Conservative pact declared that from 1958 to 1974—four electoral periods[25]—the two parties would alternate in the presidency, share legislative seats equally, as well as divide appointive positions within the state between them on an equal basis.

This pact's success is seen in the fact that the two main parties have continued to confine their struggles to the electoral arena. But it has also generated substantial costs. Not having to contest elections for 16 years meant that both the Conservatives and Liberals lost contact with citizens, especially the country's poor. Some have argued that this gave insurgent groups, such as the Fuerzas Armadas Revolucionarias de Colombia (FARC, or Revolutionary Armed Forces of Colombia), an opportunity to strengthen themselves and let new kinds of political violence—first guerrilla insurrection and later struggles between guerrillas and paramilitaries—take shape in Colombia.[26]

Venezuela's Pact of Punto Fijo was long seen as the model for democratic pacts everywhere. Before 1958, Venezuela had known only three years (1945–1948) of anything but authoritarian rule since independence. Punto Fijo was a classic pact of the genre. Engineered by the two biggest, pro-democratic parties (Acción Democrática [AD, or Democratic Action], the social democrats; and Comité para Electores Independientes [COPEI, or Committee of Independent Electors], who were Christian democrats), the pact excluded the communists, who had been in the forefront of struggles against dictatorships for years, gave the established elites (military, industrial, agricultural, ecclesiastical) guarantees that their interests would not be gravely harmed and extended benefits to the working class and peasantry by using petroleum revenues to fund redistributive programs.

Until oil prices plummeted in the 1980s, the political system built on the pact worked well. However, declining government revenues led to skyrocketing public debt and eventually to a structural adjustment program. Structural adjustment brought popular protests, Hugo Chávez's failed coup in 1992, and the collapse of the Punto Fijo system by 1998, when that same Chávez won the presidency in a landslide. This pact's weakness was the near-monopoly of power it concentrated in AD and COPEI, creating what came to be called a *partydocracy*. In the end, the two main parties had become so set in the ways of the pact that they were unable to mobilize their objectively substantial resources to address Venezuela's economic and social problems effectively.

Nicaragua has a rich if not always savory history of pacts. We have already seen the beneficial effects of that country's nineteenth-century deal between Conservatives and Liberals that brought Nicaragua three decades of peace and stability. However, *pact* became a term of opprobrium due to the use of pacts by the Somoza family dictatorship (1936–1979). The Somozas' Partido Liberación Nacional (PLN, or Nationalist Liberal Party) made deals with its opponents in the Conservative party that guaranteed the latter a share of legislative seats and government posts—first a third but later 40 per cent—in return for accepting fraudulent electoral results. The dictatorship got to claim that it ran competitive elections—the opposition won a third of the seats—and the opposition got what Nicaraguans call quotas of power—positions in government and access to patronage—that would let the party survive.

Nicaragua's latest experience with pacts began in 2000 when the governing Liberals (Partido Liberal Constitucionalista [PLC, or Constitutionalist Liberal Party]) and the largest opposition party, the Sandinistas (Frente Sandinista de Liberación Nacional [FSLN, or Sandinista National Liberation Front]) allied to pass a series of constitutional amendments and important changes to several ordinary laws. The effect of these changes was to reduce the accountability of the president, put ordinarily nonpartisan positions such as Supreme Court appointments under the direct control of the two parties, and make permanent the leading positions of the Liberals and Sandinistas (the two parties had taken 90 per cent of the vote in the 1996 national elections) by making it extremely difficult for other political parties to form. Unlike elections under the pacts struck between the Liberals, the party of the Somozas' dictatorship, and their Conservative opponents from the 1940s to the 1970s, though, electoral outcomes were not predetermined.

While the Colombian and Venezuelan pacts are now defunct, the Nicaraguan pact still functions. However, it did not produce the results that the more powerful of its signatories, the PLC, expected. The FSLN was able to combine clever use of its quotas of power with advantages gained from conjunctural crises within the Liberal party to gain control of the judiciary. This produced court decisions favoring the Sandinistas, increasing the power they controlled. The party then capitalized on an unprecedented four-way electoral race in 2006 to win the presidency. Now the senior partner, the FSLN continues to use its pact with the PLC to pursue its goals.

Pacts were hailed by theorists in the 1980s and 1990s as the way to move from authoritarian rule to democracy. Venezuela's experience suggests that even arrangements that succeed in establishing democracy can fail. The Colombian pact produced unintended consequences that arguably have weakened democracy there. And what has happened in Nicaragua may be taken as evidence that pacts between or among the powerful can be used to secure the goals of the pact partners instead of seeking the common good.

After Bureaucratic Authoritarian Military Dictatorships: Argentina, Brazil, Chile, and Uruguay

We have already seen that the four bureaucratic authoritarian military regimes of the Southern Cone made graceful exits from power. All four militaries were left unpunished for their many violations of human rights and with their institutional integrity undamaged. It is now more than 20 years since the last of these, Chile's Pinochet, surrendered office, and the political panorama existing in the four countries is hardly what the military wanted: in 2009, all four states are not only democratic but also have left-of-center presidents. This is not to say that the period since the withdrawal of the military has been easy in any of these states, as a quick examination of the four cases will attest.

Argentina has had the rockiest road. After its failed invasion of the Falkland Islands, a British possession claimed by Argentina, the military turned the state back to civilians. The first elections, in 1983, were won by Raúl Alfonsín, a Radical.[27] Alfonsín, however, had grave problems with a military that was near revolt over attempts to bring torturers to justice and an economy that spun out of control due to hyperinflation. In 1989, Carlos Menem, a Peronista, succeeded Alfonsín, settled the military question temporarily by giving most of those involved the functional equivalent of a pardon, and controlled inflation with a tough austerity program and by pegging Argentina's peso to the US dollar. Although this gave Argentina stable prices for more than a decade and made the country the darling of international bankers, when the US dollar rose in value through the 1990s, Argentina's industrial economy suffered and a grave crisis was at hand.

Elections in 1999 brought the Radicals back to power, this time in alliance with the left-of-center Frepaso (Front for a Country in Solidarity), and made Fernando de la Rua president. Almost immediately, de la Rua faced the consequences of Menem's refusal to alter his austerity policies: high unemployment and a 4 per cent fall in gross domestic product (GDP). The full crisis hit just before Christmas 2001, when fear of currency flight led to the government ordering banks to limit withdrawals and abandon the convertibility of pesos into dollars. Massive demonstrations followed, soon turning violent. De la Rua resigned; in fact five presidents served in December 2001. In 2002, even though parity with the dollar was abandoned, Argentina's GDP fell by 10 per cent and many turned to barter to get by. Through all this turmoil, however, Argentina remained democratic.

Things improved in 2003, and that year's election brought the Peronista Nestor Kirchner to office. Kirchner's heterodox, expansionist policies saw the economy grow by roughly 10 per cent annually, even though unemployment and poverty remained high. In 2007, Kirchner declined to seek a second term and was succeeded by his wife, Cristina Fernández de Kirchner.

Although less dramatic than Argentina's, Brazil's post-dictatorship history is hardly uneventful. Full civilian rule was restored via indirect presidential elections in 1985. The first directly elected president under the new democratic system, Fernando Collor de Mello, was impeached for fraud and would have been convicted had he not resigned just before the final vote in 1992. His vice-president, Itamar Franco, finished the term, with his greatest achievement being to have named Fernando Henrique Cardoso, one of the founders of the dependency school of political economy (Chapter 8), finance minister. Despite making his academic reputation as a radical sociologist, Cardoso masterminded a tough austerity policy (the Plano Real, after a new currency, the *real*) that stabilized the nation's economy and paved the way for his election as president in 1994 as a centrist.

As president, Cardoso accelerated the privatization program that was part of the Plano Real and succeeded in getting the constitution amended to allow him a second consecutive term. Although this was controversial, as Latin Americans have come to associate extended presidential terms with authoritarian rule, it allowed Cardoso more time to lay the foundations for a successful economic policy. Equally important, FHC, as he was called during his years in office, proved a successful diplomat. Being on good terms with world leaders such as Bill Clinton helped Cardoso raise Brazil's international profile, a trend continued by the country's next president, the leftist Luiz Inácio Lula da Silva, leader of the Workers' Party.

Winning the presidency on his fourth try (he had already lost to Collor and then twice to FHC), Lula surprised many observers. Not only did he continue the economic policies set down by his predecessor, but Lula was also able to take significant initiatives in social policy. Two of the latter have become well known: Fome Zero (Zero Hunger) and the Bolsa Família (Family Budget). Both are cash transfer programs that aim to increase the purchasing power of the poor and can be seen as steps toward a form of guaranteed minimum income. Fome Zero gives unconditional grants to very poor families to allow them to buy more food. Bolsa Família gives money to a broader group of the poor on the condition that their children go to school and get all their required childhood shots. Moreover, Lula assumed a leading role at the World Trade Organization conference in 2003, where he played a key role in bringing together other big developing countries, such as India and South Africa, to oppose the positions on agricultural subsidies put forth by the wealthy countries.

A relatively successful first four years did not spare Lula a run-off to win re-election in 2006. He has shown no interest in a third term, perhaps institutionalizing a two-term presidency in Brazil. That a labor radical can become president of Brazil without provoking a strong reaction from the military and can then secure policies that are both moderate and progressive should be seen as auguring well for the country's democratic prospects.

Despite having a long tradition as both a constitutional and democratic government, for the first decade following the restoration of democracy it seemed that Chile would be hobbled by authoritarian holdovers—elements of the Pinochet constitution of 1980 that limited the reach of democratic government. Among the institutions were lifetime senate appointments for ex-presidents, designated senators-for-life (which included retired chiefs of all the armed services), special privileges for the military (including designating their own chief of staff), and the binomial electoral system (Chapter 6) that favored parties of the right. Despite these advantages, since 1989 Chile has been governed by an alliance of parties of the left and center (the Concertación). The parallel alliance of parties of the right (the Alliance for Chile) has done well in municipal elections but has yet to take power nationally.

The remnants of the military regime began to weaken when ex-President Pinochet, then a senator-for-life, was arrested in London on charges of violating human rights (Chapter 6). Although the former dictator never stood trial, the fact of being charged and having to resort to a plea of mental incapacity to avoid judgment changed the correlation of political forces in favor of the left. The clearest proof of this was the approval of a series of constitutional amendments in 2005 that did away with all the authoritarian holdovers, except the binomial electoral system.

Although the right has yet to govern nationally in Chile, the ruling Concertación, which groups Socialists, Christian Democrats, and two smaller parties, has maintained substantially intact the free-market model installed during the dictatorship. Chile's economy is the most robust in Latin America and has made a successful adjustment to the demands of globalization. In particular, it has taken advantage of its location in the southern hemisphere to specialize in the provision of out-of-season fresh produce to the north. Nevertheless, the Concertación has restored enough of the Chilean welfare state to let the country reduce its rate of poverty to the lowest in Latin America: 13.7 per cent in 2006.[28] What the government has been unable to do is move the country from a resource-based to a knowledge-based economy or take effective steps toward redressing Chile's highly unequal income distribution.

Chile's current president, Michelle Bachelet, is not only the first woman to govern the country, but she is also a victim of torture whose father, an air force general, was killed by the dictatorship. In one sense, she can be seen marking the end of the dictatorship and the turning of a page in Chilean political history. However, the closeness of election results—the last two presidential races had to go to run-offs—points not just to an ideologically divided society but also to the existence of a significant reservoir of support for the military regime. The next step in Chile's return to democracy would seem to be electing a president from the Alliance, the coalition of the right, to permit the country's conservatives to demonstrate that they can govern effectively within a democratic order.

Uruguay, the last case, has the highest levels of support for and satisfaction with democracy in Latin America (Table 7.2). This is in keeping with the country's democratic reputation, which dates from the end of the nineteenth century and the election of José Batlle y Ordoñez as president. Under his guidance, Uruguay became known as "the Switzerland of South America," due principally to Batlle's construction of the continent's first welfare state. As a result, the country developed important social legislation, such as the eight-hour day, the recognition of women's rights, and Latin America's first divorce law.

Batlle's reforms were not universally welcomed, and opposition to them led to an episode of dictatorship. In 1933, President Gabriel Terra suspended the constitution, dissolved the legislature, and imposed strict press censorship. The 1930s, in fact, brought dictatorships, some of them admittedly short-lived, to all Latin American countries except Colombia,

Costa Rica, and Mexico. Nonetheless, Uruguay retained its reputation as one of Latin America's model democracies until the late 1960s, when escalating urban guerrilla warfare saw the government declare a state of emergency. Democracy came to an end in 1973 with the seizure of power by the armed forces. After losing a referendum in 1980 that would have enshrined a constitution drafted by the dictatorship, the military regime began a liberalization that led to the return of civilian rule in 1985.

Once again a democracy, Uruguay returned to its familiar two-party politics that pitted the more liberal Colorados against the more conservative Blancos. As in Argentina, the new government, presided by the Colorado Jorge Sanguinetti, had to address the question of whether members of the military should be prosecuted for human rights abuses. The administration granted the soldiers an amnesty to put an end to military unrest. In 1989, a public initiative led to the holding of a referendum on the amnesty, which upheld the government's original position. That was not the end of the story, for in 2006 and 2007 a number of leading figures from the dictatorship were brought to trial, bringing Uruguay into line with Argentina and Chile.

Uruguay's 2004 elections returned a president from outside the historic two-party framework, Tabaré Vázquez, who led his Frente Amplio (FA, or Broad Front), a left-wing coalition, to majorities in the house and senate as well. Among the members of the FA now in congress or the cabinet are some former guerrillas who have embraced democratic politics.[29]

To summarize, all four former dictatorships now have elected governments from the left and all but Chile have seen power change hands between parties. Moreover, the most obvious residues of their authoritarian pasts are disappearing.

A Special Case: Mexico

When the Partido Revolucionario Institucional (PRI, or Institutional Revolutionary Party) governed Mexico between 1929 and 2000, the country was known as "the perfect dictatorship." What made it perfect was that Mexico did not look like a dictatorship, even though it vested nearly total powers in the hands of the president, who was always a member of the PRI. In terms more reminiscent of the analytical discourse of political science, the PRI regime featured:

· a hegemonic party that monopolized state power by excluding others, while permitting a licensed opposition;
· control of the presidency, congress, state governors and legislators, and many municipal governments thanks to electoral rigging;

- a president who had tremendous power for his six-year term (including the power to name his successor) but who then exited political life;
- state control over important economic resources that gave the governing party an enormous pool of funds and jobs;
- a willingness to use coercion less frequently than in a dictatorship but more readily than in a democracy;
- an important reserve of legitimacy stemming from the PRI's identification with the Mexican Revolution and its strongly nationalist foreign policy.

So how could it lose power?

In one sense, the PRI's decline begins in 1982 when Mexico declared that it could not continue paying its foreign debt, then $82 billion.[30] This opened the door to structural adjustment policies that began shrinking Mexico's public sector, thereby reducing the PRI's ability to use government employment to co-opt support. As well, austerity policies made it increasingly difficult for the Mexican government to meet the demands of the poor. The more specifically political side of the equation began with the 1988 presidential election. Not only was this widely regarded as having been stolen by the governing party, but it also saw Cuauhtémoc Cárdenas, son of the legendary president Lázaro Cárdenas (1934–1940), lead his newly formed Partido de la Revolución Democrática (PRD, or Party of the Democratic Revolution) against the PRI.

Things got even worse for the PRI in 1994. On New Year's Day, when Mexico's entry into the North American Free Trade Agreement (NAFTA) with Canada and the United States took effect, the Ejército Zapatista de Liberación Nacional (EZLN, or Zapatista National Liberation Front) rebelled in the southern state of Chiapas, destroying the country's image as a peaceful, well-governed society. Just a few months later, the PRI's presidential candidate and assured winner of the 1994 elections, Luis Donaldo Colosio, was assassinated. He was replaced at the head of the PRI ticket by his campaign manager and ex-minister of education, Ernesto Zedillo.[31]

Zedillo, something of an outsider, then carried out electoral reforms that made possible the election in 2000 of Vicente Fox, the candidate of the Partido Acción Nacional (PAN, or National Action Party). In fact, the star of those elections was the Instituto Federal Electoral (IFE, or Federal Electoral Institute), which handled the vote flawlessly. The results were universally accepted, and Mexico launched forth into a new era of competitive electoral democracy with substantial optimism. After six years, however, Fox had proven to be less than totally effective in managing a minority congress and had been able to do little to address the needs of Mexico's poor, who had been paying for the country's economic restructuring since

1982. The outcome was the 2006 election, outlined in Chapter 1, which tarnished the IFE's reputation and left president-elect Felipe Calderón of the PAN with a weakened mandate.

Besides competitive elections, Mexico also has the makings of a three-party system (PAN, PRD, and PRI) and a highly fractionalized electorate. Combine this with the lack of run-offs in cases where a presidential election leaves the winner without a majority of the vote—something that was simply impossible while the PRI controlled Mexico's politics from 1929 to 2000—and a repetition of 2006's highly conflictive election is possible. The step forward of competitive elections has been matched by a step back in the form of electoral results that make Mexico a particularly difficult country to govern.

The Oldest Democracy: Costa Rica

Since the civil war of 1948, Costa Rica has been a democracy. By 2009, it had completed 60 years of continuous democratic rule, making it Latin America's oldest democracy. What is more, its democracy was, for more than 30 years, not just electoral but social as well. Its indicators of social well-being matched or exceeded those of Cuba, proving that social equity could be achieved through free elections and the rule of law. Costa Rica was a model for what should be possible in Latin America.

Behind this record of good government was the Partido Liberación Nacional (PLN, or National Liberation Party), which became the political vehicle for the victors of 1949. The party's chief, José Figueres, had led the insurrection against the government of the day and on taking power committed himself and his followers to a political regime inspired by the New Deal, the program of US president Franklin Roosevelt in the 1930s. The PLN identified itself as social democratic, expanded a welfare state that had been begun even before 1949, continued Costa Rica's tradition of emphasizing education, and during the 1950s and 1960s worked to bring down dictatorships throughout the Caribbean Basin.

To finance its ambitious social programs, the PLN and the various right-of-center parties who won the presidency at least every eight years[32] relied on foreign aid, as well as sales of coffee, sugar, and bananas—the classic basket of exports of an after-dinner country, the label often applied to exporters of those commodities. The oil shock of the 1970s hit Costa Rica hard, forcing it into a structural adjustment program. By the mid-1980s, the Costa Rican welfare state was but a shadow of its former self, and the country, led by the social democratic PLN, turned to embrace the market. Economically, this transition has been successful, as Costa Rican GDP per capita has grown rapidly and the nation has diversified its economic base to include a broad range of services, a substantial tourism sector, and some high-tech industries.

Politically, however, the picture is more somber. The two PLN governments of the 1980s stabilized both the economy and the political system, although only at the cost of shrinking the welfare state. Further, the leader of the second of these administrations (1986–1990), Óscar Arias, put Costa Rica in the international spotlight by brokering the Esquipulas Peace Accords that brought to an end the guerrilla wars that had rocked Central America during the 1980s.[33] After 1990, the magic ended. In Chapter 6 we saw that the three men who held the country's presidency during the 1990s had either served time for corruption or had chosen exile over facing Costa Rican justice. Further, along with the decline of the welfare state, the country has also seen its infrastructure start to crumble, crime rates soar, and its once-famed education system fail to produce the well-trained young people necessary to let Costa Rica shift into a knowledge-based economy.

There is, though, some good news. Costa Rican citizens remain stubbornly democratic and will mobilize themselves to defend what they think is right. For example, in 2000, massive demonstrations halted plans to privatize the state-owned telephone and electric company. Then in 2007, public resistance to the country's entry into the Central American Free Trade Agreement (CAFTA) forced a referendum, which the pro–free trade forces won.

The Outlier: Cuba

In a way, Cuba has always been Latin America's outlier. To begin with, it was the last country to attain independence from Spain (1898). Further, its independence was unlike any other in the hemisphere, as it was strictly controlled for three decades by the United States. Then, in 1959, Fidel Castro led his *barbudos* (bearded men) to power, nationalized US–held firms without compensation—although other companies whose Cuban assets were nationalized were paid. He soon afterward repelled an invasion organized by the CIA and then declared Cuba communist and allied with the Soviet Union. For the next three decades, Castro not only represented the reality of Third World socialism to many Latin Americans but also worked to extend the reach of Marxism by word and deed. Not only has the Havana regime defied Washington for a half-century by existing in the face of diplomatic pressures and an embargo, but during the 1980s many Cubans also fought and died trying to make Marxist regimes in first, Ethiopia, and later Angola, secure from their enemies.

Many thought that the days of the revolution and its leader were numbered when the Soviet Union, Cuba's biggest aid donor and customer, ceased to exist in 1991. Castro, however, proved resourceful. Cuba developed what has become a booming tourism sector, made important advances in biotechnology and pharmaceuticals, and experimented timidly with market reforms, which were soon rolled back. Nevertheless, Cuban living standards suffered. Food became more expensive and less readily available, and those who had access to dollars via remittances from relatives in the United States were able to access goods out of the reach of Cubans who depended wholly on their salaries in pesos.

What remained constant was the political system. Although Castro's government has provided Cubans with free health care and education, subsidized food, and a level of social and economic equality unmatched in the hemisphere, it has remained a one-party state. Cubans, that is, cannot turn the Communists out or even select a different cohort of Communists to govern them. And until illness and age forced Castro to leave office in 2008 (see Chapter 1), Cuba was also a personal dictatorship, like so many others that have flourished over the years in Latin America. To emphasize this side of Castro's politics, US sociologist Irving Louis Horowitz has long called Fidel a Communist *caudillo*.[34]

A window on political change opened in Cuba when Raúl Castro formally succeeded his older brother as president in February 2008. Obviously, the main lines of the regime remain unchanged. The Communist Party still holds a legal monopoly on state power and the security forces keep a tight rein on dissidents. However, there are signs of a relaxation of some of the most restrictive regulations of the past that will permit a more open society. In April 2008, for example, Cubans received the right to own cell phones and to travel abroad without getting an exit visa. Whether this leads to full competition for posts within the Communist Party or even interparty competition is a question that future events will answer.[35] The future will also tell us if the Cuban Revolution can be more successful than the Chinese in combining economic growth with social and economic equity.

Problems of Latin American Democracy in the Early Twenty-First Century

Twenty-first-century Latin American democracy is electoral democracy. This means that elections decide who governs. It need not and often does not mean that other attributes of liberal, constitutional democracy are present. For example, while governments and governors are held accountable at elections—vertical accountability—there are few mechanisms of horizontal accountability—courts, legislatures, other levels of government—to make them explain their actions and stay within the limits of the law between elections. As a result, citizens' rights may be less secure, courts may be less able to render justice, and legislatures may not actually represent the views of the people.

Counterbalancing these limitations are the highest levels of media freedom ever known in Latin America and the rise of an increasingly self-reliant and capable civil society. This latter point deserves elaboration.

Civil society is the name given to all the political organizations that are formed by citizens, are independent of government, and which pursue some public objective. Although there is no agreement regarding exactly what organizations get included in civil society—for example, whether formally constituted pressure groups belong—there is no question that democratic government demands that citizens be able to form organizations to pursue their goals and to have some reasonable chance of influencing government to turn their demands into law. Formal political institutions, governments and political parties, cannot monopolize the political sphere in a democracy. Too often in Latin America's past revolutionary governments have declared themselves vanguards, able to interpret the people's will without letting the people express that will freely, and even more conventional elected governments have sought all claims on the state channeled through them. This pluralization of political power in the region may be the most important and enduring effect of democracy's third wave.

If the pluralization of politics is to persist, however, it will have to offer opportunities to historically underrepresented and even unrepresented sectors, such as women, indigenous people, and the poor, to use government to advance their own agendas. Doing so will require that political parties both recruit more individuals from these groups to serve as legislators and incorporate them into the decision-making structures of the party and the policy-making structures of the state. Moreover, it will require that parties recognize that movement politics are legitimate vehicles for making demands on the state and for expressing collective interests. Put differently, the ambit of politics has to be widened to permit more entrants and deepened to let those entrants make new and possibly unconventional claims.

But what if reigning economic doctrine isolates most of economic policy from the public's demands? It is this question that the Bolivarian Group (see Text Box 7.3)—Venezuela, Bolivia, Ecuador, and Nicaragua—sought to address. Although their objective is admirable, the fact that each of the four countries builds its politics around a strong leader with a propensity for personalist rule is troubling. The United Nations Development Programme's proposal for a citizens' democracy, a way to organize and manage a society to make it easier to extend and safeguard individuals' rights and freedoms, is doubtless what all democrats, everywhere, want to see. Just how to configure a political system to make a citizens' democracy work is the central question, and one that political science can help answer.

Further Readings

Collier, Paul. *Wars, Guns, and Votes: Democracy in Dangerous Places.* New York: Harper Collins, 2009.

Phillip, George D.E. *Democracy in Latin America.* Malden, MA: Polity Press, 2003.

Discussion Questions

① Why does it appear that more Latin American states have not been more successful in establishing durable democratic government? What factors would have to be addressed to let this happen?

② We often distinguish real democracies, those that produce egalitarian social outcomes, from formal or procedural ones, those whose definition of democracy stops at free elections, legal equality among citizens, and the rule of law. Why should the two forms not automatically coexist? What would need to happen to make sure that they do?

Notes

1. Peter H. Smith, *Democracy in Latin America: Political Change in Comparative Perspective* (New York: Oxford University Press, 2005) 28.

2. These are Australia, Belgium, Canada, Denmark, France, Luxembourg, the Netherlands, New Zealand, Sweden, Switzerland, the United Kingdom, and the United States. None of them had universal suffrage in 1900, so democracy in these countries deepened and broadened throughout the last century. One could arguably include Norway in this group, even though it became independent of Sweden in 1905; Finland, which declared its independence from Russia in 1917; and Ireland, whose effective independence from Britain dates from 1920. The minimum is 12, the maximum, 15.

3. Joseph Schumpeter, *Capitalism, Socialism, and Democracy*, 5th ed. (London: George Allen and Unwin, 1976).

4. See Guillermo O'Donnell, "Democratic Theory and Comparative Politics," *Studies in Comparative International Development* 36:1 (2001): 5–36.

5. For a sophisticated liberal democratic defense of economic democracy, see Robert A. Dahl, *A Preface to Economic Democracy* (Berkeley, CA: University of California Press, 1985).

6. United Nations Development Program, *Democracy in Latin America: Towards a Citizen's Democracy* (New York: United Nations Development Program, 2004). http://democracyreport.undp.org; hereafter UNDP, *Democracy*.

7. UNDP, *Democracy*, 100–102.

8. UNDP, *Democracy*, 102–130.

9. There is a useful discussion of the question of conceptualizing democracy in David Collier and Steven Levitsky, "Democracy with Adjectives: Conceptual Innovation in Comparative Research," *World Politics* 49:3 (1997): 420–431.

10. The system is described in Arturo Cruz, Jr., *Nicaragua's Conservative Republic: 1858–93* (Houndmills, UK: Palgrave, 2002).

11. Smith, *Democracy*, 19–43.

12. Samuel Huntington, *The Third Wave* (Norman, OK: The University of Oklahoma Press, 1991).

13. Adrian Leftwich, "Governance, Democracy and Development in the Third World," *Third World Quarterly* 13:3 (1993): 605–624, treats this question.

14. Poverty and indigence are defined in terms of being able to provide a specific market basket of goods. A more familiar and striking definition classes as poor those living on less than $2 per person per day, while the indigent get no more than $1 per person daily. Poverty is examined in more detail in Chapter 8.

15. United Nations Economic Commission on Latin America, *Social Panorama of Latin America*, 2007 (Santiago, Chile: ECLAC, 2007). www.cepal.org/cgi-bin/getProd.asp?xml=/publicaciones/xml/9/30309/P30309.xml&xsl=/dds/tpl-i/p9f.xsl&base=/tpl-i/top-bottom.xslt; hereafter ECLAC, *Social Panorama*.

16. Juan Linz and Alfred Stepan, eds., *The Breakdown of Democratic Regime.* (Baltimore, MD: Johns Hopkins University Press, 1978).

17. Guillermo O'Donnell, Phillipe Schmitter, and Laurence Whitehead, eds., *Transitions from Authoritarian Rule* (Baltimore, MD: Johns Hopkins University Press, 1986).

18. Valerie Bunce, "Comparative Democratization: Big and Bounded Generalizations," *Comparative Political Studies* 33:6–7 (2000): 703–734.

19. Terry Karl, "Petroleum and Political Pacts: The Transition to Democracy in Venezuela," *Transitions from Authoritarian Rule,* eds. O'Donnell, Schmitter, and Whitehead (Baltimore, MD: Johns Hopkins University Press, 1986), 196–219.

20. The key case here is Ecuador, which has seen three presidents fail to finish their constitutional terms since 1996. Nevertheless, elections remain the only way to take power legally and legitimately.

21. Populist policies in North America included agricultural marking boards, cooperatives, and government-run public utilities to assure that farm families had electricity and phones.

22. For an introduction to Latin American populism, see Michael L. Conniff, ed., *Populism in Latin America* (Tuscaloosa, AL: University of Alabama Press, 1999).

23. Bunce, "Comparative Democratization."

24. The results of municipal elections in Nicaragua in 2008, which saw Daniel Ortega's Frente Sandinista de Liberación Nacional capture the mayor's chair and control of the councils in 105 of the country's 146 municipalities, have been criticized as fraudulent; see Roger Burbach, "Et Tu, Daniel? The Sandinista Revolution Betrayed," *NACLA Report on the Americas* 42: 2 (March–April): 2009. http://nacla.org/node/5562?editionnid=5552&issuename=Revolutionary%20Legacies%20in%20the%2021st%20Century&issuenum=2&volume=042&issuemonth=March/April&issueyear=2009&lilimage=.

25. It was extended until 1978.

26. Nazih Richani, *Systems of Violence: The Political Economy of War and Peace in Colombia* (Albany, NY: State University of New York Press, 2002).

27. The Radicals of Argentina (Radical Civic Union, or the UCR) are not radicals in the North American sense. They are more like the Liberal Party of Canada or the US Democrats—ideologically centrist.

28. ECLAC, *Social Panorama,* 54.

29. Martin Weinstein, "The Left's Long Road to Power in Uruguay," *From Revolutionary Movements to Political Parties: Cases from Latin America and Africa,* eds. Kalowatie Deonandan, David Close, and Gary Prevost (New York: Palgrave Macmillan: 2007), 67–80.

30. It would be roughly two and a quarter times that much in 2008 dollars. See Federal Reserve Bank of Minneapolis, *What Is a Dollar Worth?* www.minneapolisfed.org/Research/data/us/calc.

31. Mexico does not have a vice-president, thus there was no vice-presidential candidate to take Colosio's place.

32. Since 1949, no Costa Rican political party has held the presidency for more than two consecutive terms, eight years. The PLN, though, did control the legislature from 1953 to 1982.

33. The matter is discussed further in Chapter 10.

34. Irving Louis Horowitz and Jaime Suchlicki, eds., *Cuban Communism: 1959–2003* (New Brunswick, NJ: Transaction Publishers, 2003).

35. For a clear statement of what it would take for a one-party regime to be democratic, see C.B. Macpherson, *The Real World of Democracy* (Toronto: CBC, 1964).

8

Political Economy and Economic Policy in Latin America

Economics is concerned with how a society organizes the production and distribution of goods and services. It is easy to imagine how politics could affect economics. It is just as easy to envision how economics might affect politics. We use a number of different approaches when talking about the relation between economics and politics: textbook economics, economic history, economic policy, and political economy. Each needs an introduction.

Textbook economics are what professors teach and students learn in economics courses. They are based on several principles that are shared by all in the profession yet cover a vast array of concrete phenomena. Textbook economics are important not only because they are the foundation of how many of us understand the abstract workings of an economy but also because of their policy impact. Policymakers tailor their plans to accord with what economic theory tells them about how the economy works.

That is why it is important to remember that the economics found in textbooks is not always the same. In the 1950s, when political science began looking seriously at Latin America, economists in North America were generally Keynesians. John Maynard Keynes (pronounced *canes*) was a twentieth-century English economist who argued forcefully and successfully for an active government role in managing a country's economy. This was to be done by adjusting taxes, government spending, and interest rates to raise or lower spending by consumers and investors to keep an economy growing steadily. Keynesian theory came into vogue during the 1930s, when the then-current textbook model, classical free-market economics, had no solution to the Depression. However, when the Keynesian view of the world had no answers to the slump of the 1970s, it ceded its place in the texts to a revised form of free-market economics often called neoliberalism. To further complicate matters, Marxists had their own textbooks that patiently and persuasively explained why capitalism was destined to fail.

Economic history sounds simpler and safer. After all, history has already happened. However, the different theoretical orientations that populate economics have their own interpretation of history. To overstate matters, a Marxist view would stress class struggle and history's inexorable march toward communism, while a free-enterprise theorist would note the beneficent effects of the working of the unregulated market through time. Yet it is imperative to know economic history to properly understand the politics of a place, any place.[1]

History matters in economics just as in any other social science. That is because sectors of an economy rise and fall, as do regions of a country where those sectors are important. As Chapter 3 describes, elites linked to established sectors often maintain their political influence even as their economic weight declines. Of equal importance, long reliance on a particular economic sector, such as the automotive industry in Michigan and Ontario, can lead politicians to overlook opportunities for economic diversification or to protect an industry when it might be better to push it toward change. In any case, knowing the economic history of a country or an entire region of countries is an essential part of what is necessary to understand politics in Latin America.

Although economic theory and economic history are commonly used approaches to the study of the economics of Latin America, political scientists feel far more at home talking about *economic policy*. Obviously, this includes the national budget, but also takes in areas such as banking regulation, competition policy, and consumer protection legislation, to mention just a few. There are numerous ways to examine public policy, but one of the most common is to look at how Latin American governments have managed their economies—the ends sought as well as the tools used. And the central question there is how to account for changed policies.

In making Latin American economic policy, as in other areas of the region's political life, external models have had great influence. Sometimes these models have been adopted freely by national elites. This was true in the eventual triumph of free trade and Latin American nations' enthusiastic participation in the global economy as producers of primary products in the nineteenth century. However, at other times, especially since 1900, economic policy has been imposed by external forces, most often the government of the United States. Again, we see why a historical perspective on Latin American politics pays real dividends.

One lesson that emerges from this brief overview of approaches to studying the economic side of Latin American politics is that it would be self-defeating to try to treat politics and economics as distinct phenomena, separated by a firewall. Prescriptions for advancing the region's economic development have always recognized that government has a role to play, even when that role is limited to setting the rules that permit the economy to prosper. Yet much of political science forgets this. Only political economy bears the politics-economics nexus constantly in mind, because it is consciously interdisciplinary. Political economy examines how the structure of an economy (concentration of wealth, sectoral balance, and so on) affects what governments do and how governmental decisions (taxes, spending, and so on) influence how an economy works.

As with economic theory, history, and policy, political economy also divides along ideological or programmatic lines. One of these is the neo-liberal variant of free-market economics. It gives special attention to failed interventionist policies and has been prominent since the 1970s. Another variant is Marxist, and it obviously emphasizes the structural causes of capitalism's weaknesses. A third, older school is historical in orientation, and thus inclined to be less theoretical and favor description. This chapter tries to balance the contending views, which necessarily means that it comes out more descriptive than theoretical and does not fully embrace the positions associated with any particular school.

In fact, the aim of this chapter is to present the current state of the economies of both Latin America as a region and in a few selected countries. It will discuss questions of structure (for example, which sectors are rising or falling), performance (issues such as growth, poverty, and inflation), and policies (especially the theories behind the policies).

The Latin American Economy Today: Some Data and Interpretations

Sixty years ago, shortly after the end of World War II, although Latin America was a relatively poor region, that poverty was relative to Europe, North America, and Australia and New Zealand. Indeed, the wealthiest countries of Latin America were arguably better off than still-unreconstructed Europe, and even middle-income countries were ahead of Spain and Portugal. In the first decade of the twenty-first century, that is no longer the case. In fact, not only has Latin America been left behind economically by its former colonial masters, but even countries that six decades earlier were far poorer than anywhere in Latin America (possibly excepting Haiti), especially the nations of East and Southeast Asia, are also now better off. What happened?

Answering the foregoing requires three pieces of information. The first is simply the current economic status of the countries of Latin America. The second is similarly straightforward, as it concerns Latin America's historical economic status as a region. Only the last part is more complex, as it has to do with explanations for Latin America's economic performance and the related prescriptions for its improvement.

Data

Answering the first question—the current economic status of Latin American countries—is best done by considering national income statistics. These refer only to an economy's growth and how much bigger it has become, and need not say anything about its development or how diversified and sophisticated an economy is. The first set of statistics (Table 8.1)

Table 8.1 National GDP per Capita, 2005

Country	GDP ($US)	PPP ($US)	Classification
Argentina	4,728	14,280	Upper-Middle Income
Bolivia	1,017	2,819	Lower-Middle Income
Brazil	4,271	8,402	Upper-Middle Income
Chile	7,073	12,027	Upper-Middle Income
Colombia	2,682	7,304	Lower-Middle Income
Costa Rica	4,627	10,180	Upper-Middle Income
Cuba	n/a	4,500*	Lower-Middle Income
Dominican Republic	3,317	8,217	Lower-Middle Income
Ecuador	1,608	4,440	Lower-Middle Income
El Salvador	2,467	5,255	Lower-Middle Income
Guatemala	2,517	4,568	Lower-Middle Income
Haiti	500	1,663	Low Income
Honduras	1,151	3,430	Lower-Middle Income
Mexico	7,454	10,751	Upper-Middle Income
Nicaragua	954	3,647	Lower-Middle Income
Panama	4,788	7,605	Upper-Middle Income
Paraguay	1,400	5,070	Lower-Middle Income
Peru	2,838	6,039	Lower-Middle Income
Uruguay	4,848	9,962	Upper-Middle Income
Venezuela	5,275	6,632	Upper-Middle Income
Canada	34,484	33,375	
United States	41,890	41,890	
Portugal	17,376	20,410	
Spain	25,914	27,169	

* Estimate.

Source: Adapted from UNDP, *Human Development Report, 2007/2008.* 277–279; World Bank, World Development Report 2008, 333; and CIA *Factbook, 2008.*

Text Box 8.1 Measuring Income

The most common measure of income is gross domestic product (GDP). It is the market value of all final goods produced in a place during a specified time, normally a year, but occasionally a quarter. It also includes the value added at intermediate stages. Formerly, gross national product (GNP) was widely used. GNP is calculated by adding GDP to net income received by residents from nonresident sources (for example, foreign investments). A third measure, gross national income (GNI), is very similar to GNP and is used in some reports by the World Bank.

Any of these measures can be presented in nominal terms (that is, the value of a country's production expressed in an international currency, usually $US, at existing exchange rates). However, a better way to assess the standard of living that a nation's income provides is to use the purchasing power parity (PPP) exchange rate. This rate considers how much a given basket of goods costs in different countries in their home currencies. A simple PPP is the "Big Mac Index" used by the British magazine *The Economist*. It asks what McDonald's charges for a Big Mac in different countries and uses this as a rough-and-ready indicator of what the "real" exchange rate between two currencies should be. PPP-adjusted per capita income figures are especially useful in giving a more realistic picture of levels of well-being in poor countries, as a dollar or Euro generally buys more goods and services in a poor country than it does at home.

---

simply shows current figures for gross domestic product (GDP and for the purchasing power parity, or PPP value of that amount (see Text Box 8.1). Three points stand out. First, Latin America is substantially poorer than its two North American neighbors and its European colonizers. Nevertheless, the World Bank classifies all Latin American countries as either upper-middle-income or lower-middle-income countries, except Haiti, which is a low-income country. Second, nominal per capita incomes in Latin America understate the population's purchasing power, in some cases significantly. Third, per capita incomes vary widely among countries. Each point merits a closer look.

First, Latin America is home to middle-income countries, those with per capita incomes between $905 and $11,115 annually in 2005.[2] What is striking is that none of the countries makes it into the ranks of the wealthy. The economic historian Angus Maddison's data[3] show that in the past some countries did reach that plateau—for example, Argentina in the 1920s and Venezuela in the 1970s—but they could not hold their places. These are primary product exporters, and as world demand for their products goes, so go their economies. Or as an early twentieth-century Costa Rican president said, "Our best finance minister is a high price for coffee."

To the extent that this is true, a significant part of the region's economic prospects and problems are tied to foreign demand for raw materials.

A second point that emerges concerns the difference between nominal incomes and PPP incomes. There are only four cases—Chile, Mexico, Panama, and Venezuela—where the PPP is not at least twice the nominal income. This implies low consumer prices, but low consumer prices suggest the likelihood of low wages. In that case, most people will have little money with which to consume goods and services and drive the economy. This is consistent with the extreme levels of income inequality found in Latin America that we saw in Chapter 3.

Finally, if Haiti is excluded as an outlier, the top per capita income in Latin America (Mexico) is about eight times higher than the bottom (Nicaragua). In the old European Union (EU) of 15 countries, the ratio is little more than 5:1, with Luxembourg's $79,851 leading and Portugal's $17,376 trailing.[4] However, the new EU of 27 countries has Bulgaria at the bottom, with a per capita income of $3443, 1/23 of Luxembourg's. Thus there is a relative equality among Latin American states, which is consistent with all but one of them being middle income countries.

GDP is often used as the principal indicator of development, but it is better seen as an indicator of economic growth. That is, GDP tells us whether the economy is producing more or less activity that can be measured in money terms. It does not tell us whether there is new activity, greater efficiency, or whether the growth is the result of speculation or an international boom. Neither does it say anything about the uses to which income is put or how it is distributed.

Students of development, who examine how countries or regions increase their material well-being and make their economies more sophisticated, have always had reservations about using GDP, or any other measure of national income, to gauge development. Yes, income measures are easily available and are generally calculated the same way everywhere. Moreover, they are intuitively easy to grasp, as long as we accept that more money is better than less. Yet, as noted above, GDP can obscure important facets of a country's material status. For that reason, the United Nations Development Program (UNDP) developed its Human Development Index (HDI). The HDI combines measures of literacy and education, life expectancy, and GDP to get a broader picture of how development is progressing in a country.

Table 8.2 shows that although no Latin American country is classified as a high-income country by the World Bank (>$US11,116 per capita in 2005), eight make it into the high HDI rank. Although the benefits in terms of living standards of a high HDI are intuitively easy to grasp, higher levels of human development should also bring more purely economic benefits. A better educated and healthier population should give a country an edge in securing economic growth. This certainly has been the case of the Four

Table 8.2 Latin American Countries Classed by Income Category and Human Development Rank

Income Class/HDI Class	High	Medium	Low
High (>$US11,116)*			
Upper middle ($3,596–$11,115)*	Argentina, Brazil, Chile, Costa Rica, Mexico, Panama, Uruguay	Venezuela	
Lower middle ($905–$3,595)*	Cuba	Bolivia, Colombia, Dominican Republic, Ecuador, El Salvador, Guatemala, Honduras, Nicaragua, Paraguay, Peru	
Low (<905)*		Haiti	

* Annual per capita gross national income, 2005.

Source: UNDP, *Human Development Report, 2007–2008,* 230–232; World Bank, *World Development Report, 2008,* 333.

Asian Tigers—South Korea, Singapore, Taiwan, and Hong Kong—which grew rapidly in the last quarter of the twentieth century.

Historical Data

From the foregoing, it is clear that Latin America is a region of middle-income countries (19/20), which are also nations showing medium levels of human development (12/20). Compared to the world's high-income countries, this will not look very good. This brings us to the key point: namely, whether Latin American economies are performing satisfactorily, slowing down, or falling behind. Historian Stephen Haber asserts that the income gap separating Latin America and the North Atlantic nations first appeared in the nineteenth century and was maintained through the twentieth.[5] He observes that "[i]n 1800 per capita income in the United State was slightly less than twice that of Mexico and roughly the same as in Brazil. By 1913 US GDP was four times that of Mexico and seven times that of Brazil."[6]

Table 8.3 indicates that other patterns exist that suggest Latin America continued to fall behind, even in the twentieth century. It compares four Latin American economic leaders—Argentina, Brazil, Chile, and Mexico—to two Asian miracle economies, as well as to Spain and Portugal. Until 1960, the four Latin American countries, among the largest and most developed, compared favorably to their foreign competitors. However,

Table 8.3 Per Capita GDP in Four Latin American Countries, Japan, South Korea, Portugal, and Spain (in International 1990 Dollars[7])

Year	Argentina	Brazil	Chile	Mexico	Japan	South Korea	Portugal	Spain
1900	2,756	678	1,994	1,366	1,180	n/a	1,706	1,302
1920	3,473	963	2,130	1,823	1,696	1,081	2,712	1,290
1940	4,161	1,250	3,139	1,822	2,874	1,441	2,020	1,605
1960	5,539	2,335	4,320	3,155	1,476	1,005	3,022	2,956
1980	8,206	5,198	5,738	6,289	13,478	4,302	9,203	8,044
2000	8,544	5,392	9,539	6,877	21,069	14,343	15,269	14,022

Source: Adapted from Angus Maddison, *The World Economy.* Paris: OECD, 2006. 445–447, 520–522, 558–562.

over the next 20 years there are dramatic reversals. The wealthiest Latin Americans begin falling behind both the Asian and Western European comparative cases, and by 2000, the Latin Americans are left in the dust.

Obviously other countries could have been chosen and a different picture would have emerged. However, the turnaround relative to the late-industrializing Asians and the long-stagnant European former colonial masters is dramatic. More importantly, it suggests why the management of Latin American economies is a source of concern.

Poverty

Few still hold that poverty is a sign of divine disfavor. Rather, poverty reduction is a priority for most governments, in rich countries as well as in poor ones. In Latin America, addressing poverty became a pressing issue in the 1990s. The 1980s were the region's "lost decade," when the economies of all nations except Colombia experienced negative growth: in other words, their economies shrank. One result was extremely high levels of poverty and extreme poverty. In the 1990s, the International Monetary Fund (IMF) and the World Bank (WB), the international financial institutions (IFI) that administered Structural Adjustment Programs (SAPs), began demanding that poverty-reduction programs be included as part of the conditions governments had to meet to get loans.[8] Poverty had to be on the policy agenda.

In both the United States and Canada, measuring poverty is a controversial topic. In Latin America, although each country has its own poverty line, there are two measures that can be applied internationally. Each

Table 8.4 Poverty and Indigence in Urban and Rural Latin America (%)

	Total Poor*	Urban Poor	Rural Poor	Total Indigent	Urban Indigent	Rural Indigent
1980	40.5	29.8	59.9	18.6	10.5	32.7
1990	48.3	41.4	65.4	22.5	15.3	40.4
2000	42.5	35.9	62.5	18.1	11.7	37.8
2005	39.8	34.1	58.8	15.4	10.3	32.5

* Includes indigent.

Source: Adapted from, ECLAC, *Social Panorama of Latin America, 2006.* 59; and *Social Profile of Latin America,* 2005. 64.

distinguishes poverty from extreme poverty or indigence. One definition comes from the World Bank, and classes the proportion of the population living on $2 per day as living in poverty, and those living on $1 per day as living in extreme poverty (both as PPP figures). The other is set by the United Nations Economic Commission on Latin America (ECLAC, or CEPAL, its Spanish initials), which defines poverty as not having the per capita income to afford a market basket of basic goods (food, shelter, clothing) and indigence as falling short of being able to afford even food. Table 8.4 presents poverty and indigence data on Latin America, compiled from ECLAC statistics.

These data, especially the 1990 figures, point to the reverses suffered in the region during the 1980s as well as to the recovery since then. Yet it is disheartening to see that 1980 poverty levels were not bettered until 2005. For Latin America's poor, the lost decade became a lost quarter-century. Equally troubling is the persistence of indigence, above all in rural areas. Although these region-wide numbers are revealing, they necessarily obscure differences between nations. Table 8.5 presents poverty and indigence statistics for 18 countries. These show that a few countries—notably Brazil, Chile, Costa Rica, Ecuador, and Mexico—have made great strides in reducing poverty. Similarly, Argentina has regained ground lost in its 2002 meltdown and Venezuela and Peru are moving in positive directions. Unfortunately others—including Bolivia, Colombia, and Paraguay—have stagnated.

Although there is no ready explanation for this intraregional variation, there appear to be two factors in play. One is simply economic reactivation: growth has returned, even if not all countries appear to have shared equally in the recovery. The second is effective public policy. Here one can point to Chile, where two decades of governments attentive to the question of poverty have made an impact. Where both elements reinforce one another—once again, as in Chile, but also in Brazil and more recently

Table 8.5 Poverty and indigence in 18 Latin American Countries, 1990-2006 (% of Population)

Country	Around 1990*		Around 2002†		Around 2006‡	
	Poverty	Indigence	Poverty	Indigence	Poverty	Indigence
Argentina	21.2	5.2	45.4	20.9	21.0	7.2
Bolivia	52.6	23.0	62.4	37.1	63.9	34.7
Brazil	52.6	23.0	37.5	13.2	33.3	9.0
Chile	38.6	13.0	18.7	4.7	13.7	3.2
Colombia	n/a	n/a	50.6	23.7	46.8	20.2
Costa Rica	26.3	9.9	20.3	8.2	19.0	7.2
Dominican Republic	n/a	n/a	44.9	20.3	44.5	22.0
Ecuador	62.1	26.2	49.0	19.4	39.9	12.8
El Salvador	n/a	n/a	48.9	22.1	47.5	19.0
Guatemala	69.1	41.8	60.2	30.9	n/a	n/a
Honduras	80.8	60.9	77.3	54.4	71.5	49.3
Mexico	47.7	18.7	39.4	12.6	31.7	8.7
Nicaragua	73.6	48.4	69.4	42.4	n/a	n/a
Panama	39.9	13.1	25.3	8.9	30.8	15.2
Paraguay	43.2	13.1	61.0	33.2	60.5	32.1
Peru	n/a	n/a	54.8	24.4	44.5	16.1
Uruguay	17.9	3.4	15.4	2.5	18.5	3.2
Venezuela	39.8	14.4	48.6	22.2	30.2	9.9

* 1989–1993   † 2000–2002   ‡ 2005–2006

Sources: Adapted from ECLAC, *Social Panorama of Latin America,* 2005, 70–71; and *Social Panorama of Latin America,* 2007. 11.

in Venezuela—poverty can be reduced. Countries unfortunate enough to have neither experienced strong economic growth nor had governments pursuing sound and vigorous antipoverty policies have made less progress. What emerges from this overview of poverty is that simply depending on the tides of market forces to "raise all boats," as it were, is unlikely to make deep or rapid inroads into reducing poverty.

What Happened and What to Do About It

Deciding how Latin America fell behind is directly related to prescribing what Latin America should do to remedy its economic problems, from slow growth to poverty. Since independence, every country in Latin America has experimented with different policy frameworks and global approaches to development. These have had as their objective not just making countries richer (that is, raising national income) but also making economies more sophisticated and diversified. There has long been a sense that at least Latin America's big countries ought to be on the same economic and social level as the world's most advanced economies. That they are not is obvious, but why they are not is a perpetual dilemma.

Understanding what to do requires a sense of what has already been done—that is, you have to know what went wrong before you can fix it. It also helps to understand why things happened as they did. Addressing both issues requires looking at economic history and political economy. It will also demand anticipating some of the questions treated more fully and systematically in the next chapter, because a sense of how international economic relations works is needed too.

Positivism

In Spanish America, though not Brazil, roughly the first half-century after independence was the era of the *caudillo*, which was described in Chapter 2. Politically, the *caudillo* period was characterized by instability and recurrent warfare. Obviously, there were economic consequences. Investment, domestic and foreign, were withheld, capital was destroyed, lives were lost, and serious, systematic building of a nation's economy was delayed until order was restored for the long term. Where foreign incursions and international war were added to internal disruptions, as in Mexico and Central America, matters were even worse. When peace finally came there was a lot of catching-up to do.

To guide them in making up lost ground, Latin Americans turned to a foreign model. They had done this generally unsuccessfully in the past when seeking a political path for the newly independent states and would do so again many times in the future, with mixed results at best. This time, however, they got it at least partly right, as they chose positivism. This nineteenth-century philosophy-cum-action plan came from French philosopher Auguste Comte (1798–1857) and was very influential in Latin America between 1870 and 1914. Positivism called for applying the scientific method to the management of society and the practice of politics. Doing so required giving technical experts enormous power in authoritarian states. In short, it was a technocratic political philosophy, the first of several that Latin Americans would see put into operation in their nations.

The economic policies of positivism were aimed at establishing the conditions for best-practice, late-nineteenth-century capitalism to work. As in earlier episodes of liberal rule, Church lands not actively used for religious purposes and communal lands were expropriated and sold to individual buyers, generally wealthy ones. To this was added infrastructure development, notably in transportation: railroads, ports, and whatever else was needed to get exports to market. Not usually classed as infrastructure but also part of this economic wave was a rapid development of banking, including some central banks. And certain kinds of processing industries—for example, those producing chilled meat—also began to grow.

Although manufacturing played a smaller role in Latin America's late-nineteenth-century economic boom than it did in North America or Western Europe, the resulting overall growth was impressive. Clayton and Conniff report some eye-catching figures.[9] Between 1870 and 1900, Argentina's exports grew sixfold, the same amount that Brazil's foreign trade increased from 1833 to 1889. Mexico outperformed both South American countries by seeing its export figures rise eightfold in value and sevenfold in volume. Latin America was the reservoir of raw materials for the industrializing world to the north. Many of the products were foodstuffs—meat and wheat from Argentina; coffee from Central America, Brazil, and Colombia; sugar from Cuba; and bananas from Central America—but there were also minerals, especially from Mexico and Chile.

Being an exporter of raw materials (staples) brings benefits but also costs. When demand is high, national income grows; and if this growth is well managed it generates four vital linkages: *forward*, or processing; *backward*, or building the tools necessary to harvest the raw materials; *final demand*, or what wages and profits generated by the sector are spent on; and *revenue*, or money government gets to build schools, hospitals, and highways. In other words, being a raw material exporter can be a country's springboard to further development. Turning to the disadvantages, the most obvious is dependence on others for your well-being. If demand for oil or bananas falls, then having vast oil reserves and extensive banana plantations will not generate much income.

Unfortunately, that is precisely what happened to Latin American exporters in 1914, when World War I broke out. Although Mexico, Central America, and the Caribbean had stable markets in the United States, most South American countries had stronger ties to Europe. Thus when hostilities began in August 1914, and Europe's great powers put their economies on a war footing, much of Latin America saw the demand for its exports fall. The entry of the United States into the conflict in 1917 extended the hardship to countries whose exports had flowed north instead of east.[10] World War I, therefore, brought to an end 40 years of rapid, sustained economic growth in Latin America.

Import Substitution Industrialization (ISI)

Reconstruction after World War I and the return to what US president Warren G. Harding called "normalcy" led the export-dependent economies of Latin America toward recovery. Alas, within a decade the world was plunged into the Great Depression, the most profound economic crisis of the twentieth century. World trade ground to a halt as countries looked to save their own industries, investments, and jobs, making "beggaring thy neighbor" the economic policy of choice. Country after country turned to autarky, or self-sufficiency.[11] This was true of Stalin's Russia, Hitler's Germany, and Franco's Spain. Latin America, too, chose autarky; but although there was no shortage of dictatorships in the region during the middle third of the last century, it was less a particular form of autocratic rule there than a specific economic policy that defined the region's approach to self-sufficiency. That policy was import substitution industrialization (ISI).

ISI does just what its name suggests: it is a policy to expand industry by producing at home finished goods that were formerly imported. The logic is impeccable. The country needs to diversify its economy to reduce its dependence on raw material exports. There is an established market for certain goods that are imported. Some of these goods, say, tractors or televisions, are relatively easy to manufacture—they are not the highest of high-tech products. Therefore, that is where the nation's manufacturing sector should start. To make sure that the sector prospers, however, it will be necessary to protect it with quotas, subsidies, or, most commonly, tariffs. Thus protected, the sector can grow and become profitable, modernizing and diversifying the economy, and bringing into being new economic actors to counterweigh the raw material producers.

Intellectual legitimation for ISI came from the structuralists.[12] This was a school of economic theory that was indigenous to Latin America and that flourished after World War II. Led by Argentine economist Raúl Prebisch, who directed the UN's Economic Committee for Latin America (ECLAC/CEPAL), the school argued that Latin America, similar to other developing areas, occupied the periphery of the world economy, whereas the industrialized nations formed the center The periphery was structurally different from the center: it depended more on the primary sector, had weaker financial institutions, suffered from deteriorating terms of trade—meaning that their exports bought ever fewer of the center's products—and it could not count on private capital to overcome these weaknesses. Decisive, vigorous state action was needed to correct the imbalance. ISI filled the bill perfectly.

At first glance, ISI looks a lot like the tariffs that the United States, Canada, and much of Europe used to industrialize in the nineteenth century.[13] It is worth noting that Latin America had long had very high tariffs; and although they were more often originally justified as mechanisms to raise revenues than to protect domestic firms, they had a protective effect as well.[14] However, John Rapley, an expert in economic development studies, believes that ISI was based on a different concept. Where the North

American tariffs were infant industry tariffs (IIT), designed to allow new industries to find their competitive feet, ISI aimed at creating an industrial sector where none previously existed.[15]

Latin American countries moved vigorously into ISI in the 1930s. The Depression, followed by World War II, and then the Bretton Woods international trade regime, in place from 1944 to 1971 (see Chapter 9), provided favorable conditions for the policy to work. Further, and despite the well-founded warnings of free traders that tariffs raise costs that are passed on to consumers as higher prices, Latin American ISI produced good economic results into the 1960s (see Text Box 8.2). Mexico, Brazil, Argentina, and Chile did especially well by this policy. However, in the 1970s, the age of the first oil shocks, stagflation, and the first signs of the debt crisis, things went bad quickly. Though clearly not all of this was the fault of ISI, the 1970s ended ISI as surely as 1914 laid positivism to rest.

Modernization

After World War II, the Third World came into existence as a great wave of decolonization began to sweep over Africa, Asia, and the Caribbean. Although all Latin America was already independent and was home to several relatively wealthy states, it, too, became part of this new bloc. The arrival of so many new states led researchers and policymakers in the developed world, above all in the United States, to reflect on how those countries could be made richer, more democratic, and more firmly aligned with the West against the communist nations. Essentially, modernization theory prescribed a capitalist road to development that reflected established practices in the developed capitalist world in the 1950s. As the dominant economic policy model was Keynesian, modernization theory was consistent with a state that actively managed its country's economy. Unlike the neoliberal Washington Consensus of the 1980s and 1990s, it did not seek an idealized free market, though it was fully capitalist and strongly inclined toward free trade.

Though important, economic questions were not at the center of modernization theory. To become modern—which meant having a democratic government and a capitalist economy that was managed for the public good—a country also needed the appropriate values.[16] Economy, polity, and outlook would all change together, each reinforcing the other to produce countries that functioned much like the world's wealthiest democracies. In fact, modernization theory was built on an idealized reading of the histories of the Western European and North American democracies. There was even a standard recipe for the poorer nations of Latin America and the rest of the world to follow.

To start, a country would bring in the most modern firms from abroad. This is something Latin American ISI policies were comfortable with, as

Text Box 8.2 Assessing ISI

Like every other economic policy ever tried anywhere, import substitution industrialization produced a mixed record of successes and failures. It is important to remember this truism, because ISI became the scapegoat for all Latin America's economic problems when the international financial institutions brought their radical free-markets prescription to bear in the 1980s. First, we need to recall that it was a response to a pressing problem: the shutdown of global trade in the Depression that marked the second time in less than 20 years that the world trading system had failed Latin American countries (along with all other export-oriented nations). Second, industry grew in the ISI period. In fact, manufacturing output increased by 6.8 per cent annually from 1945 to 1972,[17] meaning that it doubled roughly every 11 years. We can say, then, that it was a successful conjunctural policy that outlasted its conjuncture; but that criticism applies to every policy any government has ever made.

ISI's failures were, however, substantial and built into the institutional structure that surrounded the policy. Rather than examine its purely economic weaknesses, it is better to look at its political defects. There are always vested interests that will support an economic policy that benefits them, even if it harms the larger community. In the case of ISI, those vested interests were the owners and employees of the firms that produced substitutes for imports. Concentrated in cities, often in the capital, these interests were ideally placed to resist any attempts by government to change the rules. The workers, generally unionized, took to the streets, while the owners mused publicly through the business press about the losses they would suffer and made personal contact with their friends in office. Even unelected governments found this combination irresistible. It was only the application of outside pressure in the 1980s, in the form of IMF and World Bank conditions for access to loans, that shifted the correlation of forces and terminated a policy that had grown counterproductive.

that is how Argentina, Brazil, and Mexico, among others, got auto industries. These firms would open state-of-the-art plants and hire locals to fill all the jobs from the least skilled hourly worker to middle management. Doing this would, theoretically, create a class of well-paid professional managers, as well as a similarly highly paid, unionized workforce. Then the efficiency and profitability of the firm would show other enterprises how to do things. Before long, local businesses would have adopted the best practices of the foreign firm, leaving the country a more efficient economy and a growing middle class alongside a modern working class. The modern sectors, social and economic, would challenge and displace the old elites,

> **Text Box 8.3** The Alliance for Progress
>
> It is more common to view the Alliance for Progress (AFP), initiated in 1961, as a US foreign policy initiative designed to assure that the Cuban Revolution did not extend beyond the island's shores rather than to see it as a development policy. Yet much of the AFP's content was geared to development, even if development was just another weapon in the Cold War. Among the most evident developmental elements were land reform, which would necessarily entail a dramatic redistribution of rural property, a large role for comprehensive development planning, and a commitment by the United States to provide unprecedented volumes of financial aid. Taking these steps, it was believed, would assure that more Latin Americans resisted the blandishments of communism.
>
> In the end, unfortunately, the AFP's developmental side got sidetracked and the democratic political systems that development was to support never materialized. In fact, the 1960s saw a strong swing back to military dictatorships throughout the region. The growing war in Vietnam pushed democratic development in Latin America off Washington's radar. As a consequence, the Alliance for Progress is now remembered as an anticommunist implement in the West's Cold War strategy and not as a prime example of what the theory of modernization looked like when put into practice.

increasingly come to dominate government, and build democracy—the political system most in tune with their modern values.

Although things did not work that way anywhere, it was not for want of trying. Latin America was the laboratory for a very ambitious policy experiment undertaken by the US government: the Alliance for Progress (see Text Box 8.3). In the end, however, the foreign firms produced fewer benefits than predicted, and thus the new, democratic working and middle classes did not grow as expected. As a result, the old elites retained power; democracy was rolled back; and while the economy of the region did expand, that, too, fell short of what was promised. In the end, the failure of modernization to live up to its promises led to a radical rethinking of how economic and social development could be achieved. Dependency theory was the fruit of that exercise.

Dependency

Dependency theorists take the position that underdevelopment is the product of unequal power relations between the center, the big capitalist countries that dominate the world economy, and the periphery, the poor countries of the Third World and hence all of Latin America. Their argument is that the countries of the center—which curiously extends to include developed staples exporters such as Canada, Australia, and Norway—have created a system in which the raw-materials producers of the periphery become dependent on the center, thus incapable of charting their own developmental course. The explanation is structural and inherent in the nature of capitalism and the realities of international relations. Dependency is the result of power relations between the very strong and the very weak.

Whereas other theories of development, which are actually conceptual explanations for why a country or region has a low level of economic and human development, see the world's poor countries at an earlier stage of development than the rich, dependency sees the global economic and political system, dominated by the center, as preventing the development of the periphery. In fact, it argues that, beginning with colonization, the center underdeveloped the periphery in order to have cheap and ready access to raw materials.

This perspective also asserts that the center opposes the installation of democratic governments in the periphery. Authoritarians keep order and, to the extent that they incorporate local business elites, those governments and their supporters do very well from the dependent relation with the center. Addressing the problems demands confronting structural deficiencies, which include weak financial systems and capital shortages, as well as the more predictable problems of illiteracy, poverty, and poor health; but this demands more freedom of action than relations with the capitalist center permit. The solution, in long run, is finding a noncapitalist road to development. By the 1970s, the inability of policies based on modernization theory to produce many tangible, positive results certainly made dependency explanations plausible.

Latin American thinkers were at the forefront of dependency thinking. Though not precisely a *dependencista*, Raúl Prebisch, the first director of the UN's Economic Commission for Latin America (ECLAC/CEPAL) who was introduced earlier in conjunction with ISI, was instrumental in developing the structuralist economic theory that was the forerunner of dependency. He introduced the terms *center* and *periphery* into economic analysis, and also pointed out the worsening terms of trade between rich and poor countries, which resulted in poor countries needing to export more raw materials to get the same quantity of manufactured goods. By the 1970s, the leading figures of the dependency school were Brazilians (see Text Box 8.4), although dependency analysts were most numerous in North America and Western Europe.[18]

Although dependency perspectives offered a useful corrective to the too-sanguine views of modernization thinkers and reminded everyone of the realities of international relations, they produced few concrete results. Stephen Haber's review of the tenets of dependency analysis finds that they are frequently wrong when applied to Latin America as a whole,

---

Text Box 8.4 The Dependency Theorist Who Became President of Brazil

Fernando Henrique Cardoso was president of Brazil between 1994 and 2002, having served earlier as his country's finance minister from 1993 to 1994. As finance minister, FHC, as he is universally known in Brazil, introduced tough measures that brought the country's once seemingly intractable inflation under control. Then, as president, he oversaw the privatization of many state-owned enterprises, such as the telephone companies. If we said nothing more about Cardoso, everyone would label him a conventional, pro-business president who embraced the typical neoliberal policy agenda. That conclusion, however, would be mistaken.

Cardoso was not a career politician. He began his professional life as a sociologist, indeed as a Marxist and the co-author of one of dependency theory's seminal texts.[19] His conception of dependency was not as stark as some, though, as FHC believed that capitalism and development were not antithetical, only that capitalist development brought fewer benefits to the periphery than to the center. And some argue that his Marxism allowed Cardoso to analyze problems in a fresh way and arrive at unconventional solutions.[20] In short, FHC was a pragmatic politician who used all the resources at his disposal to confront the grave crises facing Brazil during his tenure as finance minister and later as president.

---

although they carry more explanatory weight in the cases of the small Central American and Caribbean countries.[21] Nevertheless, the notion of outside predators hampering Latin American economic development still thrives and is a central part of the critique of the Washington Consensus and its neoliberal policy prescriptions.

The Washington Consensus and Structural Adjustment: Neoliberal Political Economy

From the 1930s through to the 1970s, diagnoses of Latin America's economic ills and prescriptions for their remedy all involved an active, interventionist state. This is unsurprising, as the laissez-faire political economy that brought good results in the decades preceding World War I had stopped working and everyone was turning to government as the new solution. Everything changed with the arrival of the debt crisis of the 1980s. The state presence shrunk and market-friendly policies replaced government intervention, marking the coming of neoliberal political economy to Latin America in the form of the Washington Consensus.

Although the first experiment with market orthodoxy came in the 1970s from General Augusto Pinochet's dictatorship in Chile, and so was autochthonous, in the rest of Latin America the policy was imposed as a political condition for getting loans from the World Bank and IMF. Although earlier models, particularly modernization, also had foreign roots, they were more freely chosen by governments. This latest economic panacea for Latin America had more in common with the solutions put forth in the 1920s when "money doctors" went to Latin America to correct problems arising from foreign debts.[22]

John Williams, an economist with a think tank in Washington, DC, gave the name "the Washington Consensus" to a set of policies that Washington-based financial institutions—notably the World Bank, the IMF, and the US Treasury—backed as the way to solve the Third World's debt crisis (thus Latin America's too) and assure that there would not be another one. The policies were built around straightforward fiscal conservatism: cut budget deficits; privatize state enterprises; reduce tariff protection; emphasize export development; cut subsidies; reduce regulations; and broaden the tax base.[23] The dimensions of the crisis, marked by hyperinflation in many countries as well as extremely high foreign debt burdens, seemed to justify a radical approach. It is not just a coincidence that in the 1980s, the decade of the apogee of conservative economic policy in the United States and Great Britain, that the radical approach was market orthodoxy.

Because this latest economic prescription for Latin America is so closely linked with an international debt crisis, its detailed examination is deferred to the next chapter. However, there are a few things that should be noted here. The policies making up the Washington Consensus are essentially those that the IFIs had prescribed as part of their structural adjustment programs (SAP) since the 1970s. SAPs were supposed to work in two separate but closely linked steps: stabilization and structural adjustment proper.

Stabilization addresses inflation. Policy makers know of one sure way to control inflation and that is through austerity policies that bring a slowdown of economic activity, even a recession. Government spending is slashed, meaning that government workers are laid off and projects that require public financing, such as work on schools and roads, are shelved. State-owned enterprises are sold, both to raise money and to put them into what are thought more appropriate private hands. Money saved goes to pay down foreign debts, because the interest paid to service those debts could be better used to pay for public services or lower taxes. This part of the process generally lasted for only a few years and had reasonable success.

Structural adjustment, per se, has not done as well. This part of the program is to set the economy on a new foundation that ensures steady growth, which proponents of SAPs argue can only be accomplished by finding a niche in the world economy, producing some good or service more efficiently (relatively more cheaply) than do other countries. This sounds a lot like what Latin America did before 1914. However, now there are many more competitors, and even stronger financial administration, which is also part of a SAP, has not assured success.

Overall, the results generated by the Washington Consensus to date suggest that Latin America has not yet found its way to prosperity. It is true that some nations have used the policies to strengthen their economies and move forward; Mexico, Costa Rica, and Brazil come to mind. Others, such as Nicaragua, Honduras, or Ecuador, may have got better fiscal administration out of the bargain but not much else. So, more developed countries, with sufficient material resources and good administrative practices in both the public and private sectors, have done relatively well, while other countries have not. This is hardly better than the record posted by ISI when that policy was working well in the 1950s and helps explain why there is a backlash against neoliberal economic politics now that parallels what happened to ISI a generation ago.

Conclusion: The Next Installment

As the next chapter in Latin America's economic history is now being written, it is impossible to do more than highlight the signs of change. From the mid-1980s until the end of the 1990s, the proponents of market orthodoxy had a near-monopoly on electoral success in Latin America. Presidential candidates who campaigned on anti-neoliberal platforms, such as Alberto Fujimori in Peru in 1990, quickly embraced the realities of SAP politics once elected. Parties, too, were swept up in the move to reduce government's economic role: the Partido Revolucionario Institucional (PRI, or Institutional Revolutionary Party) in Mexico, the Partido Liberación Nacional (PLN, or National Liberation Party) in Costa Rica, and the Peronistas in Argentina all abandoned their historic ties to state-centered economic policies, adopting the Washington Consensus instead. Of course, their international indebtedness left them little choice. Chile's Socialists and Christian Democrats, joined in the Concertación, the country's center-left electoral alliance, and maintained market-friendly policies partly to maintain the confidence of the business sector and the right generally, but also because those policies were producing good results.

Things began to change in 1998, the year Hugo Chávez brought his Movimiento V (Quinta) República (MVR) to power in Venezuela. Resolutely anticapitalist, Chávez promised to bring his country and the world twenty-first-century socialism, and the Venezuelan leader has made neoliberal trade policies a special target. Five years later, Nestor Kirchner became Argentina's president and set about moving that country out of its worst economic crisis since the Depression by ignoring the policy prescriptions of the Washington Consensus; his wife, Cristina Fernandez de Kirchner, elected to succeed him in 2008, is following the same trajectory. Then the Pink Tide elections of 2005 and 2006 added three more anticapitalists to the roster of Latin American presidents: Evo Morales of Bolivia, Rafael Correa of Ecuador, and Daniel Ortega of Nicaragua. To this group of five leaders we can add another five who are less root-and-branch socialists but are far from being advocates of market economics, at least in their social policies. These are: Luiz Inácio Lula da Silva, Brazil; Michelle Bachelet, Chile; Tabaré Vázquez, Uruguay; and probably the two left-of-center presidents elected in Guatemala and Paraguay in 2008, Álvaro Colom and Fernando Lugo, respectively. This puts 10 of Latin America's 19 elected presidents outside the circle of market orthodoxy.[24] Cuba, of course, remains firmly Communist and as yet untouched by trends and tendencies in capitalist political economy.

The pendulum is swinging away from the free-market policies of the Washington Consensus and the SAPs. This should come as no surprise. Like every other economic policy, market orthodoxy did not deliver as promised. And when a policy does not live up to its billing, people tend not to salvage and repair but to scrap and replace. That only five of 19 elected presidents are taking their countries in a clearly statist or conventionally socialist direction is perhaps evidence that democratic forces in other countries have been able to countervail the power of wealth sufficiently to permit a compromise settlement that has more of the characteristics of Keynesian managed capitalism. All of this suggests that Latin America has yet to find its economic magic elixir; and unless it is very, very different from anywhere else in the world, it never will.

Since late 2008, however, Latin America has had more to worry about than abstract economic models, the policies that flow from them, and the results those policies produce. As in the 1930s, the world is again in the grip of a grave economic crisis. Should this be a multiyear phenomenon, as it appears to be in its early days, Latin American nations will face serious economic disruptions and possibly political and social challenges as well. Demand for Latin America's exports will fall, lowering profits and depressing domestic investment. Foreign investment will also fall, as a generally bearish outlook comes to dominate investors in the wealthier countries of the world. Unemployment will rise, causing increased hardship among the poorer classes and perhaps sparking political unrest. So far, this sounds like a replay of the 1930s, but there is a new element at work in this the first decade of the twenty-first century: remittances from Latin Americans working abroad—Mexicans and Central Americans in the United States, Brazilians in Portugal, and people from the Andean states in Spain—will also fall as these emigrants take pay cuts or lose their jobs. As tough as things promise to be in Canada and the United States, it is a good bet that they will be tougher in Latin America.

Further Readings

Sachs, Jeffrey. *The End of Poverty: Economic Possibilities for Our Time.* New York: Penguin, 2006.
Sen, Amartya. *Development as Freedom.* New York: Random House, 2000.
Todaro, Michael P., and Stephen C. Smith. *Economic Development.* 10th ed. Upper Saddle River, NJ: Pearson, 2008.

Websites

Inter-American Development Bank: www.iadb.org
United Nations Development Program: www.undp.org
United Nations Economic Commission for Latin America and the Caribbean (ECLAC): www.eclac.org

Discussion Questions

① If South Korea, Taiwan, Malaysia, China, and now India can find formulas to spur economic development, why has no Latin American country been able to do so? Examining a political economy approach that consciously includes both political and economic factors should prove helpful.

② Aside from ISI, the economic models that Latin American governments have adopted have come from outside the region. What are the costs and benefits of using imported policy models?

Notes

1. Basic sources include Victor Bulmer-Thomas, *The Economic History of Latin America Since Independence* (Cambridge: Cambridge University Press, 1994); Rosemary Thorp, *Progress, Poverty and Exclusion: An Economic History of Latin America in the 20th Century* (Washington, DC: Inter-American Development Bank, 1998); Victor Bulmer-Thomas, John A. Coatsworth, and Roberto Cortés Conde, eds., *The Cambridge Economic History of Latin America,* 2 vols. (Cambridge: Cambridge University Press, 2006.

2. World Bank, *World Development Report, 2008* (Washington, DC: World Bank, 2007) 333.

3. Angus Maddison, *The World Economy* (Paris: OECD, 2006) 520–522.

4. UNDP, *Human Development Report, 2007–2008* (Houndmills, UK: Palgrave Macmillan, 2007) 277–278.

5. Stephen Haber, ed., *How Latin America Fell Behind: Essays on the Economic Histories of Brazil and Mexico* (Stanford, CT: Stanford University Press, 1997).

6. Stephen Haber, "Introduction: Economic Growth and Latin American Economic Historiography," *How Latin America Fell Behind,* 1.

7. International or Geary-Khamis dollars are a hypothetical unit of currency with the same purchasing power as the US$ in the United States. Thus they are a PPP income measure. International dollars are usually fixed in 1990 values to provide a benchmark for historical comparisons.

8. IFIs and SAPs are considered briefly farther along in this chapter and figure prominently in the next.

9. Lawrence A. Clayton and Michael L. Conniff, *A History of Modern Latin America* (Fort Worth, TX: Harcourt Brace & Company, 1999) 125.

10. Where the exports could serve as war material or where an economy was closely integrated into the US system, as with Cuba, the shock was lessened.

11. See Jeffry A. Frieden, *Global Capitalism: Its Fall and Rise in the Twentieth Century* (New York: Norton, 2006) Chapter 9.

12. Two articles published in 2005 put structuralism in contemporary perspective: Joseph L. Love, "The Rise and Decline of Economic Structuralism in Latin America: New Dimensions," *Latin American Research Review* 40:3 (2005): 100–125 and John H. Coatsworth, "Structures, Endowments, and Institutions in the Economic History of Latin America," *Latin American Research Review* 40:3 (2005): 126–144.

13. This point is well argued by Werner Baer, "Import Substitution and Industrialization in Latin America: Experiences and Interpretations," *Latin American Research Review* 7:1 (1972): 95–122.

14. John Coatsworth and Jeffrey Williamson, "Always Protectionist? Latin American Tariffs from Independence to the Great Depression," *Journal of Latin American Studies* 36:2 (2004): 205–232. Revenue tariffs were also used in Canada and the United States.

15. John Rapley, *Understanding Development: Theory and Practice in the Third World*, 3rd ed. (Boulder, CO: Lynne Rienner Publishers, 2007) Chapters 1–4, provides an informative discussion of ISI and IIT. See also Bulmer-Thomas, *Economic History*, Chapters 7–9; Thorp, *Progress and Poverty*, Chapters. 4–6; and Frieden, *Global Capitalism*, Chapter 13.

16. To get the flavor of modernization theory, see the following: Daniel Lerner, *The Passing of Traditional Society* (New York: Macmillan, 1958); Gabriel Almond and James Coleman, eds., *The Politics of Developing Areas* (Princeton, NJ: Princeton University Press, 1960); W.W. Rostow, *The Stages of Economic Growth: A Non-communist Manifesto* (Cambridge: Cambridge University Press, 1960); Cyril E. Black, *The Dynamics of Modernization: A Study in Comparative History* (New York: Harper and Row, 1966); and Samuel P. Huntington, *Political Order in Changing Societies* (New Haven, CT: Yale University Press, 1968).

17. Thorp, *Progress and Poverty*, 322.

18. Fernando Henrique Cardoso and Enzo Faletto, *Dependency and Development in Latin America* (Berkeley, CA: University of California Press, 1979) and Andre Gunder Frank, *Capitalism and Underdevelopment in Latin America: Historical Studies of Chile and Brazil* (New York: Monthly Review Press, 1967).

19. Cardoso and Faletto, *Dependency and Development*.

20. Ted Goertzel, "Still a Marxist," *Brazzil* (April 1997). www.brazzillog.com/pages/blaapr97.htm.

21. Haber, *How Latin America Fell Behind*, 10–14.

22. Paul Drake, *Money Doctors, Foreign Debts, and Economic Reforms in Latin America from the 1890s to the Present* (Wilmington, DE: SR Books, 1994).

23. The full list is found in John Williamson, ed., *Latin American Adjustment: How Much Has Happened?* (Washington, DC: Institute for International Economics, 1990) Chapter 2.

24. Even centrist leaders elected since 2006, such as Alan García of Peru, Óscar Arias of Costa Rica, and Martín Torrijos of Panama, appear more disposed to employ statist solutions to economic problems today than would have been the case 10 or 15 years previously.

9

International Political Economy: The Politics of Latin America's International Economic Relations

Despite the experiments in self-sufficiency described in the last chapter, the states of Latin America live by trade. To reap the maximum benefit from that trade, each state deals with a variety of partners. Some of these are other Latin American states, often neighbors. Others lie beyond the region. Among the latter have often been the world's most powerful economies. In the nineteenth century, both Britain and the United States were key players, joined at times by France and Germany. Throughout most of the twentieth century, the United States cast the longest economic shadow over Latin America, above all in Central America and the Caribbean. As the twenty-first century dawns, China, the world's emerging economic powerhouse, is carving out a place for itself as well, though it has far to go before it can challenge Washington's dominance.

When we think of international political economy in relation to Latin America, what automatically comes to mind are the links between Latin American countries and the economic great powers. Ties with lesser economic forces throughout the world—Canada, for instance—and intraregional economic relations get moved to the back of the line. This produces a misleading picture of the region's international economic relations.

Regional economic integration, on and off the agenda for half a century, is particularly strong early in the twenty-first century. This takes two forms: subregional, multilateral free trade agreements (FTA), like the one that brings together Central America and the Dominican Republic; and the more ambitious if still unrealized integration projects of Mercosur and Alternativa Bolivariana para las Américas (ALBA), both of which we treat below.[1] Further, since the 1980s, international financial institutions (IFIs) such as the World Bank, International Monetary Fund (IMF), and the Inter-American Development Bank (IADB) have played key roles in Latin American economic life. Obviously, transnational corporations also have to figure in the analysis. Finally, to present the fullest possible picture of international economic forces active in the region, some note should be taken of the role of non-governmental organizations (NGOs) and even remittances sent by expatriates working abroad. The empirical landscape thus is quite complicated. Whether this complexity helps or hinders individual countries and the region as a whole is a question to which we shall return at the end of the chapter.

What was said about the interaction of politics and economics in Chapter 8 applies to the subject of this chapter with equal force. There is, first, a distinction to be made between formal or textbook international economics and a state's policy on foreign trade and foreign economic relations more broadly. Since the days of Adam Smith and David Ricardo, conventional liberal capitalist economic theory has propounded the benefits of free trade and international specialization according to the theory of comparative advantage. We expand these themes below, but for now it is important to note that those principles have only rarely guided governments' policy thinking in the international economic realm.

Moreover, the same ideological divisions found in all thinking about economics apply to international economics and trade politics. In fact, the resurgence of a modified version of dependency theory, with a strong antiimperialist tinge, that emanates from the Bolivarian Group (Venezuela, Bolivia, Ecuador, and Nicaragua) adds a dimension not found in domestic politics. When dealing with prescriptions for ameliorating a country's foreign economic policy, therefore, it is necessary to bear in mind that this is a politically charged theme. Not only are there specific sectors, interests, and social groups that benefit from or are harmed by any given policy, but there are also beliefs in play about just what is the morally right way to do things.

International Political Economy

Like political economy in its wider sense, international political economy (IPE) focuses on how economics affects politics and how politics impacts economics. That is, it treats politics and economics as inseparable, even if the specific nature of their interaction differs from case to case. Being centered in the international sphere, however, IPE is especially attentive to state actions, because nation-states are the primary actors in international politics. A look at the main lines of policy identified by IPE shows this clearly.

Nationalist Models

Mercantilism is the oldest of the schools of IPE that we consider, with roots reaching back to the earliest days of the nation-state. For convenience, we can put its origins in sixteenth-century Western Europe. The core of the theory justifying this policy is that states accrue power through trade, making international commerce another power resource. In its original form, mercantilism sought to accrue gold and silver, literally the stuff of money, explaining why Spain's conquistadors sought gold as well as God and glory. Underlying this view is the sense that international trade is a zero-sum game in which what I win, you lose. Therefore, to build a strong country, a state must do all it can to maintain large trade surpluses, exporting a higher value of goods and services than it imports, and thus have more wealth at its disposal. Since my surplus is your deficit, the argument is that I become stronger and you become weaker.

Other forms of nationalist IPE, although often called mercantilist, differ in one important respect from the original. Instead of aiming principally to accrue bullion, since the end of the 1700s an equally important objective has been building national industries. In 1791, Alexander Hamilton, the first US Secretary of the Treasury, sent Congress his *Report on Manufactures*. That document called for subsidizing industry and using a system of tariffs (taxes on imports) to generate revenue for the government and provide an element of protection for growing manufacturers.[2] Forty-six years later, Friedrich List, a German economist, published *The National System of Political Economy*, in which he argued that the state must act to ensure the full, balanced development of a nation's economy, even if this means foregoing short-term trade advantages.[3]

As Chapter 8 noted, Latin American nations turned to tariff-protected import substitution industrialization (ISI) in the mid-twentieth century. However, the most famous and successful practitioners of nationalist IPE in the twentieth century were found in Asia. The so-called Asian Model was based on the policies Japan used to modernize and industrialize its economy and society in the late nineteenth century and then employed to rebuild after World War II. This system is best described as a blend of private capital with a strongly interventionist state: capitalism but not free-market capitalism. Governments direct investment, picking strategic sectors of industry or commerce to receive the greatest amounts of capital mobilized by banks. The state also wants strong export firms, again making a decision to use public policy to build world-class industries rather than waiting for the market to do the selection. Between roughly 1960 and 1990, South Korea, Taiwan, Singapore, and Hong Kong (while it was still a British colony) adapted this model to their needs and successfully developed. A third generation, led by Malaysia, Indonesia, and Thailand, embraced the Asian Model in the 1980s but with less success (see Text Box 9.1). No Latin America country has used this model.

Free-Market IPE

Free-market or liberal IPE describes situations in which a state conducts its international economic relations essentially in conformity with the prescriptions of orthodox, textbook economics. We examine the concepts underlying this school of international political economy later in this chapter.

Text Box 9.1 The Asian Model

When we think of the Asian model, there are normally two things that come to mind. The first is its success. The recovery of Japan after World War II, the rise of South Korea and Taiwan from agricultural backwaters to prosperous nations producing top-quality high-tech goods, and the more recent emergence of Malaysia as a burgeoning economic force all point to how well the model works. The fact that Asia's two newest and most powerful economic engines, China and India, fall outside the Asian model in many respects can almost be overlooked.

The second factor that stands out is the way the model operates. This approach to export-led development builds on a close relationship between the state and large firms. If large firms do not exist, the state fosters their growth. In this system, the state is very active, directing capital into areas that governments believe are necessary for the nation's development. It is this characteristic that leads to the Asian Model being called *mercantilist*.

Although the regimes that first implemented the Asian Model were either authoritarian or restrictive democracies of some kind, the system has produced fairly equal income distributions, good educational results, and very effective land reform in the cases of Japan, Taiwan, and South Korea. Running the Asian Model requires a strong state with an able bureaucracy. It also demands an international trade regime—the rules that govern international trade—that accepts high levels of state economic intervention. The first requirement helps explain why the model has not been more widely used in Latin America, while the second suggests why it is not widely used anywhere early in the twenty-first century.

Nevertheless, it is important to introduce its philosophical underpinnings and note its history in Latin America.

At the heart of market economics is the idea of individual freedom, in particular the freedom individual people have to arrange their economic lives as they wish. Obviously, this is a very abstract goal and in real life only the wealthiest organize their material existence without regard to material obstacles. The point of liberalism, the political ideology that encompasses market economics, was different. It targeted legal barriers to freedom. In the economic context, an example would be the controls over international trade imposed by mercantilism. These, liberal thought argued, not only limited people's freedom in the economic sphere but were also bad economics. Restrictions on trade impose costs on society in the form of higher prices and a reduced selection of goods. True, those who are sheltered by the rules do very nicely indeed, but the nation suffers.

To address both the above ills—constrained freedom and inefficient economics—free-market IPE proposes a specific trade regime.[4] At the heart of that regime is free trade. Ideally, a free-trade world would see all countries trading with one another on a completely equal legal footing; and consumers would not have to pay extra taxes in the form of tariffs when buying foreign products. In practice, minimizing those legal impediments and extra charges is an acceptable substitute. To make a free-trade regime work as theory predicts it should, states must find their niche in the global economy. They do that by concentrating on producing goods and services at which they are especially efficient; that is, a state should discover what it does relatively better than anyone else and concentrate on that.[5] Finally, all countries should have an external orientation, meaning that their economies should look for opportunities to trade and not concentrate on just the internal market, as Latin America did under ISI.

Latin America has had two extended periods in which it has worked within a free-market trade regime. The first was the 1870 to 1914 boom era described in Chapter 8. This was the golden era of global free trade, and Latin America knew sustained export-led growth. The second period began with debt crisis—the lost decade of the 1980s—and continued through the 1990s, the age of structural adjustment. Now, in the first decade of the twenty-first century, pushed by a commodities boom driven by rapid industrial growth in China and India, Latin America has again taken off: in the middle of the decade (2003–2007), growth for the region averaged a healthy 5.2 per cent annually.[6] However, as both this latest spurt and the long boom prior to 1914 were both linked to strong demands for primary products, it may be unwise to attribute too much to the nature of the rules governing the international economy.

Socialist IPE

There is certainly a socialist IPE, especially if by socialist we mean Marxist or Marxist-leaning. A centrally planned economy that gives little or no room for private businesses, even tiny family ones, and a radical redistribution of wealth are its hallmarks. It is also true that states with this political identity have traded more with each other than with capitalist countries. Whether this produces a socialist IPE is open to question. We know that within the framework of the Council of Mutual Economic Assistance (CMEA, or Comecon), the old Soviet Bloc economic union, Cuba specialized in producing raw materials, notably sugar and nickel, much as it had when the United States was its economic lodestar.[7] We also know that the three Latin American countries that had avowedly socialist governments that were either fully Marxist or Marxist-inspired—Cuba since 1959, Chile from 1970 to 1973, and Nicaragua in the 1980s—were all targeted for extreme economic pressure by Washington.

Cuba's situation is the most dramatic. Since 1962, the US government has maintained an economic embargo against Cuba. The Kennedy administration took this step, which extended economic sanctions begun in 1960 by President Eisenhower, in response not only to Cuban nationalization of American property without compensation (businesses headquartered in other countries, including Canada, were also expropriated but their owners were paid) but also to the Castro government's alignment with the Soviet Union. Over the years, the embargo has at times been relaxed to allow US citizens to visit the island, but it has also been stiffened to impose penalties on US firms whose foreign branches trade with Cuba. The suspension of economic relations with the United States for nearly five decades has not brought down the Communist regime there.

Nicaragua's situation was different. Although the Sandinista Revolution of 1979 brought down an old US ally, the Somoza family dictatorship (1936–1979), the revolutionaries were more patient. They initially nationalized only the property of the Somoza family and their closest associates, still an impressive 20 per cent of the country's arable land; and even though the Sandinistas never disguised their aim to build socialism, they moved slowly and generally tried to minimize the resulting friction.[8] Despite that, the Reagan administration imposed an embargo in 1985, declaring the Sandinista state a threat to American national security, and maintained it until the revolutionaries lost power in the elections of 1990. While economic distress contributed to the Sandinistas' defeat, another of Washington's policies, the low-intensity counterrevolutionary war it sponsored, was what most convinced Nicaraguans to abandon the revolutionary experiment.

The administration of Chilean president Salvador Allende, elected in 1970 and overthrown by the military on September 11, 1973, is the last case. Allende was a Marxist, although he belonged to the Socialist Party, and was determined to use a narrow, minority victory to construct the Chilean road to socialism. There was no embargo, but President Nixon ordered the CIA to apply pressure to "make the economy scream." A combination of increasing economic chaos and the Allende administration's growing popularity at the polls moved the military to topple the government.

This brief review of relations between the US government and the three Marxist governments that Latin America produced in the twentieth century makes two points clear. First, international political economy is embedded in international economic relations. Second, international economic relations are first and foremost international relations. They are about the exercise of power in the relations between states.

The Economic Essentials

International economics provides a series of concepts with which one must be familiar in order to be able to follow the arguments made by the various schools of IPE and of international economic relations in general. There are four concepts—free trade, comparative advantage, balance of payments, and exchange rates—that are critical and only one is even remotely difficult to grasp.

Free trade is the cornerstone of orthodox (capitalist) thinking about international economics. Impediments to free trade, such as tariffs and nontariff barriers (for example, product standards, safety, environmental, and labor regulations, or quotas), keep the international economy from working at peak efficiency. If the world's political leaders were all economists, free trade would have been the universal trade policy since sometime in the nineteenth century. Obviously it has not been because policymakers have been less concerned about making the global economy work at top efficiency than how well their own national economies do.

Besides wanting to see international trade less encumbered, free trade also promotes international specialization, which is another point on which governments hold different views than academic economists. The key concept here is comparative advantage and it does not mean quite what common sense might expect it to. No one questions that if country A is a very efficient cucumber grower and bad at making digital widgets, and country B is great with digital widgets and can hardly grow a cucumber, then A should grow cucumbers, B should make widgets, and they should both trade one for the other. But the theory of comparative advantage says that even if A is better at both, trade can still make sense. That would happen if, for instance, in country A you gave up 100 cucumbers to get a digital widget, while in country B, you have to give up 90. In that case, B should specialize in digital widgets because it gives up fewer cucumbers to get one.

Once again, world trade does not follow that prescription closely, and some theorists even question the real utility of comparative advantage as an analytical tool.[9] For example, Michael Porter, a Harvard Business School professor, argues that comparative advantage is too narrowly based to capture the determinants of national economic success. He proposed looking at a country's competitive advantage, which focuses mainly on the structure and behavior of a nation's business firms. Government plays a significant role by creating conditions that encourage firms to innovate. By stretching the concept a little we can see the Cuban government's decision to emphasize tourism and pharmaceuticals after the collapse of the Soviet Union in 1991 as one example, and the Chilean government's work to position that country as a provider of out-of-season fruit to the northern hemisphere and farmed salmon and wine to the world as another case where competitive advantages were produced.

We saw above that the promoters of a nationalist IPE, such as Hamilton and List, were suspicious of free trade, fearing that it stifled the economic growth of emerging nations. Similarly, there are many who see today's expansion of free trade within the framework of globalization as responding mainly to North American corporate agendas. However, free trade can be an attractive policy option for poor countries. Certainly, Latin America's export-led growth around the turn of the twentieth century might not have occurred without relatively free trade. The same is true of the manufacturing miracles of Asia over the last six decades. Further, where free trade does not exist, as in agricultural products, governments of poor countries demand its application.

A third conceptual building block of international economics that has significant political repercussions is the balance of payments (BoP). The BoP is simply the difference between the value of what a country exports and what it imports.[10] If you export more than you import, which was the cardinal rule of mercantilism, your trade balance is positive. If the opposite occurs, your trade balance is negative. It can also be in balance, with neither surplus nor deficit. World trade is always in balance, but some countries have surpluses, at times very large ones—think of China in the first decade of the twenty-first century—and others deficits, which can also be very large.

If a country has a deficit, even a temporary one, it must finance it either out of its international reserves (its holdings of foreign currency or gold) or by borrowing. Countries normally borrow by selling their bonds on the international market, although highly indebted states with chronic deficits may be unable to do so. They must go outside the market and seek loans from the international financial institutions (IFI). This has been a common problem in Latin America and one that we examine below in the context of structural adjustment.

Even countries with a persistent surplus can cause problems for the international economy. Not only is one country's surplus another's deficit, but consistent surpluses also drive up the value of a country's currency, which can lead to inflation, rising imports, and pressure on domestic firms. Recently, countries such as China, Russia, Norway, and the United Arab Emirates have set up sovereign wealth funds, which look to invest surpluses in productive assets overseas. As yet, no Latin American nation has established such a fund.

The fourth and last concept is exchange rates. At its simplest, this is just the rate at which one currency, say, Canadian dollars, exchanges for another, for example, Honduran lempiras. It does not take long for complications to arise, however. Should a country fix the value of its currency in terms of some other so that a lempira always buys the same amount of Canadian dollars? Or should it let its currency float, rising and falling according to market conditions? Alternatively, a country could maintain multiple exchange rates: one for businesses, another for individual citizens, and a third for tourists. Persuasive arguments have been made for each of these options and others besides. The question is important because an overvalued currency can lead to a fall in exports—which is

Balance of Payment

Exchange rates

Text Box 9.2 Rebranding the National Currency

Changing the name of a Latin American country's currency to accompany a substantial devaluation is a longstanding practice. Since independence in 1822, Brazil has had 11 different currencies, 6 of which saw one unit of new currency replace at least 1,000 of the old.[11] Argentina has had 10, 2 of which replaced 10,000 of the old money. Peru has had only 3 different currencies, but when the nuevo sol replaced the inti in 1991, it took 1 million of the old to buy 1 of the new.

In Nicaragua, the story is a little different. As in Peru, there have been only three currencies, two cordobas and a cordoba oro, although the latter is conventionally called a cordoba as well. The first change occurred in 1988 when the Sandinista government sought to reel in galloping inflation by introducing a new cordoba that was worth 1,000 old ones. The change was fruitless, as inflation for 1988 climbed to roughly 34,000 per cent. To keep up with rising prices, the government had to change the face value of the already-depreciated new currency. Thus a 10 cordoba note eventually resurfaced as a 1 million cordoba note. Three years later a new government introduced the cordoba oro, worth 5 million cordobas. Because the government was slow getting the new money into circulation, the old currency continued to be accepted and was baptized the cordoba *chanchero*, or "pigsty cordoba," by the public. As well, US dollars were accepted for some time as quasi-legal tender.

Finally, there are countries that have adopted the American greenback as their national currency. In Panama it is called the balboa; and while coins bear the visages of Panamanian heroes, the bills are US currency. El Salvador adopted the dollar in 2001. Ecuador did so in 2000 but has begun to contemplate returning to its historic currency, the sucre.

basically what produced the Argentine crisis of 2002 (see below), whereas an undervalued one produces trade surpluses that invite retaliation and may make necessary imports too expensive. Moreover, the repeated bouts of hyperinflation, which minimally means an accumulated inflation of 100 per cent over three years, have caused several Latin American countries to reinvent their currencies in an attempt to start afresh (see Text Box 9.2).

Latin America in the World Economy to 1982

Since being colonized by the Spanish and Portuguese, Latin America has been an exporter. Obviously, it is natural that colonies export to the imperial center those high-value products that often explain the colonizer's interest in a place. All Western European colonial empires of the modern age—England, France, the Netherlands, and Belgium, as well as Spain and

Portugal—did so. Actually, it seems unlikely that there ever was an imperial power that did not turn its colonies into purveyors of goods to meet the metropole's wants and needs.[12]

What Spanish America sent back to Spain were first and foremost silver and gold: the bullion that was the object of mercantilist policy. As well, the Spanish colonies produced dyestuffs (indigo and cochineal) and some foodstuffs (cacao for chocolate) for export. Though most exports went to Spain, there was active intercolonial trade in food, mules, and cattle to support the mining industry. As was normal in colonial settings, trade with foreigners was forbidden; however, equally normally, a lively contraband trade existed. Like those of the Spanish colonies, Brazil's economy was adapted to the needs of its metropole. The content of the trade was somewhat different, however, as it began with dyewood (brazilwood), then moved quickly to sugar, which Spanish America did not develop. In the eighteenth century, the discovery of gold and diamonds led to the export of those precious commodities. Portugal sought to monopolize trade with its American colony, using Brazil's vast wealth to balance Lisbon's foreign trade accounts. In this regard, the two Iberian empires were alike.

As a result, both the Spanish and Portuguese American colonies had their economies shaped by decisions made in capitals thousands of miles distant. However, the Iberian colonies differed little from their British American counterparts in this respect. Colonies were expected to serve the needs of the stronger states that administered them. Further, the entire range of a colony's commercial links was centered in and on the metropole. Accordingly, unless there was significant domestic economic development in a colony that was not export-related, as was true of England's North American possessions, colonies had little opportunity to develop the banking systems that would be needed to support post-independence economic development.

At independence, all Latin American states entered the global economy as specialists in the production of primary products and have retained that specialization to the present.[13] This is neither surprising—most Latin American states have relatively low population densities and a good stock of raw material—nor is it a sentence to perpetual underdevelopment—as the experiences of Australia, Canada, and New Zealand make clear. Yet no Latin American nation has had the economic success of those former British colonies. This is attributable in great part to the political instability that wracked most Latin American countries in their first decades of independence, which both set back development and delayed the full entry of Latin American nations into the rapidly expanding world trading system of the first half of the nineteenth century. Another consequence of extended instability was an almost chronic inability to raise capital domestically or attract it internationally. These problems were substantially overcome during the boom period from roughly 1870 until 1914.

Text Box 9.3 Coffee Comes to Costa Rica

Sometime around the turn of the nineteenth century, the first coffee plants came to Costa Rica. With few precious metals and a native population too sparse to constitute the base of servile labor needed for plantation agriculture, this was the poorest of Spain's Central American colonies. Poverty meant neglect by the metropole and allowed Costa Rica alone among Spain's American possessions, to develop a smallholder society. This is not to say that there were not rich and poor, only that the bulk of an admittedly small population, about 50,000 at independence in 1821, was independent farmers.

Such a small population could hardly generate from private sources the capital needed to promote coffee production, which demands a five-year wait for the coffee plants (*matas*) to mature before they bear fruit. Government intervention, first from municipalities and then from the national government, was both needed and quickly forthcoming. Aid took the form of tax breaks and a policy of giving title to anyone who raised coffee for five years on what had been ungranted public land. As a result, Costa Rica came to have many small-scale, independent farmers raising coffee on their own land. Further, although there were some coffee barons with large plantations and who also owned the processing plants (*beneficios*), a chronic shortage of labor in the lightly populated country meant that people who picked coffee (and there needed to be a lot of them) received good wages.

All of this would have gone for naught if there had been no market for the coffee. Fortunately, in 1843 a British captain, William Le Lacheur, looking for more cargo to make his homeward voyage profitable, took on Costa Rican coffee. From then until the end of the 1800s, when the banana trade started, coffee accounted for more than 90 per cent of the nation's exports.[14]

Even prior to the good times, however, some Latin American countries did develop new exports, send them to the world, and enjoy a few moments of prosperity. In Costa Rica, that new export was coffee. This commodity became the country's principal export for more than a century; and because of the peculiar array of social and demographic factors present in that Central American state, the new crop strengthened social equality, something coffee cultivation did not always do elsewhere (see Text Box 9.3). A somewhat different result was produced in Peru, where the hot new export was guano, seabird droppings.

Between 1840 and 1880, Peru was the world's only exporter of guano, which was used as a fertilizer. Unlike most raw materials, it did not require a great deal of either capital or labor to extract. Although production was almost totally in British hands, guano generated substantial royalties, which the state used for public works, raising public salaries—including the military's—and consolidating the nation's domestic public debt, which greatly benefited the Peruvian bond-holding class. As the guano deposits came to be worked out, production slowed, and revenues fell. By 1880, guano production ceased to be an important part of Peru's economy. In 2008, however, guano mining made something of comeback, as soaring petroleum prices made once-uneconomic sources of fertilizers profitable again.[15]

The end of *caudillo* rule brought most countries stability by the last third of the nineteenth century. With political stability came economic recovery, as production and investment could resume without the fear that all would be wiped out in the next civil war. This put the region in a position to participate in the late-nineteenth-century wave of industrialization in Europe and North America. As well, new technologies, notably refrigerated ships, made new exports feasible. Thus chilled beef was shipped from Argentina and bananas from Central America. To this list, one may add the rubber from the Amazon for tires that the start of the automobile age made a necessity and the nonferrous metals—copper from Chile and tin from Bolivia—that new industries demanded. Finally, there were industrial spinoffs, especially in the larger countries. For example, Argentina's chilled beef exports demanded slaughterhouses, which led to Buenos Aires being called "la nueva Chicago," but other industries grew as well: metalworking, glass, paper, and textiles.[16]

Although the period from 1870 to 1914 is linked with laissez-faire, the international trade regime then in place was not purely free trade. Tariffs were common. Some, as in Latin America, were to generate revenues; others, such as those in Canada and the United States, were frankly protective. Where the free market reigned was in balance of payments. The gold standard, which demanded the settlement of international debts in gold, meant that a debtor could not run repeated trade deficits. The value of its currency would fall, imports would drop, exports rise, and balance be restored. A creditor country would automatically pass through a mirror-image process that would bring its international balances back into line. While this worked well for the system, the gold standard had a deflationary effect overall and often left Latin American countries in difficult circumstances.[17]

Perhaps if World War I had not begun in 1914, Latin America could have accumulated the capital needed for at least the larger countries to have made the transition to industrial economies. That did not happen, and as was described in Chapter 8, the response was to move to import substitution industrialization (ISI). Exports, however, did not end with the coming of ISI but contributed to the very healthy 6 per cent per annum growth rate in the region from 1950 to 1980, a figure bettered only by East Asia.[18] After 1973, though, things began to fall apart.

Rising oil prices coming after the October 1973 oil shock were the culprit and they affected Latin America in several ways. First, countries that were oil importers—all but Mexico, Venezuela, Ecuador, and Colombia—faced huge increases in energy costs, as the price of oil quadrupled in just a few months. Therefore governments either had to accept serious economic slowdowns or borrow to cover the rising costs. Borrowing, the usual course, brought the shock's second effect into play.

Oil producers were awash in oil revenues and placed these funds with major foreign banks in Europe and the United States. The banks then had to find ways to turn these deposits into loans in order to make a profit. Cash-hungry states in Latin America and elsewhere were the answer to the banks' prayers, just as the banks' loans appeared to save the borrowing countries from recession. Sadly for both, more complications were on the way.

Although the worst of the oil price shock had been absorbed within a few years, there were lingering effects in the form of rising inflation and rising unemployment: stagflation. This unprecedented phenomenon reduced demand in the developed economies, which affected most imports, at the same time that interest rates rose to control inflation, further dampening demand. For Latin American nonpetroleum producers, the foregoing led to greater borrowing, as countries were not getting sufficient returns from their exports. When their loans were renegotiated, the new borrowing came with interest rates three to four times higher than the original. Further, improvident oil producers, here Venezuela and Mexico, also borrowed lavishly, counting on oil revenues to continue climbing. Unfortunately, decreasing demand in the north combined with new oil supplies coming online from the North Sea to send oil prices plummeting after 1980. Latin America's great debt crisis of the 1980s was at hand.

Neoliberal IPE: Structural Adjustment, the Washington Consensus, and Globalization Since 1982

The Mexican government's announcement in 1982 that it was suspending payments on its foreign debt set the Third World debt crisis in motion. However, the shift to a new international trade regime, under whose rules the crisis would be managed, had already begun. This new system, called either neoliberal, to indicate its return to the free-market policies of classical liberalism, or the Washington Consensus, because international financial institutions (IFIs) headquartered in Washington (the IMF and the World Bank, as well as the United States government) all backed it, was the latest form of free-market IPE to dominate the world economy (see Text Box 9.4). Although modified in certain respects since then, it continues as the reigning outlook of the developed capitalist world today.

Text Box 9.4 The Washington Consensus

By the end of the 1980s, general agreement about the best economic policies to prescribe had emerged among those who funded the programs designed to resolve the economic problems of countries swept up in the debt crisis. John Williamson, an economist with the Institute for International Economics, a think tank in Washington, DC, identified 10 key areas and labeled them the Washington Consensus, because the most important players were located in the US capital: the IMF, the World Bank, and the US government. Included were:

- balanced budgets
- elimination of subsidies
- tax reform
- exchange rates and interest rates set by the market
- trade liberalization in the form of reduced tariffs
- deregulation, including loosening controls on foreign investment
- privatization of state enterprises
- increased legal security for property rights

These formed the core of the policy reforms demanded by structural adjustment programs, whose goal was to cause debtor nations to dedicate more resources to paying down their debts and reentering the world economy as full trading partners. Too often applied in a one-size-fits-all manner, these policies, unremarkable in themselves, often resulted in more pain than gain. This was true not only in Latin America but in other countries, such as Russia, as well. By the end of the twentieth century, the consensus had weakened and more emphasis was being given to social concerns.

Neoliberalism marked a radical change of direction in international economic policy. In the 1960s, it was accepted that governments should follow Keynesian principles and play an active role in managing capitalist economies, but the failure of that policy to cope with the 1973 oil shock and the stagflation that followed brought a change. Voters in the United Kingdom elected Margaret Thatcher's Conservatives in 1979, and their counterparts in the United States chose Ronald Reagan and the Republicans in 1980. Both leaders believed that only returning to the economic policies of the free market would restore the economic health of their nations and the world. Domestically, this meant deregulation, balanced budgets, cuts to social programs, and a general reduction of the state's economic and social footprint. Internationally, the prescription was for the greatest possible liberalization of international trade: lower tariffs, floating currencies with

{ 220 }

Table 9.1 Total External Debt as Percentage of National Income by Country and Year

Country	1980	1985	1990	1995	2006
Argentina	35.6	84.2	46.0	35.8	58.6
Bolivia	93.3	184.9	106.8	81.3	49.0
Brazil	30.6	48.7	26.0	22.9	18.7
Chile	45.2	143.3	67.4	45	37.9
Colombia	20.9	42	45.4	32.1	26.9
Costa Rica	59.5	120	68.1	43.1	31.9
Dominican Republic	31.5	82.5	60.5	38.5	29.6
Ecuador	53.8	77.5	122.7	83.9	41.9
El Salvador	25.9	46.6	45.6	28.6	50.4
Guatemala	14.9	27.5	38.1	25.2	15.7
Honduras	61.5	82.4	138.5	115.6	45.7
Mexico	30.3	55.2	43.8	61.2	19.5
Nicaragua	112.2	217.9	6993.3	676.8	84.8
Panama	89.3	104.9	140.4	83.3	62.2
Paraguay	20.7	59.4	39.1	24.6	36.9
Peru	51.0	89.4	68.2	59.5	33.3
Uruguay	16.5	80.7	55.0	29.5	52.1
Venezuela	42.1	59.1	70.3	47.5	24.7

Sources: Constructed from World Bank, *World Debt Tables, 1990, 1996.* Washington: World Bank, 1990, 1996; World Bank, *Global Development Finance, 2001, v.2.* Washington: World Bank, 2001, 2008.

values set by market forces, and freedom for capital to flow unimpeded to wherever the most profitable investments were found.

These values became the benchmarks of the new international economic order. Further, where in the past the rules of the international economy would have been enforced by nation states, the agents assuring adherence to these norms were the multilateral lenders, another and more specific name for IFIs such as the IMF and the World Bank. Their instruments were structural adjustment programs (SAP) and conditional loans, which made access to concessional, ultra-low interest loans contingent on implanting a SAP's recommendations.

Table 9.2 Latin American Inflation Rates by Country, 1970-2005

Country	1971–1980	1981–1990	2000–2006
Argentina	133.9	416.9	12.2
Bolivia	21.0	263.4	6.0
Brazil	38.6	327.6	9.3
Chile	188.1	20.5	6.8
Colombia	22.3	25	6.7
Costa Rica	15.7	22.9	9.8
Dominican Republic	9.1	24.5	18.6
Ecuador	13.8	38	10.4
El Salvador	10.7	17.4	3.1
Guatemala	10.5	15.9	7.1
Honduras	8.1	6.8	7.8
Mexico	18.1	66.5	6.7
Nicaragua	12.8	583.7	7.6
Panama	7.5	2.4	1.7
Paraguay	12.7	25.1	10.7
Peru	30.1	287.3	3.5
Uruguay	65.1	64.4	10.1
Venezuela	14	21.2	6.3

Sources: Constructed from World Bank, *World Development Report, 1993.* 238–239. Washington: World Bank 1993; and *World Development Report, 2008.* 240–241. Washington: World Bank, 2008.

Neoliberalism's Tools: Structural Adjustment Policies

Chapter 8 introduced the concept of SAPs to help explain why Latin America returned to free-market economic policies in the 1980s and 1990s. SAPs have two objectives: resolve current problems emerging from serious fiscal imbalances—chronic government deficits—and making structural corrections that minimize the recurrence of such imbalances. Regarding the former, there were two issues that were critical. One was a country's level of foreign indebtedness (Table 9.1), while the other was inflation (Table 9.2). Unless inflation was controlled, economic growth would be jeopardized, and without growth, a country would find it hard to pay down its debts, restore its credit rating, and divert funds from debt servicing to more productive uses.

Figures for external debt as a proportion of national income do not always give the full story, as a country with very high export revenues can finance its debt service (paying interest and paying down the principal) relatively easily. Nevertheless, as the levels of debt approach or exceed a nation's total income, the chances of default increase. This has certainly been the case in the past in Latin America, where there were waves of defaults on foreign loans in the 1820s, 1870s, and 1930s.[19] So, to avoid another round of defaults that might have threatened the world banking system, SAPs were put into place by both main multilateral lenders.

Inflation had been a chronic problem in many countries, as Table 9.2 indicates. This had two negative consequences for nations where inflation was historically high. On the one hand, it hurt the poor, whose earnings rarely kept pace with price rises; on the other, high inflation discouraged both savings and investment. In fact, the inability of governments in Latin America to manage inflation led to capital flight, as those with money shifted their wealth offshore.[20] As with reducing foreign debt, the strictures of the SAPs appear to have worked to control inflation.

However, because of their commitment to reducing expenditures, Structural Adjustment Programs are also associated with across-the-board cuts to health and education, reductions in public sector employment, and the elimination of subsidies on what is often called the *canasta básica*, the market basket of basic consumer goods such as cooking oil, milk, and rice. Further, the trade liberalization policies demanded by the SAPs increasingly placed Latin American countries in direct competition with countries in other regions that produced raw materials and were trying to build export industries based on low labor costs. In fact, the prescription for restoring growth and building new wealth was simply to adapt to the demands of globalization by maximizing a country's comparative advantage in the world economy. In a few cases this led to new markets for new exports: Colombia now sells cut flowers to the world, Costa Rica exports pineapples, and Brazil and Argentina both now export soybeans. Not inconsequential gains but certainly not a passport to the ranks of high-income countries.

Looking backward, it appears that SAPs had greater success securing conformity with economic orthodoxy than in actually restructuring Latin American economies to secure better performance, though they certainly reined in galloping inflation where it existed. This leads to the conclusion that if accepting a SAP had not been the prerequisite for getting concessional loans, it is improbable that states anywhere would have taken the multilaterals' offer. In fact, the results of the programs were sufficiently disappointing even to the IFIs that by the mid-1990s they had adjusted structural adjustment itself.

Two new programs marked the shift and though neither abandoned the tenets of the market, both recognized that the desperately poor, among both people and states, were often worse off after receiving the assistance of the Word Bank and the IMF. One program demanded that recipient countries prepare Poverty Reduction Strategy Papers (PRSP) before receiving loans. Although the new program began in 2000 with the promise that it would give states more ownership over their adjustment processes, early evaluations suggest that it has not fulfilled expectations.[21] The second new policy was the Highly Indebted Poor Countries Initiative (HIPC). Begun in 1996, the initiative can potentially cover 42 countries, although only 27 have qualified to date; only two are in Latin America: Honduras and Nicaragua. To qualify for the HIPC, a country must have a SAP, be poor and highly indebted, and meet a series of other requirements, including having a poverty reduction plan. The payoff is that the country will have forgiven 80 per cent of its debt that is held by the Paris Club countries (a group of the leading creditor states), with a strong possibility that other creditors will do the same. However, this benefit comes at the cost of devoting a substantial proportion of a country's revenues to debt reduction, thereby risking greater impoverishment.[22]

In fact, looking at the record of SAPs in Latin America presents a picture that is uninspiring at best and frankly appalling at worst. Argentina is the worst case (see Text Box 9.5), yet it is interesting because it shows the government staying with a policy that had exhausted its usefulness. That is, Argentina repeated the same error with its neoliberal reforms that it and its neighbors had made a generation earlier with import substitution industrialization (ISI).

Free Trade: Regional and Hemispheric

Although structural adjustment aimed at opening up countries to free trade, it did not specifically promote free trade agreements. Nevertheless, since the late 1980s Latin America has seen a proliferation of regional and bilateral free trade deals. There has even been work toward a hemispheric free trade area, which was initiated by the United States and supported by Canada. However, it has not prospered, due to resistance from Latin America. If nothing else, autarky is off the table and every country in the hemisphere recognizes the utility of trade.

The most successful and interesting of the free trade arrangements are the regional deals. The North American Free Trade Agreement (NAFTA)—linking the United States, Canada, and Mexico—is the best known to North Americans. It owes its importance to historically nationalist Mexico's agreement to enter into a free trade deal involving the United States, *el coloso del norte*. Potentially more significant is the Mercosur (Mercosul in Portuguese). In 1991 Argentina, Brazil, Paraguay, and Uruguay signed the Treaty of Asunción, creating the Common Market of the South. Bolivia, Chile, Colombia, Ecuador, and Peru are associate members, while Mexico

Text Box 9.5 Argentina: From Stardom to Collapse

In the mid-1990s, Argentina was the reigning star of structural adjustment. The first six years after the country's return to democracy in 1983 had proven economically traumatic. Growth stopped, inflation soared, and jobs were jeopardized. Things were so bad that the incumbent president, Raúl Alfonsín, left office early so that the newly elected Carlos Menem could take over and try his hand. Although a Peronista, a member of a party that had always favored a strong state presence in the economy, Menem quickly embraced the neoliberal policies of structural adjustment. His action was not unprecedented, as both Mexico's Partido Revolucionario Institucional (PRI) and Costa Rica's Partido Liberación Nacional (PLN) had made the same move in 1982.

Argentina acted rapidly to privatize state-owned enterprises, deregulate the economy, cut public spending, lay off thousands of public sector workers, and, the key to Menem's success, peg the peso to the US dollar. This last policy was critical to the success of the administration's anti-inflation policy, as it gave investors confidence that the government would have to continue its market-friendly, austerity policies if the two currencies were to remain at par. Inflation did drop; falling from 5,000 per cent annually in Alfonsín's last years to 1.5 per cent in 1995, and investor confidence was restored as the Buenos Aires stock market boomed. But the now–very expensive peso undermined Argentina's industrial exports, leading to the closure of many manufacturing firms, which only added to the country's unemployment problem. Still, voters were happy enough with seeing inflation whipped that they first let Menem amend the constitution to let him seek a second consecutive term and then reelected him.

Unable to seek a third successive term, Menem ceded power to Fernando de la Rua of the Radicals (Unión Cívica Radical, UCR), a centrist party, in 1999. By December 2001, de la Rua was presiding over perhaps the greatest economic crisis in Argentina's history. Businesses failed, unemployment grew, and bank accounts were frozen. Working- and middle-class Argentines took to the streets to demand the government's removal. Although the president declared a state of siege, he could not control the situation and resigned on December 20, 2001. Three presidents later, Eduardo Duhalde, a Peronista, took office on January 1, 2002, becoming Argentina's fifth president in less than two weeks. Duhalde managed to stabilize the economy but only after seeing the peso drop to a third of its former value and the economy shrink by 11 per cent. Nevertheless, he finished the term begun by de la Rua. In 2003, the people of Argentina elected Nestor Kirchner their president. Kirchner made a clean break with the neoliberal policies of the past and gave the country four years of solid growth.

is an observer. Venezuela signed a membership agreement in 2006 and in 2009 is still waiting for its application to be ratified by all members. Mercosur is a customs union that sets a common tariff, indicating a higher level of economic integration than that found in free trade areas such as NAFTA. Mercosur, therefore, is a step toward realizing the historic dream of Latin American unity. Other regional economic organizations include the Community of Andean Nations (Bolivia, Colombia, Ecuador, and Peru, with Chile as an observer) and CAFTA-DR, linking the five Spanish-speaking states of Central America and the Dominican Republic.

Lastly, there are an increasing number of bilateral free trade agreements. Canada has concluded pacts with Chile and Costa Rica; the United States has ratified accords with Chile, and Central America and the Dominican Republic; Mexico with 12 other Latin American states; Chile with Costa Rica, El Salvador, and, more significantly, the People's Republic of China and the European Union. Other countries have also struck bilateral free trade deals, both within Latin America and outside the region, and numerous pacts have been signed and await ratification by the respective national legislatures.[23]

Conclusion: Current Trends

It has been more than 25 years since Mexico's debt problems brought structural adjustment to Latin America. In that time, the Washington Consensus has lost most of its shine. Citizens throughout the region have begun again to elect left-of-center governments that are looking for different development models. Beyond these general trends, two developments relate directly to the international political economy of Latin America.

The first is that Latin America is generating its own development model for the first time in 50 years. This is the Alternativa Bolivariana para las Américas (ALBA), and it is Venezuelan president Hugo Chávez's answer to neoliberal development projects. ALBA is intended to be the alternative to the Free Trade Area of the Americas (FTAA), the US-initiated, neoliberal-leaning project for intra-hemispheric free trade. By late 2008, it had only five member states (Venezuela, Cuba, Bolivia, Nicaragua, and Honduras) and four with observer status (Ecuador, Uruguay, the Dominican Republic, and St. Kitts); however, it marks a dramatic departure from the norms of international trade, as ALBA's objective is promoting social development rather than merely liberalizing trade.[24] Venezuela has also pledged $1 billion to the Bank of the South, a Latin American–based multilateral lender envisioned as a counterweight to the IMF and World Bank. It will provide funding for projects to build "cooperative advantages," fight poverty, and preserve Latin America's autonomy.[25] How much of this becomes concrete and actually influences the course of Latin American development and the shape of the international political economy is an open question, especially given the serious global economic recession that began late in 2008. International economic relations change slowly and unpredictably. Nonetheless, having a serious alternative to the existing order issuing from Latin America and having a bit of an economic base with which to work constitute a dramatic shift away from the status quo.

The other development has been the commodity boom spurred by demand in China and India. Up to now, China has been the more important to Latin America. The Asian giant buys iron, copper, soybeans, and petroleum—materials it needs to fuel its industries—and sends Latin America manufactured goods ranging from cars to textiles. This of course is business as usual. However, China is also sending parts for assembly to Latin American factories, integrating the region into Chinese global supply chains. Again, this is all very new and what will happen when China suffers its first serious reverse is unknowable. However, Latin American countries are getting another chance to build their economies by riding the coattails of an economic power on the rise. This ought at least to lessen trade dependency on North America and open new opportunities for some Latin American firms; however, it is again necessary to observe that the worldwide slump prevailing in 2009 could undermine the region's prospects much as the Depression of the 1930s did.

Further Readings

Balaam, David, and Michael Veseth. *Introduction to International Political Economy*. Upper Saddle River, NJ: Prentice Hall, 2007.
Fitzgerald, E.V.K. *Global Markets and the Developing Economy*. London: Palgrave Macmillan, 2003.

Discussion Questions

① How much of Latin America's relatively weak position in international economic relations is due to domestic factors in each country? How much can be attributed to external factors—for example, international trade rules or the foreign policies of great economic powers, such as the United States?

② Which seems to be a better option for a Latin American country looking to develop its economy through international trade: leveraging its natural resources or developing new specialties in manufacturing or services?

Notes

1. There are also bilateral free trade agreements, which have been energetically pursued by Mexico and Chile. These, too, are considered further later in the chapter.

2. Alexander Hamilton, "Report on Manufactures," *The Theoretical Evolution of International Political Economy: A Reader*, eds. George Crane and Abla Amawi (New York: Oxford University Press, 1991) 37–47.

3. Friedrich List, *The National System of Political Economy*, tr. and ed. W.O. Henderson (London: Cass, 1982).

4. A trade regime refers to all the laws and regulations governing international trade, as well as to the institutions—global and regional international organizations focused on world commerce—that are built to make and apply those rules.

5. The catch is that although free trade makes the whole system more effective, it need not necessarily make any given country better off.

6. ECLAC, "Table 2.1.1.1," *Statistical Yearbook for Latin America and the Caribbean, 2007* (Santiago, CL: ECLAC, 2007) 85. For less optimistic figures, see José de Gregorio, "Economic Growth in Latin America: The Recent Experience," paper prepared for the conference: Latin America's Total Factor Productivity Puzzle, Santa Barbara, CA, 2007. www.bcentral.cl/jdegredo/pdf/jdg22092007/pdf.

7. Soviet foreign aid to Cuba was significant; the most frequently quoted figure is about $3 billion annually in the late 1980s. However, this high level of support aside, Communist foreign trade practice left Cuba producing the same raw materials for export as it did under capitalism.

8. Rose J. Spalding, *Capitalists and Revolution in Nicaragua: Opposition and Accommodation, 1979–1993* (Chapel Hill, NC: University of North Carolina Press, 1994) and Phil Ryan, *The Fall and Rise of the Market in Sandinista Nicaragua* (Montreal, QC: McGill-Queen's University Press, 1995) are useful sources of information.

9. Michael E. Porter, *The Competitive Advantage of Nations* (New York: Free Press, 1990).

10. Though we generally think of balance of payments referring to trade in goods and services, it also applies to capital flows.

11. For Brazil, see "History of Brazilian Currency," www.gwu.edu/~ibi/Statistics%20PDF%20Files/Brazilian%20Currencies.pdf; for Argentina, "Argentine Peso," www.spiritus-temporis.com/argentine-peso/history-of-the-argentine-currency-system.html; for Peru, Mike Hewitt, "The History of Money: Peru," *Goldseek*, February 3, 2009, www.news.goldseek.com/GoldSeek/1233678265.php; for Nicaragua, "Billetes y monedas," *Banco Central de Nicaragua*, www.bcn.gob.ni/moneda/.

12. A case might be made that the formal empire the United States acquired after the Spanish–American War was motivated more by strategic interests, namely having coaling stations for the navy and secure outposts in strategic locales. This need not preclude a conventional colony-imperial-center trading relationship; however, it would suggest that economic advantage was a secondary motive in conquering lands and creating colonies.

13. For figures see, Harry E. Vanden and Gary Prevost, *Politics of Latin America: The Power Game* (New York: Oxford University Press, 2006) 148–149.

14. For more details, see Carolyn Hall, *El café y el desarrollo historic-geografico de Costa Rica*, 3rd ed. (San José, CR: Editorial Costa Rica, 1982) and Ivan Molina and Stephen Palmer, *The History of Costa Rica* (San José, CR: Editorial de la Universidad de Costa Rica, 1998).

15. Simon Romero, "Peru Guards Its Guano as Demand Soars Again," *New York Times* (30 May 2008). www.nytimes.com/2008/05/30/world/americas/30peru.html.

16. Fernando Ricchi, *Chimneys in the Desert: Argentina during the Export Boom Years* (Stanford, CT: Stanford University Press, 2005).

17. Jeffry A. Frieden, *Global Capitalism: Its Fall and Rise in the Twentieth Century* (New York: W.W. Norton, 2006) 111–116. Of course, the greatest nineteenth-century battles over the gold standard occurred in the United States in the 1890s.

18. Population increase made net economic growth closer to 2.5 per cent per capita.

19. Carlos Marichal, *A Century of Debt Crises in Latin America: From Independence to the Great Depression, 1820–1930* (Princeton, NJ: Princeton University Press, 1989).

20. Manuel Pastor, "Capital Flight from Latin America," *World Development* 18:1 (1990): 1–18.

21. Geske Dijkstra, "The PRSP Approach and the Illusion of Improved Aid Effectiveness: Lessons from Bolivia, Honduras and Nicaragua," *Development Policy Review* 23 (2005): 443–464.

22. David R. Dye and David Close, "Patrimonialism and Economic Policy in the Alemán Administration," *Undoing Democracy: The Politics of Electoral Caudillismo*, eds. David Close and Kalowatie Deonandan (Lanham, MD: Lexington Books, 2004) 119–142, examine the HIPC as it worked in Nicaragua.

23. A full list of all free trade agreements is available through WorldTradeLaw.net. www.worldtradelaw.net/fta/ftadatabase/ftas.asp.

24. See Paul Kellogg, "Regional Integration in Latin America: Dawn of an Alternative to Neoliberalism?" *New Political Science* 29:2 (2007): 187–209.

25. "What is ALBA?" www.alternativabolivariana.org/pdf/alba_mice_en.pdf (accessed 26 June 2008).

10

Latin American International Relations

Thinking about International Relations

Political science students who take courses in international relations (IR) quickly learn the moral of Thucydides' "The Melian Dialogues": The strong do what they will; the weak do what they must. Applying this dictum to Latin America gives rise to a series of complications. One is that not all Latin American states are equally strong or weak. Brazil, Mexico, Argentina, Chile, and now Venezuela all are at least "middle powers," on a par with Canada, Spain, or Australia. Cuba has punched far above its weight in international affairs for a half-century now, thanks to its symbolic importance as a revolutionary regime and the exceptional abilities of Fidel Castro as a politician. Were Colombia, the third most populous state in the region, ever to overcome its grave internal problems, it, too, might accede to the ranks of middling powers. Then there are the rest: small, poor states that have few resources to bring to the global table. Before dismissing them as lacking international importance, though, we must recall that "weak" and "poor" are relative concepts. These states interact with one another, not just with bigger powers. Presumably their behavior among their peers reflects the more equal distribution of capacity among the actors.

To talk sensibly about Latin American states as international actors and of the international ties of the region and the states that compose it demands a multifaceted approach. To begin with, it is necessary to review the basic themes used in the study of politics among nations. Because the international political system has different traits than any national system, the analysis of IR uses different concepts and has various perspectives. From this foundation, the chapter moves on to the relations between the states of the region and the world's great powers—most obviously the United States—then considers relations among the Latin American states before examining some contemporary trends.

The Basics of International Relations

International politics are literally anarchic: there is no central governing authority in the international system. Because there is no central authority, there is no body responsible for enforcing laws. And because there is neither an officially designated law enforcement mechanism, nor a law-making or law-adjudicating one either, every actor in the international political system has to look out for itself. This is called the principle of self-help and it is the only sure means of defense in a war of each-against-all.

What causes the international system to work this way is the concept of national sovereignty. States, sometimes called nation-states, are the principal actors in the international system, and every state, great or small, possesses sovereignty. That means that no one can interfere with the internal operations of a state. States have governments that make laws that their citizens can be forced to obey; but there is no global government that makes laws that states must follow.

There is, though, global governance. In practice, states cooperate on some issues and generally act according to widely accepted principles. This gives an element of order to the international system and makes it possible for states and their citizens to carry out many daily tasks with a reasonable degree of security. However, this is not law but convention.

Thinking about international relations divides into two analytical schools: realism, the more influential, especially among practitioners; and liberal internationalism (see Table 10.1). Realism emphasizes power, national interest, and conflict between and among states. Liberal internationalism, or idealism, stresses cooperation, the role of nonstate actors in world affairs, and the part taken by international governmental organizations (IGOs)—for example, the United Nations—and international non-governmental organizations (INGOs), such as the Red Cross/Red Crescent.[1] Both schools work from abstract models and each describes some parts of international politics better than the other does. So combining the most relevant aspects of realism and idealism is generally necessary to get a thorough, accurate picture of reality.

Realism argues that states are the actors that count in international politics and that national security is the preeminent concern of states. Because there is no law to constrain power, every state has to build and preserve as much capacity as it can to protect itself and promote its national interest. Accordingly, a state has to accumulate power, which is the ability to get what it wants out of its relations with other states. Thus realism stresses the conflictual side of international relations and sees this struggle taking place within the international system. How power is distributed within that system influences how states relate to each other.

Logically and empirically, the international system can have one of three basic structures, depending on how power is concentrated: multipolar,

Table 10.1 Realism and Liberal Internationalism: A Quick Comparative Overview

	Realism	Liberal Internationalism
International System	Anarchic; each state for itself	States interdependent
State	Main actor; seeks power to secure the national interest	States predominate but IGOs + INGOs + other non-state actors are also significant
Peace	Strength brings peace	Law and shared goals bring peace
Global Governance	If and to the extent strongest states want it	Necessary, real, and growing stronger

Source: Adapted from Eric Mintz, David Close, and Osvaldo Croci, *Politics, Power and the Common Good: An Introduction to Political Science.* 2nd. ed. Toronto: Pearson Educational Publishing, 2008. 489.

bipolar, and unipolar. In a multipolar system, power is relatively dispersed among four or more states.[2] An example of a multipolar international system is the balance-of-power system that prevailed in the nineteenth century. There were several relatively equally powerful states that dominated international affairs: Great Britain, France, Germany, the Austro-Hungarian Empire, the Ottoman Empire, and Russia. As long as no state or bloc of states became too powerful, the system was stable and peace was maintained. However, the system broke down with the start of World War I (1914–1918) and did not regain its former effectiveness in the inter-war period.

A bipolar system is the second possibility. The best example of this system was the standoff between the United States and the Soviet Union during the Cold War (1946–1991). During that period, states aligned with either Washington or Moscow. While neutrality was imaginable, the realities of the situation made choosing sides almost mandatory. This was certainly so in Latin America. Until the Cuban Revolution of 1959, Washington was unchallenged. Moscow gained a second ally for a while after the success of the Sandinista Revolution in Nicaragua in 1979, although the Sandinistas were careful to maintain solid ties with the West, even if the United States government was hostile.

Finally, there can be a unipolar system, in which one state dominates the rest of the world. Something like this existed after the collapse of the Soviet Union (1991), when the United States emerged unquestionably as the world's preeminent power. The defining characteristic of this system is that the only superpower can and does act unilaterally. In a bipolar system, one superpower countervails the other, while in a multipolar system a state needs to line up allies. Washington's failure to consolidate a rapid victory in Iraq suggests that the international system's unipolar moment may have passed. However, in the western hemisphere, the United States is still the only superpower.

Besides a global international system there are regional subsystems. Latin America is part of the inter-American system, but there is also a purely Latin American system, which excludes the United States. A state such as Brazil can have middling importance on the world stage but be a significant actor in inter-American affairs and a substantial power within Latin America.

Where realists focus on conflict, liberal internationalists concentrate on cooperation. Like realists, idealists acknowledge that states usually cooperate because it is in their interest to do so. Among the policy areas where interstate cooperation exists are certain technical areas (civil aviation or telecommunications), economics and trade (the World Trade Organization), and national security (various collective security organizations, such as NATO). The growth of problems that cannot be addressed within the territorial boundaries of a single state, like climate change or disease control, suggests that international governance will grow. Latin America has a number of regional IGOs, including the Organization of American States, the Pan-American Health Organization, the Sistema Económico Latinoamericano (SELA, or Latin American Economic System), as well as several regional and sub-regional trading blocs, such as Mercosur. There is also the recently formed (2008) Unión de Naciones Suramericanas (UNASUR, or Union of South American Nations), which includes a South American Security Council, a collective security organization. On the whole, however, international cooperation within the region has been slow to develop beyond the bilateral level.

When dealing with international politics, then, we need to work with different expectations. This is true even when our interest is foreign policy —the choices a state makes about how to relate with other international actors. At one level, foreign policy is like any other public policy. It is made by a government with specific priorities and values. And like all public policy, foreign policy occasionally bumps up against unbending reality and has to change its goals and methods.

Nevertheless, foreign policy brings special challenges. The most obvious of these emerges when foreign policy deals with high politics: issues of war and peace, national defense, and at times even national survival. Even when the stakes are not as high, dealing with other states presents special challenges (for example, power disparities and irreconcilable agendas). Although similar problems present themselves in the domestic domain, governments generally have more tools at their disposal in seeking an acceptable solution. This can make foreign policy a particular challenge for governments with limited resources.

Latin America and International Relations Theory

When you study international relations in the United States, you learn a lot about great powers and how they act because the United States has been one of the world's great powers for nearly 70 years. The international politics of great powers also receive substantial attention in Canada, a middle power, because that country has been very active in world affairs for more than 60 years. As a result, most North Americans have a perspective on international affairs that reflects being at or close to the heart of international politics. Things are different in Latin America.

Since independence, the states of Latin America have been parts of the international system. However, although they are legally the equals of any other state, geographical marginality—former US secretary of state Henry Kissinger said that nothing important happens south of 40 degrees north latitude, roughly where Washington, DC, is located—combines with having no substantial world powers within the region to relegate the nations of Latin America to the sidelines in international affairs. Most of the time, Latin American states are the objects of international action and not the subjects defining world politics.

Given the differences between North America and Latin America, it would be surprising if they did not have different perspectives on international politics. This is especially true since the academic study of international relations has for more than 60 years been dominated by practitioners from the United States. Arlene Tickner has surveyed academic international relations in Latin America and the Caribbean and found that they differed from the US-influenced norm in several important ways.[3]

First, although no one questioned the lawlessness of the international order, Latin Americans saw a hierarchical structure to world politics: there were the great powers, the core of the system, at the top, followed by a slightly larger number of second-level, supporting players, and then everybody else followed. Second, dependency theory has had a marked influence, reflecting the sensitivity of those in the region (and elsewhere in the Third World) to the reality of often having your nation's fate substantially controlled by foreigners. Evidence of the impact of dependency thinking is found in the concept of autonomy. Although it has much in common with sovereignty, a keystone of conventional IR, autonomy gives greater stress to the ways the international system and foreign actors impinge on a state's ability to develop economically. There are other examples of how those on the margins of the world adapt mainstream concepts to conform better to their realties (see Text Box 10.1.). Finally, Tickner notes that Latin American scholars have shown little interest in the intradisciplinary debates that occasionally rock academic IR in North America and Western Europe.

Text Box 10.1 Making Realism More Realistic

The academic study of international relations has European roots, but its greatest growth came in the United States after World War II. Its concepts revolve around the high politics of war and peace, and the objects it studies are great powers whose actions can change the shape of the world. What does this have to say to Latin America or any other poor, marginalized part of the world? The theories of *peripheral realism* and *subaltern realism* are two responses to this question.

Carlos Escudé of Argentina developed the concept of peripheral realism. He argues that there is a hierarchy of power in the international system, and while a very few states, such as the United States, set the rules, most have the rules imposed on them As a result, for these peripheral states, realism means avoiding conflict with great powers and defining the national interest in terms of development.[4]

Subaltern realism is associated with Mohammed Ayoob, a native of India who teaches in the United States. The essence of this concept is that among weaker states, domestic concerns play a significant part in shaping international goals and postures. Ayoob thus stresses the interplay of domestic and international factors in explaining how the weak act in world affairs.[5]

Both authors suggest that traditional perspectives in academic IR and in actual foreign policy-making err in assuming that all states have identical aims as international actors. Esucudé and Ayoob point out that those with less power necessarily tie their foreign objectives to internal goals. However, this leaves open the question of how peripheral or subaltern states act when dealing with each other.

International Politics within Latin America

When we think of Latin American international relations, what normally comes to mind is how the states of the region deal with the world's great powers. This is understandable because of the complex and conflictive relationship the United States has had with Latin America. However, one can argue that most interstate relations for Latin American countries are intraregional and therefore take place between and among the Latin American states themselves. These relations, like all international relations, have both conflictive and cooperative elements. To canvass what for most Canadians and Americans is the little-known terrain of international politics between and among the states of Latin America, we highlight historically important conflicts and attempts at cooperation within the region. We start with conflict.

Recent Interstate Conflict in Latin America

On March 2, 2008, Colombian troops destroyed a camp of the Fuerzas Armadas Revolucionarias de Colombia (FARC, or Revolutionary Armed Forces of Colombia), a powerful guerrilla group financed by kidnapping and drugs. In the attack, the Colombian forces killed Raúl Reyes, the guerrillas' second-in-command, and seized a number of computers that contained material implicating the Venezuelan and Ecuadoran governments as the guerrillas' collaborators. This was a great coup for the Colombians and would have been greater if the camp had not been in Ecuador. And since the Colombians were not in hot pursuit of the FARC (that is, not pursuing them into Ecuador from Colombia), this was a clear case of Colombia violating Ecuador's sovereignty. Rafael Correa, Ecuador's president, protested vigorously.

Things got hotter when Venezuelan president Hugo Chávez entered the picture. Chávez was a friend of the FARC—only two months earlier he had campaigned to have the FARC declared a belligerent force and not an illegal insurgency, an action that would have made the guerrillas a state in formation and afforded them certain legal privileges. Even so, the Venezuelan's response was unexpectedly forceful, as he ordered the chief of staff of Venezuela's military to move troops to the Colombian border. Fortunately, Álvaro Uribe, the Colombian president, did not respond in kind. Even more fortunately, at a meeting of Latin American presidents held shortly after the flare-up, President Leonel Fernández of the Dominican Republic got Chávez and Uribe to shake hands and move their dispute to a more conventionally diplomatic forum.[6]

This tripartite dispute, between Colombia on the one side and Ecuador and Venezuela on the other, was unmistakably high politics. The stakes were sovereignty and national security. Military force had been employed by one actor, albeit against an insurgent, and armed forces mobilized by another. Headlines around the world warned of a possible war among the three South American states. Although none of the states involved were major international actors, the confrontation that arose was very much the stuff of realist international relations.

One explanation for its peaceful resolution comes from the democratic peace hypothesis (see Text Box 10.2). It would emphasize that the fact that all three parties to the conflict were democracies, albeit ones with particularly strong presidents, contributed to its pacific resolution. Alternatively one could argue that once President Chávez reflected a little, he backed away from his ideological stance and adopted a more pragmatic posture, while President Correa's anger may also have cooled, and President Uribe managed to stay calm. What mattered was that all three proved open to compromises. Sometimes, though, willingness to compromise is absent or only emerges after costly conflict or painstaking mediation by

> **Text Box 10.2** The Democratic Peace Hypothesis
>
> Democracies do not fight other democracies. That is the essence of the democratic peace hypothesis. This hypothesis—and like any hypothesis it can be tested and either confirmed or disconfirmed—is derived from two sources. One is the historical record of the last two centuries, which shows remarkably few wars between states that would have been considered democratic. The other is Immanuel Kant's 1795 essay, *Perpetual Peace*. Currently, there is substantial debate among theorists of international relations regarding the democratic peace hypothesis. Critics believe that the growing number of democracies heightens the possibility of armed conflict between democracies (for example, border conflicts). Proponents argue that the more open and pluralistic decision-making mechanisms of democracies will continue making war between democratic states rare.

outsiders. This is what happened in the Beagle Channel dispute between Argentina and Chile, which began when both states were ruled by military dictatorships.

The Beagle Channel lies at the southernmost tip of South America, and Argentina and Chile had disputed rights to this waterway connecting the Atlantic and Pacific since 1902.[7] In 1971, the definition of the boundary between the two states was referred to the International Court of Justice (ICJ) and to arbitration by Queen Elizabeth II of England.[8] Her decision, issued in 1977, was rejected by Argentina because it gave a number of islands to Chile. Bilateral negations failed, as did a Chilean call for ICJ mediation.

On December 9, 1978, Argentina dispatched warships to the Beagle Channel, and Chile did the same. Two days later, Pope John Paul II called for continued talks, and by December 23, both parties had accepted papal mediation. As both dictatorships boasted of their Catholic identities, they could hardly refuse John Paul II's offer. Before the Pope's representative could bring the parties to an agreement, however, Argentina invaded the Falklands in 1982 (see below). The Argentines' crushing defeat at the hands of the British spelled the end of the dictatorship and a democratic government under Raúl Alfonsín was elected in 1983. By 1984 a treaty had been signed.

A little more than a decade later, in 1995, the Cenepa conflict between Ecuador and Peru actually did lead to war.[9] Peru and Ecuador had fought three earlier wars (in 1829, 1859, and 1941) over their ill-defined boundary east of the Andes in the Amazonian lowlands, the last costing Ecuador roughly half its territory. Although the 1942 Treaty of Rio de Janeiro defined most of the new border, it left a 47-mile (78 km) strip unspecified. Peru argued that the boundary was the Condor Mountain Range.

Ecuador, though, asserted that it was the Cenepa River, which gave it both a little more territory and, since the Cenepa flowed into a tributary of the Amazon, a basis for claiming unrestricted access to the great river.

What generated the conflict was the decision by both states to set up armed border posts in the disputed region, something that had created a minor, nonlethal, conflict in 1981. This time, however, each country mobilized some 5,000 soldiers and sent aircraft in to provide close support. Fighting occurred between January and March 1995, and both combatants suffered significant casualties: there were an estimated 500 battle deaths, with a disproportionate number being Peruvian. The war's outcome effectively ratified the original Peruvian position, with slight modifications. A treaty embodying those provisions was ratified by both states in 1998.

It should be noted that this war occurred while Ecuador was democratic, and although Peru's president had become increasingly authoritarian, he had been freely elected in 1990. It is probable that the nature of this border conflict, festering for more than a century and a half, outweighed whatever effect democratic governments might have had.

The last militarized conflict to be presented is the Soccer War, fought between El Salvador and Honduras in 1969. It is called the Soccer War because it broke out after El Salvador defeated Honduras to qualify for the 1970 World Cup. However, the war's roots are found not in rowdy fans but a 1969 Honduran law that took land from Salvadoran immigrants and gave it to Hondurans.[10] Throughout the twentieth century, land-hungry Salvadoran peasants had migrated to the neighboring and relatively lightly populated Honduras. When the law was adopted in 1969, it was estimated that about one-fifth of the peasant population of Honduras was of Salvadoran descent. The Honduran land law dispossessed thousands of Salvadorans, who were forced to emigrate. Anti-Salvadoran feelings had been high in Honduras and now anti-Honduran sentiments grew rapidly in El Salvador.

Fighting began on July 14, 1969, when the army of El Salvador invaded Honduras. Although it lasted only four days, it is estimated that 250 troops and 2,000 civilians died, while about 100,000 people were displaced. Almost all these losses occurred in Honduras. As well, the roughly 130,000 Salvadorans who then left Honduras to return to very difficult conditions in El Salvador should be counted as unofficial casualties. Unlike the three other cases treated here, this conflict was neither a classical border dispute nor did it grow out of a border incident. Rather, it pitted immigrant against native-born in a struggle for ever scarcer resources.

Less dangerous disputes have also arisen between Latin American states. Two cases illustrate what those have been like. Uruguay and Argentina have been embroiled in a dispute since 2005 over the former's decision to allow paper mills to be built along the Río Uruguay, which forms part of the boundary between the two states.[11] Argentina claimed that Uruguay's government acted illegally in giving the project the go-ahead without referring it to the joint Argentina-Uruguay commission that is supposed to control development along the river. Then there is the pollution problem, which will be familiar to anyone who has ever passed through a mill town. Not only is there the signature rotten egg smell, but the toxic chemicals used in papermaking are also dumped into the river. Argentine citizens living along the river reacted with protests, while Uruguayan authorities closed access to bridges crossing the river, halting both protesters and normal vehicular traffic. Then in November 2007, Uruguay's president, Tabaré Vázquez, gave the mills the green light. Buenos Aires continued to protest officially and Argentines facing the mills did so informally. However, Vázquez and his government acted to defend their view of Uruguay's national interest.

The second case concerns Nicaragua's Río San Juan boundary with Costa Rica.[12] Most riparian boundaries are set mid-channel to allow both parties free access. The Rio San Juan is different. The Cañas-Jerez Treaty (1858) gave Nicaragua the river all the way to the Costa Rican shore but guarantees Costa Rica navigation rights. In 1888, the Cleveland Award, issued by US president Grover Cleveland, revisited the issue, establishing that Costa Rica could not put gunboats on the river, though it was allowed to protect its commercial vessels as they used the San Juan. Over time, a modus vivendi was reached that saw Costa Rican authorities inform their Nicaraguan counterparts when they were putting armed patrols on the water (for example, when going to relieve isolated police outposts along the river). However, Costa Rica began ignoring this practice, and on July 15, 1998, Nicaragua issued an order prohibiting Costa Rican officers from carrying weapons on the San Juan. Costa Rica responded by refusing Nicaraguan officials the right to land on Costa Rican soil.

Costa Rica was in the wrong, and the issue might have been resolved quickly had Nicaraguan president Arnoldo Alemán not treated it as an affront to his country's national sovereignty. However, his administration was facing scandals and Alemán may have wanted to divert attention. For whatever reason, the conflict remained unresolved for nearly two years. A settlement was reached only after a round of summit diplomacy, involving Alemán and Costa Rican president Miguel Ángel Rodríguez, with the occasional mediation of the Secretary-General of the Organization of American States. These efforts restored the *status quo ante*.

Boundary issues are plainly important sources of international tension within Latin America. However, arms races can also threaten the peace. Scarcely a year goes by when there are not articles in the international press describing a new arms race in Latin America. In 2008, it was Venezuela, on a multibillion-dollar arms-shopping spree in Russia, that was in the news, but Brazil, Chile, Peru, and Colombia have made similar headlines over the last 10 years. Although overall spending on arms in

> **Text Box 10.3** The Security Dilemma
>
> If I, as the ruler of country X, feel threatened militarily by my neighbors, my most logical course of action is to acquire more effective weapons and mobilize more troops so that my nation will be more secure. However, if I do that, my neighbors will then feel the same insecurity that I had felt. As those states are also governed by rational, logical men and women, they, too, will get better weapons and deploy more military personnel. Then I am back where I started. That is the security dilemma: In making my state secure, I must make others insecure. As they make themselves more secure, my state again becomes insecure.

Latin America and the Caribbean fell from 1.5 per cent of GDP in 1997 to 1.3 per cent in 2006,[13] there is still concern that one country's increased arms expenditures will cause its neighbors to boost theirs (see Text Box 10.3). This is partly because some countries have raised their defense budgets considerably. Venezuela's budget, for example, increased by 35 per cent between 2004 and 2006.[14] Given the frequency of border conflicts throughout Latin America over the last half-century, an arms race could be a dangerously destabilizing force.

Looked at in comparative perspective, Latin American military budgets do not appear particularly large.[15] In 2005, only nine spent over 1 per cent of GDP on defense, but two of those, Chile—rebuilding its forces—and Colombia—engaged in a counterinsurgent war, dedicated 3.8 per cent of their nations' income to the military. This is still below Washington's 4.1 per cent; however the United States was fighting in both Iraq and Afghanistan at the time. Nevertheless, a glimpse at the weapons that some of the states are buying (see Table 10.2) indicates the level of sophistication that some of these militaries possess. And we must remember that as late as 1990, Argentina and Brazil were pursuing the development of nuclear weapons.[16]

Interstate Cooperation in Latin America Since 1960

Despite what the foregoing material suggests, there are also instances of international cooperation among the countries of Latin America. The best known evidence of this is Mercosur and the other free trade treaties that were discussed in Chapter 9. By lowering tariffs and encouraging broader economic integration these efforts can help advance cooperation between states. Having shared economic interests should give governments another strong reason to keep international conflicts from arising and move quickly to resolve those that do appear. Nevertheless, the fact that the

Table 10.2 Selected Arms Orders and Deliveries, Latin America, 2007

Country	Purchases (Source)
Brazil	21 fighters (France, United States) 35 helicopters (Russia) 270 main battle tanks (Germany)
Chile	3 frigates (United Kingdom) 28 fighters (United States) 100 main battle tanks (Germany)
Venezuela	24 fighters (Russia) 100,000 AK-47 assault rifles (Russia) factory to build AK-47s (Russian licence) 47 helicopters (Russia)

Sources: Compiled from International Institute of Strategic Studies, *The Military Balance, 2008*, 100–101; Stockholm International Peace Institute, *SIPRI Yearbook 2007*, 287.

Uruguay–Argentina dispute over paper mills involved Mercosur partners did not facilitate reaching a settlement.

Equally familiar is the Organization of American States (OAS). Although all Latin American states are members (Cuba, though, has been suspended since 1962), the OAS had been so dominated by the United States that it was seen through much of the twentieth century as a cat's paw for Washington. This image began to change in 1979 when the OAS rejected US initiatives to send a multilateral peacekeeping force to Nicaragua to thwart the soon-to-be-successful Sandinista revolutionaries. Since then, the OAS has established the Inter-American Court of Human Rights, been involved in election monitoring, and conducted peace-building operations in Central America, the Caribbean, and Colombia. Most recently, the organization was instrumental in bringing under control the tensions that arose when Colombia violated Ecuadoran territory to attack guerrillas in 2008.

Perhaps more interesting are the instances of cooperation that grow out of conflicts. In 1997, the Nicaraguan navy detained 11 Honduran fishing boats operating illegally in Nicaraguan waters in the Gulf of Fonseca, a body shared by El Salvador, Honduras, and Nicaragua. Although use of the Gulf is governed by a 1901 treaty, neither Nicaragua nor Honduras had clearly defined their boundaries in the Gulf, creating ideal conditions for border conflicts. Illegal fishing often produces strong responses from states whose stocks are being poached, because it depletes a common property resource: the Cod War between Iceland and Britain (1958) saw shots fired, and the Canada–Spain Turbot War (1995) apparently came close to that. In this case, Honduran naval patrols tried to free the boats and their 14 crew, prompting the Nicaraguan forces to open fire. Luckily, there were no casualties. In the wake of this incident, representatives of the militaries of the three countries agreed to conduct coordinated patrols. There have been no further serious confrontations, suggesting that conflicts sometimes teach states to cooperate.

Another Central American example deals with states seeking peace. However, this is not about warring states negotiating a peace treaty but rather about the nations of Central America working together to end insurgent wars in El Salvador, Guatemala, and Nicaragua in the 1980s. The process evolved through a series of steps. Between 1983 and 1985, it was known as the Contadora Process. In 1986, it became known as the Esquipulas Process, taking its name from the Guatemalan town where its first meeting was held. In February 1987, President Óscar Arias of Costa Rica proposed a peace plan. This eventually became the Esquipulas II Accord. Although rejected by the United States because it recognized that the Sandinista government of Nicaragua had been democratically elected in 1984, the initiative led to the beginning of talks that eventually bought peace to the region.[17]

The Contadora–Esquipulas Process is important for three reasons. First, it dealt with high politics: peace, war, and national security. Second, it went against the express wishes of the United States, the dominant power in the western hemisphere. Third, it was carried out by small, poor, weak states, thus doing precisely what the weak are supposedly incapable of doing in world affairs.

The final example of interstate cooperation in post-1960 Latin America is perhaps less edifying than any of the above. We know that like-minded states often find it easier to collaborate among themselves on matters of international significance. Thus we frequently see Canada working with Australia or Sweden in international affairs. But like-minded does not necessarily mean democratic. Operation Condor involved the cooperation of the intelligence agencies of the military dictatorships of Argentina, Bolivia, Brazil, Chile, Paraguay, and Uruguay, and occasionally those of Ecuador and Peru. From 1975 to 1983, the participants in Operation Condor shared intelligence on, and more importantly carried out assassinations of, political opponents. It is doubtful that liberal internationalists have Operation Condor in mind when they speak of international cooperation, although that is clearly what it was.[18]

From Independence to 1960

Conflict in Latin America usually conjures up images of coups and revolutions, not wars between states. However, the period from independence to 1960 saw several serious and significant interstate conflicts. One of these, the 1941 war between Ecuador and Peru, we have already alluded to, but there are four others that merit a closer look: the National War, 1856 to

1857; the War of the Triple Alliance, 1864 to 1870; the War of the Pacific, 1879 to 1883; and the Chaco War, 1932 to 1935.[19]

In the National War, Costa Rica, Honduras, El Salvador, and Guatemala, along with some Nicaraguans, fought the government of Nicaragua. However, that government was not in Nicaraguan hands. Since 1821, Nicaragua had been convulsed by an effectively endless civil war between Liberals from León and the Conservatives of Granada. In 1855, the Liberals decided to swing the odds in their favor by bringing in mercenaries (then called filibusters) from the United States. William Walker, a soldier of fortune, brought his 57-man American Phalanx to Nicaragua. Walker quickly defeated the Conservatives, then turned on the Liberals, set himself up as president, and began working to have Nicaragua admitted to the Union as a slave state.

Costa Rica was the first to declare war on the mercenaries, inflicting heavy losses on Walker before its army was struck by cholera and had to withdraw. El Salvador, Guatemala, and Honduras soon joined the fight. In May 1857, after suffering repeated defeats and having no easy means of escape, Walker surrendered to the commander of a US Navy sloop standing off the Nicaraguan coast. Three years later, Walker returned to Central America, landing in Honduras. This time he was captured by the British and turned over to the Hondurans, who executed him.

The War of the Triple Alliance had more conventional belligerents, as all four states involved were governed by their own nationals. However, it was unusual in one important respect: a small poor country, Paraguay, confronted three neighbors, Argentina, Brazil, and Uruguay. Eventually the Paraguayans were worn down, losing at least half their total population and about 55,000 square miles (150,000 sq. km) of territory to Argentina and Brazil.

Among the war's causes were boundary disputes between Paraguay and both Argentina and Brazil, as well as Argentine and Brazilian designs on Uruguay. When a Uruguayan president friendly to Brazil was installed in 1864 with Brazilian assistance, Paraguay's president, Francisco Solano López, responded by declaring war on Brazil. This obviously brought Uruguay into the conflict on Brazil's side. A little later López also declared war on Argentina. Although Paraguay probably had the strongest army of any of the four belligerents, perhaps even outstripping the other three combined, the country succumbed after the long war. This was the bloodiest war in South American history, with a minimum of 300,000 deaths among soldiers and civilians.

Although less costly in terms of lives, the War of the Pacific (1879–1883), involving Chile, Bolivia, and Peru, gave rise to consequences still felt today. This, too, grew from a border conflict, this time in the nitrate-rich Atacama Desert. The precipitant was a decision by Bolivia to abrogate unilaterally a treaty that obligated it to share tax revenues with Chile in a territory under Bolivian jurisdiction but worked by Chileans. A secret treaty signed by Peru and Bolivia in 1873 that obligated the signatories to guarantee each other's territory and independence brought Peru into the war.

Chile was more developed economically and politically. It had built a stronger navy and a more professional army. As a result, Chile's forces prevailed, although they were outnumbered two to one. Chile annexed Bolivia's coastal province—leaving that country landlocked—as well as the southernmost Peruvian province. Obtaining these areas (and losers ceding territories to winners was a common outcome of nineteenth-century wars) increased Chile's nitrate reserves, which drove the country's economy for the remainder of the 1800s. Although the cessions were defined by treaty, to this day Bolivia continues pressing Chile for the restoration of sovereign access to the sea.

This question of maritime access was also a partial cause of the Chaco War (1932–1935) between Paraguay and Bolivia. The Chaco was a vast, thinly populated wilderness separating Bolivia and Paraguay. Although the region, about 100,000 square miles (260,000 sq. km) was legally Bolivian, such settlement and development that occurred had been undertaken by Paraguay (for example, permitting the settlement of Canadian Mennonites in the Chaco in the 1920s). However, the discovery of oil on the western fringes of the Chaco in Bolivia made La Paz want to makes its legal claims real, if only to get access to the Paraguay River and have a port from which to ship its oil.

Bolivia appeared to have the advantage when hostilities began in 1932: it was larger, wealthier, and had a more modern military. Yet these advantages were offset by having to fight in unfamiliar territory and having an army composed mainly of indigenous conscripts with low morale. In the end, Paraguay triumphed and received the Chaco, which proved not to have oil. Of greater consequence, Bolivia's defeat in the Chaco War led to an extended period of political unrest that culminated in the Bolivian Revolution of 1952.

Latin America's interstate conflicts, both modern and historic, arose from material causes, not ideological ones. Which state controls a given territory determines whose citizens will benefit from that territory: this has been the logic of the many boundary disputes. The Soccer War was different and offered a preview of what analysts such as Thomas Homer-Dixon[20] predict will be tomorrow's wars. It was certainly about access to resources, but instead of being about where a border was drawn, the conflict between El Salvador and Honduras erupted from a dispute between land-hungry immigrants from the former occupying land that the equally impoverished citizens of the latter sought in order to improve their lives.

The World and Latin America

When most of us think of Latin America in world affairs, we think of the relations between the states of the region and the world's great powers. Over the past century this has meant principally the United States, but during the Cold War it also included the Soviet Union. Before that it was Britain and France, and now China is entering the picture. However, there are also nonstate international actors, notably the UN and its agencies, along with the international financial institutions (IFIs) and some international non-governmental organizations (INGOs), which have had important roles in Latin American affairs since the 1980s. And even middle powers such as Canada, a NAFTA member, occasionally assume a measure of prominence.

In all of these cases, the assumption is that the Latin American state is always the weaker party, destined to do what it must, while the foreign actor does what it will. Although there are exceptions, this has generally been the case. What changes with time is the means by which the greater power chooses to exercise its influence. It would be foolhardy to say the age of direct foreign military intervention is past; however, it does seem that this option now comes farther down the list of alternatives than a century ago.

The Europeans

In the nineteenth century, European powers played a substantial role in Latin American affairs. Although their presence declined through most of the twentieth century, since the 1980s, Europe's presence has risen again, thanks to the economic resurgence of Spain and Portugal, as well as to the interest of the European Union in expanding trade ties.

Of the original colonizers, Spain has had the greater impact. In the 1860s, for example, Spain was invited by Dominican dictator Pedro Santana to annex the Dominican Republic. Madrid did so and occupied the island from 1861 to 1865. However, almost continuous insurrection led the Spanish to rescind the annexation and withdraw. Then in 1865 and 1866, Spain was involved in a war with Peru and its Chilean ally, called either the Guano War or the Pacific War. This was a naval conflict that grew from a conflict between Basque guano miners and Peruvians. A Spanish naval squadron, which was on a scientific mission off the coast of Peru, sought to protect its nationals, and mishandled diplomacy led to war. While the Spanish were successful militarily, a shortage of ammunition and a belief that the South Americans had been taught to respect Spaniards led the Europeans to withdraw. From that time until the 1980s, relations between Spain and Latin America were relatively low key and built mostly around cultural ties.

French influence was especially felt in Mexico. In 1837, in order to collect claims against Mexico for damages suffered by French citizens, France sent a squadron to the Gulf of Mexico. French troops landed, captured towns and forts, and eventually received the money sought. Because one of the claimants was a baker, this intervention became known as the Pastry War.

Much more dramatic was the French occupation of Mexico from 1862 to 1867. The pretext was Mexico's failure to pay foreign debts, an issue that figured prominently in Latin America's nineteenth-century relations with the United States, but Emperor Napoleon III's dreams of a new French empire in America also played a part. Thus, although Britain and Spain joined France in a punitive expedition to seize the customs house at Veracruz along with the import and export duties paid there, the first two soon left. France, however, stayed, conquered the country, and put a Habsburg archduke on a newly created Mexican throne as Emperor Maximilian I. Mexican nationalists, led by Benito Juárez (whom the French had forced from the presidency), resisted the new regime. Perhaps more importantly from the French perspective, after the end of its Civil War in 1865, the United States, with a million men still under arms, made its displeasure known. In 1867, Napoleon III withdrew the French military, but Maximilian stayed on, surrendered to the Mexicans, and was executed by a firing squad.

As the greatest power of the nineteenth century, Britain naturally had a notable presence in Latin America. In large part, this was economic, and the country was particularly strong in Argentina and Chile. However, between 1655 and 1860 it claimed a protectorate over the Miskito Indians who inhabited the Mosquito Coast of eastern Nicaragua. Although London transferred suzerainty (control over foreign but not internal affairs) over the region to Managua in 1860, the Miskito resisted and Nicaragua did not assume full control until 1893.

More memorable than the above is the Falklands War, April 2 to June 24, 1982. The Argentine military dictatorship that had seized power in 1976 was facing increasing internal unrest in early 1982. To boost its popularity the junta decided to invade the Falkland Islands, known as the Islas Malvinas in Argentina, the country that had long claimed them. These islands in the South Atlantic have been claimed variously by Britain, France, Spain, and Argentina but had been a British colony since 1834. Argentina's rulers believed that retaking the Malvinas would not only be popular but also easy, expecting that London would recognize a fait accompli and negotiate their transfer to Buenos Aires. However, the government of the United Kingdom decided to fight. The resulting Argentine defeat soon brought an end to the dictatorship, and although Argentina retains its claims to the islands, these claims are now made peacefully.

The United States of America

The United States has been the most important foreign power in Latin America for more than a century. Even before that, it was the most powerful actor in the Caribbean and Mexico. The Clayton–Bulwer Treaty (1850) between the United States and the United Kingdom recognized the fact of US dominance in Central America, while the Mexican War (1846–1848), which in Mexico is known as the War with the United States or simply the US Intervention, gave proof of Washington's might along its southern border. The United States has long been the western hemisphere's dominant power. The power disparity between that country and the states of Latin America has always been great, all the more so since Washington's dominance in the hemisphere has not been seriously challenged for more than a century and a half. This has allowed the makers of US foreign policy unusual latitude in defining their relations with their weaker southern neighbors.

Frequently this freedom has seen power used in ways that vexes Latin Americans. The list of invasions, interventions, veiled overthrows, lesser cases of subversion, and intimidation is long. To facilitate understanding of more than 200 years of US–Latin American relations, we adopt the framework used by Peter Smith and divide that history into three periods:[21]

- a regional edition of the long nineteenth century—the era of imperialism and great power rivalry throughout world politics, lasting in this case from 1790 to World War II;
- the Cold War, from 1946 to the end of European Communism in 1991;
- the still-undefined present—an era that began with the United States as the only superpower but that within 10 years saw Washington confronting a hitherto unimaginable array of actors, including international terrorist groups.

During this first period, Latin America was, in the words of political scientist Lars Schoultz, beneath the United States, both on the map and how it was viewed in terms of the intelligence and moral character of its people.[22] This condescension was not unique to the United States. The British gave us the "white man's burden," while the French had their *mission civilisatrice*. Were there such a thing as a truly detached perspective, it might conclude that the United States differed from the two Europeans mainly in that its colonial expansion before 1898 happened mostly in physically adjacent territories and at the expense of Native Americans and Latin Americans. Thus an essential step to understanding US–Latin American relations is to shed the blinders of American exceptionalism—whether seen positively or negatively—and treat Washington's behavior as that of any other great power.

The usual landmarks of the first 150 years of relations between the United States and Latin America are the Monroe Doctrine; the Mexican War; various attempts to annex Cuba or Nicaragua as slave states; interventions in many parts of the Caribbean Basin; and the Good Neighbor Policy. The first of these, the Monroe Doctrine (1823), declared that European states could not establish new colonies anywhere in the Americas and that the United States viewed attempts to do so as threats to its national interest. It is unlikely that the United States in 1823 could have done a great deal to stop renewed colonization had Britain not found Washington's principle congenial: London did not want to lose the markets it had recently opened in the new Latin American republics. Nevertheless, Washington had staked its claim to be the arbiter of international affairs in all the Americas, an audacious if understandable act by an emerging power.

Most treatments of the Mexican War (1846–1848) and the various attempts to annex Cuba put them in the context of Washington's nine-teenth-century drive for territorial expansion.[23] That is, domestic political dynamics—here, the push to open land for settlement—drove foreign policy. In the case of the war with Mexico, which cost Mexico half its territory, the root cause was the presence of US settlers in the Mexican territory of Texas. The Texans declared independence from Mexico in 1836, and in 1845, Texas became a state, which the Mexicans had long warned would lead to war. Cuba's position was different, because there were no US settlers. Rather, the island was attractive due to its potential to become a slave state and maintain the political weight of the slaveholding interests before the Civil War and because its location made it appear critical to the defense of the United States once Washington became a plausible global actor in the 1890s.

International factors were more important in the policy of intervention and occupation that developed between 1898 and 1934. Justification for intervening in Cuba, Haiti, the Dominican Republic, Honduras, Mexico, Panama, and Nicaragua came from the Roosevelt Corollary to the Monroe Doctrine. Enunciated by President Theodore Roosevelt, this doctrine saw the United States guarantee order and the payment of debts throughout the Americas, thereby denying extra-hemispheric powers a pretext for in-tervention. However, beyond protecting US interests, policies derived from the Roosevelt Corollary were to promote democracy and, in the words of President Woodrow Wilson, "teach [the Latin Americans] to elect good men."

These interventions thus were not just about political stabilization and seeing that bills were paid. There were also public works projects (roads, public health, schools), programs to reform and modernize the security forces, and attempts to lay the foundations for electoral democ-racy. Unfortunately, these came with rigid controls. In Nicaragua, the most obvious of these was the presence of Marines from 1909 to 1926

> **Text Box 10.4** The United States in Nicaragua
>
> José Santos Zelaya, the Liberal dictator who was Nicaragua's president from 1893 to 1909, first attracted Washington's attention because he meddled in his neighbors' affairs. Then, when Panama was chosen over Nicaragua as the transisthmian canal route, he set about trying to interest Germany and Japan in the Nicaraguan route. Eventually, in 1909, the United States backed a Conservative-led revolution that ousted Zelaya. The result, however, was not democratic stability, the objective of the Roosevelt Corollary, but two decades of civil war, followed by a guerrilla insurgency, and Marines stationed in Nicaragua until 1934. There were, though, two honest elections, in 1928 and 1932, the first of which saw power change hands peacefully between parties for the first time ever in Nicaragua's history. The United States also demobilized the partisan armies of the civil war and replaced them with the more professional National Guard. But only three years after the United States withdrew, the Somoza family began its two-generation dictatorship, using the National Guard as a key instrument.

and 1927 to 1934 (see Text Box 10.4). Haiti had Marines from 1915 to 1934, the Dominican Republic from 1916 to 1924; and while Cuba had less experience with occupation, it did have the Platt Amendment. That provision, literally an amendment to an appropriations bill, gave the US government the right to intervene in Cuban affairs when it deemed it necessary to preserve Cuba's independence, prohibited Cuba from ceding land to any other foreign state, limited its treaty-making abilities, and gave the United States rights to a naval base in Guantanamo Bay. It was made part of the 1901 Cuban constitution in order to end the US occupation of the island. It was abrogated in 1934, except for the provisions regarding Guantanamo Bay.

Although any great power wants its backyard quiet and orderly, Washington's insistence on promoting democratic rule set the United States apart from even other democratic states 100 years ago. For all its stress on democracy, though, direct intervention and military occupation were the key ingredients in a policy designed to give the United States mastery over the hemisphere. On that score, the United States and the European colonial powers were quite similar. Latin Americans were relieved when President Franklin D. Roosevelt abandoned his cousin's Corollary in 1934 and instituted the Good Neighbor Policy of nonintervention.

Washington's hemispheric policy during the Cold War had anticommunism as its focus. This easily translated into support for dictators who provided political stability and repressed left-wing politics, whether nationalist, socialist, or genuinely communist. Despite this, in 1959 the

Cuban Revolution brought Fidel Castro to power; Castro soon aligned himself with the Soviet Union. The United States had various responses.

One was reform. The 1960s brought the Alliance for Progress (see Text Box 8.3), which sought to promote democracy and social and economic reform. A decade later, the Carter administration (1976–1980) emphasized human rights and negotiated a treaty handing control of the Panama Canal to Panama.

More common were US intervention and the overthrow of governments thought too leftist. The list includes Guatemala (1954), the Dominican Republic (1965), and Panama (1989). Further, the Bolivian Revolution of 1952 was destabilized; Cuba is still a target of Washington's pressure; and military overthrows of elected governments in Brazil (1964), Argentina (1966 and 1976), Uruguay (1973), and Chile (1973) were accepted with equanimity.[24] Additionally, the Nicaraguan Revolution of 1979 was the target of low-intensity conflict (LIC), which involved organizing and supporting insurgents to weaken a targeted government.

There were also major in-country, counterinsurgent (CI) training operations in Guatemala and El Salvador, plus CI instruction for officers from many countries at the School of the Americas, originally located in Panama and then shifted to Fort Benning, Georgia. Similarly, there were generally high levels of tolerance for anticommunist dictators wherever they arose. However, particularly troublesome dictators, such as the Dominican Republic's Trujillo (1930–1961), could be isolated; and toward the end of the period they were encouraged to leave power (Haiti's "Baby Doc" Duvalier) or respect election results that spelled the end of their rule (Chile's General Augusto Pinochet).

In this instance, Latin American policy fell within a broader foreign policy framework. Nevertheless, Washington's preoccupation with Latin America never flagged. This does not appear to be the case today. Since the September 11, 2001, attacks against the United States and particularly after the Bush administration launched the Iraq War in 2003, Latin America has fallen below Washington's radar. This has permitted Venezuela's left-populist leader, Hugo Chávez, to mount a boisterous and active anti-American foreign policy, even aligning himself closely with Iran, one of the states forming President George W. Bush's "Axis of Evil." Even the world's sole superpower cannot pay attention to everything, and Latin America is less of a threat to US national security than the wars in Iraq and Afghanistan or Iran's pursuit of nuclear weapons. Since taking office in 2009, President Barack Obama has not only faced the same set of security problems in southwest Asia but also confronted a global economic crisis, so he, too, has dedicated little time to Latin America. The dangerous thus trumps the merely annoying, which is what IR theory would predict.

> **Text Box 10.5** Middle Powers
>
> Great powers are easy to identify. They have more military might, economic capacity, and diplomatic influence than do other states. There can never be more than a few great powers at one time. Middle powers are states with middling power, capacity, and influence. Some of them—for example, Australia, Canada, and Sweden—prefer operating in multilateral institutions, working to stabilize and legitimize the world order. However, Latin American middle powers—such as Argentina, Brazil, Chile, Mexico, and now Venezuela—appear more oriented toward regional affairs and interested in reforming the existing order. In short, although all middle powers share similar levels of power and capacity to act in international politics, they do not all use that power in the same way.

Other Actors

Some of the international relations of Latin American states are conducted with lesser powers, emerging powers, and nonstate actors, principally international governmental organizations (IGOs) and international financial institutions (IFIs). To consider a sample case representing the lesser powers, we will examine Canada. Canada is perhaps the model for a middle power (see Text Box 10.5): a politically and economically significant state that is respected internationally but that is not a significant world power. Moreover, it is North American, a signatory, along with Mexico and the United States, of the North American Free Trade Agreement (NAFTA) and though allied with the United States has pursued an independent foreign policy.

Yet Ottawa's role in hemispheric affairs began late, with Canada only becoming a full member of the Organization of American States (OAS) in 1990; Latin America has yet to occupy a sure and significant place in Canada's foreign policy. An active and reasonably effective actor in the region during the Conservative Brian Mulroney government (1984–1993), Canada has since retreated to its earlier, less engaged status. Although the reasons underlying Canada's failure to engage more fully with Latin America are complex, one factor is the country's longstanding preference for multilateral diplomacy and working through IGOs. This may lead Ottawa to undervalue bilateral relations, which are important to Latin American states. As well, its active promotion of the Free Trade Area of the Americas (FTAA, see Chapter 9), a project initiated by Washington, may also have affected how Canada is perceived by Latin Americans.[25]

Another new actor in Latin American affairs is the People's Republic of China (PRC). Although the Republic of China (Taiwan) and the PRC have competed for recognition by and commercial access to Latin American countries for some time, it is only with the latter's economic miracle since 1990 that Beijing has become a significant force. Between 1993 and 2003, China's trade with Latin America grew sevenfold.[26] What China offers Latin America is new markets for raw materials exports. This is a mixed blessing. Although the greater revenues will be welcome, selling more primary products will not necessarily help countries develop. In Africa, China's diplomatic weight is greater, partly because it offers a lifeline to pariah states, such as Sudan. At the moment, this possibility does not exist in Latin America.

Finally, a brief mention of the role of nonstate actors, principally the IFIs, such as the World Bank and International Monetary Fund, is neces- sary to round out this overview of Latin America's foreign affairs. During the 1980s and 1990s, the World Bank and International Monetary Fund effectively prescribed the economic and social policies that Latin American states could adopt (see Chapter 9). These nonstate actors, IFIs, held sov- ereign states in their thrall. However, the IFIs still had less power than did the great powers that intervened in Latin America until the 1930s. Debts used to be collected by seizing customs receipts and governments changed by force of arms. However bad structural adjustment was, it did not include having foreign troops present.

Agencies of the United Nations have also played important roles in Latin America in the last years of the twentieth century. Particularly noteworthy are three missions instrumental to the Central American peace process: MINUGUA, the UN Verification Mission in Guatemala (1994–2004); ONUSAL, the UN Observer Mission in El Salvador (1991–1995); and ONUVEN, the UN Mission for the Verification of Elections in Nicaragua (1989–1990). Although the states involved had to accept the missions, the UN's presence facilitated the search for peace.

Conclusion

Examining Latin America's international relations leads to two conclu- sions. One is that while strong states really do generally get the better of weak states, how they do so changes over time and from one strong state to another. Thus although direct intervention is an option (in 2003, neo- conservative writer Max Boot spoke of "imposing the rule of law, prop- erty rights, and other guarantees, at gunpoint if necessary"),[27] it is more likely that economic sanctions, attempts to impose diplomatic isolation, and subversion, perhaps by setting up an insurgency, would be the chosen instruments. Further, what the United States did in the Latin American nations where it intervened in the first third of the twentieth century—car- rying out public works and organizing technically clean elections—seems not to have had a parallel among the European empires. This only means that each great power seeks to achieve mastery in different ways, but that point is worth remembering.

The other conclusion is that interstate relations among the weak, such as between El Salvador and Honduras, are every bit as complex as great power politics. Moreover, the weak also practice the high politics of national security, war, and peace, and they pursue their national interest with the fervor of a superpower. Even small, weak states have the potential to chart their own course in the world, even if not in the same way or to the same degree as a great power.

Further Readings

Kacowicz, Arie M. *The Impact of Norms in International Society: The Latin American Experience, 1881–2001.* Notre Dame, IN: Notre Dame University Press, 2005.

Oelsner, Andrea. *International Relations in Latin America: Peace and Security in the Southern Cone.* New York: Routledge, 2005.

Tickner, Arlene B., and Ole Waever, eds., *International Relations Scholarship Around the World.* New York: Routledge, 2009.

Discussion Questions

① This chapter presented the concept of sovereignty as it is used in international relations. When involved in international affairs, Latin American countries, especially smaller ones, often stress quite strongly their rights as sovereign nations. Why might they do this? Do they make more of the notion of sovereignty than does Canada or the United States?

② Given what we know about the role of violence as a political instrument in the domestic politics of Latin American states, is the level of conflict among Latin American states greater than one might expect, less, or about what we might expect?

Notes

1. IGOs are composed of and controlled by governments. INGOs are established and run by individuals and groups from civil society. Although INGOs often have links to governments, they normally remain independent of governments.

2. A minimum of four states is required for a multipolar system, as a three-state or tripolar system would always line up two against one and be inherently unstable.

3. Arlene B. Tickner, "Hearing Latin American Voices in International Relations Studies," *International Studies Perspectives* 4 (2003): 325–350.

4. Carlos Esucudé, "An Introduction to Peripheral Realism and Its Implications for the Interstate System: Argentina and the Condor II Missile Project," *International Relations Theory and the Third World*, ed. Stephanie Neuman (New York: St. Martin's Press, 1998) 55–76.

5. Mohammed Ayoob, "Subaltern Realism: International Relations Theory Meets the Third World," *International Relations Theory and the Third World*, ed. Stephanie Neuman (New York: St. Martin's Press, 1998) 31–54.

6. A few months later, in July 2008, Chávez's position on the FARC had changed completely, as he called for them to lay down their arms and return to civilian life. This happened after the death, by natural causes, of the FARC's longtime leader, Manuel Marulanda, the desertion of many FARC soldiers, and a stunning operation by the Colombian government to free several high-profile hostages, including former Colombian Green Party presidential candidate Íngrid Betancourt, who had been held by the guerrillas for years.

7. James Garrett, "The Beagle Channel Dispute: Confrontation and Negotiation in the Southern Cone," *Journal of Interamerican Studies and World Affairs* 27:3 (1985): 81–109.

8. Interstate disputes are often arbitrated by another head of state. It is unlikely that the arbiter does more than act as a top level intermediary and signify his or her consent to the final document, which will be the work of experts. However, the principle that only sovereigns can deal as equals with other sovereigns is preserved.

9. David Scott Palmer, "Overcoming the Weight of History: 'Getting to Yes' in the Peru-Ecuador Border Dispute," *Diplomacy and Statecraft* 12:2 (2001): 29–46. For an examination of all the Ecuador-Peru border clashes, see Robert L. Scheina, *Latin America's Wars*, vol. 2 (Dulles, VA: Brassey's Inc., 2003) 114–125.

10. There are two sources to consult. One is Thomas P. Anderson, *The War of the Dispossessed: Honduras and El Salvador, 1969* (Lincoln, NB: University of Nebraska Press, 1981). This is the academic standard. The other book is Ryszard Kapuscinski, *The Soccer War*, tr. William Brand (New York: Vintage Books, 1986). Kapuscinski was one of the twentieth century's greatest political journalists.

11. For background, see Kate Donovan, "A Beneficial Uruguayan Paper Mill: Pulp Fiction?" (Washington, DC: Council on Hemispheric Affairs, 2007). www.coha.org/2007/01/a-beneficial-uruguayan-paper-mill-pulp-fiction.html and "Argentina-Uruguay Row Hits Summit," *BBC News* (9 November 2007). http://newsvote.bbc.co.uk/2/hi/americas/7088050.shtml.

12. For background information, see José Luis Rocha, "The Rio San Juan: Source of Conflicts and Nationalism," *Envio* 292 (November 2005). www.envio.org.ni/articulo/3112.

13. International Institute of Strategic Studies, *The Military Balance, 2008* (London: Routledge, 2008) 59.

14. Stockholm International Peace Research Institute, *SIPRI Yearbook, 2007* (New York: Oxford University Press, 2007) 287.

15. Data in this paragraph are from *SIPRI*, 319–320.

16. Shirley Christian, "Argentina and Brazil Renounce Atomic Weapons," *The New York Times* 29 November 1990. http://query.nytimes.com/gst/fullpage.html.

17. Jack Child, *The Central American Peace Process, 1983–1991: Sheathing Swords, Building Confidence* (Boulder, CO: Lynne Rienner Publishers, 1992).

18. John Dinges, *The Condor Years: How Pinochet and His Allies Brought Terrorism to Three Continents* (New York: New Press, 2004) and J. Patrice McSherry, *Predatory States: Operation Condor and Covert War in Latin America* (Lanham, MD: Rowman and Littlefield, 2005).

19. For details on the first three conflicts, see Robert L. Scheina, *Latin America's Wars*, vol. 1 (Dulles, VA: 2003) 229–233, 313–332, 375–388; for the fourth, see Scheina, *Latin America's Wars*, vol. 2, 85–106.

20. Thomas F. Homer-Dixon, *Environmental Scarcity and Violence* (Princeton, NJ: Princeton University Press, 1996).

21. Peter H. Smith, *The Talons of the Eagle: The Dynamics of U.S.–Latin American Relations* (New York: Oxford University Press, 1996).

22. Lars Schoultz, *Beneath the United States: A History of U.S. Foreign Policy toward Latin America* (Cambridge, MA: Harvard University Press, 1998).

23. Schoultz, *Beneath the United States*, 14–58 and Smith, *Talons*, 20–27.

24. Kristian Gustafson, *Hostile Intent: U.S. Covert Operations in Chile, 1964–1974* (Washington, DC: Potomac Books, 2007) uses newly declassified documents to argue that although the United States certainly wanted Salvador Allende, Chile's Marxist president (1970–1973) out, the coup that overthrew him was a purely Chilean affair.

25. Useful introductions to Canada's relations with Latin America can be found in Jean Daudelin, "Foreign Policy at the Fringe: Canada and Latin America," *International Journal* 58 (2003): 637–666; Peter McKenna, *Canada and the OAS: From Dilettante to Full Partner* (Ottawa, ON: Carleton University Press, 1995); and Brian J. R. Stevenson, *Canada, Latin America, and the New Internationalism: A Foreign Policy Analysis, 1968–1990* (Montreal, QC: McGill-Queen's University Press, 2000).

26. Jaime Heine, "China's Claim in Latin America: So Far, a Partner not Threat" (Washington, DC: Council on Hemispheric Affairs, 25 July 2008). www.coha.org/2008/07/china's-claim-in-latin-america-so-far-a-partner-not-a-threat.

27. Quoted in Andrew Bacevic, *The New American Militarism: How Americans Are Seduced by War* (New York: Oxford University Press, 2005) 39.

11

Latin America in Comparative Perspective

How does Latin American politics look when compared to the rest of the world? Is it more or less democratic? Does it, on the whole, incline more toward extremely strong executives or personality-based parties than most other regions? Do key institutions—constitutions, courts, bureaucracies, legislatures, among others—evidence any idiosyncratic patterns that stand out from the norm? How different do things look if we put Latin American politics, or the politics of a particular Latin American state, up against, say, Canada and the United States, as we have done often in the text, instead of sub-Saharan Africa or Southeast Asia? What, that is, does comparative politics tell us about Latin America that we have not yet encountered?

Chapter 1 introduced two distinct but related ways to study the politics of Latin America: area studies and comparative politics. Throughout the book, both approaches have been used, sometimes together, according to which was best suited to illustrate a particular point. This chapter returns to these concepts for a closer look at Latin American politics through a comparative perspective. It will do so by taking a few of the themes investigated in earlier chapters, issues already shown to be important in Latin America—history, institutions, democracy, and political economy—and seeing what these phenomena look and act like in other settings.

Beyond setting this material out, this chapter has three objectives. First, by comparing politics in Latin America to what exists elsewhere, this final chapter aims to deepen your knowledge of Latin America because you will see its politics from a different angle. Second, it will sharpen your analytical skills in comparative politics. Third and finally, if all works as planned, by the end of this chapter you will be convinced that to be a good Latin Americanist you also have to be a good comparativist.

Comparing Polities and Politics

We make comparisons every day. Should I buy this car or that one? Is our goalie better than theirs? Our comparisons are grounded in relevant criteria. Thinking about two cars, we find out which vehicle is more reliable, more fuel efficient, cheaper, which dealer has the better reputation for service, and the like. When we turn to the goalies, we use goals allowed per game, percentage of shots blocked, and how each one plays under pressure. We look for things we need to know in order to make our comparisons meaningful. This principle extends to comparative politics.

Politics and polities (nation-states, states or provinces within federal nation-states, and the various forms of local government) can be compared in various ways. First, we can look at the same polity at different times to see what changes have occurred and what forces underlay those changes. Second, we can examine case studies of a single political system, done to highlight some special aspect of that polity. Third, we can compare a small number of polities, the small-n study, which again usually centers on some specific institution or attribute shared by the political systems under study. These first three tend to rely on qualitative methods and suppose a substantial degree of familiarity with the places studied. Finally, we can make comparisons of many polities—generally 20 or more cases, large-N studies, which use quantitative methods to search for relations between selected variables. Large-N studies operate at the highest level of abstraction—they necessarily ignore details about specific countries or regions—and are thought to be better suited for theory-building than the other approaches. None of the foregoing is particularly suited to comparing regions, say, Latin America and southern Europe, but all can be used in this context.

Strategies for Comparison

Comparing the same polity or same institution at two different times is a sometimes overlooked strategy, yet it can yield valuable insights. An easy way to see this at work is to look at a country today and 50 years ago, in 1959. For example, in 1959 Canada had no political parties dedicated to having the province of Quebec secede from Canada; in 2009 there are two, one of them with seats in the national Parliament. In 2009, an African American is president of the United States; in 1959, African Americans living in the country's south were not only kept from voting or holding office, but they were also subject to laws enforcing the segregation of black people from white. Fifty years ago, the idea that Mexico's Partido Revolucionario Institucional (PRI, or Institutional Revolutionary Party) could be defeated was laughable, but by 2009 the PRI had lost two straight presidential elections. The list could go on, but it will end here with the cases of Portugal and Spain. In 1959, each was governed by genuine fascists. Everyone knew that Portugal's António de Oliveira Salazar and Spain's Francisco Franco would not be alive in 2009, but very few experts would have predicted that both countries would have become thriving democracies by then. Those experts would have looked at Spanish and Portuguese history and declared that the future held more authoritarian governments for both nations. Looking at these changes from the perspective of comparative politics, we can ask why and how they came to pass.

In-depth studies of one polity may seem out of place in comparative politics, but without a thorough analysis of, say, Costa Rican political parties, we either have to exclude Latin America's senior democracy from comparative studies of political parties or use sketchier data that could lead to faulty conclusions. Clearly, we want these country studies to use methods that can be adopted by researchers elsewhere and to employ concepts and categories found in other research, to ensure comparability. However, there is little doubt that there are many gaps in our knowledge of how political institutions and processes work in many places and that this limits the ability of political science to develop theories. Perhaps in a perfect world local political scientists would do those studies. Nevertheless, there is a solid argument for having, perhaps, Brazilian political scientists examine federalism in Canada and the United States precisely because they automatically bring a comparative perspective to the task.

More easily recognizable as the stuff of comparative politics are focused comparisons among a small sample of polities. For instance, we could examine three small democracies in the developing world, such as Costa Rica, Trinidad and Tobago, and Mauritius. Among the themes that could be considered are the party system, social and economic policy, presidential versus parliamentary systems, and the role of the courts. Of course, both Trinidad and Tobago and Mauritius have more recent colonial histories and were formerly British possessions, which adds another possible line of inquiry.

When doing small-n studies, care must be exercised in selecting cases. One option is to look at most similar cases, while another is to examine those that are most different. Either option, however, can fall victim to selection bias. This problem arises when the cases selected for analysis produce results that are unrepresentative of the larger class of cases. Thus, although the three cases proposed above for a study of democracy in small developing countries may be inherently interesting and produce striking findings, those results may not be characteristic of the political systems in that class.

Finally, it is possible to compare many countries. It is probably easiest to use this approach with aggregate data, but that is not a prerequisite. Using aggregate data, such as income or government spending figures, it is possible to discover whether there is a relationship between levels of political violence and income inequality or what factors correlate with greater human rights protection. An example of a large-scale study that would *not* use aggregate data would be to ask whether having a certain percentage of women in a national legislature (the usual threshold is 30 per cent) produces more laws beneficial to women or whether parliamentary democracies are less stable than presidential democracies.

The methods we have just seen are complex, and this leads naturally to asking whether such studies pay off in terms of what we can learn about politics in Latin America. Rod Hague and Martin Harrop[1] offer four reasons why comparative politics are useful. First, they let us find out more about more places, and the more we know about how Latin America, considered as a region or as countries within the region, converges with or diverges from other places, the better our sense of how Latin American politics functions. Second, comparison improves our ability to classify political phemomena. For example, military coups are a class of political event, so seeing how Latin American coups measure up against coups elsewhere tells us more about both coups and their role in Latin American politics.

A third contribution of comparative politics is that they increase our capacity for explanation. If we know more about coups as a class of political action, we should be able to explain better why they occur, which lets us propose hypotheses to test. The ability to predict is Hague and Harrop's fourth argument for the value of comparative politics. If the hypothesis that as per capita income rises, the incidence of coups falls[2] is confirmed, we can then make predictions about when coups might occur. Applied to Latin America, this finding would lead us to ask whether there were some income threshold above which coups ceased to occur, thereby letting us make predictions about the future of coups in Latin America.

Some Comparisons

In the first 10 chapters of this book, comparisons were carried out on several levels. Some were between or among states within Latin America; others considered states outside the region; while still others made inter-regional comparisons. The purpose of this section is to make more focused comparisons centered on themes that were stressed as particularly necessary for developing an understanding of Latin American politics. These are:

- the role of history and its effects, including path dependence and off-path changes;
- the question of democracy, which has a historic dimension but also takes in transitions and consolidation;
- formal and informal institutions, which in practice means machinery of government and parties; and
- modes of political participation, including the role of violence as a participatory device.

History

Two obvious cases for comparison come to mind when thinking about Latin American history. The first is other postcolonial regions. In Chapter 2, we compared the British North American colonies, now the United States and Canada, with Latin America, noting how both the later origins of the British colonies and the greater levels of self-government afforded them eased their passage into the ranks of constitutional democracies. Both areas were part of the first modern wave of decolonization, which we can date from 1776 to 1825, acknowledging that this omits Canada, the Dominican Republic, Cuba, and Panama.

Turning to Africa, we have to remember that European colonialism did not last nearly as long in Africa as in Latin America (about 80 years on average, compared to more than 3 centuries) and ended much more recently, between 1956 and 1994, or 1980 if we do not count the arrival of majority rule in South Africa.[3] However, the era of the *caudillos* in Latin America bears a disturbing resemblance to postindependence Africa. Goran Hyden, a political scientist whose work centers on Africa, presents data demonstrating that it is only since 1990 that electoral defeat and retirement have begun to approach armed overthrow as the common method for African leaders to leave office,[4] a situation similar to that described in Chapters 2 and 4. And Africa is not alone. Much of Asia knew military rule or party dictatorships until near the end of the twentieth century. These cases point to problems with what 40 years ago was called nation-building but which might better be seen as studies in attempts to unite divided societies in newly formed states. Interestingly, Latin America has known more instances of secession and state breakup: Gran Colombia devolved itself into Colombia, Venezuela, and Ecuador; Central America split from Mexico almost immediately after independence, while the Central American Union finally failed in 1840; the department of Nicoya abandoned Nicaragua to become part of Costa Rica in 1824; and Panama left Colombia in 1903.[5]

Looking at the histories of Spain and Portugal since most of their American colonies became independent (1825) is also instructive because for many years Iberian and Ibero-American politics closely paralleled each other. There have been experiments in radical democracy, such as the two Spanish republics (1868 and 1931); monarchies (the Portuguese ending in 1910, and the Spanish in 1931, although it was restored in 1975); civil wars (Portugal, 1820–1832; Spain, the Carlist Wars in the nineteenth century and the 1936–1939 Civil War); dictatorships and military governments (Salazar and Franco); and periods of civic oligarchy dominated by rural bosses that differed from Latin American oligarchic democracies. Yet the Portuguese Revolution of 1974 set that country on a new path, while the death of Franco let Spain change its trajectory equally dramatically. In Latin America electoral democracy has become the almost universal governing model since democratic transitions began in 1982 in El Salvador. These two sets of histories show plainly that big off-path changes are as possible as they are unpredictable.

Looking at the history of more than one polity or region should reveal what is really distinctive about the place and what characteristics it shares with other political systems. We can then ask why these unique and shared traits exist and how they give political systems their individuality. And by looking at several political systems, we can also ask how significant political change, such as the changes in Spain and Portugal in the 1970s, can occur.

Democracy

Along with the citizens of a handful of other nations, Canadians and Americans take democracy for granted. If the states of Latin America had been lucky in the nineteenth century, their citizens would be in that group too. Unfortunately for the Latin Americans, even barebones electoral democracy did not become the rule everywhere—except in Cuba—until the end of the twentieth century (see Text Box 11.1).

If compared to long-established constitutional democracies, an imaginary median Latin American state would show a slower expansion of the suffrage, less recognition of civil liberties, more periods of political violence (civil wars and insurrections), greater reliance on coercion, and higher levels of politicized justice. More important than this list, is how we explain the differences. How much weight goes to poverty, recalling that even the relatively wealthy Argentina has had plenty of dictatorships in its past? Is focusing on the continued dominance of nondemocratic elites a better explanation for the differences? Should we look at the inability of many countries to develop strong government institutions that were congruent with democratic rule? And what about the places that made it democratically? Obviously Costa Rica belongs here, but Colombia, Chile, Uruguay, and Venezuela have long spells as electoral democracies, although those four have also had extended periods where democracy was either suspended or operated in ways that people from Canada and the United States would not recognize immediately as democratic. If setting even long-standing Latin American democracies up against the Netherlands or France seems too implausible, why not compare them to India or the British Caribbean states, which have been democratic since independence?

Easier to accept are comparisons with countries that became democratic during the so-called Third Wave. Democracy's Third Wave began with the Portuguese Revolution of 1974 and looks to have reached a steady state since 1994, when apartheid ended in South Africa. If we exclude Costa Rica, which has maintained constitutional democratic rule since 1949, the remaining basket of Latin American states are a good base for comparisons with other Third Wave democracies. Within that class, the best comparisons are regions with similar per capita incomes and levels of human

Text Box 11.1 Democracy in Latin America in 2009

All Latin American states currently declare themselves democratic. Cuba is an outlier here because its democracy is that of a socialist revolutionary vanguard whose objective will only be achieved when society is no longer divided along class lines. Four other states, the so-called Bolivarians—Venezuela, Bolivia, Ecuador, and Nicaragua—want a twenty-first-century socialism and are using electoral democracy to try to get it. Moving toward the center of the ideological spectrum, we find a number of social democratic countries—Argentina, Brazil, Chile, Guatemala, and Uruguay; and probably El Salvador and Paraguay. These six are distinguished by acknowledging that they work within a capitalist framework, but all demand that government take an active role in redistributing society's costs and benefits more equally. The remaining nine nations have governments that can be classified as centrist or rightist, depending on the degree to which each still embraces increasingly discredited neoliberal policy prescriptions, as well as the extent to which each crafts a foreign policy independent of Washington's. Although many would argue that Cuba does not belong on a list of democracies, this classification is otherwise unremarkable.

Grouping Latin America's polities by the ideological color of their democracies suggests a series of comparisons that can be made with states outside the region. Cuba has far fewer peers than it did 25 years ago, but the world's remaining one-party Communist systems—the People's Republic of China, Laos, Vietnam, and the Democratic People's Republic of Korea—could still be examined. Similarly, measuring Cuba against an ideal-type socialist revolution would be rewarding and comparing its politics to those of other one-party states, such as Eritrea, could also provide useful insights.

The Bolivarians find their peers among a heterogeneous group of other states seeking rapid social change: South Africa, Iran, and perhaps Nepal, now that it has a Marxist government. Another plausible comparison would be with Zimbabwe, an experiment in radical democracy gone wrong. Finally, the fact that this new political model is especially strong in Latin America is itself a question that merits examination.

Latin America's social democrats need to be examined in the company of other social democrats, meaning Western European countries. However, their performance on social and economic measures should be compared to what the four Bolivarians have achieved, as well as with Latin America's centrist and right-of-center democratic states. We would also want to compare the latter group with the states of ex-Communist Europe and the electoral democracies of Africa and Asia, perhaps excluding India, due to its size and complexity.

It is unlikely that the findings of such comparative analyses would be definitive, but they would give a better sense of which factors make Latin American political systems unique and which elements they share with their ideological counterparts in other parts of the world.

development. That means excluding most of Africa—although Chile's experience with uninterrupted rule by the Concertación since 1989 could offer a useful perspective on Botswana's single-party dominant democracy, and an examination of the democracy built by post-revolutionary regimes in Mozambique and Nicaragua would also be instructive.

Set against the remaining cases—which come from Europe and Asia— Latin American states stand out for having been independent longer than any of the others, except its colonizers, Spain and Portugal, as well as Greece and Russia. As independent states, all Latin American countries have acquired some experience with some form of democracy—oligarchic in the nineteenth century, liberal or radical-revolutionary in the twentieth. And the symbols of democracy, from representative government to individual rights and freedoms, have figured prominently in the discourse of the region leaders since the early 1800s. It is therefore odd that Latin America finds itself in the midst of newcomers, and it is again necessary to ask the questions raised above when comparing the region's polities to the world's historic democracies.

Nevertheless, late starters such as South Korea, Taiwan, Slovenia, and Poland look as solidly democratic as Latin America's stalwarts. On the other hand, there are significant disappointments among the more recent arrivals, not least the "color revolutions" of Ukraine (orange) and Georgia (rose). Perhaps the more important task for political science will be to follow attentively what happens to democracies with little more than a generation of practical experience as they face the challenges brought by the global economic crisis that started in September 2008. In the global Depression of the 1930s, democracies founded in the 1920s fared badly: only the Republic of Ireland survived unscathed. Economic hardship turns people onto the streets to protest, and protest often frightens the forces of order into substituting authoritarian systems for democracy. Hard times also throw up nondemocratic governments as short cuts to recovery. It could happen again.

Institutions

Government and politics need a framework, and institutions provide a big part of the framework. You have already encountered institutions in both their informal and formal guises in Chapter 4 and Chapter 6 respectively, and probably remember that political science does not define institutions as most of us would in everyday use. While political science (and other social sciences too) see institutions as repeated patterns of interactions designed to influence people's behavior, our common sense says that institutions are organizations with some kind of recognized legal status and that political institutions are closely linked to, even officially part of, the state. The former explains what institutions do; the latter looks at how they are structured. In Chapter 6 we chose to deal with this definitional problem by bearing both views in mind but moving quickly to look at examples of what observers of politics class as political institutions. The same strategy applies here as we consider executives and parties.

Executives

Latin American politics is notorious for producing extremely powerful presidents who arrogate power to themselves and do all they can to remain unaccountable to other parts of government—and often even to the voters. In 2009, as for the decade before, this "hyperpresidentialism" is symbolized by President Hugo Chávez of Venezuela. But is this hyperpresident distinctively Latin American? And is hyperpresidentialism limited to presidents or are there prime ministers who should be included in a class of "hyperexecutives?" If so, then extremely powerful executives leap the parliamentary–presidential system divide.

To start with the United States, since 1968 two presidents have been seen as pushing their powers beyond constitutional limits: Richard Nixon (1969–1974) and George W. Bush (2001–2009). Similarly, French presidents under the Fifth Republic (1958–) have also been quite powerful and given to personalizing power. Charles de Gaulle (1958–1969) was particularly well known for a personalistic style of governing, as to a lesser extent is Nicolas Sarkozy (2007–). Russia's first two post-Communist presidents, Boris Yeltsin (1991–1999) and Vladimir Putin (2000–2008) were also disposed to personalized rule, perhaps Putin more than Yeltsin. None of these presidents, each of whom arrogated significant prerogatives to himself, is from an underdeveloped country. Were the list to be extended to include African and Asian states that have become independent since the end of World War II in 1945, the list would be dramatically longer. Hyperpresidentialism is not a peculiarly Latin American trait.

Prime ministers can also be adept at centralizing power. In 2008, Russia's past president Vladimir Putin became the country's prime minister and continued exercising nearly as much power as he had as president. Canadian prime ministers have been depicted as presidentializing their office since the late 1960s. At the end of the twentieth century, when Jean Chrétien was prime minister, the process reached the point where Jeffrey Simpson could title his book on Chrétien's time in office *The Friendly Dictatorship*;[6] Donald Savoie's treatment of the same subject has the less dramatic but still revealing title of *Governing from the Centre: The Concentration of Power in Canadian Politics*.[7] British prime ministers Margaret Thatcher (1979–1990) and Tony Blair (1997–2007) were also known for wielding near-presidential power. This is natural, of course, because a prime minister with a solid, disciplined majority in the legislature (true in all these cases) has more control over the political agenda than most presidents.

Hyperexecutivism is a real phenomenon, and analyses of Latin American chief executives must reach beyond the region's boundaries in order to understand why and how political executives amass power.

Parties

Political parties in Latin America have three characteristics that strike observers. First, many of them are personalistic vehicles, whose principal purpose is to deliver the party leader to power. Second, and linked to the first, parties are evanescent—they do not last very long. Third, in many countries, parties have come to be even politically relevant only recently because the power to rule came so seldom from competitive elections. In this last respect especially, Latin America resembles Africa.[8] Yet it is precisely what does *not* stand out that is now more important: Latin American political parties are increasingly like those in most other electoral democracies because more Latin American countries *are* electoral democracies. An obvious question is whether the same thing has happened to the same extent in Africa.

There are, however, comparisons beyond Africa. The growth of electoral democracy in Latin America means it is useful to compare campaign strategies, candidate selection, leadership selection, and constituency relations in the 19 republics that hold meaningful elections (Cuba is the outlier) with those in any other electoral democracy. Dividing the region between the countries where electoral democracy was established before the 1970s—Chile, Colombia, Costa Rica, Uruguay, and Venezuela—and the rest would provide interesting contrasts, both within Latin America and with the rest of the world. The latter group could be especially usefully compared to Eastern Europe, as those states, too, are learning the workings of democratic government.[9]

Although less common than in the past, parties designed as personal electoral vehicles still exist in Latin America. Hugo Chávez organized the Movimiento V (Quinta) República (MRV, or Movement for the Fifth Republic), which brought him to power, and later formed the Partido Socialista Unido de Venezuela (PSUV, or United Socialist Party of Venezuela), which is very much Chávez's creation, though it has clearer programmatic aims. Chávez's initiatives remind us of Juan Domingo Perón, president of Argentina from 1946 to 1955 and from 1973 to 1974, whose Partido Justicialista (or Justicialist Party—which is always called the Peronistas) not only served its founder well but also continues as one of the two principal parties in Argentina 35 years after his death. Further, Ecuador and Bolivia have parties that were either formed specifically for an election (Ecuador) or that have been strongly influenced by the personality of the leader (Bolivia). These cases could be profitably analyzed alongside

Vladimir Putin's United Russia and Silvio Berlusconi's Forza Italia to gain further insights into how personalist political parties function.

Two-party systems and the closely related 2+ party[10] systems are quite common in Latin America. This is somewhat surprising, since all countries except Chile, with its binomial system, use either proportional electoral systems or mixed proportional-plurality systems in legislative elections, which should make it easier for more parties to win seats. In this respect, the Latin American polities resemble Spain, except that the latter has a parliamentary system and the former are all presidential systems. In Latin America, presidential elections are held under either a majority or a plurality system, depending on the country. Eastern Europe, however, produces a higher proportion of multiparty systems and states there have presidential–prime ministerial constitutions, thus opening the way for studies of the effects of electoral systems on party systems, as well as examining the relationship of presidential versus parliamentary government and party systems. Clearly, a comparison of the party systems found in Latin American states to those of Spain and the several countries of Eastern Europe raises interesting questions.

There are obviously many other institutions, formal and informal, we could examine: legislatures, courts, local governments, corruption, and the role of violence as a political instrument all come to mind. Whether considering Latin America's institutions in comparison to historic democracies or newer democracies in Eastern Europe, Africa, Asia, or Portugal and Spain, the exercise would teach us more about both the regions compared and the institutions examined.

Participation

During the 1950s and 1960s, political science essentially identified political participation with voting and working through parties. Now, citizen action through civil organizations and social movements form part of the picture. Although this may appear unconventional, based on what we know about the character of Latin American politics over the last nearly two centuries, many forms of political violence—especially guerrilla warfare and revolutionary insurrection—should be included as unconventional and highly contentious forms of political participation. With that in mind, the near-disappearance of armed groups as political actors in early twenty-first-century Latin America is noteworthy. Thus one very useful study would examine the frequency of what Charles Tilly and Sidney Tarrow, political scientists who have long studied movement and protest politics, called "lethal conflict,"[11] especially armed insurgencies, throughout the world. The results would indicate if what we find in Latin America is part of a global trend or is the product of local factors.

Undertaking comparisons of the role of civil society and social movement politics is similarly obvious and necessary. Chapter 5 dealt with how new forces enter the ranks of political actors in Latin America, so examining what ethnic minorities, women, and the urban and rural poor have done to win a place in the political systems of other regions is a natural step. One might compare the recent emergence of First Nations in Latin American politics with the struggles of the Romani in Eastern Europe.[12]

Similarly, examining the role of women in politics in other democratizing regions[13] will bring to light the effects of local influences on women's participation in Latin American political life.

Turning finally to voting turnout, also called the *participation rate*, political scientists Tatiana Kostadinova and Timothy Power[14] examined turnout in Latin American and Eastern European transitional democracies in the 1990s. They discovered that Latin American elections showed consistently lower participation, by about 20 per cent, than did Eastern Europe. To explain this, the authors suggested that four factors might be in play, all of which show how history affects politics: (1) the origins of the nondemocratic regime—foreign in Eastern Europe but domestic in Latin America; (2) its nature—totalitarian in Eastern Europe but more conventionally authoritarian in Latin America; (3) the longer continuous nondemocratic experience in Eastern Europe; and (4) the generally slower, negotiated transitions in Latin America versus the rapid breakdowns in Eastern Europe.

Kostadinova and Power also found that although the transition election, the first after the fall of an authoritarian regime, has very high turnout, participation declines rapidly afterward in both regions. A useful next step would be to compare the turnout in Latin America's transitional states with those in nations where no transition election occurred during the Third Wave: Costa Rica, Colombia, and Venezuela. If there is a general downward trend in participation, then there may be a more general disengagement from politics underway in the region.

Policy

Microsoft makes software. Ferrari makes really fast cars. Governments make public policy. Naturally enough, we judge a producer by its product. But the range of products made by Microsoft or Ferrari look very limited when compared to what a government puts out. National governments have to deal with everything from weights and measures to climate change, treating health care, foreign policy, and a lengthy array of other dauntingly complex issues along the way. As all national governments make public policies, the potential number of comparisons is 195: the 192 members of the United Nations, plus Kosovo, the Vatican, and Taiwan (the Republic of China).

However, at least as important as with whom comparisons are made is what is being compared. One of the topics treated in Chapter 6 was the bureaucracy in Latin American governments, where it was noted that these were proportionally smaller, relative to a country's population, than in wealthier democracies. As bureaucrats in those wealthier democratic states are important contributors to the making of public policy and not just its application, they are part of a political system's policy capacity: its ability to research, plan, and implement effective programs. One line of comparative research, then, would look at the policy roles of Latin American public services, setting them against both least-like cases (such as Canada, France, or Sweden) and most-like cases, or at least more similar ones from Eastern Europe, the smaller, mid-income Asian states (Malaysia, for example) or the larger Caribbean nations (Trinidad and Tobago or Jamaica). The same sort of comparison could be made with political parties to assess their roles as generators of policy ideas.

Another way to approach policy questions is to examine discrete policy areas. Three of these are particularly relevant to Latin America: economic development, antipoverty programs and social policy, and foreign policy. We begin with foreign policy and will concentrate on comparisons that are waiting to be made.

Foreign Policy

Chapters 9 and 10 presented different aspects of the foreign policy of Latin American states, but important questions remain. Intraregionally, it would be useful to know whether the region's smaller states (those of Central America, for example) are able to maintain a permanent, professional diplomatic corps and draw on a cadre of foreign policy professionals as the larger states (such as Mexico, Colombia, Chile, and Brazil) appear to do. Cuba, of course, is the outlier here because its diplomatic necessities are not proportional to its population. Once that information was available, interregional comparisons could be done. As well, it would be interesting to compare the foreign policy of Latin America's personalist leaders— currently, Castro and the Bolivarians—with their foreign counterparts— Zimbabwe's Mugabe and Belarus's Lukashenka, to name two—as well as with what more institutionalized regimes in Latin America do.

Economic Development Policy

In Chapter 8, we canvassed two themes that have dominated thinking about economics and economic development in Latin America since the early 1980s: structural adjustment, the adoption of neoliberal policies,[15] on the one hand, and, to a lesser extent, the region's economic decline relative to Asia, on the other. These are still viable topics for comparative

Text Box 11.2 Microfinance

Except for those few doctrinaire socialist states that severely restrict private enterprise, or simply forbid it outright (notably Cuba and North Korea), governments all over the world have to worry about how small businesses get the credit they need to start, expand, and sometimes just run. In wealthy, developed countries, we count on ordinary commercial banks. But in the world's poorer nations, those banks are notoriously reluctant to loan to the really small businesses that form important parts of their economies. We can look at two very different approaches to see what kinds of policies are available and what sorts of comparative studies are possible.

No doubt the best known microfinance program in the world is the Grameen Bank of Bangladesh. Founded in 1983 by Dr. Muhammad Yunus, winner of the 2006 Nobel Peace Prize, the bank has made small loans (about $400 to start a business) to more than 3 million clients, 90 per cent of whom are women. Ninety per cent of the bank's shares are owned by the borrowers and 10 per cent by the government of Bangladesh.

Nicaragua is taking a somewhat different approach with a program called Zero Usury (Usura Cero). Begun in 2007, this government program is open only to women. Like the Bangladesh bank, Zero Usury makes low-interest, small loans, ranging between about $175 and $1,100. Nicaraguan men needing small loans deal with private microfinancial institutions. It will be interesting to see whether the government-run Nicaraguan plan produces different results than the community-run Grameen Bank.[16]

studies, but a more fruitful line of inquiry now is looking at how nations adjust to the crisis of the early twenty-first century. What will the more radical states (Cuba, the Bolivarians, and perhaps Argentina) do that will be different from the actions taken by social democratic and centrist governments (such as Brazil, Chile, Costa Rica, and Peru) or by conservative administrations (Mexico or Colombia)? Moreover, political science will want to know how what the middle-income Latin American states do will distinguish them from both their wealthier counterparts in North America, Western Europe, and parts of Asia, as well as from the poorer countries of Africa. A particularly interesting set of studies could be done comparing the more historically statist Latin American nations with the ex-Communist states of Eastern Europe, which have been resolutely anti-statist. Opportunities for comparative studies should abound, both within Latin America and between Latin American states and those elsewhere.

Antipoverty Programs and Social Policy

Unfortunately, the economic crisis that began in 2008 will doubtlessly force governments everywhere to experiment with new antipoverty programs and social policies more generally. The Depression of the 1930s, the last global economic crisis, brought Latin America significant social reform initiatives in Chile, Colombia, and Costa Rica. If the region can avoid the wave of democratic failures that marked the 1930s and maintain the high levels of electoral democracy it has in 2009, it is reasonable to expect that a number of governments will experiment with novel approaches to poverty reduction (see Text Box 11.2). Will the more radical governments lead the way or will the center and center-left, or even the right, offer the most innovative reforms? International comparisons with middle-income Asian states (such as the Philippines), large African states (perhaps South Africa), and similar systems in Eastern Europe (perhaps Romania but also Poland) would also be instructive.

We should also remember that, at least in North America, the Depression set the women's movement back substantially—thus political scientists should be analyzing what happens to the women's and indigenous people's movements in Latin America, and elsewhere for that matter. Eighty years ago, it was easy for authorities to forget those who were marginalized for other than solely economic reasons and concentrate on material recovery. We will want to know whether the more democratic climate and higher levels of mobilization in Latin America early in 2009 will preserve hard-won gains.

Conclusion: Area Studies and Comparative Politics Revisited

While the list of topics for comparison could have been extended, the value of comparison has been pretty well demonstrated. Not only that, it is clear that interregional and interstate comparisons are plausible on a number of levels. Looking at other new democracies and setting Latin America up against other developing areas are obvious approaches. However, showing that there are reasonable comparisons to be made with wealthier states that have longer democratic histories is useful and might prod some political scientists to look seriously at such questions. And of course there are the intra–Latin American comparisons that were made in every chapter of the book that have always been the natural, if overlooked, starting point.

Viewing Latin American politics in the context of the politics of other regions and countries makes three valuable contributions to the study of the region. First, it enhances our understanding of Latin America and its constituent nations by letting us see them from a different perspective. Second, this exercise increases our knowledge of other countries because we have another standard against which to measure their performance. Finally, comparing polities or groups of polities gives us a clearer comprehension of the concepts according to which the political systems are being compared, because we have more empirical data—plain old facts—to let us make sense of abstract concepts.

Comparison considerably enriches area studies by adding perspective, and area studies—here Latin American studies—do the same for comparative politics by adding depth. Knowing a lot about other countries deepens one's perspective on the political world. For example, most studies in comparative politics center on one country, and thus are no different in that respect than analyses of Canadian or US politics. Yet political scientists whose specialty is Italy will also be well informed about most of the rest of Western Europe and will certainly be well acquainted with the largest states: France, Germany, and the United Kingdom. When those political scientists check a concept against their mental files to see how it applies to the cases they know best, comparison is automatic. So once again, having more facts helps to clarify concepts, here by adding cases to deepen understanding.

Knowing more about more polities, current or historical, also makes us more cautious and more conscious of the limits within which we work as interpreters of the political world. In practice, this may take the form of looking to construct middle-range theories,[17] which lie between detailed descriptions of discrete phenomena and attempts to build a unified theory of politics. Middle-range theories can be limited by place or time or to a specific aspect of politics, perhaps armed movements. Thinking in terms of these theories demands addressing some part of reality and devising a theoretical account that links that part to other elements of political knowledge. Doing so clearly builds theory, but it also yields a product that is concrete enough to be used by policy makers, which reminds us that political science is also about trying to make governments work better.

Further Reading

Smith, Peter H., ed. *Latin America in Comparative Perspective: New Approaches to Methods and Analysis*. Boulder, CO: Westview Press, 1995.

Thompson, Alex. *An Introduction to African Politics*. 2d. ed. Abingdon, UK: Routledge, 2004.

Green, December, and Laura Luerhrmann. *Comparative Politics of the Third World: Linking Concepts and Cases*. 2d. ed. Boulder, CO: Lynne Rienner Publishers, 2007.

Discussion Questions

① How can we say that a study of one country—for example, Argentina—can be called comparative politics? What makes it comparative? Why do we think it is enough to look at a question, such as military intervention, that exists in other countries, describe its status in Argentina, and analyze why it was such a significant factor for so many years?

② What are the benefits and drawbacks of attempting to compare the politics of Latin America as a region to the politics of, say, Eastern Europe? Would it be different if we were looking at some particular institution, such as parties or elections? What would we gain and lose if we took one country from each region, perhaps Bulgaria and Paraguay?

Notes

1. Rod Hague and Martin Harrop, *Political Science: A Comparative Introduction*, 5th ed. (New York: Palgrave Macmillan, 2007) 83–85.
2. John B. Londregan and Keith T. Poole, "Poverty, the Coup Trap, and the Seizure of Executive Power," *World Politics* 42:2 (1990): 151–183.
3. Ethiopia and Liberia were never colonized.
4. Goran Hyden, *African Politics in Comparative Perspective* (New York: Cambridge University Press, 2006) 19.
5. Despite having all current national boundaries drawn by colonizers without regard to potential problems of governability for successor states, sub-Saharan Africa has yet to see a successful case of secession. In Asia, breakups were more common: British India was split into India and Pakistan, and then Bangladesh seceded from Pakistan. Later, Singapore left what is now Malaysia.
6. Jeffrey Simpson, *The Friendly Dictatorship* (Toronto, ON: McClelland & Stewart, 2001).
7. Donald Savoie, *Governing from the Centre: The Concentration of Power in Canadian Politics* (Toronto, ON: University of Toronto Press, 1999).
8. M.A. Mohamed Salih, ed., *African Political Parties* (London: Pluto Press, 2003).
9. See Paul Webb and Stephen White, eds., *Party Politics in New Democracies* (Toronto, ON: Oxford University Press, 2003).
10. A 2+ party system has two parties that dominate politics, but those parties normally only take 75 per cent of the vote between them, and there is usually a third party that captures at least 10 per cent of the vote. In such systems, legislative majorities are hard to secure.
11. Charles Tilly and Sidney Tarrow, *Contentious Politics* (Boulder, CO: Paradigm Publishers, 2007) 135–161.
12. Peter Vermeersch, *The Romani Movement: Minority Politics and Ethnic Mobilization in Contemporary Central Europe* (New York: Berghahn Books, 2006).
13. For example, Anne Marie Goetz and Shireen Hassim, eds., *No Shortcuts to Power: African Women in Politics and Policy Making* (London: Zed Books, 2003) and Richard E. Matland and Kathleen A. Montgomery, eds., *Women's Access to Political Power in Post-Communist Europe* (Oxford: Oxford University Press, 2003).
14. Tatiana Kostadinova and Timothy J. Power, "Does Democracy Depress Participation? Voter Turnout in Latin American and European Transitional Democracies," *Political Research Quarterly* 60 (Fall 2007): 363–377.

15. There are many publications treating this theme, but useful starting points are Stephan Haggard and Robert R. Kaufman, eds., *The Politics of Economic Adjustment: International Constraints, Distributive Conflicts, and the State* (Princeton, NJ: Princeton University Press, 1992) and Kurt Weyland, *The Politics of Market Reform in Fragile Democracies: Argentina, Brazil, Peru, and Venezuela* (Princeton, NJ: Princeton University Press, 2002).

16. For details on the Grameen Bank, see Muhammad Yunus, *Banker to the Poor: Micro-Lending and the Battle Against World Poverty* (New York: Public Affairs, 1999). To find out more about Zero Usury, consult the website of the Nicaragua Network at www.nicanet.org, which provides thorough coverage of Nicaraguan affairs.

17. Robert Merton, *Social Theory and Social Structure, enlarged ed.* (New York: The Free Press, 1968).

Bibliography

Almond, Gabriel, and G. Bingham Powell. *Comparative Politics: A Development Approach*. Boston, MA: Little Brown, 1966.

Almond, Gabriel, and James Coleman (Eds). *The Politics of Developing Areas*. Princeton, NJ: Princeton University Press, 1960.

Álvarez Argüello, Gabriel, and Joan Vintro Castells. "Constitutional Evolution and Institutional Change in Nicaragua." *The Sandinistas and Nicaraguan Politics Since 1979*. Eds. David Close and Salvador Mati i Puig. University Park, PA: Penn State University Press, forthcoming.

Amado, Jorge. *The Violent Land*. New York: Knopf, 1965.

American Political Science Association. *Membership Data: Current APSA Members, 2004*. http://apsanet.org/imgtest/APSAdata.pdf (accessed 30 January 2007).

Anderson, Charles W. *Politics and Economic Change in Latin America: The Governing of Restless Nations*. New York: Van Nostrand Reinhold Company, 1967.

Anderson, Thomas P. *The War of the Dispossessed: Honduras and El Salvador 1969*. Lincoln, NB: University of Nebraska Press, 1981.

Andrews, George Reid. *Afro-Latin America, 1800–2000*. New York: Oxford University Press, 2004.

"Argentina-Uruguay Row Hits Summit." *BBC News*, 9 November 2007. http://newsvote.bbc.co.uk/2/hi/americas/7088050.shtml (accessed 26 June 2008).

Atkinson, Michael. "Governing Canada." *Governing Canada: Institutions and Public Policy*. Ed. Michael Atkinson. Toronto, ON: Harcourt, Brace, Jovanovich Canada, 1993.

Ayoob, Mohammed. "Subaltern Realism: International Relations Theory Meets the Third World." *International Relations Theory and the Third World*. Ed. Stephanie Neuman. New York: St. Martin's Press, 1998, 31–54.

Bacevic, Andrew. *The New American Militarism: How Americans Are Seduced by War*. New York: Oxford University Press, 2005.

Baer, Werner. "Import Substitution and Industrialization in Latin America: Experiences and Interpretations." *Latin American Research Review* 7:1 (1972): 95–122.

Baharona, Elena Martinez. "Nicaragua's Politicized Judiciary." *The Sandinistas and Nicaraguan Politics Since 1979*. Ed. David Close and Salvador Mati i Puig. University Park, PA: Penn State University Press, forthcoming.

Banco Central de Nicaragua, "Billetes y monedas" *Banco Central de Nicaragua* (2009). www.bcn.gob.ni/moneda (accessed 5 September 2009).

Bastos, Agusto Roa. *I, the Supreme*. Tr. Helen Lane. New York: Vintage Books, 1987.

Bates, Robert. "Area Studies and Political Science: Rupture and Possible Synthesis." *Africa Today* 44:2 (1997): 123–131.

Bates, Robert. "Area Studies and the Discipline: A Useful Controversy?" *P.S. Political Science and Politics* 30:1 (1997): 166–169.

Bates, Robert. "Letter from the President: Area Studies and the Discipline." *Newsletter of the APSA Organized Section on Comparative Politics* 7:1 (1996): 1–2.

Beckett, Ian. *Modern Insurgencies and Counter-insurgencies*. London: Routledge, 2001.

Berryman, Phillip. *Liberation Theology: Essential Facts about the Revolutionary Religious Movements in Latin America*. New York: Pantheon, 1987.

Bjornlund, Eric. *Beyond Free and Fair: Monitoring Elections and Building Democracy*. Washington, DC: Woodrow Wilson Center Press; Baltimore, MD: Johns Hopkins University Press, 2004.

Black, Cyril E. *The Dynamics of Modernization: A Study in Comparative History*. New York, NY: Harper and Row, 1966.

Blustein, Paul. *And the Money Kept Rolling In (and Out): Wall Street, the IMF, and the Bankrupting of Argentina*. New York: Public Affairs, 2005.

Branford, Sue, and Jan Rocha. *Cutting the Wire: the Story of the Landless Movement in Brazil*. London: Latin American Bureau, 2002.

Bruneau, Thomas C., and Scott D. Tollefson (Eds.). *Who Guards the Guardians and How: Democratic Civil Military Relations*. Austin, TX: University of Texas Press, 2006.

Bulmer-Thomas, Victor. *The Economic History of Latin America since Independence*. Cambridge: Cambridge University Press, 1994.

Bulmer-Thomas, Victor, John A. Coatsworth, and Roberto Cortés Conde (Eds.). *The Cambridge Economic History of Latin America*, 2 vols. Cambridge: Cambridge University Press, 2006.

Bunce, Valerie. "Comparative Democratization: Big and Bounded Generalizations." *Comparative Political Studies* 33:6-7 (2000): 703–734.

Bunce, Valerie. "The Tasks of Democratic Transition and Transferability." *Orbis* 52:1 (2008): 25–40.

Burbach, Roger. *The Pinochet Affair: State Terrorism and Global Justice*. London: Zed Books, 2003.

Burbach, Roger. "Et Tu, Daniel? The Sandinista Revolution Betrayed." *NACLA Report on the Americas* 42:2 (March–April 2009). http://nacla.org/node/5562?editionnid=5552&issuename=Revolutionary%20Legacies%20in%20the%202021st%20Century&issuenum=2&volume=042&issuemonth=March/April&issueyear=2009&lilimage= (accessed 2 March 2009).

Burns, E. Bradford. *A History of Brazil*, 2nd ed. New York: Columbia University Press, 1980.

Burton, Michael, Richard Gunther, and John Higley. "Introduction: Elite Transformations and Democratic Regimes." *Elites and Democratic Consolidation in Latin America and Southern Europe*. Eds. John Higley and Richard Gunther. Cambridge: Cambridge University Press, 1992, 1–37.

Bushnell, David. *The Making of Modern Colombia: A Nation in Spite of Itself*. Berkeley, CA: University of California Press, 1993.

Capgemini and Merrill Lynch. *World Wealth Report, 2008*. www.ml.com/media/100472.pdf (accessed 21 August 2008).

Camara, Helder. *The Spiral of Violence*. London: Sheed and Ward, 1971.

Campbell, Bruce B., and Arthur D. Bremmer (Eds.). *Death Squads in Global Perspective: Murder with Deniability*. New York: St. Martin's Press, 2000.

Cardoso, Fernando Henrique, and Enzo Faletto. *Dependency and Development in Latin America*. Berkeley, CA: University of California Press, 1979.

Carothers, Thomas. *Aiding Democracy Abroad: The Learning Curve*. Washington, DC: Carnegie Endowment for International Peace, 1999.

Carothers, Thomas. *Critical Missions: Essays on Democracy Promotion*. Washington, DC: Carnegie Endowment for International Peace, 2004.

Cheibub, José Antonio. *Presidentialism, Parliamentarism, and Democracy*. New York: Cambridge University Press, 2007.

Chilcote, Ronald, and Joel Edelstein (Eds.). *Latin America: The Struggle with Dependency and Beyond*. Cambridge, MA: Schenkman Publishing, 1974.

Child, Jack. *The Central American Peace Process, 1983–1991: Sheathing Swords, Building Confidence*. Boulder, CO: Lynne Rienner Publishers, 1992.

Christian, Shirley. "Argentina and Brazil Renounce Atomic Weapons." *The New York Times*, 29 November 1990. http://query.nytimes.com/gst/fullpage.html (accessed 24 July 2008).

Clayton Lawrence A., and Michael L. Conniff. *A History of Modern Latin America*. Fort Worth, TX: Harcourt Brace and Company, 1999.

Cleaver, Harry M., Jr. "The Zapatista Effect: The Internet and the Rise of an Alternative Political Fabric." *Journal of International Affairs* 51.2 (1998): 621–40.

Close, David. "President Bolaños Runs a Reverse, or How Arnoldo Alemán Wound Up in Prison." *Undoing Democracy: The Politics of Electoral Caudillismo*. Eds. David Close and Kalowatie Deonandan. Lanham, MD: Lexington Books, 2004, 167–181.

Close, David. *Nicaragua: The Chamorro Years*. Boulder, CO: Lynne Rienner Publishers, 1999.

Close, David. "Undoing Democracy." *Undoing Democracy: The Politics of Electoral Caudillismo*. Eds. David Close and Kalowatie Deonandan. Lanham, MD: Lexington Books, 2004, 1–16.

Coatsworth, John H. "Structures, Endowments, and Institutions in the Economic History of Latin America." *Latin American Research Review*. 40:3 (2005): 126–144.

Coatsworth, John, and Jeffrey Williamson. "Always Protectionist? Latin American Tariffs from Independence to the Great Depression." *Journal of Latin American Studies* 36:2 (2004): 205–232.

Collier, David, and Steven Levitsky. "Democracy with Adjectives: Conceptual Innovation in Comparative Research." *World Politics* 49:3 (1997): 420–431.

Collier, David (Ed.). *The New Authoritarianism in Latin America*. Princeton, NJ: Princeton University Press, 1979.

Conniff, Michael (Ed.). *Populism in Latin America*. Tuscaloosa, AL: University of Alabama Press, 1999.

Craske, Nikki. *Women and Politics in Latin America*. New Brunswick, NJ: Rutgers University Press, 1999.

Crick, Bernard. *In Defence of Politics*. London: Weidenfield and Nicholson, 1962.

Cruz, Arturo, Jr. *Nicaragua's Conservative Republic, 1858–93*. Houndmills, UK: Palgrave, 2002.

Dahl, Robert A. *A Preface to Economic Democracy*. Berkeley, CA: University of California Press, 1985.

Daudelin, Jean. "Foreign Policy at the Fringe: Canada and Latin America." *International Journal* 58 (2003): 637–666.

Davis, Madeleine (Ed.). *The Pinochet Case: Origins, Progress, and Implications*. London: Institute of Latin American Studies, 2003.

Dealy, Glen. *The Public Man: An Interpretation of Latin American and Other Catholic Countries*. Amherst, MA: University of Massachusetts Press, 1977.

Dealy, Glen. "The Tradition of Monistic Democracy in Latin America." *Journal* of the *History of Ideas* 35 (1974): 616–630.

de Gregorio, José. "Economic Growth in Latin America: The Recent Experience." Paper prepared for the conference: Latin America: Total Factor Productivity Puzzle, Santa Barbara, CA, 2007. www.bcentral.cl/jdegredo/pdf/jdg22092007/pdf (accessed 3 June 2008).

Diederich, Bernard. *Somoza*. New York: New York Press, 1981.

Dijkstra, Geske. "The PRSP Approach and the Illusion of Improved Aid Effectiveness: Lessons from Bolivia, Honduras and Nicaragua." *Development Policy Review* 23 (2005): 443–464.

Dinges, John. *The Condor Years: How Pinochet and His Allies Brought Terrorism to Three Continents*. New York: New Press, 2004.

Deonandan, Kalowatie. "The Caudillo Is Dead: Long Live the Caudillo." *Undoing Democracy: The Politics of Electoral Caudillismo.* Eds. David Close and Kalowatie Deonandan. Lanham, MD: Lexington Books, 2004, 183–198.

Deutsch, Karl. "Social Mobilization and Political Development." *American Political Science Review* 15:3 (1961): 493–514.

Domhoff, G. William. *The Power Elite and the State: How Policy Is Made in America.* New York: A. de Gruter, 1990.

Donovan, Kate. "A Beneficial Uruguayan Paper Mill: Pulp Fiction?" *Washington: Council on Hemispheric Affairs* 2007. www.coha.org/2007/01/a-beneficial-uruguayan-paper-mill-pulp-fiction.html.

Drake, Paul. *Money Doctors, Foreign Debts, and Economic Reforms in Latin America from the 1890s to the Present.* Wilmington, DE: SR Books, 1994.

Dye, David, and David Close. "Patrimonialism and Economic Policy in the Alemán Administration." *Undoing Democracy: The Politics of Electoral Caudillismo.* Eds. David Close and Kalowatie Deonandan. Lanham, MD: Lexington Books, 2004, 119–141.

Dye, David R. *Democracy Adrift: Caudillo Politics in Nicaragua.* Managua, NI: Prodeni, 2004.

Dye, Thomas. *Top-Down Policymaking.* New York: Chatham House, 2001.

Eakins, Marshall. *The History of Latin America: Collision of Cultures.* New York: Palgrave Macmillan, 2007.

ECLAC. *Statistical Yearbook for Latin America and the Caribbean, 2007.* Santiago, CH: ECLAC, 2007.

Eisinger, Peter. "The Conditions of Poorest Behavior in American Cities." *American Political Science Review* 67 (1973): 11–28.

El Salvador, Tribuna Suprema Electroral, *Elecciones 2009. Resultados Electorales Diputados.* http://elecciones2009.tse.gob.sv/page.php?51 (accessed 15 March 2009).

Engerman, Stanley, and Kenneth Solokoff. "Factor Endowments, Institutions, and Differential Paths of Growth among New World Economics: A View from Economic Historians of the United States." *How Latin America Fell Behind: Essays on the Economic Histories of Brazil and Mexico.* Ed. Stephen Haber. Stanford, CT: Stanford University Press, 1997, 260–304.

Epstein, Edward, and David Pion-Berlin (Eds.). *Broken Promises? The Argentine Crisis and Argentine Democracy.* Lanham, MD: Lexington Books, 2006.

Escobar-Lemmon, Maria, and Michelle Taylor-Robinson. "How Electoral Laws and Development Affect the Election of Women in Latin American Legislatures: A Test 20 Years into the Third Wave of Democracy." Paper presented to the 2006 Annual Meeting of the American Political Science Association, Philadelphia, PA.

Esucudé, Carlos. "An Introduction to Peripheral Realism and Its Implications for the Interstate System: Argentina and the Condor II Missile Project." *International Relations Theory and the Third World.* Ed. Stephanie Neuman. New York: St. Martin's Press, 1998, 55–76.

Farcau, Bruce. *The Coup: Tactics in the Seizure of Power.* New York: Praeger Publishers, 1994.

Fitch, J. Samuel. *The Armed Forces and Democracy in Latin America.* Baltimore, MD: Johns Hopkins University Press, 1998.

Frank, Andre Gunder. *Capitalism and Underdevelopment in Latin America: Historical Studies of Chile and Brazil.* New York: Monthly Review Press, 1967.

Frank, Dana. *Bananeras: Women Transforming the Banana Unions of Latin America.* Boston, MA: South End Press, 2005.

Franko, Patrice. *The Puzzle of Latin American Economic Development.* Lanham, MD: Rowman and Littlefield Publishers, 2003.

Frieden, Jeffry A. *Global Capitalism: Its Fall and Rise in the Twentieth Century.* New York: W.W. Norton & Company, 2006.

Gamson, William. *Power and Discontent.* Homewood, IL: Dorsey Press, 1968.

Gamson, William. *The Strategy of Social Protest.* Homewood, IL: Dorsey Press, 1975.

Garrett, James. "The Beagle Channel Dispute: Confrontation and Negotiation in the Southern Cone." *Journal of Interamerican Studies and World Affairs* 27:3 (1985): 81–109.

Gaskill, Newton. "Rethinking Protestantism and Democratic Consolidation in Latin America." *Sociology of Religion* 58:1 (Spring 1997): 69–91.

Gibson, Edward, and Tulia Falletti. "Unity by the Stick: Regional Conflict and the Origins of Argentine Federalism." *Federalism and Democracy in Latin America.* Ed. Edward Gibson. Baltimore, MD: Johns Hopkins University Press, 2004, 226–254.

Goertzel, Ted. "Still a Marxist." *Brazzil.* April 1997. www.brazzillog.com/pages/blaapr97.htm (accessed 24 May 2008).

Goetz, Anne Marie, and Shireen Hassim (Eds.). *No Shortcuts to Power: African Women in Politics and Policy Making.* London: Zed Books, 2003.

Gutiérrez, Gustavo. *A Theology of Liberation: History, Politics, Salvation.* Maryknoll, NY: Orbis Books, 1973.

Gunther, Richard, José R. Montero, and Juan Linz (Eds.). *Political Parties: Old Concepts and New Challenges.* Oxford: Oxford University Press, 2002.

Gustafson, Kristian. *Hostile Intent: U.S. Covert Operations in Chile, 1964–1974.* Washington, DC: Potomac Books, 2007.

Haber, Stephen (Ed.). *How Latin America Fell Behind: Essays on the Economic Histories of Brazil and Mexico.* Stanford, CT: Stanford University Press, 1997.

Haber, Stephen. "Introduction: Economic Growth and Latin American Economic Historiography." *How Latin America, Fell Behind: Essays on the Economic Histories of Brazil and Mexico.* Ed. Stephen Haber. Stanford, CT: Stanford University Press, 1997, 1–33.

Haggard, Stephan, and Robert R. Kaufman (Eds.). *The Politics of Economic Adjustment: International Constraints, Distributive Conflicts, and the State.* Princeton, NJ: Princeton University Press, 1992.

Hague, Rod, and Martin Harrop. *Political Science: A Comparative Introduction.* 5th ed. New York: Palgrave Macmillan, 2007.

Hall, Carolyn. *El café y el desarrollo historic-geografico de Costa Rica.* 3rd ed. San José, CR: Editorial Costa Rica, 1982.

Hamill, Hugh M. (Ed.). *Caudillos: Dictators in Spanish America.* Norman, OK: University of Oklahoma Press, 1992.

Hamill, Hugh (Ed.). *Dictatorship in Spanish America.* New York: Knopf, 1966.

Hamilton, Alexander. "Report on Manufactures." *The Theoretical Evolution of International Political Economy: A Reader.* Eds. George Crane and Abla Amawi. New York: Oxford University Press, 1991, 37–47.

Hartz, Louis. *The Liberal Tradition in America.* New York: Harcourt, Brace and World, 1955.

Hartz, Louis (Ed.). *The Founding of New Societies: Studies in the History of the United States, Latin America, South Africa, Canada, and Australia.* New York: Harcourt, Brace and World, 1964.

Hayden, Tom. *The Zapatista Reader.* New York: Nation Books, 2002.

Heine, Jaime. "China's Claim in Latin America: So Far, a Partner not a Threat." Washington, DC: *Council on Hemispheric Affairs.* www.coha.org/2008/07/china's-claim-in-latin-america-so-far-a-partner-not-a-threat (accessed 25 July 2008).

Helmke, Gretchen, and Steven Levitsky. "Informal Institutions and Comparative Politics: A Research Agenda." *Perspectives on Politics* 2:4 (2004): 725–740.

Hewitt, Mike, "The History of Money: Peru," *Goldseek*. 2009. www.news.goldseek.com/GoldSeek/1233678265.php.

Hirschman, Albert O. *The Strategy of Economic Development*. New Haven, CT: Yale University Press, 1958.

"History of Brazilian Currency." www.gwu.edu/~ibi/Statistics%20PDF%20Files/Brazilian% Currencies.pdf (accessed 26 June 2008).

Holden, Robert. *Armies without Nations: Public Violence and State Formation in Central America*. New York: Oxford University Press, 2005.

Homer-Dixon, Thomas. *Environmental Scarcity and Violence*. Princeton, NJ: Princeton University Press, 1996.

Horowitz, Irving Louis, and Jaime Suchlicki (Eds.). *Cuban Communism: 1959–2003*. New Brunswick, NJ: Transaction Publishers, 2003.

Htun, Mala. "Women, Political Parties and Electoral Systems in Latin America." *Women in Parliament: Beyond Numbers. A Revised Edition*. Eds. Julie Ballington and Azza Karam. Stockholm: International IDEA, 2006, 112–121.

Huber, Evelyne, and Michelle Dion. "Revolution or Contribution? Rational Choice Approaches in the Study of Latin American Politics." *Latin American Politics and Society* 44:3 (2002): 1–28.

Huneeus, Carlos. *The Pinochet Regime*. Boulder, CO: Lynne Rienner Publishers, 2007.

Huntington, Samuel. *Political Order in Changing Societies*. New Haven, CT: Yale University Press, 1968.

Huntington, Samuel. *The Third Wave*. Norman, OK: The University of Oklahoma Press, 1991.

Hyden, Goran. *African Politics in Comparative Perspective*. New York: Cambridge University Press, 2006.

Institute of Petroleum. "Where Is the Oil?" www.energyinst.org.uk/education/natural/3.htm (accessed 7 January 2007).

International Crisis Group. *Bolivia's New Constitution: Avoiding Violent Confrontation*. Latin American Report No. 23 (2007). www.crisisgroup.org/home/index.cfm?id=5044&l=1 (accessed 2 September 2007).

International Idea. "Global Database of Quotas for Women." www.quotaproject.org (accessed 22 February 2008).

International Institute of Strategic Studies. *The Military Balance, 2008*. London: Routledge, 2008.

International Parliamentary Union. *Women in Parliaments: World Classification*. www.ipu.org/wmn-e/classif.htm (accessed 22 February 2008).

Johnson, Chalmers. "Preconception vs. Observation, or the Contributions of Rational Choice Theory and Area Studies to Contemporary Political Science." *PS: Political Science and Politics* 30:2 (1997): 170–174.

Johnson, Harold B., Jr. (Ed.). *From Reconquest to Empire: The Iberian Background to Latin American History*. New York: Alfred A. Knopf, 1970.

Kampwirth, Karen. *Feminism and the Legacy of Revolution: Nicaragua, El Salvador, Chiapas*. Athens, OH: Ohio University Press, 2004.

Kampwirth, Karen. *Women and Guerrilla Movements: Nicaragua, El Salvador, Chiapas, Cuba*. University Park, PA: Pennsylvania State University Press, 2002.

Kapuscinski, Ryszard. *The Soccer War*. Tr. William Brand. New York: Vintage Books, 1986.

Karl, Terry. "Petroleum and Political Pacts: The Transition to Democracy in Venezuela." *Transitions from Authoritarian Rule*. Eds. Guillermo O'Donnell, Phillipe Schmitter, and Laurence Whitehead. Baltimore, MD: Johns Hopkins University Press, 1986, 196–219.

Kellogg, Paul. "Regional Integration in Latin America: Dawn of an Alternative to Neoliberalism?" *New Political Science* 29:2 (2007): 187–209.

Klaiber, Jeffery. *The Church, Dictatorships, and Democracy in Latin America*. Maryknoll, NY: Orbis Books, 1998.

Klare, Michael T., and Peter Kornbuth (Eds.). *Low Intensity Warfare: Counterinsurgency, Proinsurgency, and Antiterrorism in the Eighties*. New York: Pantheon, 1988.

Kliksberg, Bernardo. "Public Administration in Latin America: Promises, Frustrations and New Examinations." *International Review of Administrative Sciences* 71:2 (2005): 309–326.

Kholi, Atul, et al. "The Role of Theory in Comparative Politics: a Symposium." *World Politics* 48:1 (1995): 1–49.

Kostadinova, Tatia, and Timothy J. Power "Does Democracy Depress Participation? Voter Turnout in Latin American and European Transitional Democracies." *Political Research Quarterly* 60 (2007): 363–377.

Langer, Erick D., and Elena Munoz (Eds.) *Contemporary Indigenous Movements in Latin America*. Wilmington, DE: SR Books, 2003.

Lasswell, Harold. "The Garrison State." *American Journal of Sociology* 46 (1941): 455–468.

Lavarin, Asuncion. "Suffrage in South America: Arguing a Difficult Case." *Suffrage and Beyond: International Feminist Perspectives*. Eds. Caroline Daley and Melanie Nolan. New York: New York University Press, 1994, 184–209.

Leftwich, Adrian. "Governance, Democracy and Development in the Third World." *Third World Quarterly* 13:3 (1993): 605–624.

Lerner, Daniel. *The Passing of Traditional Society*. New York: Macmillan, 1958.

Lewis, Paul H. *Authoritarian Regimes in Latin America: Dictators, Despots, and Tyrants*. Lanham, MD: Rowman and Littlefield, 2006.

Linz, Juan, and Alfred Stepan (Eds.). *The Breakdown of Democratic Regimes*. Baltimore, MD: Johns Hopkins University Press, 1978.

Linz, Juan, and Arturo Valenezuela (Eds.). *The Failure of Presidential Democracy: The Case of Latin America*. Baltimore, MD: Johns Hopkins University Press, 1994.

Liss, Sheldon B. *Fidel: Castro's Social and Political Thought*. Boulder, CO: Westview Press, 1994.

List, Friedrich. *The National System of Political Economy*. Tr. and ed. W.O. Henderson. London: Cass, 1982.

Lomax, Derek. *The Reconquest of Spain*. London: Longman, 1978.

Lomnitz, Claudio. "Latin America's Rebellion: Will the New Left Set a New Agenda?" *Boston Review* 31:5 (September–October 2006): 7. http://bostonreview.net/BR31.5/lomnitz.html.

Londregan, John B., and Keith T. Poole. "Poverty, the Coup Trap, and the Seizure of Executive Power." *World Politics* 42:2 (1990): 151–183.

Love, Joseph L. "The Rise and Decline of Economic Structuralism in Latin America: New Dimensions." *Latin American Research Review* 40:3 (2005): 100–125.

Loveman, Brian. *For La Patria: Politics and the Armed Forces in Latin America*. Wilmington, DE: Scholarly Resources, 1999.

Loveman, Brian, and Thomas Davies (Eds.). *Apolitical Politics*. 3rd ed. Wilmington, DE: Scholarly Resources, 1997.

Lustick, Ian. "The Disciplines of Political Science: Studying the Culture of Rational Choice as a Case in Point." *PS: Political Science and Politics* 30:2 (1997): 175–179.

Lynch, John. *Argentine Dictator: Juan Manuel de Rosas, 1829–1852*. Oxford: Clarendon Press, 1981.

Lynch, John. *Caudillos in Spanish America, 1800–1850*. Oxford: Clarendon Press, 1992.

Macpherson, C.B. *The Real World of Democracy*. Toronto, ON: CBC, 1964.

Maddison, Angus. *The World Economy*. Paris, FR: OECD, 2006.

March, James, G., and Johan P. Olsen. "The New Institutionalism: Organizational Factors in Political Life." *American Political Science Review* 78:3 (1984): 734–749.

Marichal, Carlos. *A Century of Debt Crises in Latin America: From Independence to the Great Depression, 1820–1930*. Princeton, NJ: Princeton University Press, 1989.

Martin, Bernard. "From Pre- to Postmodernity in Latin America: The Case of Pentecostalism." *Religion, Modernity and Postmodernity*. Eds. Paul Heelas, David Martin, and Paul Morris. Oxford: Blackwell Publishers, 1998, 102-145.

Martin, David. *Pentecostalism: The World Their Parish*. Oxford: Blackwell, 2002.

Martin, David. *Tongues of Fire: the Explosion of Protestantism in Latin America*. Oxford: Basil Blackwell, 1990.

Matland, Richard E., and Kathleen A. Montgomery (Eds.). *Women's Access to Political Power in Post-Communist Europe*. Oxford: Oxford University Press, 2003.

Maybury-Lewis, David (Ed.). *The Politics of Ethnicity: Indigenous People in Latin American States*. Cambridge, MA: Harvard University David Rockefeller Center for Latin American Studies, 2002.

McClintock, Cynthia. *Revolutionary Movements in Latin America: El Salvador's FMLN and Peru's Shining Path*. Washington, DC: United States Institute of Peace Press, 1998.

McKenna, Peter. *Canada and the OAS: From Dilettante to Full Partner*. Ottawa, ON: Carleton University Press, 1995.

McSherry, J. Patrice. *Predatory States: Operation Condor and Covert War in Latin America*. Lanham, MD: Rowman and Littlefield, 2005.

Mecham, Lloyd. *Church and State in Latin America: A History of Politico-ecclesiastical Relations*. Chapel Hill, NC: University of North Carolina Press, 1966.

Merton, Robert. Social Theory and Social Structure, enlarged ed. New York: The Free Press, 1968.

Mill, John Stuart. *Considerations on Representative Government*. 1861. Whitefish, MT: Kessinger Publishing, 2004.

Mills, C. Wright. *The Power Elite*. New York: Oxford University Press, 1956.

Mintz, Eric, David Close, and Osvaldo Croci. *Politics, Power, and the Common Good: An Introduction to Politics*. Toronto, ON: Pearson, 2005.

Molina, Ivan, and Stephen Palmer. *The History of Costa Rica*. San José, CR: Editorial de la Universidad de Costa Rica, 1998.

Molloy, Ivan. *Rolling Back Revolution: The Emergence of Low-Intensity Conflict*. Sterling, VA: Pluto Press, 2001.

Montgomery, Tommie Sue. *Revolution in El Salvador: from Civil Strife to Civil Peace*. 2d ed. Boulder, CO: Westview, 1995.

Movimento dos Sem Terra. "About the MST." *MST*. www.mstbrazil.org (accessed 5 March 2008.

"The New Titans: A Survey of the World Economy." *The Economist*, 16 September 2006: 12.

Nevitte, Neil, and Santiago Canton, "The Role of Domestic Observers." *Journal of Democracy* 8:3 (July 1997): 47–61.

Nicaragua Network. www.nicanet.org (accessed 29 April 2009).

North, Douglass. *Institutions, Institutional Change and Economic Performance*. Cambridge: Cambridge University Press, 1990.

Nossal, Kim. "A Question of Balance: The Cult of Research Intensitivity and the Professing of Political Science in Canada." *Canadian Journal of Political Science* 39:4 (2006): 735–754.

O'Donnell, Guillermo. "Democratic Theory and Comparative Politics." *Studies in Comparative* International Development 36:1 (2001): 5–36.

O'Donnell, Guillermo. *Modernization and Bureaucratic-Authoritarianism*. Berkeley, CA: University of California Press, 1972.

O'Donnell, Guillermo, Phillipe Schmitter, and Laurence Whitehead (Eds.). *Transitions from Authoritarian Rule*. Baltimore, MD: Johns Hopkins University Press, 1986.

Oppenheimer, Andres. "Report on Wealthy Latins Is a Bit Troubling." *Miami Herald*, 17 August 2008. www.miamiherald.com/news/columnists/andres-oppenheimer/ story/645347.html (accessed 31 August 2008).

Palmer, David Scott. "Overcoming the Weight of History: 'Getting to Yes' in the Peru-Ecuador Border Dispute." *Diplomacy and Statecraft* 12:2 (2001): 29–46.

Panitch, Leo, and Colin Leys (Eds.). *The Socialist Register*. Halifax, NS: Fernwood Publishers, various years.

Pastor, Manuel. "Capital Flight from Latin America." *World Development* 18:1 (1990): 1–18.

Perez, Andres. *Entre el estado conquistador y el estado nación: providencialismo, pensamiento político y estructuras de poder en el desarrollo histórico de Nicaragua*. Managua, NI: Fundacion Frederich Ebert, 2003.

Pew Forum on Religion and Public Life. "Historical Overview of Pentecostalism in Brazil." http://pewforum.org/surveys/pentecostal/countries/?CountryID=29 (accessed 21 September 2007).

Pierson, Paul. "Increasing Returns, Path Dependence, and the Study of Politics." *American Political Science Review* 92:4 (2000): 251–267.

Pion-Berlin, David (Ed.). *Civil-Military Relations in Latin America: New Analytical Perspectives*. Chapel Hill, NC: University of North Carolina Press, 2001.

Pion-Berlin, David. "The National Security Doctrine, Military Threat Perception, and the 'Dirty War' in Argentina." *Comparative Political Studies* 21:3 (1988): 382–407.

Polk, William R. *Violent Politics: A History of Insurgency, Terrorism, and Guerrilla War, from the American Revolution to Iraq*. New York: Harper, 2007.

Porter, Michael E. *The Competitive Advantage of Nations*. New York: The Free Press, 1990.

Project on Extrajudicial Executions. www.extrajudicialexecutions.org (accessed on 12 May 2008).

Quigley, Carroll. *The Evolution of Civilizations: An Introduction to Historical Analysis*. New York: Macmillan, 1961.

Rapley, John. *Understanding Development: Theory and Practice in the Third World*. 3d ed. Boulder, CO: Lynne Rienner Publishers, 2007.

Remmer, Karen. *Military Rule in Latin America*. Boston, MA: Unwin Hyman, 1989.

Ricchi, Fernando. *Chimneys in the Desert: Argentina during the Export Boom Years*. Stanford, CT: Stanford University Press, 2005.

Richani, Nazih. *Systems of Violence: The Political Economy of War and Peace in Colombia*. Albany, NY: State University of New York Press, 2002.

Rocha, José Luis. "The Rio San Juan: Source of Conflicts and Nationalism." *Envio* (November 2005): 292. www.envio.org.ni/articulo/3112 (accessed 21 July 2008).

Roht-Arriaza, Naomi. *The Pinochet Effect: Transnational Justice in the Age of Human Rights*. Philadelphia, PA: University of Pennsylvania Press, 2005.

Romero, Simon. "Peru Guards Its Guano as Demand Soars Again." *The New York Times*, 30 May 2008. www.nytimes.com/2008/05/30/world/americas/30peru.html (accessed 30 May 2008).

Roquie, Alain. *The Military and the State in Latin America*. Berkeley, CA: University of California Press, 1987.

Ross, John. *¡Zapatista! Making Another World Possible: Chronicles of Resistance, 2000–2006*. New York: Nation Books, 2006.

Rostow, W.W. *The Stages of Economic Growth: A Non-communist Manifesto*. Cambridge: Cambridge University Press, 1960.

Rus, Jan, and Miguel Tinker Salas. "Introduction: Mexico 2006–2012: High Stakes, Daunting Challenges." *Latin American Perspectives* 33:2 (March 2006): 5–15.

Ryan, Phil. *The Fall and Rise of the Market in Sandinista Nicaragua*. Montreal, QC: McGill-Queen's University Press, 1995.

Salih, M.A. Mohammed (Ed.). *African Political Parties*. London: Pluto Press, 2003.

Sanderson, Stephen K. *Revolutions: A Worldwide Introduction to Political and Social Change*. Boulder, CO: Paradigm Publishers, 2005.

Saney, Isaac. *Cuba: A Revolution in Motion*. Black Point, NS: Fernwood Publishing, 2004.

Sarmiento, Domingo F. *Life in the Argentine Republic in the Days of the Tyrants, or Civilization and Barbarism*. Tr. Mary Mann. 1868. New York: Haffner Publishing, 1960.

Savoie, Donald. *Governing from the Centre: The Concentration of Power in Canadian Politics*. Toronto, ON: University of Toronto Press, 1999.

Scheina, Robert L. *Latin America's Wars*. 2 vols. Dulles, VA: Brassey's, 2003.

Schedler, Andreas, Larry Diamond, and Marc F. Plattner (Eds.). *The Self-Restraining State: Power and Accountability in New Democracies*. Boulder, CO: Lynne Rienner Publishers, 1999.

Schoultz, Lars. *Beneath the United States: A History of U.S. Foreign Policy toward Latin America*. Cambridge, MA: Harvard University Press, 1998.

Schumpeter, Joseph. *Capitalism, Socialism, and Democracy*. 5th ed. London: George Allen and Unwin, 1976.

Simpson, Jeffrey. *The Friendly Dictatorship*. Toronto, ON: McClelland & Stewart, 2001.

Skidmore, Thomas E. *The Politics of Military Rule in Brazil, 1964–85*. New York: Oxford University Press, 1988.

Sluka, Jeffrey A. (Ed.). *Death Squad: The Anthropology of State Terror*. Philadelphia, PA: University of Pennsylvania Press, 2000.

Smith, Peter H. *Democracy in Latin America: Political Change in Comparative Perspective*. New York: Oxford University Press, 2005.

Smith, Peter H. *The Talons of the Eagle: The Dynamics of U.S.-Latin American Relations*. New York: Oxford University Press, 1996.

Spalding, Rose J. *Capitalists and Revolution in Nicaragua: Opposition and Accommodation, 1979–1993*. Chapel Hill, NC: University of North Carolina Press, 1994.

Spiritus-Temporis, "Argentine Peso" 2009. www.spiritus-temporis.com/argentine-peso/history-of-the-argentine-currency-system.html.

Steinmo, Sven, Kathleen Thelen, and Frank Longstreth (Eds.). *Structuring Politics: Historical Institutionalism in Comparative Analysis*. New York: Cambridge University Press, 1992.

Stephen, Lynn. *Women and Social Movements in Latin America: Power from Below*. Austin, TX: University of Texas Press, 1997.

Stevenson, Brian J.R. *Canada, Latin America, and the New Internationalism: A Foreign Policy Analysis, 1968–1990*. Montreal, PQ: McGill-Queen's University Press, 2000.

Stokes, William. "Violence as a Power Factor in Latin American Politics." *Western Political Quarterly* 5:3 (September 1952): 445–468.

Stockholm International Peace Research Institute. *SIPRI Yearbook, 2007*. New York: Oxford University Press, 2007.

Stromquist, Nelly P. *Feminist Organizations and Social Transformation in Latin America*. Boulder, CO: Paradigm Publishers, 2007.

Taussig, Michael. *Law in a Lawless Land: Diary of a "Limpieza" in Colombia*. New York: New Press, 2003.

Teichman, Judith. *The Politics of Freeing Markets in Latin America: Chile, Argentina, and Mexico*. Chapel Hill, NC: University of North Carolina Press, 2001.

Thelen, Kathleen. "Historical Institutionalism and Comparative Politics." *Annual Review of Political Science* 2 (1999): 369–404.

Thomas, Hugh. *The Cuban Revolution*. New York: Harper Torchbooks, 1977.

Thorp, Rosemary. *Progress, Poverty and Exclusion: An Economic History of Latin America in the 20th Century*. Washington, DC: Inter-American Development Bank, 1998.

Tickner, Arlene B. "Hearing Latin American Voices in International Relations Studies." *International Studies Perspectives* 4 (2003): 325–350.

Tilly, Charles, and Sidney Tarrow. *Contentious Politics*. Boulder, CO: Paradigm Publishers, 2007.

United Nations Development Programme. *Human Development Report, 2007–2008*. Houndmills, UK: Palgrave Macmillan, 2007.

United Nations Development Programme. *Democracy in Latin America: Towards a Citizens' Democracy*. New York: United Nations Development Program, 2004. http://democracyreport.undp.org (accessed 5 March 2008).

United Nations Economic Commission on Latin America. *Social Panorama of Latin America, 2007*. Santiago, CH: ECLAC, 2007. www.eclac.cl/publicacines/xml/9/30309/PSI2007_Sintesis_Lanzamiento.pdf (accessed 3 April 2008).

United Nations High Commissioner for Human Rights. Reports of the Special Rapporteur on Extrajudicial, Summary, or Arbitrary Executions. www2.ochr.org (accessed 9 April 2008).

United States Army. *Counterinsurgency*. FM3-24. Washington, DC: Department of the Army, 2006. *Political Database of the Americas*. http//pdba.georgetown.edu (accessed 20 September 2007).

USAID Center for Democracy and Governance. *USAID Handbook on Legislative Strengthening*. Washington, DC: United States Agency for International Development, 2000.

Van Cott, Donna Lee. *From Movements to Parties in Latin America: The Evolution of Ethnic Politics*. New York: Cambridge University Press, 2005.

Van Cott, Donna Lee. *The Friendly Liquidation of the Past: The Politics of Diversity in Latin America*. Pittsburgh, PA: University of Pittsburgh Press, 2000.

Vanden, Harry E., and Gary Prevost. *Politics of Latin America: The Power Game*. New York: Oxford University Press, 2006.

Vanden, Harry. "Brazil's Landless Hold Their Ground." *NACLA: Report on the Americas* 38:5 (2005): 21–27.

Vermeersch, Peter. *The Romani Movement: Minority Politics and Ethnic Mobilization in Contemporary Central Europe*. New York: Berghann Books, 2006.

Vincent, Isabel. "Where Even the Good Are Bad." *Maclean's* 121:4–5 (4–18 February 2008): 33–35.

Washbrook, Sarah (Ed.). "Special Issue on Rural Chiapas Ten Years after the Zapatista Uprising." *Journal of Peasant Studies* 32:3–4 (July/October 2005).

Watkins, Melville. "A Staple Theory of Economic Growth." *Canadian Journal of Economics and Political Science* 29 (1963): 141–158.

Webb, Paul, and Stephen White (Eds.). *Party Politics in New Democracies*. Toronto, ON: Oxford University Press, 2003.

Weinstein, Martin. "The Left's Long Road to Power in Uruguay." *From Revolutionary Movements to Political Parties: Cases from Latin America and Africa*. Eds. Kalowatie Deonandan, David Close, and Gary Prevost. New York: Palgrave Macmillan, 2007, 67–80.

Wesson, Robert, et al. *The Latin American Military Institution*. New York: Praeger Publisher, 1986.

Weyland, Kurt. *The Politics of Market Reform in Fragile Democracies: Argentina, Brazil, Peru, and Venezuela*. Princeton, NJ: Princeton University Press, 2002.

"What Is a Dollar Worth?" Federal Reserve Bank of Minneapolis. www.minneapolisfed.org/Research/data/us/calc (accessed 15 April 2008).

"What Is ALBA?" www.alternativabolivariana.org/pdf/alba_mice_en.pdf (accessed 16 June 2008).

White, Richard Alan. *Paraguay's Autonomous Revolution: 1810–1840*. Albuquerque, NM: University of New Mexico Press, 1978.

Wiarda, Howard, and M. MacLeish Mott. "Introduction: Interpreting Latin America's Politics on Its Own Terms." *Politics and Social Change in Latin America: Still Tradition?* 4th ed. Eds. Howard Wiarda and Margret MacLeish Mott. Westport, CT: Praeger Publishers, 2003, 1–2.

Wiarda, Howard (Ed.). *Authoritarianism and Corporatism in Latin America*. Gainesville, FL: University Press of Florida, 2004.

Wiarda, Howard J., and Howard F. Kline (Eds.) *Latin American Politics and Development*. 6th ed. Boulder, CO: Westview Press, 2007.

Wickham-Crowley, Timothy P. *Guerrillas and Revolution in Latin America*. Princeton, NJ: Princeton University Press, 1992.

Williamson, John. *Latin American Adjustment: How Much Has Happened?* Washington, DC: Institute for International Economics, 1990.

Wilson, Suzanne, and Leah A. Carroll. "The Colombian Contradiction: Lessons Drawn from Guerrilla Experiments in Demobilization and Electoralism." *From Revolutionary Movements to Political Parties: Cases from Latin America and Africa*. Eds. Kalowatie Deonandan, David Close and Gary Prevost. New York: Palgrave Macmillan, 2007, 81–106.

Wolf, Eric, and Edward Hansen. "Caudillo Politics; A Structural Analysis." *Comparative Studies in Society and History* 9:2 (1967): 168–179.

World Bank, *Global Economic Prospects 2007*. http://web.worldbank.org/WBSITE/EXTERNAL/EXTDEC/EXTDECPROSPECTS/EXTGBLPROSPECTS/0,,contentMDK:20675180~menuPK:615470~pagePK:2904583~piPK:2904598~theSitePK:612501,00.html (accessed 15 January 2007).

World Bank, *World Development Report, 2008*. Washington, DC: World Bank, 2007.

WorldTradeLaw.net. www.worldtradelaw.net/fta/ftadatabase/ftas.asp (accessed 26 June 2008).

Wright, Angus, and Wendy Wolford. *To Inherit the Earth: The Landless Movement and the Struggle for a New Brazil*. Oakland, CA: Food First Books, 2003.

Yunus, Muhammad. *Banker to the Poor: Micro-Lending and the Battle against World Poverty*. New York: Public Affairs, 1999.

Index

A

absolute monarchies, 83, 92, 141
accountability, 141, 167, 179
Afghanistan, 2, 9
Africa, 11, 17, 105, 153, 253
  decolonization, 16, 196
  military, 69
African slave trade, 27
Alemán, Arnoldo, 86, 147, 240
Alessandri, Arturo, 35
Alfonsín, Raúl, 40, 172, 225, 238
Alianza Bolivariana para las Américas
  (ALBA), 207, 226
Alianza Renevadora Nacional (ARENA)
  (Brazil), 90
Alianza Republicana Nacionalista
  (ARENA) (El Salvator), 39, 112
Allende, Salvador, 91, 113, 212
Alliance for Progress (AFP), 10, 198, 251
Amado, Jorge, *The Violent Land*, 57
American exceptionalism, 144, 248
American Popular Revolutionary
  Alliance (APRA) or Alianza Popular
  Revolucionaria Americana, 151
American Revolution, 29–31
Anderson, Charles W., 31, 106–7
Antonio, Carlos, 88
Araujo, Arturo, 39
area studies approach, 12–15, 18–19, 257
Argentina, 6, 34, 63, 72, 115–16, 189, 224
  austerity programs, 172
  auto industry, 197
  Beagle Channel dispute, 238
  British economic presence, 247
  cabinet ministers, 143
  constitution, 225
  coups, 40, 97
  currencies, 172, 215, 225
  democracy, 39–40, 166, 172, 263
  deregulation, 225
  economic crisis (2001), 36, 40, 127,
    172, 215, 225
  exports, 34, 194, 223
  Falkland Islands, 40, 171, 238, 247

  federalism, 140
  Guerra Sucia, 40, 47, 147
  ISI model, 38
  judiciary, 147
  Madres de la Plaza de Mayo, 120
  middle classes, 127
  middle power, 231, 252
  military regime (1976-1983), 40–41, 71,
    73, 90, 243
  nuclear weapons and, 241
  organized labor, 126–27
  poverty reduction, 191
  presidential reelection, 225
  privatization, 225
  structural adjustment program, 40,
    224–25
  War of the Triple Alliance, 244
Argentina / Uruguay paper mill dispute,
  239–40
Arias, Óscar, 178, 243
Aristide, Jean-Bertrand, 98
Aristotle, 83, 159
Armies without Nations (Holden), 78
arms race, 240–41
Asia, 16, 105, 196. *See also* names of
  specific Asian countries
Asian Model, 209–10, 219–20
Asian tigers, 189
al-Assad, Bashar, 87
Australia, 8, 37, 199, 216, 231, 252
Austro-Hungarian Empire, 233
autarky, 37, 195, 207
authoritarian political systems, 12, 32, 101,
  108, 157
authority of *concepts,* 158
autonomy, 10, 123, 235. *See also* national
  sovereignty
Autonomy Statute (1987), 122
Ayoob, Mohammed, 236
Aztec empire, 28

B

Bachelet, Michelle, 53, 118, 143, 174, 203
Bahamas, 7

land reform, 60–61
nationalization of US property, 178, 212
post-Fidel, 3–4
power in international relations, 231
raw materials for Soviet Bloc economic union, 211
remittances (US dollars), 179
social and economic equality, 179
support for Marxist regimes, 178
tourism, 178, 213
US economic pressure, 211–12, 251
US intervention, 249, 251
Cuban Communist Party, 4, 178–79
Cuban exile community (Miami), 3
Cuban Revolution, 31, 60, 127, 198, 233, 251
social revolution, 99
currency, 213–14
floating currencies, 220
gold standard, 211
rebranding national currency, 215
US dollar, 172, 215
cuts to public spending. *See* structural adjustment programs (SAPs)

D
Da Silva, Luiz Inácio, 5, 42, 68, 126, 203
role at World Trade Organization meeting, 173
social policy, 173
De Gaulle, Charles, 265
De la Rue, Fernando, 225
Dealy, Glen Caudil, 82
death squads, 39, 100, 127
debt crisis, 38, 196, 200–202, 211, 219, 223
debt (foreign debt) (table), 221
decolonization, 16, 196, 261
dedazo ("pointing a finger"), 81
democracies
economic elites in, 62
electoral democracies, 163, 177, 179, 261
formal democracies, 160
historic democracies, 91–92, 157–58
historical institutionalism, 80
political change within, 107, 115, 158–59, 261
democracy and democratization, 2, 44, 105, 114, 157–80, 264
accountability and, 141
association with hard times, 164
citizens' democracy, 160–61, 180

comparative politics, 262–64
constitutional democracy, 7, 11, 16, 261–62
democratic revolutions, 60
democratic strengthening, 144
democratic transitions, 17, 165–66
direct democracy, 160
electoral competition within the elite, 38
electoral democracy, 5, 148, 157–58, 163, 167, 262, 266
factor endowments encouraging, 30
impeded by personalized rule and violence, 101
liberal democracy, 159–60
oligarchic democracy, 161
pacted democracy, 166, 168–70
radical democracy, 261
Third Wave, 17, 41, 150, 163, 180, 262
in tune with modern values (modernism), 198
Democracy in Latin America (UNDP), 160
Democratic Action (AD) Acción Democrática, 151–52, 170
democratic peace hypothesis, 237–38
Democratic People's Republic of Korea, 263
Denmark, 58
dependency theory, 16–17, 172, 198–200, 208, 235
depression of 1930s. *See* Great Depression
deregulation, 220, 225. *See also* structural adjustment programs (SAPs)
development studies, 16
Díaz, Porfirio, 34–35, 98, 110
dictators and dictatorships, 11, 33, 35, 41, 83–84, 87–91, 113, 200. *See also* names of individual dictators
comparisons, 261
economic elites in, 62
Dirty War, 40, 120, 147
divorce, 66, 174
domestic election observer groups, 149
Dominican Republic, 6–7, 11, 86
bilateral agreements, 226
free trade agreements, 178, 207, 226
independence, 158
US intervention, 249–51
Dominican Republic-Central American Free Trade Agreement (CAFTA-DR), 178, 226
drug lords *(cocaleros)*, 96, 124
drugs and drug trade, 113, 237
cocaine, 2, 124, 139

First Nations. *See* Indigenous peoples
Fome Zero (Zero Hunger), 173
foreign investment (1870s), 34–35
foreign policy (Latin American countries), 234, 269
 independent of Washington, 4–5, 10, 251, 263
Forza Italia, 267
Fox, Vicente, 176
fragment theory, 25
France, 6, 8, 35, 70, 97, 207, 215, 233, 246
 occupation of Mexico, 247
Francia, José Gaspar Rodríguez, 33, 88
Franco, Francisco, 163, 195, 261
Franco, Itamar, 172
free media and oppositional activity, 15, 158–59, 179
free trade, 208, 210–12, 214
 golden era of global free trade (1870–1914), 211
 North American corporate agenda, 214
 regional and hemispheric, 224, 226
 suspicions of, 213
Free Trade Area of the Americas (FTAA), 226, 252
free-market economics, 183
free-market economies, 4–5, 174
free-market IPE, 209–11, 219
free-market principles, 17, 185
French Revolution, 31
Frieden, Jeffery, 37
The Friendly Dictatorship (Simpson), 265
Front for a Country in Solidarity (Frepaso), 172
Fujimori, Alberto, 68, 202
Funes, Maricio, 112

G

Gabon, 84
Gadaffi, Muammar, 87
Gaitán, Jorge Eliécer, 42, 96
García, Anastasio Somoza, 94
GDP, 186–88, 190
general theory, 16
Germany, 6, 35, 195, 207, 233
Gini index, 55
global economic crisis (2008), 2, 90, 114, 128, 203, 227
 comparative politics approach, 270
 fall of oil prices, 5
 impact on democracy, 264
 impact on social policy, 271

Global Economic Prospects (2007), 10
global governance, 232, 234
globalization, 213, 223
God, 27, 209
Godoy, Virgilio, 119
gold (and other minerals), 27, 209, 216
gold standard, 211
golpe de estado. See coups
"good governance," 164
Good Neighbor Policy, 249–50
Goulart, João, 90
Governing from the Centre (Savoie), 265
government, 135–36. *See also* state
Grameen Bank of Bangladesh, 270
Gran Columbia (1821-1830), 70
Granada, 7, 27, 43, 59, 94, 162, 244
Granma, 4
Great Britain. *See* United Kingdom
Great Depression, 40, 183, 195–97, 271
 effect on democracy, 264
 interruption of trade, 34, 36–37
Grito de Dolores (Cry of Dolores), 63
gross domestic product. *See* GDP
gross national income (GNI), 187
guano, 217–18
Guano War (or Pacific War), 246
Guantanamo Bay, 250
Guatemala, 6, 53, 66
 constitutions, 137
 death squads, 127
 democratic revolution (1944-1954), 31, 60
 insurgent wars, 243
 in National War, 244
 Protestants, 67–68
 social democracy, 263
 term limits for executives, 141
 UN Verification Mission, 153, 253
 US counterinsurgent (CI) training operations, 251
 US intervention (1954), 251
Guerra Sucia (dirty war), 40, 47, 147
guerrilla insurgencies, 39, 42, 106–7, 109–10, 170, 243
 as political participation, 267–68
 women in, 120
Gunther, Richard, 51
Gutierrez, Gustavo, *A Theology of Liberation,* 65

H

Haber, Stephen, 189, 199
Hague, Rod, 260

The Violent Land (Amado), 57
Von Clausewitz, Karl, 108

W

Walker, William, 43, 94, 244
War of a Thousand Days, 42, 95
War of the Pacific, 244
War of the Supremes, 95
War of the Triple Alliance, 33, 244
War on Terror, 2
wars of independence, 14, 24, 109
Washington Consensus, 36, 38, 72, 196,
    200–203, 219–20
wealth, concentration of, 56. *See also*
    income inequality
Weber, Max, 83, 135
Wiarda, Howard, 82
Williams, John, 201
Williamson, John, 220
Wilson, Woodrow, 249
Wolf, Eric, 34
women, 53, 112, 117–21, 180
    contentious forms of participation,
        119–20
    low interest loans, 270
    political participation, 268
    quota laws, 118, 128
    representation in legislatures, 118–19
    set back after Great Depression, 271
women presidents in Latin America, 53,
    118–19, 174
women's issues, 123
women's rights, 174
women's vote, 117
women's vote (national elections) (table),
    118
Workers' Party (Brazil), 5, 42, 173
working class, 37, 110, 112, 167, 170. *See
    also* lower classes
World Bank, 187, 190, 197, 201, 207,
    219–20, 224
    definitions of poverty, 191
    Global Economic Prospects (2007), 10
    role in economic and social polices of
        Latin America, 153
World Trade Organization, 234
World War I, 233
    interruption of trade, 34, 36–37, 194,
        211
World War II, 195–96, 210
World Wealth Report (2008), 55

Y

Yeltsin, Boris, 265
Yrigoyen, Hipólito, 39
Yunus, Muhammad, 270

Z

Zapatista National Liberation Army
    (EZLN), 121–22, 176
    transnational support, 123
    use of the Internet, 123
    women in, 120
Zedillo, Ernesto, 176
Zelaya, José Santos, 34, 44, 60, 94, 111,
    250
Zero Usury, 270
Zimbabwe, 84, 263, 269